Against the Modern World

Against the Modern World

Traditionalism and the Secret Intellectual
History of the Twentieth Century

MARK SEDGWICK

UNIVERSITY PRESS

2004

OXFORD
UNIVERSITY PRESS

Oxford   New York
Auckland Bangkok Buenos Aires Cape Town Chennai
Dar es Salaam Delhi Hong Kong Istanbul Karachi Kolkata
Kuala Lumpur Madrid Melbourne Mexico City Mumbai Nairobi
São Paulo Shanghai Taipei Tokyo Toronto

Copyright © 2004 by Oxford University Press, Inc.

Published by Oxford University Press, Inc.
198 Madison Avenue, New York, New York 10016

www.oup.com

Oxford is a registered trademark of Oxford University Press

Library of Congress Cataloging-in-Publication Data
Sedgwick, Mark J.
Against the modern world : Traditionalism and the secret intellectual
history of the twentieth century / Mark Sedgwick.
p. cm.
Includes bibliographical references and index.
ISBN 0-19-515297-2
1. Guénon, René. 2. Tradition (Philosophy) I. Title.
B2430.G84 S39 2003
194—dc21 2002153340

9 8 7 6 5 4 3 2 1
Printed in the United States of America
on acid-free paper

Turning and turning in the widening gyre
The falcon cannot hear the falconer.
Things fall apart, the centre cannot hold,
Mere anarchy is loosed upon the world,
The blood-dimmed tide is loosed, and everywhere
The ceremony of innocence is drowned.
      William Butler Yeats, "The Second Coming"

Preface

This book is a biography of René Guénon and a history of the Traditionalist movement that he founded, two subjects that have been almost unknown to the outside world. In January 1996, when I started the research on which this book is based, I had read one of Guénon's books but had no idea of his importance, or that there was any such thing as a Traditionalist movement. To help orient the reader, the book starts with a prologue that shares parts of my own voyage of discovery with the reader in somewhat impressionistic fashion, and with some identities concealed. The remainder of the book conforms to normal scholarly standards and answers most of the questions raised in the prologue. Traditionalism itself is defined in chapter 1.

Because this book is a history of René Guénon and the Traditionalists, it follows events from their point of view. First Guénon himself is placed center stage, and then those who in one way or another followed him. This central position may seem to exaggerate the Traditionalists' historical importance, but it is the Traditionalists themselves who are the subject of this book, not the periods and countries in which they lived. The Traditionalist movement has never been systematically surveyed before, and so my first objective has been to establish what the movement was, who belonged to it and in what ways, and what they did. There is some assessment of Traditionalism's importance in larger contexts, but that is not my main purpose.

A survey of a movement as large as Traditionalism presents certain organizational difficulties for a historian, especially once Traditionalism has split into several branches and then into subbranches, all of which proceed more or less independently of each other. The need to follow developments in several different domains makes strict chronological order impossible. My principle, therefore, has often been to adopt a partly thematic approach, following developments to their conclusions even when doing so means then going backward in time to pick up earlier developments of a different variety. This approach sometimes results in chronological jolts, but I hope that the reader will hold on.

Some further caveats are required. All history is to some degree a work of reconstruction, but because of the novelty of this subject, the secrecy surrounding much Traditionalist activity, and the need of certain people to keep quiet about their activities during the period of European fascism, some sections of this book depend more on guesswork than is usual. The grounds for my reconstructions are always given in the endnotes, but what is presented in the main text is generally not the process but the conclusion of my reconstruction.

Some of the journeys made for this book have taken me through intellectual territory regarded by many as beyond the pale, into landscapes dotted with such features as anti-Semitism, terrorism, and fascism. We will even briefly visit the SS in Nazi Germany. As readers follow me through this territory, they are asked to remember that the fact that I do not explicitly condemn an idea or a practice does not mean that I endorse it. In most historical works, this would go without saying. Nobody would suppose that writing about Robespierre implies an endorsement of the Terror, and it is possible to write on Marxist theory without being expected repeatedly to condemn the activities of the OGPU and the NKVD. I see no reason why one should not write about other theories on the same basis, and that is what I do here. When we visit the SS, we will do so in the company of the Italian baron Julius Evola, an important Traditionalist, and will see that organization though his eyes—as a body with interesting possibilities. This approach should not be taken to mean that I myself see the SS in this way. I do not.

Since one of the most important sources for information used in this book is the Internet, it is appropriate that there is a companion website to this book, www.traditionalists.org, which carries updated information, photographs, copies of some original documents, Traditionalist bibliographies, and links to Traditionalist websites. Any reader who can expand on, elucidate, or correct any aspect of this book is invited to visit the website and e-mail me. The site also carries some additional material intended primarily for interested scholars.

In writing a book of such wide scope as this one, I have had to enter into numerous areas where I have little scholarly right to be. I have done my best to understand the background to Traditionalist activities in a variety of areas and eras, but I make no claim to expertise on all the places and periods covered in this book. Also I am even more than usually indebted to many colleagues for their suggestions, assistance and comments. In particular I would like to thank Boris Falikov, H. T. Hansen, Klaus Kreiser, Jean-François Mayer, Shahram Pazuki, Bryan Rennie, Ottavia Schmidt, Stephen Shenfield, and PierLuigi Zoccatelli, and also all the French scholars who helped me, especially Jean-Baptiste Aymard (who was most helpful despite his disagreement with many of my interpretations), Jean-Pierre Brach, Stéphane Dudoignon, Antoine Faivre, Jean-Pierre Laurant, Bernadette Rigal-Cellard, and Thierry Zarcone. I would also like to thank all the others who helped the project along with suggestions, enthusiasm, or both; the American University in Cairo for a grant that made possible my research in Morocco and Iran; Russell Sender, attorney, of Goldman Sender; and Cynthia Read, my editor at the Oxford University Press, for her support and her humor in the face of adversity. I would further like to thank my interviewees: this book could never have been written without their time, patience, and generosity. Finally, I would like to thank my wife, Lucy, for many things, and not least for her penetrating comments on the manuscript of this book.

Many of the people dealt with in this book were known by more than one name. My practice has been to refer to them by whichever name is most frequently used in my sources. Alternate names, as well as dates of birth and death, are given in the index.

In general I translate loosely and for sense, trying, for example, to make the English title of a work published in another language sound like a real book title. I have usually used the most appropriate English approximations for Islamic technical terms rather than the Arabic original. In the rare cases where the original has been retained, a longer explanation than that found in the main text is given in the glossary (along with brief definitions of certain English technical terms).

When transliterating from Arabic, I have used the standard *International Journal of Middle East Studies* system but have omitted diacritical marks. The reader who knows Arabic will be able to reconstruct these easily; the reader who does not know Arabic would find them meaningless and distracting. When transliterating names of Arabic origin from Persian or Russian, I have transliterated the Arabic original for the sake of consistency: thus "Jamal" rather than "Dzhemal."

Contents

PART IV   Traditionalism and the Future

List of Main Characters

Pouvourville, Albert de (1861–1940). Taoist imperialist and Guénon's second important master.

Encausse, Gérard (1865–1916). Founder of the Martinist Order and Guénon's first major mentor.

Aguéli, Ivan (1869–1917). Swedish Sufi and painter.

Charbonneau-Lassay, Louis (1871–1948). Catholic antiquarian, friend and patron of Guénon, and first master of the Fraternity of the Cavaliers of the Divine Paraclete.

Sebottendorf, Rudolf von (1875–1945). German occultist and Mason who established the political party Adolf Hitler transformed into the Nazi Party.

Eberhardt, Isabelle (1877–1904). Franco-Russian Sufi and writer.

Maritain, Jacques (1882–1973). Catholic philosopher, once a patron of Guénon.

Chacornac, Paul (1884–1964). Guénon's publisher.

Thomas, Georges-Auguste (1884–1966). Second master of the Fraternity of the Cavaliers of the Divine Paraclete.

Séligny, Paul de (1903–?). Mauritian, resident in France. Cult leader and guru.

Reyor, Jean (1905–88). Guénon's devoted early disciple, editor of *Etudes traditionnelles* until 1961.

Vâlsan, Michel (1907–74); Romanian, later resident in France. First Schuon's *muqaddam* in Paris and then shaykh of an independent Alawiyya Sufi order. Editor of *Etudes traditionnelles* from 1961 until his death.

Burckhardt, Titus (1908–84). Swiss. Schuon's closest and earliest associate, and his *muqaddam* in Basel.

Lings, Martin (1909–) English. First Guénon's associate in Cairo, then Schuon's *muqaddam* in London.

Pauwels, Louis (1920–97). French writer and publisher specializing in the occult.

Hartung, Henri (1921–88). French, later resident in Switzerland. Briefly a follower of Schuon, later progressive public intellectual.

Pallavicini, Felice (1926–), Italian. Italian shaykh of a Traditionalist Sufi order in Milan, derived from the Idrisi Ahmadiyya.

Freda, Franco. Italian political traditionalist.

Jamal, Gaydar (1947–). Russian Islamist.

Against the Modern World

Prologue

It was dark save for the beam of a flashlight some floors up. Damp had mixed with smoke, and water was still running and dripping. A fireman passed me as I climbed anxiously up the stairs, but I let him pass without speaking to him, since my Russian is poor. Before going into the building where I was staying, I had already established that the fire had started on the roof. Tramps, they said, from the nearby Kurskaya rail station. I hoped that was the case, and nothing more sinister.

My Russian is poor, but the Russians I'd come to Moscow to interview were all cultivated men who spoke several languages. "Dugin is incredibly erudite, brilliant in his way. . . . The main thing to remember is that all these people are 100 percent insane," said an addendum to my introduction to one of these leaders, e-mailed to me by an American scholar, a Sovietologist when there was a Soviet Union, and then a collector of monarchists and fascists and "patriots" from the fringes of Russian politics. Dugin taught himself perfect French and quite reasonable English, plus two or three other European languages, while working as a street-sweeper during the closing years of the USSR. His former colleague Edvard Limonov had learned his almost perfect English while living in New York as a Soviet defector, a dissident novelist. And doing what else? Limonov's most famous book, *It's Me, Eddie*, was clearly autobiographical, but also fictional. It had been sitting unread on my bookshelf in Cairo since I'd put it down after reading a few pages years before, shortly after I first moved to Egypt. Later, when I'd finally realized why Limonov's name kept ringing a bell, I'd found his book again and read it, entranced. Limonov was describing the disorientation and disenchantment of the Soviet emigré, respected as poet in his own country even if rejected by the system, but neither needed nor respected in the West. He was also describing the experience of every emigré in the West, an experience I now recognized in some of my Egyptian friends, and the experience of every dissident, not just Soviet ones. Alexander Solzhenitsyn hadn't much liked the book, though, I later discovered (he described Limonov as "a little insect who writes pornography").

The sound of falling water was growing quieter as I reached the top of the stairs. The apartment I was staying in was more or less intact. The plaster had fallen from the ceiling in the kitchen, and the floor was half an inch deep in water, but that was all. My host's girlfriend's diminutive cat was still alive even if terrified, and my interview notes had been protected by the clear plastic folders in which I kept them. All remained legible save for a single sheet of background on conservative Communists and radical democrats. That night the cat crept into bed with me, burrowed beneath the blankets, as light and soft as a bird against my stomach.

It probably really was the tramps from the Kurskaya rail station, despite my fears. Moscow was beautiful that summer, but still a long way from home and help, and I had been meeting some strange people. Dugin had indeed been erudite, and charming too, but I'd never gotten further than a brief telephone call with Limonov, and even that had taken days to arrange. His reluctance to see me probably had something to do with the fact that Western journalists and scholars invariably wrote about him and Dugin as being threats to world peace, leaders of a frightening following of skinheads and punks, the personifications of the nightmare of a reborn Third Reich armed with nuclear weapons. Of course, any Russians who claim that their party—the National Bolshevik Party that Dugin and Limonov had founded—combines the best elements of Nazism and Stalinism are going to have PR difficulties with the Western public.

"I like people like that," said Natalya, the writer who had done most of the recent stories on Dugin and Limonov in the *Moscow Times.* "They're fun, different. Not like the other politicians." Natalya had taken me to one of Moscow's luncheon clubs, a stylish but largely empty restaurant in retro style, the music and decor from the early Brezhnev years. Access for members only, through an unmarked steel door, opened by a steely ex-KGB man in a dark suit. Natalya had progressed from being an occasional helper to American journalists in Leningrad, through the University of California and an internship on the *Los Angeles Times,* to being the personification of the best aspects of the New Russia. Irreproachably liberal, full of light and hope, partying and writing with equal zest, she had nothing of the fascist about her. But an explorer of alternatives? Yes. As we left the club she picked up a colorful sticker: "There are all sorts of strange people about nowadays. . . . And I like it." The reference was not to Dugin but to the increasing numbers of people living in Moscow without Moscow residence permits, the Muscovite equivalent of the West's immigrant problem.

In the center of Moscow another former colleague of Dugin's, Gaydar Jamal, lived behind another steel door, this one to an apartment in a smart building near the American Embassy. Jamal's door was opened not by an ex-KGB man but by a young Tartar with a shaven head, who later served Jamal and me thin coffee in cracked cups with saucers that didn't match. There were several other such young men in the almost unfurnished apartment, either doing nothing in general or doing nothing while I was there. Jamal and I talked of Dugin, of Islam, of our grandparents, of jihad, of Jamal's contacts with the Taliban, of modernity and tradition.

Although I could imagine Jamal's young Tartars getting up to all sorts of things, he and I got on well. He had even promised to look me up the next time he was in Cairo—not a prospect I really relished, both because of the implications for my file with the Egyptian security services of a visit from a high-profile foreign Islamist, and because I could imagine my wife's reaction when Jamal and his entourage dropped in unannounced. Dugin and I had got on well enough too. There had been no skinheads at his office, just a secretary looking forward to getting home, the inevitably stony-faced Russian janitor in her late fifties, and a man who looked as if he might be in the book trade, sitting on a sofa and leafing through the catalog of Dugin's publications. Dugin, I later realized, had by then already left the National Bolsheviks far behind and was embarked on the route that would lead him to a possibly even more frightening alliance with the Kremlin. Limonov, in contrast, ended up in jail.

Although almost all my notes remained legible despite the fire and water in my borrowed apartment, I had to get a new copy of Evola's *Riding the Tiger*, a book I'd brought with me to read while waiting for interviews to materialize. Evola, Baron Julius. Artillery officer, avant-garde painter, magician. Died in Rome, 1974. His books were discovered in the Lenin Library in Moscow by Jamal and a few other Soviet dissidents shortly after the Cuban missile crisis. The librarians who had let Evola's books onto the open shelves could never have looked inside their covers and had not realized how dangerous they were. In Italy in the 1970s, it is said, you got into more trouble if the police found Evola's books during a search of your apartment than if they found plastic explosives.

Evola was tried in Italy in 1951 for "plotting to reestablish Fascism," but he was acquitted. It was a ridiculous charge: mere Fascism had always been far too tame for Evola. True, he'd worked with Mussolini on Italy's racial laws, but the Fascists had finally summoned him home from Berlin and withdrawn his passport. His views were simply too extreme for them. Evola was to Mussolini as Trotsky was to Stalin—but who has heard of him? Well, the Italian anti-terrorist police, for a start. He just now scored 12,600 hits from an Internet search on google.com; Trotsky leads, admittedly, with 137,000 hits.

I myself had never heard of Evola until I asked Shaykh Abd al-Wahid Pallavicini how he became Muslim. That was how my research into Traditionalism started, in Milan in the winter of 1995–96, while I was interviewing the Italian shaykh of a Sufi order composed solely of Italian converts to Islam. I'd first heard of Pallavicini and the Italian Sufis at a conference in Khartoum, chatting with an Italian colleague outside the conference hall where we lingered to warm up between sessions. That conference hall was one of the few places in the Sudan that had working air conditioning, and the conference organizers were determined to use it to the full. The hot Sudanese sun and sand and silence provided occasional relief between tedious sessions in the fridge inside. As we shivered in the semi-darkness, Sudanese scholars one after another gave paper after paper on subjects in which they themselves had no great interest but which they thought might interest a foreigner and open the gates to the gold mine of a research grant from abroad.

"If you're working on the Idrisis," said my Italian colleague, "we have some in Milan." One of the aspects of the Idrisi Sufi order that interested me at that point was how it had spread, and so a few months later, during the cold January of 1996, I flew from Cairo to Milan. Some of Shaykh Pallavicini's followers met me at the airport, treating me with the greatest of respect because I came from the Orient. Well, had just come from the Orient—I was born in London, actually, with a surname that suggests distant Viking ancestry. I, in turn, treated Shaykh Pallavicini with the deepest respect too. That is how you treat Sufi shaykhs, and interviewing Sufi shaykhs was part of my business as a historian of Islam. I'd never met an Italian shaykh before, but it seemed safest to approach him more as a shaykh than as an Italian. During our interview Pallavicini told me that he had become Muslim in Switzerland in 1952, having been sent to a Sufi shaykh there by Evola. He'd contacted Evola as the Italian translator of the works of a French writer, René Guénon, whom he had been reading.

So perhaps my research didn't really start that winter, since I'd already heard of René Guénon, even though the name Evola then meant nothing to me. Perhaps my research had started ten years before, in 1986, on the second day of my first trip to Cairo. I was visiting a school friend who had gotten a job teaching freshman writing at AUC, the American University in Cairo, and my friend took me to lunch at the AUC cafeteria. We carried our trays from the cash register to a vacant table and sat down. "Those are the converts over there," remarked my friend, enjoying playing the part of guide, indicating a table toward the opposite side of the room. There were four men sitting around a small table, all with full beards, all dressed in dark clothes—or did they just look dark? After only two days in Cairo, I probably still associated Islam with darkness. How could a Westerner convert to Islam? The four men were talking quietly, their meal finished, leaning forward toward each other. What could they be talking about?

A year later I had moved to Cairo and was myself teaching at AUC, and I got to know one of those converts, a Danish citizen whose mother tongue was German but who spoke perfect American English and was often mistaken for an American. Once an ambulance driver in Hamburg, once a spiritual seeker in Sri Lanka, he had taught English at the American University of Beirut and there had met a Turkish Sufi shaykh and had become Muslim on the spot. He was not so dark, on closer acquaintance. Rather, he was a man with bright eyes and an irreverent sense of humor, who easily became a friend and remains one today. One day in the 1980s he lent me a book by René Guénon, who he said was a French convert to Islam who had lived in Cairo for many years. The book looked innocent enough—a Penguin paperback with an AUC library shelfmark on the spine. The date stamp inside indicated that the book was approximately twelve years overdue, as I pointed out. The convert smiled. "That is far too valuable a book," he said, "to be trusted to the library. Make sure you give it back to me."

It was a strange, difficult book, not about Islam at all. Rather, it was about time and quantity and quality and Aristotle, about Gog and Magog and the coming end of the world. It was a worrying book, and I found it hard to dismiss.

"How can you read this stuff?" asked the school friend who had pointed out the table of converts at lunch the previous fall.

"Guénon?" said another AUC professor. "Read this." And he gave me a book by Frithjof Schuon. A Swiss this time, and another shaykh, I was told. A different author from Guénon, lent to me by a different type of man, Alan Gould. Once a Beat poet, Gould radiated energy rather than humor, jetting in and out of Saudi Arabia and speaking—after decades in the Middle East—the most truly awful Arabic I've ever heard.

That was really how it started, with two converts to Islam teaching at AUC, and with two authors, both Europeans said to be Sufi shaykhs, but neither author, paradoxically, writing much about Islam. Though I couldn't see why, relations between the Guénon-reading convert and the Schuon-reading convert seemed cooler than I would have expected. Anyhow, when both names came up again in Milan—Schuon was the Swiss shaykh to whom Pallavicini was sent after reading Guénon—I was intrigued.

Guénon and Schuon clearly were important for one aspect of the Western encounter with Islam: not for the "clash of civilizations" encounter, but for its opposite—defection. Guénon's books were the major cause of conversion to Islam in Italy, according to the proprietor of one of Milan's major Islamic centers whom I interviewed. Ali Schutz ran a restaurant serving Middle Eastern cuisine which doubled as an exhibition space and occasional lecture hall. It was attached to a busy shop selling prayer carpets, scarves for Muslim women, incense burners, framed pictures of the Kaba in Mecca, Korans, and other books, including a shelf of Guénon's works in both French original and Italian translation. Ali himself was not a great fan of Guénon, "but that's what people want to read, and it's useful, it brings people to Islam."

So, an easy enough picture, except perhaps that Evola didn't really fit. "A sort of Fascist philosopher," said an Italian scholar I visited, "who thought that Islam was a spiritual race." I didn't learn much more; the scholar was suffering from severe influenza, had been reluctant to meet me at his apartment during the weekend, and clearly wanted to finish our interview as quickly as possible. I got up to go, and as I did so caught sight, in a poorly printed pamphlet open on his desk, of a blurry photograph of smiling men in SS uniform. I looked closer, questioning. "A Muslim contingent in the SS," answered my reluctant host. "I do some work on that sort of thing too." Then I was in the street, looking for a delicatessen to buy some treats to take back to Cairo with me. Two panettoni for the price of one (it was a fortnight after Christmas), and some porcini mushrooms. Mission accomplished. I had a chapter to add to my book on the spread of the Idrisi Sufi order, and some edible trophies of my trip.

My picture of Guénon and Schuon as Islamic writers was one that survived for some time. On the plane home from Milan I read a short biography of Guénon that one of Pallavicini's followers had given me. It talked briefly of Guénon's foolish youth, of his membership in various occultist groups in Paris, and then of his 1910 conversion to Islam at the age of 24. Guénonianism, as I was beginning to call it, seemed to be about Islam in the West. Schuon had been a reader and follower of Guénon. There was also Martin Lings, a follower first of Guénon and then of Schuon. I'd met Lings once when he came to Cairo to collect a prize from President Hosni Mubarak for a biography of the Prophet Muhammad he'd written; it was quite an achievement for an Englishman to write about the Prophet of Islam, to be translated into Arabic, and even to win a prize. Lings had entertained me and two others in his room at the Meridien hotel. Quintessentially English as he manipulated milk jug and teapot, speaking in the clipped accent of his generation, Lings talked about traditional and modern architecture. The Nile flowed past outside; Lings wore a *galabiyya* robe, and his guests were sitting on a hotel bed, but otherwise we might have been in Surrey.

In addition to Lings there was Seyyed Hossein Nasr, I learned—another known name, the author of *Ideals and Realities of Islam,* published by the AUC Press, that had been given to me by Rana, another AUC professor, its margins heavily annotated. Rana was beautiful and tragic, tortured by problems of every variety. Was she feminist first, or patriotic Arab opponent of Western cultural imperialism? Was she a daughter of the Nile, or alumna of Emmanuel College, Cambridge? Was she oppressed as a woman and a member of a once and forever subject race, or a wealthy employer of several servants at her splendid villa? Was she Muslim or freethinker? Scholar or novelist? Married or free? I don't know what part Nasr's book played in her struggles. Years later, when I met her in the street and we drank a difficult coffee together, striving and failing to break through a decade of silence to rediscover the intimacy we'd once shared, she was a divorced novelist, writing not in English but in Arabic, winner that year of a prestigious gold medal.

Once Shaykh Pallavicini had revealed to me that Schuon led a Sufi order, it was easy enough for me to find that order. Schuon's order was secret for most of its existence, but it is hard to keep entirely secret anything involving hundreds of people over more than seventy years. The secret was guarded most closely from the "profane," from irreligious modern Westerners. Living in Cairo and being familiar with Sufism and Islam, I was coming at it from the unguarded rear. Fragments I'd already heard here and there began to make sense. Rumors surrounding a dozen known figures, people who looked like Sufis but acknowledged membership in no known order, settled into place. I realized why a brilliant young Dutch scholar who had joined an Egyptian Sufi order in Alexandria had then left it for an unspecified destination. I now understood what it was that linked certain individuals I knew or knew of, who had always seemed to be more than just good friends: it was a secret Western Sufi order that for three quarters of a century had never admitted even its name, the Maryamiyya.

Slowly I began to piece together the links between Guénon and Schuon and an ever increasing number of Western writers about Islam, most of them open or secret converts to Islam. Library catalogs revealed books and publishers and journals. An interesting scholarly article had almost taken its final form when someone mentioned Andrew Rawlinson, a retired English academic living in France, and his forthcoming book, *Western Masters in Eastern Traditions*.

Rawlinson sent me the relevant sections of the draft of his book, from which a very different picture of Schuon emerged. Rawlinson saw Schuon not as a pious Sufi but as a charlatan, possibly self-deceiving and certainly deceiving others. He seemed to think that any Western convert to Islam must be somehow crazy, something that by then I knew was not the case. I politely questioned Rawlinson's view of Schuon. One morning, I found a stout envelope in my mailbox from Rawlinson, containing copies of some photographs. I sat at my desk, alternately burying the photographs under other papers and taking them out again, fascinated and horrified. There was Schuon dressed up as a Native American chief, surrounded by young women in bikinis. There was Schuon naked, save for what looked like a Viking helmet. And there was a painting by Schuon of the Virgin Mary, also naked, her genitalia clearly drawn. My intended article would need substantial revision, as would many other conclusions I had come to.

This was my first puzzle. Some of the major Western authors on Islam were followers of a man who went around dressed in a feather headdress, or not dressed at all, painting some very unusual pictures. At the least, I had to take more seriously the reports of other irregularities in the Maryamiyya Sufi order—irregularities from an Islamic point of view, at least. I went to talk to Gould, the Schuon reader, in his AUC office. He mentioned the photographs before I did, guessing correctly that I must have seen them. They were stolen, part of a sordid story he didn't want to go into, he said. Any interest in them was prurient. They were irrelevant. It was my problem if I chose, wrongly, to dwell on them. As for the alleged irregularities, they were not irregular: it was my understanding of the regular that was deficient. I had an ethical problem to face, and I was not facing it well. That was the end of a friendship with a man I had liked even if I had never really understood him, a man whose kindness was as visible and as endearing as his eccentricities.

While on a visit to America I went to Washington, D.C., to see Nasr, the author of Rana's much annotated book on the *Ideals and Realities of Islam*, and of many other books as well. "He's *University* Professor of Islamic Studies," a graduate student who I knew from Cairo explained to me before I left Princeton for Washington. "I'm not sure what that is, but it's much grander than just professor, and don't forget it." Whatever it was, it entitled Nasr to his own secretary and to a suite rather than a mere office, and it was made clear (though not by Nasr himself) that I was most fortunate to be granted access to the great man. I dared not mention the photographs. Nasr took much the same line as had Gould regarding irregularities. Properly understood, he explained, there was nothing irregular. Who was I to argue with a University Professor of Islamic Studies? I didn't attempt it. And yet I was far from convinced.

Two years later, when I went to Iran during another cold winter and visited the remains of the splendid Traditionalist academy that Nasr had once run there, I realized that I had actually been fortunate to meet a great man. Whatever a University Professor may be, Nasr in Iran had been far more important than he later became in America, and he remained important in Iran even after the revolution. Rana, I discovered, was only one of countless Muslims who, unsure how to integrate their own modernity with the religion and culture into which they had been born, hoped that Nasr might help them find an answer.

My second puzzle was the Evola connection. I was beginning to understand the basis of the philosophy that Guénon had developed, a philosophy that Nasr had convinced me should be called not Guénonianism but Traditionalism, and Evola and Schuon had clearly developed the same philosophy further than Guénon himself had. But Evola didn't fit in at all, neither with the picture of Sufi piety nor with the alternative picture of an influential cult. There was, I found, already a scholarly literature on Evola, but nowhere were Guénon or religion mentioned. Instead, Evola was invariably featured as the intellectual inspiration of Far Right terrorism in Italy during the so-called "years of lead," the 1970s, when machine-gun bullets had flown far more frequently than was healthy in a Western democracy. Clearly, something was missing. Evola came out of a religious movement. He had to have a religious side to him.

My chance to discover what Evola's religious side might have been was given to me by Friedrich Müller, a professor of religious studies at a European university. Müller approached me at a conference where I'd given a paper on "Traditionalist Sufism." He was interested in Guénon and therefore in my work on him, he said. We talked, and Müller offered to arrange for me to interview a Muslim follower of Evola, "if you don't mind your name appearing somewhere in a police file," he added. As a long-term resident of Egypt, with an Egyptian police file by then at least a foot thick, I wasn't much worried by the idea of a slim and presumably elegant folder among the files of the Italian police. I met Müller in Germany, and we proceeded together by train toward the northern Italian city of Parma. Even if I wasn't worried about police folders, Müller evidently was. Every time we changed trains he would apologize for leaving me on the platform and disappear into a public telephone box. After a number of calls, he announced that the meeting was on.

Claudio Mutti's office was in a nondescript gray apartment block on the edge of Parma, a working-class district with silent streets, battered cars parked under trees, and sleeping cats. Mutti's office was a room in his mother's small apartment, not entirely insulated from the appetizing smells of Italian cooking. There was a small desk which, with its stand of rubber stamps, resembled a busy bureaucrat's. The walls were decorated with Islamic kitsch—quotations from the Koran printed on metallic paper adorned with glitter, photographs of sites in Mecca and Medina framed in cheap plastic. Behind a filing cabinet, out of character with the Islamic theme, leaned a staff on which hung a flag, a black cross bordered with white on a red field, an Iron Cross in the upper left quarter, and a swastika in the center. I later identified this as the *Reichskriegsflagge*, the Nazi War Ensign.

Mutti sat not at his desk but on a wooden kitchen chair. After chatting amicably with Müller in excellent French, Mutti turned to me and helpfully answered my questions. Any serious reader of Evola, he said, would know Guénon, though not all readers of Guénon would discover Evola. We discussed Evola's possible spiritual practice, and Mutti gave me a copy of an article in which he had explained of himself, "Why I chose Islam." From there we passed onto Evola's influence in other countries. Mutti had taught Romanian and Hungarian at an Italian university until dismissed for his political activities, I was told, and he kept in touch with Romanians and Hungarians interested in Evola. Did I remember the television pictures of Ceauşescus's trial? asked Mutti. The judge in the background in military fatigues with a white beard? A great fan of Guénon, he was, said Mutti. Perhaps I would like a copy of Mutti's book on Evola on the Eastern Front? It was produced, inscribed, received with thanks.

It was only much later that I discovered what I should have been asking

Mutti about: not the Islamic kitsch but the *Reichskriegsflagge*. Before leaving Italy, I went into a large bookstore and asked about books on the "black" terrorists, the rightists. The sales assistant looked surprised. There were plenty of books on "red" violence, he said almost hopefully, if I wanted one of those. It was really "black" violence that interested me? Well, there might be something. He found me Franco Ferraresi's thick book on *Threats to Democracy*. Italian academia is highly politicized, and Ferraresi was evidently of the Left, but among the attempts to blame rightist terrorism on a corrupt and morally bankrupt establishment, his book provided exhaustive coverage of the extreme Right in the 1960s and 1970s. When I finally got around to reading the book back in Cairo, I found, among the many groups that took their inspiration from Evola, one truly frightening in its nihilism, the group once led by Franco Freda. And among Freda's followers had been Mutti, my accommodating host in Parma. I wondered who Professor Müller had been calling to arrange that meeting.

What else were these Traditionalists? Pious Sufis or a cult, religious or political? Soon people were beginning to challenge my initial view of Traditionalism as an Islamic, or an occidental-Islamic, phenomenon. The trouble started at a conference on new religious movements in Amsterdam, where I gave a paper on "Traditionalist Sufism." That was where Müller had approached me and invited me to accompany him to Parma. It was where I had been invited to Moscow. It was also where I first came to the attention of the French.

I had discovered the Amsterdam conference on the Internet while trying to educate myself about Madame Blavatsky and the Theosophical Society. Sufi shaykhs pride themselves on their spiritual genealogy as much as Austrian grand dukes once prided themselves on their bloodlines, and as a researcher into Sufism I couldn't just dismiss Guénon's foolish youth. The key figure at first seemed to be someone referred to, always in quotation marks, as "Papus," a man whose books on the Tarot and astrology and reincarnation were still in print. Reading about "Papus" led me to the Theosophists, and memories of my early teens. At the age of 15 I read my way through the works of Paul Gallico of *Snow Goose* fame, a book that has been out of print for years. Near my school had been a dusty bookshop that sold more pens and paper than books, and on its shelves were unsold first editions of Gallico's novels, irresistibly on offer in the late 1970s at original 1960s prices. I much enjoyed *The Hand of Mary Constable* (1964): "Alexander Hero . . . is sent to New York, where a scientist is convinced that he is in touch with his dead daughter through a medium. The evidence is a cast of a hand, with the fingerprints of the dead girl in them." Ectoplasm, red spies, everything.

By the end of my research on Traditionalism, I had encountered an atomic scientist and even red spies (retired ones), but no ectoplasm. I had also learned that although there had been almost as much trickery around Blavatsky as in

Paul Gallico's novel, there was deep seriousness in Theosophy too—seriousness of consequences today, as of motivations then. At the Amsterdam conference I listened in growing fascination to the papers. I knew that religion mattered in the contemporary Middle East, that political and cultural developments there could hardly be studied without reference to Islam, but I had always assumed that this was one of the special characteristics of the region in which I lived and on which I worked. The West was different, I thought: save for some pockets of resistance in the United States, it was a postreligious world, a secular society. Yet the majority of Swedes believe that the earth is visited by alien beings, I learned, as do at least one third of Americans. According to one survey, over a quarter of French people believe in reincarnation. Professor Wouter Hanegraaff of the University of Amsterdam argued that although Western esotericism has often been ignored by scholars embarrassed at this survival from earlier times, the emergence of modernity itself is in fact intertwined with the history of esotericism. Theosophy, I learned to my astonishment, even lay at the origin of the specialty store in the fashionable Zamalek district of Cairo where my wife and I bought our organic vegetables.

Amsterdam is where I met the community of scholars studying new religious movements in the West, and also where a subsection of that community discovered me. Soon after the conference had finished, the editor of a French journal I'd never heard of e-mailed me in Cairo, asking to publish my paper on "Traditionalist Sufism." When I submitted the text, a reviewer from the Sorbonne questioned my view of Guénon as purely Muslim. At the Sorbonne, I discovered, Guénon was seen as Catholic, as part of the history of French esotericism, and as a Freemason; his Islam was thought to be almost secondary.

And so the Amsterdam conference led me to Paris, Guénon's own city. Guénon had once submitted a Ph.D. thesis to the Sorbonne and had it rejected, but even if Guénon never forgave the Sorbonne, by the end of the twentieth century the Sorbonne had rehabilitated Guénon. I made an appointment at the Section for Religious Sciences of the School of Higher Studies with Monsieur Jean-Pierre Laurant, French academia's leading authority on Guénon and the most critical reviewer of my "Traditionalist Sufism." A porter directed me to the library, a tiny paneled room with glass-fronted bookcases and creaking floors, where I found a gray-haired gentleman poring over a manuscript covered with kabbalistic charts and diagrams. The manuscript rolled and stowed, we proceeded out into the sunlight to a nearby cafe; I was soon to discover that most French scholarly discourse takes place in cafes. Monsieur Laurant's courtesy matched the venerable paneling of the library as he inquired after the progress of my researches, rather as one might ask after the health of a mutual friend. He offered a few suggestions, almost apologetically. Each, of course, turned out to open a new and wide avenue of inquiry.

One of the centers of Guénon's life in Paris had been his publisher, once called Chacornac Brothers and then renamed "Traditional Books" (Editions traditionnelles) in honor of the movement Chacornac's best-selling author had founded. Its address was printed on the front covers of countless books I had seen: 11, quai Saint-Michel, a short walk from the Sorbonne. But when I reached the quai Saint-Michel, Editions traditionnelles was no longer there. Only one esoteric bookshop survived in the quarter, the Table d'Emeraude, in the rue de la Huchette (the "medieval rue de la Huchette," according to the guidebook), one street back from the River Seine. The area was otherwise given over to tourists and postcard sellers, and to restaurants where one heard every language but French. The Table d'Emeraude bookshop was dilapidated, its staff manifestly unenthusiastic even about going to the effort of opening the cash register.

Three days later I had to suggest a place to meet with a Traditionalist Sufi shaykh who was coming from Burgundy to Paris on business involving the sale of horses (the shaykh in question ran a stud farm). Despite my earlier reception there, I chose the sidewalk in front of the Table d'Emeraude, thinking that at least I could browse profitably if the shaykh was late. He did arrive late, giving me details by cell phone of the traffic jam he was stuck in, but I had no profitable distraction while waiting for him. Since my previous visit, the Table d'Emeraude had closed down. "And had reopened as a Greek restaurant?" inquired Monsieur Laurant when I next saw him.

Following Monsieur Laurant's leads, I accumulated growing lists of names. These I investigated initially in the ultramodern National Library of France, a brand-new monstrosity with its own metro station and a computer system of a complexity that defeated its employees almost as often as its readers. From the National Library to more meetings in more cafes. "So you were the person who ordered that book," remarked a young Catholic scholar. "I wondered who it was." The young scholar, it seemed, worked part-time at the National Library. It was never quite clear to what extent some of these French scholars were studying the Traditionalist movement and to what extent they were part of it, how much I was being helped and how much I was being monitored.

More details of Guénon's interests and influence emerged from the Freemasons, especially from the archivist of the French National Grand Lodge, whom I met not in a cafe but in an office adjoining the Grand Lodge's library. There was no air of Masonic secrecy here, but rather the piles of books and papers that accumulate in the office of any active but slightly disorganized scholar. I obtained still more details from a jovial pipe-smoking monk in a three-piece suit, who ordered couscous for lunch at his neighboring North African restaurant. Yet more notes came from interviews with a French Muslim scholar who gave me an appointment at the cafe attached to the Institute of the Arab World, where we drank green tea with mint out of silvered Moroccan teapots rather than the usual small cups of coffee.

Leaving the Institute of the Arab World, I paused at various Arab-Islamic bookshops on the way back to the metro, trying to establish a rough ratio of Traditionalist to non-Traditionalist books on sale. After three such bookshops, I found myself outside Editions traditionnelles, miraculously and unexpectedly reopened in more hospitable surroundings than the streets full of Greek restaurants and tourists that had submerged its original quarter. I bought a few books and interviewed the owner, who clearly hoped I might buy one of the remaining complete sets of *Etudes traditionnelles*, Guénon's journal (I hereby wholeheartedly recommend those remaining sets to research libraries worldwide). On my way out of the shop I paused by a pile of tattered and yellowed pamphlets. "Take one if you like," said the owner, and I did. It was *The Veil of Isis* of May 6, 1891, subtitled *The Weekly Organ of the Independent Esoteric Studies Group of Paris*, price 10 centimes, "edited by 'Papus,'" "Papus," described by one enthusiastic biographer as "the Balzac of occultism," had been Guénon's first known contact with the occultist milieu. And there, together with an announcement of "Papus"'s next lecture (on "The Black Mass through the Ages"), were articles in which, years before the movement should have existed, I seemed to be reading Traditionalists. Or, putting things the right way around, something very like Traditionalism had evidently existed before Guénon.

By the time I left Paris, I had to admit that there was a lot more to Guénon than Islam, that the view of Guénon that was current in Paris was as valid as that held in Cairo. And it didn't end there. Once my article on "Traditionalist Sufism" had been published and another conference paper I gave on "Traditionalists on the Web" had been posted, appropriately, on the conference organizers' website, people began to contact me. I learned of Traditionalist occultists in Brazil, of Traditionalist philosophers in Iran, and of a Traditionalist art school in Britain. And the art school in Britain turned out to operate under the auspices of Prince Charles and to share premises with something called the Temenos Academy. The Temenos Academy, I learned, had been established by one of Britain's best-regarded poets, Kathleen Raine, and it was in correspondence with Kathleen Raine that I first encountered the name of Marsilio Ficino. This name led me to Renaissance Italy, and to the first origins of Traditionalism. Professor Hanegraaff, the scholar of esotericism, seemed to be right. Traditionalism set itself against the modern world, but it was born with modernity, in the Renaissance.

Kathleen Raine and Prince Charles were not the only well-known names that were beginning to appear in my notes. At times it felt as if I was uncovering the secret intellectual history of the twentieth century. There were Aldous Huxley and André Gide and T. S. Eliot. "How did you first encounter Traditionalism?" I asked an American professor in an e-mail. Through the works of E. F. Schumacher, he replied. Schumacher? Who else? Mircea Eliade, why not? Claimed as a Traditionalist by Mutti in his book on Evola on the Eastern Front, damned as a Fascist and anti-Semite by his enemies and by Saul Bellow, marked forever, I concluded, by his early encounter with Guénon and Evola.

Huston Smith? Thomas Merton? Of course—I was no longer surprised by anything. Jung? Why not Sartre as well? There are limits. Never Sartre, and on closer investigation Jung turned out to be from a sometimes similar, but ultimately quite different, school.

Many of those who contacted me over the next two years were former or current members of Schuon's Maryamiyya, the secret Sufi order which had ended in the "irregularities" that had first alerted me to the fact that there was more to Traditionalism than met the eye. "Do you want to know the truth about Schuon?" asked one e-mail. Yes, please, I replied—and then found myself engaged for several weeks in a difficult correspondence through which I finally managed to convince my timid volunteer that I really was an objective scholar, not a crypto-fascist. My article required some clarifications, explained another, politely, through an intermediary. Letters, faxes, and e-mails followed, as did interviews from Chicago to Geneva, as well as photocopies of hundreds of documents of one sort or another. All of these informants said either that they wanted to set the record straight, or that they wanted the truth to be known, but I began to realize that most were seeking an answer and were hoping that I might help provide it. What, they were all asking themselves, went wrong? A distinguished elderly gentleman invited me to lunch at his country house in the Swiss mountains, introduced me to his grandchildren, and then seemed reluctant to be alone with me. I finally asked one or two questions in front of his son-in-law, who had also once followed Schuon, and received only defensive and evasive answers. We reverted to generalities as the scheduled interview became a somewhat uncomfortable social visit. At the very end, as I was preparing to leave to catch my train, the elderly gentleman sought me out. "I am so sorry. Please forgive my reactions earlier. You must understand that . . . all these years . . . it is all so . . . painful." I left with nothing to add to my notes, but with great compassion for that sad gentleman. A year later, when I heard of his death, I grieved.

By then I was beginning to understand what lay behind Traditionalism. Evola's Fascist connections were interesting, but they were not the point. W. B. Yeats mattered more than Mussolini: Yeats was not himself a Traditionalist, but definitely a precursor, along with William Blake. "Things fall apart, the centre cannot hold, / Mere anarchy is loosed upon the world," Yeats had written. His "centre" was Raine's *temenos*, the sacred center, the divine and the spiritual, that essential aspect of human life which seemed to have vanished from the West. In its absence, all was falling apart, and anarchy threatened— not mere political anarchy, but a more serious, more deep-reaching anarchy. Traditionalism was the exhilarating attempt to reinstate a divine order, the response of sensitive and intelligent individuals to an alien world, to a West in which they were as much dissidents as Dugin had been in the late USSR.

The Schuon riddle was in the end the most difficult one of all, and part of the problem was to discover when the "irregularities" first began to manifest themselves. They were clearly there in the 1990s: had they started in the 1980s or 1970s? One well-informed non-Traditionalist source spoke of rumors even in the 1960s. Then another elderly gentleman, whom I shall always remember with respect and affection, got in touch with me. He bought me lunch by the edge of a lake, took me for a walk, and lent me a book, a paperback with a plain cream cover bearing only the title *Erinnerungen und Betrachtungen*, or Memories and Reflections, and the name of its author: Frithjof Schuon. Privately printed by subscription for restricted circulation, this was Schuon's own autobiography, almost amazingly frank, and it answered almost all my remaining questions. The "irregularities" had started in the 1940s, or even at the very beginning in the 1930s, or perhaps in Schuon's childhood. And that tragedy was at last explained.

Schuon's memoirs provided an explanation on a personal level, and my contacts with so many other Traditionalists, face to face or in their writings, followers of Schuon or always independent of him, provided other such explanations. A more general explanation of Traditionalism was still needed: an explanation of why it spread as it did, why it mattered so much to so many, and why it attracted some of the most important minds in modern thought. As a historian, I am of course convinced that a carefully told story is in itself a path to understanding, and that conviction underlies the book that follows this prologue. In addition, a more theoretically based analysis will be found in chapter 14. The questions discussed there include the relationship between Traditionalism and Orientalism, historical streams and counterstreams, globalization, cultural displacement, and the tactic of *entrisme*. These are all questions that writing this book has helped me to understand better, but in the end that was not really the point. This book is dedicated not to abstract questions, but to the people whose hopes and aspirations, energies and—sometimes—errors make up the history of Traditionalism.

PART I

The Development of Traditionalism

I

Traditionalism

There are many sorts of "traditionalists" and many "traditionalist" movements. In the widest sense of the word, a "traditionalist" may be no more than a conservative, possibly a nostalgic person who hankers after the customs of his or her youth. A "traditionalist" may also be someone who prefers a specific established practice over something that has replaced it, as in the case of Marcel Lefebvre, the Catholic archbishop who rejected the conclusions of the Second Vatican Council and established a schismatic church following the old Tridentine rite. He and his followers are commonly described as "Catholic traditionalists."

This book is the history of a movement that is "traditionalist" in a more precisely defined sense. The word "tradition" derives from the Latin verb *tradere*, to hand over or to hand down, and in an etymological sense a tradition is "a statement, belief or practice transmitted (especially orally) from generation to generation."[1] The Traditionalist movement with which this book deals takes "tradition" primarily in this sense, as belief and practice transmitted from time immemorial—or rather belief and practice that *should* have been transmitted but was lost to the West during the last half of the second millennium A.D. According to the Traditionalists, the modern West is in crisis as a result of this loss of transmission of tradition, as was explained in 1927 in *The Crisis of the Modern World*. The solution? Most frequently, *Oriental Metaphysics* (1939), but sometimes *Revolt against the Modern World* (1934). *Crisis of the Modern World* and *Oriental Metaphysics* were the work of René Guénon, who will be considered primarily in the first three chapters of this book; *Re-*

volt against the Modern World was the work of Julius Evola, whom we will meet later.[2]

The Traditionalists who are discussed in this book constitute a movement in the loosest sense of the word. The Traditionalist movement has no formal structure, and since the late 1940s has had no central command. It is made up of a number of groups and individuals, united by their common debt to the work of René Guénon. Though the movement is sometimes called "Guénonian traditionalism," most of those involved in it reject that title and prefer to call themselves "traditionalists," often with a small *t*; I use the title that they give themselves, but for the sake of clarity I always capitalize the *T*.

The history of Traditionalism falls into three stages, reflected in the three parts into which this book is divided. During the first stage, up to the 1930s, Guénon developed the Traditionalist philosophy, wrote various articles and books, and gathered a small group of followers. During the second stage, attempts were made to put the Traditionalist philosophy into practice, principally in two very different contexts: Sufi Islam, as an example of Oriental metaphysics, and European fascism, as a form of revolt. During the third stage, after the 1960s, Traditionalist ideas began to merge unremarked into the general culture of the West and to pass from the West to the Islamic world and to Russia.

Guénon's Works

Guénon had published his first articles by 1910 and his first book in 1921, and he continued to publish new books until 1946, as well as writing enough articles to fill a dozen posthumous collections. The essentials of the Traditionalist philosophy, however, can be found in four books published between 1921 and 1924.[3]

The first of these four books was Guénon's *L'introduction générale à l'étude des doctrines hindoues* [A General Introduction to the Study of Hindu Doctrines], published in 1921.[4] The *Introduction générale* was controversial from the start. It was recommended for publication by a distinguished French Catholic philosopher then at the start of his career, Jacques Maritain, an important figure in the early history of Traditionalism, but had previously been rejected as a doctoral thesis by an equally distinguished French Indologist then at the peak of his career, Sylvain Lévi.

Lévi rejected the *Introduction générale* (in thesis form) for three main reasons. First, it "ma[de] light of history and historical criticism,"[5] a criticism of Guénon's methodology that was in many ways justified. Guénon made no pretense of following the standard scholarly methods of Indology: for reasons examined later, his approach was theological rather than anthropological or sociological. For Guénon, Hinduism was a repository of spiritual truth, not the body of beliefs and practices modified over time that late nineteenth-century Western scholarship recognized. While this approach obviously disqualified Guénon's work for Lévi's purposes, it did not for the Catholic philosopher Maritain.

Lévi's second objection to Guénon's thesis was that it left out anything that did not fit Guénon's theory that Hinduism could be reduced to Vedanta.[6] Vedanta is one of six *darshanas* or philosophical schools of Hindusim, and draws especially on the Upanishads as the end or summation of the Vedas, the most important of the Hindu scriptures, along with the Bhagavad Gita and the Brahma-sutras. These were among the earliest Hindu texts to be translated into French and Vedanta became widely known as a result of the inclusion of two chapters of the Bhagavad Gita in the *Cours de philosophie* [Course in Philosophy] (1828) of the popular French philosopher Victor Cousin.[7] Vedanta was widely appreciated in the nineteenth-century West, mostly because it "recognize[d] no reality but the Universal Being, unique and without limiting qualification,"[8] a characteristic with obvious appeal for those brought up in a monotheistic culture. For Lévi and for later Indologists, however, there are many varieties of Hinduism other than that of Vedanta; that Guénon chose to ignore these was a consequence of the context in which he had first encountered Vedanta, discussed later. As a philosopher, Maritain would have had no views on this omission: the status of Vedanta in Hindu culture lay beyond his field.

Lévi's third objection to the thesis was that Guénon was "quite ready to believe in a mystical transmission of a primal truth [*une vérité première*] that appeared to humanity in the first ages of the world,"[9] a belief that for Lévi was self-evidently ridiculous but that Maritain evidently did not find especially objectionable.[10]

What Lévi called "a primal truth" is more commonly known as the Perennial Philosophy, and belief in the existence of the Perennial Philosophy—a belief I will call "Perennialism"—is one of three central elements in the Traditionalist philosophy that Guénon developed.

The term *philosophia perennis* (Perennial Philosophy) was coined in 1540 by a Catholic scholar[11] to describe one of the central insights of Marsilio Ficino, an important figure in the origins of Traditionalism. Ficino was a priest who was president of the Platonic Academy of Florence during the fifteenth century and one of the central figures of the Italian Renaissance.[12] He considered the fifteenth century's revival of interest in Plato to be a gift of God to provide philosophical arguments to support Christianity, and he saw Plato and Christianity as having equal authority because they were the same: "lawful religion is no different from true religion; and lawful religion is no different from true philosophy."[13] Whereas a modern Westerner might justify religion by giving it a philosophical coloring, Ficino did the reverse, giving to Platonic philosophy a religious coloring. For Ficino, God lay behind both Christ and Plato, and the

Perennial Philosophy preceded (and so united) both. All religions shared a common origin in a single perennial (or primeval or primordial) religion that had subsequently taken a variety of forms, including the Zoroastrian, Pharaonic, Platonic, and Christian.[14]

For a century and a half after Ficino, the idea that there was a Perennial Philosophy became increasingly widely accepted. Perennialism was, however, discredited in the early seventeenth century[15] and thereafter survived only at the edges of Western intellectual life. Then, in the nineteenth century, Perennialism was revived in a slightly modified form, with the newly discovered Vedas being taken as its surviving textual expression. It was in this form, as we shall see, that Guénon encountered Perennialism, and it is this form of Perennialism that is advanced in the *Introduction générale*, was rejected by Lévi, and is central to the Traditionalist philosophy.

The next two of Guénon's books that appeared after the *Introduction générale* added the second of the three central elements of the Traditionalist philosophy (the first element being what may be called Vedanta-Perennialism). Like the *Introduction générale*, these two books emerged under Catholic auspices, being derived from articles that were originally commissioned in 1921 by Father Emile Peillaube, a colleague of Maritain, for the *Revue de Philosophie* [Journal of Philosophy], which he edited.[16] The first of these articles attacked Theosophy (a religious movement discussed later in this book) and was the basis of Guénon's second book, *Le Théosophisme, histoire d'une pseudo-religion* (1921). This was followed by a similar work in 1923, *L'erreur spirite* [Spiritualist Errors].[17] Both were sophisticated demolitions of Theosophy, spiritualism, and occultism, proceeding from a familiarity with the occultist milieu that Guénon had acquired between 1906 and 1912, a period of his life discussed in the next two chapters of this book.

The principal importance of these two books for the Traditionalist philosophy is that they advanced two interrelated concepts, "counterinitiation" and "inversion." In Traditionalist use, "counterinitiation" is the opposite not of initiation as such but of initiation into a valid, orthodox tradition such as that represented by Vedanta. "Counterinitiation" is initiation into pseudo-traditions such as Theosophy, which are in fact the inversion of true tradition. Instead of leading to the Perennial Philosophy, counterinitiation leads away from it. The place of initiation in the Traditionalist philosophy (the third of the three central elements) is considered later.

More important than "counterinitiation" is the related concept of "inversion." Guénon did not invent this concept, which is present in eschatological accounts of the Anti-Christ (who is the inversion of the true Christ), but it was to become a major element of Traditionalism. Counterinitiation is the inversion of initiation, but inversion is not restricted to questions of initiation. In its fully developed Guénonian form, inversion is seen as an all-pervasive characteristic of modernity. While all that really matters is in fact in decline, people foolishly suppose that they see progress.

Inversion, the second concept advanced in these two books, is one of the most powerful elements in the Traditionalist philosophy, providing many readers of Guénon and of later Traditionalists with a persuasive explanation of much that seemed most perplexing to them about the twentieth century. To take contemporary examples, phenomena that can be explained as examples of inversion include youth fashions of apparent ugliness, the preaching of the values of "letting it all hang out" as superior to self-restraint, the existence of pedophile priests, and the photographs of Andres Serrano.[18] In the words of a contemporary Traditionalist—a young and talented European scholar of Islam—once the modern world is understood in terms of decline rather than progress, almost everything else changes, and there are not many people left you can usefully talk to.[19] Of course, a non-Traditionalist might point out that comparable examples of inversion could be found in the fifteenth century as well as the early twenty-first century, but that is not the point.

Guénon's next book completed the essentials of the Traditionalist philosophy. This was *Orient et Occident* [East and West] (1924), a call for the saving of the West from collapse by means of Oriental tradition. In the first half of this book Guénon systematically attacks the illusion of materialism and the "superstitions" of progress, reason, change (as desirable in itself), and sentimental moralizing (an Anglo-Saxon specialty):

> Modern Western civilization appears in history as a veritable anomaly among all those that we know; this civilization is the only one that was developed in a purely material direction, and this monstrous development, the start of which coincides with what is commonly called the Renaissance, has been accompanied by a corresponding intellectual regression which has reached a point where today's Occidentals no longer know what pure intellectuality might be—hence their disdain, not only for Oriental civilizations, but also for the European Middle Ages.[20]

By "pure intellectuality" Guénon means something close to metaphysics, "spirituality" or religion, which has been replaced by a superstitious cult of reason that values only that which is not really valuable—an example of inversion.

Given the identification of the Orient with tradition and the Occident with modernity, the title "East and West" could equally well have been "Traditional and Modern," and the second rather than the first pair of terms would come to be the standard ones in Traditionalist discourse. What Guénon opposes is not the West but the modern world, and what he hopes for is not the triumph of the East but to "restore to the West an appropriate traditional civilization."[21] The West, Guénon argued in *Orient et Occident*, was in grave danger—not because of "chimerical terrors" such as Bolshevism and the "Yellow Peril" (a phrase he uses in quotations, meaning Chinese and Japanese militarism), but because it was based on nothing more substantial than industrial superiority. In the absence of any real—that is, spiritual—foundations, Western civilization was in immediate danger of cataclysmic collapse into barbarism and consequent extinction through assimilation by more soundly based civilizations.[22]

Guénon was not the only one writing about the imminent collapse of the West in the 1920s: Oswald Spengler's widely read *Der Untergang des Abendlandes* [The Decline of the West] was published in two volumes between 1919 and 1922.[23] The fact that the West has not yet collapsed is not sufficient reason for dismissing Guénon as a marginal eccentric: there are even today sober voices warning of such a collapse. Again, a non-Traditionalist might point out that a sense of decline and a fear of imminent collapse is, like inversion, to be found in many ages and places and is arguably a standard human characteristic, but, again, that is not the point.

Guénon wished to avert the extinction of the West, and he devoted the second half of his book to explaining how its destruction might be avoided. What was needed was an "intellectual elite"—"intellectual" being used in a special Guénonian sense of spiritual, metaphysical—to receive "traditional teaching" by "an assimilation . . . of Oriental doctrines" (unless surviving Western forms could be found, which Guénon thought unlikely), so as to push the West toward the restoration of a traditional civilization.[24] Guénon thought this plan had only a possibility of success but believed it worth trying, since at the very least it would be of benefit to the members of the elite themselves, and

> If the elite does not have the time for sufficiently generalized activities to profoundly modify the Western mentality as a whole this elite would be the symbolic "ark" floating on the waters of the flood and could thus serve as the focal point for activities through which the West, though probably losing its autonomous existence, would however receive the bases of a new development, this time a regular and normal one. But there would still be difficult problems: the ethnic revolutions would certainly be most serious. It would be much preferable for the West to acquire a civilization appropriate to its own conditions, sparing it from being more or less unpleasantly assimilated by traditional forms that are not made for it.[25]

Guénon's proposed elite did not need to be large or organized at first, nor secret, since its activities would "by their very nature, remain invisible to the commonality, not because they are hidden from it, but because it is incapable of understanding them." Indeed, a premature attempt at organization, especially at any large organization, would be not only useless but dangerous, because of "the deviations that would inevitably occur," and because of the temptations of "immediate social action, perhaps even political action." However, there would be no harm in forming small "study groups," though the members of these would have to be careful because they would threaten "unsuspected low powers." Only once the ground had been properly prepared would a "strongly constituted organization" be needed and possible.[26]

With *Orient et Occident* the essentials of the Traditionalist philosophy are established. Though this idea is not explicit in *Orient et Occident*, the appropriate traditional doctrine for the West to assimilate in order to survive was some expression of the Perennial Philosophy, as described in the *L'introduction générale à l'étude des doctrines hindoues*, which is in fact more of an introduction to a Guénonian understanding of "Oriental metaphysics" than to Hinduism. The "unsuspected low powers" opposed to this project included counterinitiatic organizations, though once again there is no explicit reference in *Orient et Occident* to *Le Théosophisme* or *L'erreur spirite*.

This book is a history of the various attempts over the remainder of the twentieth century to put Guénon's project into action, to form his elite, and to restore "traditional civilization" to the West. "Unsuspected low powers" proved less of a problem than Guénon feared, and they barely feature in the following chapters. There were, however, many Traditionalist organizations that were in retrospect "premature"—some of them specifically oriented toward "social [and] political action"—and various "deviations" did indeed result.

Before we move on, it is necessary to give a better example of Guénon's style than the preceding quotations, which have been edited for directness. Guénon's style is often anything but direct, though it reads somewhat better in French than in English. For example, Guénon introduces this announcement: "If some people, instead of working in isolation, prefer to meet so as to constitute a sort of 'study group,' it is not there that we see a danger nor even a difficulty," with the following: "However, we do not wish to close the door on any possibility, no more on this ground than any other, nor to discourage any initiative, however little it is likely to produce valuable results and avoid ending in a simple wasting of effort; we only wish to warn against false views and too-hasty conclusions."[27]

Guénon's style, though invariably praised by Traditionalists, is hardly calculated to appeal to the "commonality," the counterpart of Guénon's elite and a group that Guénon clearly dismissed. Guénon made no attempt to communicate with those who he thought would neither understand nor appreciate his work—though, as we will see, some later Traditionalists did successfully address general audiences.

Guénon published six more books during the 1920s, of which the most important are *L'homme et son devenir selon le Védânta* [Man and His Future according to the Vedanta] (1925) and *La crise du monde moderne* [The Crisis of the Modern World] (1927).[28] The first is a development of the *Introduction générale* and the second a development of the first part of *Orient et Occident*, treating the question of the nature and role of the elite only briefly, in a postscript.

La crise du monde moderne is Guénon's masterpiece. It is one of the most frequently translated of his works, and has remained in print and generally available since publication, being today a standard part of the publisher Gallimard's popular and prestigious Folio series (the French equivalent of Penguin Modern Classics). It is probably the best starting place for any reader interested in investigating the original texts of Traditionalism.

Among the refinements introduced in *La crise du monde moderne* is more palatable terminology, with "sacred science" effectively replacing the "pure intellectuality" of *Orient et Occident*, and "profane" replacing "common." The style is also much improved. What remains of the discussion of the "intellectual elite," for example, is introduced as follows: "If everyone understood what the modern world really is, it would immediately cease to exist, since its existence, like that of all limitations, is purely negative; it exists only by the negation of traditional and suprahuman truth."[29]

The improved style and the clarity and force of *La crise du monde moderne* may well be the result of the conditions under which it was written—in a hurry. Many writers find that what is written almost without thinking on a subject that has been well digested is better than what is written painstakingly with the benefit of extensive revision, and this seems to have been the case for Guénon. The origin of the book was the suggestion by Gonzague Truc, a publisher and a friend of Guénon, that Guénon write a book summarizing their many conversations. Guénon did so, producing what Truc called "a work of inspiration."[30]

As well as being an improvement on previous works from the point of view of style and organization, *La crise du monde moderne* refines the Traditionalist concept of "inversion." In addition to a chapter on social chaos there is a discussion of individualism as both a modern superstition and a modern illusion: Guénon explains how modern "individualism" in fact destroys real "individuality." Both social chaos and individualism were issues in 1927 and remain issues today. More important, *La crise du monde moderne* starts with a discussion of the Hindu concept of cyclical time, in which the final era, the *kali yuga* (literally "fourth age," glossed by Guénon as "dark age") is a 6,000-year period of decline. It is in the *kali yuga* that we presently find ourselves (according to both Guénon and most Hindu writers). The theory of cyclical time and *kali yuga* complete one aspect of the Traditionalist philosophy by providing the explanation for the state of affairs explored by Guénon elsewhere: inversion is a characteristic of the *kali yuga*.

Guénon and the Catholics

Although the Traditionalist philosophy is not Catholic, it was Catholic sponsorship—in the form of Maritain's recommendation of the *Introduction générale* and Peillaube's commissioning of articles by Guénon for the *Revue de Philosophie*—that helped Traditionalism to emerge into the public sphere from its origins, which, as we shall see, lie in the occultist milieu of the Belle Epoque.

Guénon's contacts with Catholics started in 1909, when he was first published in *La France chrétienne* [Christian France], a periodical discussed later that specialized in attacks on Freemasons and occultists. Though *La France chrétienne* was a very different type of periodical from Peillaube's *Revue de Philosophie*, Guénon wrote on similar subjects for both publications: against what he saw as "counterinitiation" and what the Catholics saw as the enemies of the Church. Contacts between Guénon and the Catholics became deeper in 1915 when Guénon began to attend lectures at the Institut Catholique (Catholic Institute),[31] a private institution of higher education established after the Law of Separation of Church and State of 1905 had made it impossible to continue teaching Catholic theology at the (state-owned) Sorbonne. Most members of the former department of theology at the Sorbonne seceded to establish the Catholic Institute, where Peillaube was chair of the department of philosophy, and where Maritain was a professor of philosophy.

Guénon seems to have fit into the Catholic Institute as a fellow anti-secularist and anti-materialist, and after 1916 he delivered occasional lectures there, mostly on Hinduism. The general view was that he was working on what would today be called comparative religion, and in his lectures he was using terminology and ideas of non-Christian origin to describe spiritual realities, realities that were of course Christian, as some others used terminology and ideas drawn from pre-Christian Greek philosophy to the same end. Admittedly, some of his views perhaps needed to be brought closer to the doctrines of the Church.[32] If this view was wrong, Guénon never corrected it, and some later felt that they had been deceived if not betrayed, but it is not clear that they were wrong in seeing Guénon then as more or less Catholic in a conventional sense. We have little information concerning his religious practice during the 1920s, but he probably took his wife, a devout Catholic, to Mass on Sundays.

In addition to helping him publish his work, Guénon's Catholic friends seem also to have helped him in his career. Guénon's formal education had been interrupted in 1906, as we will see, but in 1914 he returned to it, obtaining a *licence* (approximately, BA) in philosophy from the Sorbonne in 1915, at the age of almost thirty. He then got his first job, as a substitute teacher at a school in Saint-Germain-en-Laye near Paris. When the teacher for whom he was substituting returned, Guénon got his second job, as a teacher of philosophy at the lycée at Sétif in Algeria for the year 1917–18.[33]

In 1919 Guénon sat for the *agrégation* in philosophy at the Sorbonne. The *agrégation* is a comprehensive examination required for teaching most subjects in French lycées and universities, and at that time it came in two parts. Guénon passed the written examination but failed the oral part. Newly introduced regulations prevented him from sitting the *agrégation* again because of his age, and so Guénon began to think in terms of a doctorate. After the refusal of his thesis by Lévi, however, Guénon had to give up all hopes of a regular academic career:[34] the Catholic Institute was now the only serious forum left open to him. Guénon's friends helped him to get a job as philosophy teacher at the Ecole des Francs-Bourgeois (a Catholic school, for which the *agrégation* was not required) in 1922.[35]

The alliance between the Catholic Institute and Guénon could not last, however. Even the *Introduction générale* worried Maritain, who inserted into someone else's review of that book the warning that "Guénon's metaphysics are radically irreconcilable with the [Catholic] faith," and added a concluding paragraph: "The remedy [for contemporary problems] proposed by Mr. Guénon—which is, frankly, a Hinduist restoration of ancient Gnosis, mother of heresies—would only make things worse."[36] That Maritain should have recommended for publication a book with which he evidently disagreed is a paradox that is explicable partly in terms of his then friendly personal relations with Guénon, and partly because as an academic philosopher he could see the interest of views that, as a believing Catholic, he could only reject.

The publication of Guénon's later book, *Orient et Occident*, distanced him further from his Catholic supporters. A review in the *Revue de philosophie* asked how Guénon could "be content with a mere philosophical entente with the Oriental world and lose all hope of seeing these people [Orientals] entering into Catholic unity."[37] A Dominican went further, warning against taking Guénon for an ally of Catholicism on the strength of his "brilliant execution of Theosophy . . . , his horror of Protestantism, and of secular and scientist morality." The Dominican concluded, "Our naivete does . . . have some limits": Guénon was clearly on the other, Oriental, side.[38] Maritain's own reaction to *Orient et Occident* is not known, but relations between Guénon and the Catholic Institute cooled and finally ceased. There is a prevalent (though unconfirmed) story that Maritain later attempted (without success) to have Guénon's works put on the Catholic Church's Index of Prohibited Books.[39]

Guénon had already been dismissed in 1921 from his post at the Ecole des Francs-Bourgeois as a result of his unorthodox views, to the disappointment of his pupils, many of whom who had enjoyed philosophy courses taught without any textbooks (Guénon said there were no good ones) which tended to concentrate on medieval esotericism.[40] For the next few years, Guénon seems to have lived off the less satisfactory income from giving private lessons in philosophy.

In 1925, however, Guénon found a new Catholic ally in Louis Charbonneau-

Lassay, an important figure in the early history of Traditionalism. Charbonneau-Lassay was an ultra-Catholic antiquarian devoted to the study of Christian symbolism, to whom Guénon was introduced by a common friend associated with *La France chrétienne*.[41] Charbonneau-Lassay had since 1922 been contributing to *Regnabit, revue universelle du Sacré-Cœur* [International Journal of the Sacred Heart], a journal established the previous year by Father Félix Anizan under the patronage of Cardinal Louis-Ernest Dubois, archbishop of Paris. At Charbonneau-Lassay's suggestion, Guénon began to contribute articles to *Regnabit* in 1925, writing on the legend of the Holy Grail and trying to demonstrate the essential unity of various traditional forms. He thus compared the Sacred Heart to the third eye of Shiva, raising a number of eyebrows; Anizan initially defended Guénon, responding that *Regnabit* was meant to be a serious journal, not a work of piety.[42] Guénon was not Anizan's only unusual contributor: he also solicited contributions from Georges-Gabriel de Noillat, leader of the Hiéron du Val d'Or Study Center. This had been established in 1873 by a Jesuit and a Spanish baron, with a number of unusual objectives, including two that prefigured Traditionalism: a Perennialist attempt at "the reconstruction of a universal sacred tradition," and establishment of a "Christian Masonry of the Grand Occident" to combat the anti-Christian Freemasonry of the Grand Orient, the most atheist of France's three Masonic "Obediences" (denominations or supreme bodies).[43]

The publication of *La crise du monde moderne* in 1927 meant the end of relations between Guénon and the Catholic Church; ironically, the passage that caused most trouble is actually Guénon's most explicitly pro-Catholic. The postscript to which the second half of *Orient et Occident* has been reduced ends with an optimistic (for Guénon) discussion of the potential role of the Church, a discussion that was absent from *Orient et Occident*, where Guénon's references to Christianity were restricted to condemnations of Protestantism. In *La crise du monde moderne*, after noting signs that a revival of sacred science had already begun, Guénon identified the Catholic Church as the natural body to place itself at the head of this movement, and he advised it to do so if it did not want to be overtaken by it.[44]

Coming on top of comparisons between the Sacred Heart and the third eye of Shiva, this statement proved too much for many Catholics, who again complained to *Regnabit*'s editor, Anizan. The editor himself evidently remained somewhat inclined toward Guénon, since he gave him a final chance, asking him to clarify his position regarding the obligation of any Catholic "to believe and to say that [Catholic] doctrine is the most complete terrestrial expression of religious truth." Guénon declined the invitation, evidently wishing neither to lie nor to make a public declaration of apostasy.[45] His participation in *Regnabit* thus ceased.

The signs of the hoped-for revival that Guénon discerned were, presumably, the group of Traditionalists that had begun to gather around him. Some of these are discussed later in this chapter; several others will be introduced in later chapters. The year in which many of these Traditionalists discovered Guénon's work was 1927, the year of the publication of *La crise du monde moderne*.

Traditionalists in the 1920s

Traditionalism in the 1920s was not yet a religious movement—there was no common practice or even belief—but rather was a philosophical movement, though a philosophy with a difference: the conviction that "if everyone understood what the modern world really is, it would immediately cease to exist." One member of the small circle of Traditionalists at this time was Jean Reyor (also widely known as Marcel Clavelle), an important figure in the history of Traditionalism, about whose origins little is known. Reyor later recalled that the general view was that the objective was to achieve understanding—wisdom, perhaps—through the study of texts, whether original sources such as the Vedas or the writings of Guénon, and to distance oneself from the modern world. At that time "integral participation in a particular traditional form did not seem imperative."[46] This view was to change after 1930, as we will see.

Traditionalists in Paris

The central point around which Traditionalism revolved during the 1920s was a journal, *Le Voile d'Isis* [The Veil of Isis], published by Chacornac Brothers, Paris's leading occultist publisher and bookseller. Guénon had met Paul Chacornac, the co-proprietor of Chacornac Brothers, in 1922 when, after finishing *L'erreur spirite*, he sold off much of his library of occultist works.[47] Chacornac, an important figure in the history of Traditionalism, described his meeting with Guénon, perhaps a little overdramatically, thus:

> One morning—it was the tenth of January 1922—we saw coming into our store on the Quai Saint-Michel a very tall man, thin, brown [-haired], approaching thirty, dressed in black, with the classic appearance of a French scholar. His long face, crossed by a small moustache, was lighted by two strangely clear and piercing eyes that gave the impression of seeing beyond appearances.
>
> With perfect politeness, he asked us to come to take away some neo-spiritualist books and pamphlets he wanted to get rid of. . . .
>
> The interior [of his apartment] was of an extreme simplicity that fitted perfectly with the simplicity of the man himself. In the salon where he received us, a picture caught our eye: it was the life-sized

portrait of an Indian woman, brown, bare-headed, wearing a dress of red velvet, with rings in her ears, whose face stood out in luminous fashion. On the mantelpiece stood an unusual Masonic clock, dating from the late eighteenth century; a piano and a large bookcase, stuffed with books, completed the decor.[48]

Chacornac kept in contact with Guénon and in 1928 decided to transform *Le Voile d'Isis*, (an occultist journal that Chacornac Brothers had been publishing since 1890) into a Traditionalist journal, edited though not directed by Guénon. The principal motive was the desire to revive a failing title rather than any real enthusiasm for Traditionalism, though a genuine enthusiasm for Guénon and Traditionalism did develop later. This transformation was to be completed in 1933 by the change of the journal's name to *Etudes traditionnelles* [Traditional Studies].[49] *Le Voile d'Isis/Etudes traditionnelles* was for many years the main point around which Traditionalists gathered, as well as the place where Guénon and most of his collaborators published their work. It was the centerpiece of a Traditionalist research project: the study of a wide variety of initiatic traditions, in the pre-Renaissance West as well as the East, along lines indicated by Guénon's own work.

Chacornac's decision to entrust his journal to the Traditionalists, taken for purely commercial reasons, aided the spread of Traditionalism in the same way that the sponsorship of the Catholic Institute had. In the 1920s Chacornac Brothers was well established as one of four publishers in Paris working with occultist and alternative religious books, publishing perhaps 300 titles a year out of a total of about 1,100 appearing annually.[50] The dominant position of Chacornac Brothers made Guénon's connection with Paul Chacornac especially useful.

In addition to *Le Voile d'Isis* there were other focal points for Guénon's followers, most notably the weekly salon held by Geneviève Jourd'Heuil, a musician who had been deeply impressed by Guénon after meeting him at the Catholic Institute.[51] It was perhaps partly because of her efforts in Rome during the 1930s that Guénon's works were never put on the Index of Prohibited Books. She remained convinced that there was no contradiction between her Catholicism and her admiration for Guénon, a view with which many disagreed. Although she failed in her attempts to bring his work to the attention of Cardinal Pacelli (later Pope Pius XII), she later claimed to have spent many long meetings with Cardinal Rampolla, then running the Office for the Propagation of the Faith, explaining Traditionalism to him.[52]

The regular contributors to *Le Voile d'Isis* included Reyor, two followers of Guénon from his occultist period (Patrice Thomas and George-Auguste Genty), some friends of Chacornac, and some people who had gotten in touch with Guénon after reading and liking his work. Typical of these was a Dr.

Probst-Biraben,[53] a schoolteacher from Constantine in Algeria who often visited Paris, who was a Freemason and a Sufi.[54] The most important contributor, after Guénon himself, was Ananda Coomaraswamy.

Coomaraswamy

Guénon's principal early collaborator was Ananda Kentish Coomaraswamy, curator of the Department of Indian Art at the Boston Museum of Fine Arts and already a distinguished art historian when he encountered the work of Guénon in the late 1920s. Coomaraswamy quickly came to the view that "no living writer in modern Europe is more significant than René Guénon, whose task it has been to expound the universal metaphysical tradition that has been the essential foundation of every past culture."[55]

Coomaraswamy's considerable reputation as a scholar was based on works such as his five-volume *Catalogue of the Indian Collections in the Museum of Fine Arts* (1923-30) and his *History of Indian and Indonesian Art* (1927)[56] and was founded on his almost encyclopedic knowledge of Indian art and his then radical approach to the subject, which was to understand works of art by placing them in their context—which meant in practice their religious context.[57] This approach reflected an understanding of religion, discussed later, that was to prove easily compatible with Traditionalism.

It is not recorded what first led Coomaraswamy to Guénon; it is possible that Coomaraswamy encountered Guénon's books in the circle that frequented a "progressive" New York bookstore, the Sunwise Turn, a circle that included Eugene O'Neill, Ernest Hemingway, and Havelock Ellis, with interests in everything from graphology to Gurdjieff—and thus, possibly, Guénon. One might wonder what a 50-year-old museum curator from Boston was doing in such circles in New York. There are two answers to this question: that Coomaraswamy was an unusual museum curator in the first place (as we will see), and that he was having an affair with a young dancer, Stella Bloch, who lived in New York even during her subsequent marriage to Coomaraswamy between 1922 and 1930.[58]

The relationship between Coomaraswamy and Guénon, which was conducted entirely by mail, filled out and rounded off the Traditionalist philosophy. Guénon provided the big ideas, and Coomaraswamy provided the scholarship—sometimes reflected in changes in Guénon's own views, sometimes in Guénon's and Coomaraswamy's own later work.[59] Coomaraswamy was the first of many scholars to become dedicated, "hard" Traditionalists.

Traditionalism transformed Coomaraswamy's writing. In 1928 he started work on the Vedas, and in 1933 he published his first purely religious work, *A New Approach to the Vedas: An Essay in Translation and Exegesis*.[60] The new approach in question, Coomaraswamy explained in his introduction, was a Perennialist one: "a translation and commentary in which the resources of other forms of the universal tradition are taken for granted."[61] From then on Coomaraswamy wrote more and more on the religion underlying the art and less and less on artistic representation of religion. For some, this change in Coomaraswamy's orientation was a disappointment. Eric Schroeder, later a historian of Persian art, recalled of his time as Coomaraswamy's assistant:

> We were constantly engaged in argument; for I was trying to revive the art historian who had become extinct in the philosopher, and he was determined to evoke the philosopher in an immature art historian. . . . Though he was perfectly generous and communicative on historical questions, he was not interested in them any more. He felt interest in present history, the industrialist rape of Asia and the prostitution of Western intellect to the contingent, but his *delight* was in metaphysics. All the waves of historical argument beat on him in vain; persistently, persistently he diverted history into the eternal categories which alone he was willing to admit.[62]

The major works of Coomaraswamy's Traditionalist period are *The Transformation of Nature in Art* (1934), comparing Oriental and medieval Western concepts, and another comparative work, *Hinduism and Buddhism* (1941). Coomaraswamy's basic thesis is, of course, one of Perennial unity—that Hinduism and Buddhism were both expressions of the original Perennial Philosophy.[63] He also wrote a number of Traditionalist articles, some published in *Le Voile d'Isis/Etudes traditionnelles*, and some (for him, more importantly) in scholarly journals such as the *Journal of the American Oriental Society* and the *Harvard Journal of Asiatic Studies*.[64] As he wrote to a fellow Traditionalist toward the end of his life: "My writing is addressed to the professors and specialists, those who have undermined our sense of values in recent times, but whose vaunted 'scholarship' is really superficial. I feel that rectification must begin at the reputed 'tip,' and only so will find its way into schools and text books and encyclopedias."[65]

This first attempt to bring Traditionalism to a scholarly audience and thence into the wider culture of the West was not a success. Coomaraswamy's reputation and stature were such that his new interests could do his career little harm, but though "it was generally realized that he had something important to say, and that it would be wise to give him a hearing . . . very few thought it was wise to take him seriously."[66] Thus while his *Hinduism and Buddhism* was reviewed in *The Harvard Journal of Asiatic Studies*, the review was not at all favorable. After correctly ascribing the origin of Coomaraswamy's attempt to demonstrate the unity of Hinduism and Buddhism to Guénon and Perennialism, the reviewer observed that "any interpretation motivated by such a fixed idea tends to force etymologies and meanings on words and passages in order to make them conform to a preconceived idea." After giving many examples of the dubious interpretations that he expected to find and had indeed found, the reviewer concluded: "Coomaraswamy minimizes the difficulties. . . . There is no real description of later Buddhism and Hinduism as historical and institutionalized religions. . . . There are some good things in the book, but . . . the author completely ignores a mass of evidence which cannot be made to fit the theory."[67]

These criticisms are strikingly close to those offered by Sylvain Lévi twenty years earlier concerning Guénon's *Introduction générale*. Of course, Coomaraswamy's scholarly reputation was based on his art history; like Maritain, he had not trained as a philologist or a historian of religion.

In 1933, as a result of an internal reorganization at the Museum of Fine Arts, Coomaraswamy became a research fellow, a move that gave him more time to devote to his research.[68] He remained in this position until his retirement in 1947 at the age of 70. At his retirement dinner he announced that he was going to follow Hindu tradition and retire to a life of contemplation in India, but before he could leave America he died. His fourth and final wife, Luisa, arranged for a funeral service to be said by a Greek Orthodox priest, after which he was cremated and his ashes scattered in the Ganges[69]—a practical expression of Perennialism.

Coomaraswamy's principal audience was in the end much the same as Guénon's, though somewhat wider. He became an established part of the Traditionalist canon, for many years second only to Guénon himself in importance as a Traditionalist writer.

Guénon's Sympathizers

Just as there was a salon for Guénon's followers, there was also a salon attended by less devoted sympathizers and by others, held by François Bonjean. Bonjean was a novelist who wrote most frequently on Morocco but was best known for a trilogy, *Histoire d'un enfant du pays d'Egypte* [The Story of a Child of the Land of Egypt] (1924).[70] Bonjean and Guénon were introduced in 1924 by a mutual acquaintance, a literary journalist. They found that their understandings of the Orient were similar, and they met frequently for some time,[71] but Guénon does not seem to have had any significant impact on Bonjean's writing. Bonjean's salon was primarily for those interested in East–West relations; it met on Friday evenings, gathering together Frenchmen and "Orientals" living in Paris. Bonjean recalled in 1951:

> I still can see Guénon, tall, thin, dripping with good faith, facing his opponents. The sight of this Occidental mounting an impassioned defense of the legacy of the Orient against playful Orientals, held both something of the piquant and of grandeur. With inexhaustible patience, he attempted to convince his audience of the existence in various parts of the Orient of centers capable of leading disciples

along the difficult and sometimes dangerous paths of "purification."[72]

It does not sound as if Guénon had much success in bringing Bonjean's Orientals to his view of the Orient. He had more success in French artistic circles.
Among those who have been identified as admirers of Guénon during the
1920s were a Cubist painter, two Surrealists, and another novelist.

The Cubist Albert Gleizes is known to have met Guénon only twice, in
1927, having previously been unaware of his work, but the two men found
much common ground.[73] Gleizes's interest in questions of modernity, tradition, and symbolism, however, was ancillary to his interest in the nature and
purpose of painting, and given the distance between the two men's ultimate
objectives, it is unsurprising that they seem to have had little impact on each
other.[74]

The Surrealist André Breton on occasion quoted from Guénon's work with
approval, but Breton's interests, like those of Gleizes, differed from those of
Guénon.[75] Another Surrealist, René Daumal, was engaged in a more specifically spiritual quest than was Breton, a quest that started with an early
chemical-induced experience of the divine while experimenting with carbon
tetrachloride in 1924.[76] Although Daumal's final spiritual destination was not
Traditionalism but Gurdjieff,[77] after reading Guénon's L'homme et son devenir
selon le Védânta in 1928, Daumal noted approvingly in his diary that Guénon
was the single Western writer on Hinduism whose hands did not change gold
into lead. "But I fear," he went on, addressing Guénon in his diary, "that the
joy of thinking may divert you from that law—historic in the widest sense—
that necessarily pushes that which there is in us of man toward revolt."[78] Daumal was right: Guénon was not interested in revolt. Daumal's fellow painter
Evola, once a Dadaist but by 1928 a neo-Pagan occultist, was interested in
revolt, however (as we will see). From this interest, deviation "necessarily"
resulted. Evola was later a Traditionalist second in importance only to Guénon
himself.

One of Daumal's friends at this time was Louis Dumont, the son of a
railroad executive whose personal revolt—dropping out of high school and
supporting himself from a variety of casual jobs—had caused his widowed
mother much grief. Dumont was introduced by Daumal to Guénon's work,
and Guénon's work led to his lifelong fascination with India. A few years later
Dumont got a job as a typist at Paris's important Museum of Popular Arts and
Traditions, an environment that played an important part in his decision to
complete his education.[79] By the 1960s Dumont was one of France's leading
sociologists; the consequences then of his early reading of Guénon in Daumal's
company are considered in later chapters.

The novelist Henri Bosco, whose work would become popular after the
Second World War and remain well known in France for the rest of the century,

was introduced to the work of Guénon by Bonjean somewhat later, in 1938. Bosco was at that time writing *Hyacinthe*, which he later described as his *livre clef*, a painstaking examination (like most of Bosco's books) of an internal spiritual journey.[80] Guénon (Bosco wrote to Bonjean) unlocked the conclusion of this book, that "salvation can only come from the *breath*, that is to say from a higher influence, anterior to us."[81] This conclusion can hardly be described as Traditionalist—indeed, another friend of Bosco's saw it as Catholic.[82] Coming as it does from a writer who by his own account read and reread all Guénon's work with dedication,[83] it serves to remind us how diffuse and indirect the effect of even an important influence can be. Were it not for the survival of Bosco's correspondence with Bonjean and for one published reference, no one would suspect that Traditionalism had mattered to Bosco. Bosco is the first known "soft" Traditionalist: someone for whom Traditionalism was evidently important but not a determining influence, and for whom it had few visible consequences. There must have been many others, even in the 1920s, for whom Guénon's books were important in ways that will remain unknown.

The Catholic antiquarian Charbonneau-Lassay was also a close associate of Guénon, continuing his friendship with Guénon even after Guénon had been excluded from *Regnabit*. He also remained on friendly terms with such Traditionalists as Reyor, and he contributed to *Le voile d'Isis/Etudes traditionnelles*.[84] His own work was little altered by his association with Guénon, however, and so cannot be described even as a "soft" Traditionalist. He was, it seems, quite simply a Catholic. The gifted son of two servants, he had been educated locally by the Brothers of Saint Gabriel, a lay fellowship. He had himself become a Brother but had left this order in 1903 when the Brothers were dissolved. He spent the rest of his life working as an engraver, local archaeologist, and historian, becoming secretary of the *Revue du Bas-Poitou* (a local journal) in 1913. His major work was the *Bestiaire du Christ* [Bestiary of Christ], a monumental work on Christian symbolism commissioned by Cardinal Dubois, the patron of *Regnabit*, on which he spent fifteen years.[85] His interest in symbolism meant that he had much in common with the Traditionalists, but that was all. As we will see, on important points he differed from them fundamentally.

2

Perennialism

The life of René Guénon falls into three phases (distinct from the three stages of the history of Traditionalism). The "Catholic" phase we have just considered was the second phase. The first phase, considered in this and the next chapter, was an "occultist" phase, during which Guénon encountered most of the sources from which he developed the Traditionalist philosophy. Our consideration of this phase will involve numerous detours through little known alleyways of Western intellectual and religious history. The third phase of Guénon's life (which he spent as a Sufi in Cairo) began in the 1930s and is considered in part II of this book. From that point there will be fewer detours.

René Guénon

René Jean-Marie Joseph Guénon was the only child of a Catholic couple living comfortably in Blois, a substantial town on the Loire known for its fine chateau. His father, a loss assessor for a local insurance company, was 56 at the time of the birth of his first and only child; René's mother was then 37. She was his father's second wife (the first had died childless). René's childhood was unremarkable. Despite somewhat delicate health, he did well at school, where he specialized in mathematics. In 1904, when he was 18, his ambitious parents sent him to the Collège Rollin in Paris to pursue further studies in mathematics with a view to entering the prestigious Ecole Polytechnique.[1]

In 1906 Guénon left the Collège Rollin, where he was doing badly. He instead immersed himself in Parisian occultism until shortly before the start of the First World War. It is not known what drew Guénon's attention to occultism, but he clearly needed some new interest, having failed to do well in his mathematical studies. Nor is it known what view Guénon's by then elderly parents took of all this. It is possible that upon coming of age in 1907 Guénon acquired an independent income, since he seems not to have needed to concern himself with earning a living until after the start of the First World War.

The occultist group that Guénon joined in 1906, and from which he derived his "Vedanta-Perennialism," was the Martinist Order. It had been established in about 1890 by Gérard Encausse (famous as "Papus"), a central figure in the early development of Traditionalism. Encausse was a physician and the son of an alternative medical practitioner who had invented the "Encausse generator,"[2] a patent machine for passing medicines through the skin by means of hot water; it had never enjoyed the success that its inventor had hoped for.[3] Encausse became a qualified physician (unlike his father) but continued the family interest in alternative therapies such as homeopathy and mesmerism. In 1887, while studying at the Faculty of Medicine in Paris, Encausse joined Isis, the Paris lodge of the Theosophical Society, one important source of the Martinist Order's Perennialism, and so of Traditionalist Perennialism.

Perennialism and the Theosophical Society

The Theosophical Society is generally known today as a "new religious movement" (what the general public calls a "sect"), but it was established in New York in 1875 for entirely serious purposes, with bylaws modeled on those of the American Geographical and Statistical Society. It was founded by a respectable lawyer and journalist then in his mid-forties, Colonel Henry Olcott.[4] Olcott wanted the Theosophical Society to carry out research in comparative religion and also to find "ancient wisdom," especially in the "primeval source of all religion, the books of Hermes and the Vedas"[5]—in other words, the Perennial Philosophy. Like Guénon, Colonel Olcott supposed that the Perennial Philosophy could be found in the Vedas; in believing that it could also be found in the books of Hermes, Olcott was following the Renaissance scholar Marsilio Ficino's original Perennialism. The Vedas were unknown to the Renaissance; Ficino instead took as the earliest expression of the Perennial Philosophy the *Corpus Hermeticum* ascribed to the probably mythical Hermes Trismegister. The *Corpus Hermeticum* was produced between the first and third centuries A.D., and accordingly shows the Christian, Stoic, and neo-Platonic influences of its time, as well as some ancient Egyptian influence. In the fifteenth century, however, it was badly misdated, being generally supposed to date from the time of Moses, or perhaps earlier.

As a result of this error in dating, the *Corpus Hermeticum* appeared to foreshadow both Christianity and Plato in prophetic fashion (as, of course, it would, having been composed *after* both Plato and Christ), and so it gave rise to the original conception of the Perennial Philosophy. When in 1614 a Geneva philologist, Isaac Casaubon, demonstrated conclusively that the *Corpus Hermeticum* was not of Mosaic but of post-Christian origin,[6] Perennialism was largely discredited. It did, however, survive and is visible, for example, in late eighteenth-century France among Freemasons based around a lodge that operated between 1761 and 1781, Les Elus Coëns. One member of this lodge was Louis-Claude de Saint-Martin, after whom Encausse named his Martinist Order. De Saint-Martin, a retired army officer and a Freemason with many mystical and some Hermetic interests,[7] believed that "All the traditions of the earth must be seen as deriving from a fundamental mother-tradition that, from the beginning, was entrusted to sinful man and to his first offspring."[8] Similar sentiments were echoed by Saint-Martin's near contemporary, Count Joseph de Maistre, who belonged to a lodge directed by Jean-Baptiste Willermoz, once of Les Elus Coëns and for a time a close associate of Saint-Martin:[9] "The true religion . . . was born on the day that [all] days were born . . . , The vague conceptions [of the ancients] were no more than *the more or less feeble remains* of the primitive tradition."[10] Perennialism, then, was still flourishing—at least in French Masonic circles—at the start of the nineteenth century.

The combination of Perennialism with Hinduism to produce Vedanta-Perennialism seems to have happened at about the same time. It is first visible in the work of Reuben Burrow, an important figure in the origins of Traditionalism. Burrow was an otherwise unknown contributor to *Asiatick Researches*, the journal of the Asiatick Society of Bengal. This society, the first Western learned association devoted to the study of the Orient, was established in Calcutta in 1784 under the presidency of "Oriental Jones"—Sir William Jones, a British employee of the Honorable East India Company, a gifted linguist, and a judge on the Calcutta Supreme Court.[11] Although the work of Oriental Jones himself is still respected, the work of some of his colleagues would today be less well received than it was at the close of the eighteenth century. In his "A Proof that the Hindoos Had the Binomial Theorem," published in *Asiatick Researches* in 1799, Reuben Burrow attempted to demonstrate the advanced state of ancient Indian mathematical knowledge, arguing backward from the state of later Indian astronomy. This notion led him to suggest a probable Indian origin for the European sciences. After some speculation about the probable location of "the Paradise of Moses," Burrow observed:

> From the aforesaid country [the Paradise of Moses] the *Hindoo* religion probably spread over the whole earth; there are signs of it in every northern country, and in almost every system of worship. In *England* it is obvious; Stonehenge is evidently one of the temples of

Boodh. . . . The religious ceremonies of the papists seem in many
parts to be a mere servile copy of those of the *Goseigns* and *Fakeers;*
the christian ascetics were very little different from their filthy original the *Braggys,* &c. . . . That the *Druids* of *Britain* were *Bramins,* is
beyond the least shadow of a doubt; but that they were all murdered
and their sciences lost, is out of the bounds of probability; it is
much more likely that they turned Schoolmasters, Freemasons, and
Fortune-tellers, and in this way part of their sciences might easily
descend to posterity, as we find they have done.[12]

Burrow here subscribes to a form of Perennialism that favors Hinduism over
Hermes, though he also connects Hinduism with Moses. His supposition that
the sciences of the brahmins and Druids survived among Freemasons suggests
that he himself might have been a Freemason, in which case he might have
encountered Perennialism in Masonic circles similar to those around the
French lodge Les Elus Coëns. This, however, is speculation. What is clear is
that from the start of the Western discovery of Hindu texts, some saw Hinduism as the "primeval source" of all religion.

Although Burrow's thesis interested some later British scholars,[13] there is
no evidence of any direct link between his work and Olcott's conviction that
the Vedas contained the Perennial Philosophy. The most likely origin of Olcott's
interest in the Vedas was the growing availability of, and interest in, translations into Western languages of Hindu texts, some of them the work of other
members of the Asiatick Society of Bengal. One of the earliest Western intellectuals to draw significantly on these translations was the American philosopher Ralph Waldo Emerson, an important figure in the origins of Traditionalism. Emerson, a one-time minister of the Unitarian Church, was, along with
Henry D. Thoreau, leader of the Transcendentalist Movement. In 1831 Emerson read the newly published English translation of Cousin's *Cours de philosophie* [*Course in the History of Modern Philosophy*], which contained two chapters of the Bhagavad Gita (Song of the Lord). The Bhagavad Gita had been
translated into English between 1824 and 1827 in the journal of the sister body
of the Asiatick Society of Bengal, the *Transactions of the Asiatic Society of London,*
and it was on this translation that Cousin drew.[14]

The Vedas and Vedanta exercised an important influence over Emerson,
and therefore on Transcendentalism. Through Transcendentalist journals such
as *The Western Messenger* and *The Dial,* they reached a wider American public.[15]
This may well be how Olcott encountered them.

Emerson also subscribed to a form of Perennialism, writing in his diary
in 1839 that for him "Bible" meant "the Ethical Revelations considered generally, including, that is, the Vedas, the Sacred Writings of every nation, and
not of the Hebrews alone." In this, and in his emphasis on the East as a source

of wisdom ("Europe has always owed to oriental genius its divine impulses," as he said in 1838 in his celebrated address to the Harvard Divinity School),[16] Emerson prefigures Olcott, and so also Encausse and Guénon. Perennialism as understood by Emerson and Cousin continued independently during the twentieth century, perhaps most famously in Aldous Huxley's *The Perennial Philosophy* (1944).[17]

Olcott might today be as respectable as Huxley had it not been for the activities of a new friend of his, Helena Petrovna Blavatsky (born Baroness von Hahn), a Russian adventurer with a dubious past, and an important figure in the origins of Traditionalism. The daughter of a Russian army officer and a proto-feminist novelist (her German surname reflected her father's Baltic origin),[18] Blavatsky when young had married and then left a Russian administrator named Nikifor Blavatsky, the vice-governor of Yerevan, Russian Armenia. She arrived in New York in 1873 after various adventures, most recently the collapse—among charges of fraud—of the Spiritist Society she had run in Egypt, where she briefly settled after travels in Europe and the Near East.[19] Olcott had met her, and evidently fallen under her spell, in 1874, when he traveled to Vermont to visit the then famous farmhouse of the Eddy brothers, where various paranormal phenomena were reported to be occurring.

The Theosophical Society originally had Olcott as its chairman, a younger lawyer as secretary, and sixteen other members, including Blavatsky. Within a month of its foundation, Blavatsky was elected "corresponding secretary," from which position she was to divert the society to her own purposes. Something of what would ensue might have been predicted from one of a number of communications Olcott received shortly after he met Blavatsky, written on green paper in gold ink and signed by a fictional Tuitit Bey of Luxor, Egypt.[20] Tuitit Bey, identifying himself as grand master of the equally fictional Mystical Brotherhood of Luxor, opened the correspondence by assuring Olcott that "Sister Helen [Blavatsky] is a valiant, trustworthy servant," and in a later letter requested Olcott to find Blavatsky an apartment in New York and to look after her.[21] Given that Olcott had spent some time earlier in his career investigating fraud (as a special commissioner at the War Department), it is hard to understand why he did not jump to the obvious conclusion that Blavatsky needed someone to pay her rent, but evidently he did not.

The Theosophical Society expanded from its original eighteen members in New York to a world-wide organization, based from 1879 in India (from 1882 at Adyar, Madras). Ultimately it had more than 500 "lodges" (branches) in over forty countries in Asia and the West, including the lodge in Paris that Encausse joined in 1887.[22] The success of the Theosophical Society in Asia was probably due mostly to the value of Western endorsement for the national cultural and religious revivals then underway, part of the nationalist reaction to European imperialism (in 1967 Sri Lanka commemorated the sixtieth anniversary of Olcott's death with a special postage stamp).[23] The expansion of the Theosophical Society in the West, on the other hand, was due chiefly to two factors: the environment of the times, and the high quality (in their final form) of Blavatsky's writings.

The spread of Theosophy owed much to the extraordinary success of two books, *Isis Unveiled* (1877) and *The Secret Doctrine* (1888).[24] Authorship of both books was attributed to ethereal sources, but both were in fact drafted by Blavatsky and then turned into publishable form by human "ghost" writers—by Olcott in the case of *Isis Unveiled*, and in the case of *The Secret Doctrine* by two English brothers who took over after Blavatsky's original choice of editor had refused the task in dismay on reading her disorganized first draft.[25] Both books did in a sense reflect the Theosophical Society's original intention to search in "the books of Hermes and the Vedas," but not in any scientific spirit. *Isis Unveiled* was extensively plagiarized from a variety of standard works on occultism and Hermeticism (134 pages from Samuel Dunlap's *Sōd, the Son of Man*, 107 pages from Joseph Ennemoser's *History of Magic*, and so on), while *The Secret Doctrine* drew heavily on John Dowson's *Classical Dictionary of Hindu Mythology and Religion*, Horace Wilson's annotated translation of the *Vishnu Purana*, and other such works.[26] This plagiarism was of a piece with Tuitit Bey's letters to Olcott, as well as with Blavatsky's claimed association with fictional Tibetan *mahatmas* (initiated adepts) of a "Great White Brotherhood" evidently inspired by the novels of Sir Edward Bulwer Lytton, British colonial secretary 1858–66 and amateur occultist, and with Blavatsky's almost compulsive manufacturing of paranormal phenomena during seances.[27] These fraudulent activities were exposed in 1884, first by an investigation carried out by the London-based Society for Psychical Research (a serious organization something like what the Theosophical Society itself might have become if left to Olcott; it numbered among its members the philosopher Henry Sidgwick, Prime Minister William Gladstone, and the poet Alfred Lord Tennyson). The impact of the damning report of this investigation was compounded by a disaffected Theosophist who revealed details of how certain paranormal phenomena were actually produced, even demonstrating the functioning of a false panel in a room at the Society's headquarters at Adyar.[28]

Ironically, Blavatsky's plagiarism may be the secret of her books' success. Tricks such as using bamboo poles to drop "materialized" letters cannot explain the popularity Theosophy enjoyed, but the reexpression in contemporary (and often fashionably pseudoscientific) terms of classic religious ideas, edited by competent writers such as Olcott, may explain it. Arguably, had Blavatsky resisted the temptation to continue the sort of tricks she presumably developed to earn a living before meeting Olcott and had so avoided scandal, the Theosophy expressed in her (plagiarized) books might have established itself as a major world religion rather than fading away during the twentieth century.[29]

The Martinist Order

Immediately on joining the Theosophical lodge Isis in Paris, Guénon's first master Encausse began to write in a French Theosophical journal—*Le Lotus, revue des Hautes Etudes Théosophiques*—not so much on Theosophy as on his other main interest, initiation, which is the third major element in the Traditionalist philosophy. According to Encausse, while Theosophy was transmitting initiations from India, where "the ancient truth still survives," contemporary Freemasonry had allowed political and material interests to drive out spiritual ones, even though its rituals derived from ancient initiations. [30] This, in slightly modified form, became the Traditionalist conception of initiation.

In general, initiation has two aspects, which can be described as exoteric and esoteric. The classic Christian initiation is baptism. Its exoteric significance is to mark one's entry into the Christian community, while (in Catholic theology) the esoteric significance is that it gives the new Christian access to divine grace, and so to the possibility of salvation, which is otherwise absent.[31] It was the esoteric aspects of non-Christian initiations such as Masonic ones that interested Encausse, and so (later) Guénon and the Traditionalists.

The origins of Masonry (or "Freemasonry"—the two terms may be used interchangeably), a practice that through Encausse contributed to Traditionalism and then was itself later modified by Traditionalism, are unclear. The most likely explanation of its emergence is the grafting of elements of Hermeticism onto preexisting trade guilds in Scotland during the sixteenth and seventeenth centuries.

Sixteenth-century Scottish stonemasons were organized into guilds, as were other craftsmen of the time, but the masons' guilds developed special characteristics because of the special nature of masons' work. While most crafts and guilds were sedentary and so could be organized relatively easily in any particular town, major building projects required the use of numerous masons drawn from various places, who often lived on site during a project. This situation gave rise to two modifications of the standard guild system. The first was on-site "lodges," temporary organizations parallel to the permanent guilds, the first of which is recorded in 1483. The second was the development of secret recognition signals to identify qualified masons—"free masons," those who had been admitted to, or "made free of," a guild. In a town, everyone in a guild easily knew who else belonged to it; this was not the case on a building project that drew masons from far afield, some of whom might not be properly qualified.[32]

Like other guilds, masons had what might be called "foundation myths" as well as trade secrets, and among those was the myth of the development of masonry before the Flood by Jabal son of Lamech, the subsequent rediscovery of the secrets of Jabal by Hermes Trismegistus, the passage of these secrets through Ancient Egypt to Jerusalem at the time of the building of the Temple, and the subsequent transmission of these secrets to Europe. References to Hermes among the Masons were evidently noted with interest by gentlemen familiar with the role ascribed to Hermes by Ficino and his successors, probably first by William Schaw, the Grand Master of Works for the Kingdom of Scotland, who in 1598–99 reorganized Scottish masonry. Schaw was a courtier from a family of courtiers, had traveled in France in 1584, and was in touch with alchemists and Hermeticists.[33]

Whether by means of Schaw or not, by the end of the seventeenth century symbolic and Hermetic lore characteristic of the Renaissance had transformed both Scottish and English masonry. From the 1630s increasing numbers of gentlemen (known as "nonoperatives") joined Scottish and English lodges, and in 1723 and 1738 the *Constitutions* of James Anderson, a Scot who had moved south, were promulgated in England, marking the start of Freemasonry as it exists today.[34] The first lodges had opened in France by 1736.[35]

While Masons may argue about the true nature and purpose of Masonry, in practice it can be observed that different groups of Masons came to follow very different objectives during the nineteenth century. One historian accurately described Masonry as "a protean institution that changes shape and content according to circumstances and membership. It could provide an institutional framework for almost any religious or political belief."[36] In the 1880s some French lodges were primarily political and often violently atheistic; some were devoted to philanthropy and good fellowship; and some were devoted to spiritual development. Encausse was addressing all these groups, but he appealed principally to those interested in spiritual development.

Within a year of joining the Theosophical lodge Isis, Encausse became involved in a quarrel with a senior French Theosophist. This led to the personal intervention of Colonel Olcott, the dissolution of Isis, and the formation of a new Theosophical lodge, Hermès, of which Encausse was appointed corresponding secretary (the same powerful position that Blavatsky held in the Theosophical Society proper). During these events, Encausse and a few followers established a monthly journal, *L'initiation*,[37] and in its first issue Encausse continued his attack on contemporary Masons, complaining of their ignorance of the symbolism contained in their own rites. Soon after, he established his Martinist Order, which was intended to be a new Masonry "on sounder bases."[38] It was not affiliated with any of the three rival Masonic Obediences then present in France.

As a complement to the neo-Masonic Martinist Order, Encausse also established in 1889 an Independent Group for Esoteric Studies, the declared purposes of which included preparing people for entry to the Martinist Order and the Theosophical Society, and spreading Perennialism, proclaiming "that truth is One, and that no school, no religion can claim it for itself alone. . . .

In every religion can be found manifestations of the single truth."[39] Guénon later joined both the studies group and the order.

Although the objectives of the Independent Group for Esoteric Studies were compatible with the ideas of Theosophy, the Martinist Order was not. The fictional Tibetan adepts from whom Blavatsky attempted to derive her authority were described as initiates, and by implication Blavatsky herself was initiated into some of their mysteries, but the giving of initiation to others through neo-Masonic orders such as the Martinist Order was never part of Blavatsky's plan.[40] Both the Martinist Order and the Independent Group for Esoteric Studies also constituted threats to Blavatsky's authority—breakaway groups were a frequent problem for the Theosophical leadership at this time. Blavatsky therefore organized the establishment of a new journal, *La revue théosophique*, in which she attacked Encausse for moving away from Theosophy toward Masonry. In response, Encausse founded a second journal, *Le voile d'Isis* [Veil of Isis], a sarcastic reference to one of Blavatsky's two major books, *Isis Unveiled*, initially to carry on a polemic against Blavatsky and the Theosophists. As we have seen, *Le voile d'Isis* later became the principal Traditionalist journal. It was published for slightly more than a century, until 1992. The original publisher of *Le voile d'Isis* was Henri Chacornac, whose son Paul transformed the journal into *Etudes traditionnelles* in 1933. Henri Chacornac had married Marie-Pauline Lermina, the daughter of Jules Lermina, a successful popular novelist who had favored occult themes and was one of the better known contributors to Encausse's *L'initiation*. Henri Chacornac was established by his new father-in-law as a publisher-bookseller (activities then commonly combined). He published the celebrated poet Paul Verlaine as well as his father-in-law and a number of other authors, and it was presumably through Lermina that Chacornac was chosen as the publisher of *Le Voile d'Isis*. After his death, his business was carried on by his two sons Paul and Louis, Paul as editor and Louis as manager.[41]

Once open hostilities had broken out between Encausse and Blavatsky, a number of Theosophists left the Theosophical lodge Hermès for the Martinist Order, and the remaining Theosophists soon dissolved Hermès. Encausse expanded his own organizations in France and abroad, until by 1900 there were hundreds of Martinist lodges and related bodies, from America to the Russian Empire.[42]

The Order of the Temple

In 1906 Guénon entered Encausse's Free School of Hermetic Sciences (as the Independent Group for Esoteric Studies had been renamed) and joined the neo-Masonic Martinist Order and an irregular Masonic lodge called Humanidad (Humanity), located in France but licensed by a Spanish rather than a French Obedience. By this time all these organizations had become generalized occultist bodies. The Free School of Hermetic Sciences was divided into a number of sections and groups, ranging from a Section for Initiatic Studies (closest to Encausse's heart) to a Group for the Paranormal and a Group for Action in the Centers of Feminine Intellectuality.[43] The paranormal section was given to tricks like those practiced by Blavatsky—the "materialization" of letters, hair, and the like.[44] In Paris the Martinist Order had four lodges: Sphinx (for general studies), Hermanubis (for the Oriental tradition), Velléda (for Masonry and symbolism), and Sphynge (artistic).[45] Lodges abroad were left very much to their own devices, some established by people who had never even met Encausse but had merely corresponded with him.[46] A later grand master of the Martinist Order, Constant Chevillon, wrote that Encausse's Martinism "was the victim of a too vast eclecticism . . . it represented in the spiritual world that which is represented in the animal world by the class of invertebrates."[47]

Encausse's activities had been connected with early feminism from the start, when there had been much reciprocal membership between Theosophists close to Encausse and the followers of Anna de Wolska, the Polish organizer of the 1889 International Congress for Feminine Works and Institutions, held in Paris. The first meetings of the Independent Group for Esoteric Studies were held at the Wolska Library, and de Wolska was Encausse's lover until 1895, when he made a respectable marriage.[48] Encausse and Martinism were linked not only to feminism but also to most of the other alternative causes of the time: homeopathy, anarchism, animal rights, and of course anything related to alternative spirituality—Masonry, hermetic occultism, Vedanta, Baha'ism, alternative science; almost anything, in fact, save Roman Catholic Christianity.

The concept of the "cultic milieu," developed by sociologist Bryan Wilson, is very helpful in understanding this conglomeration of alternatives. According to Wilson, there exists in modern Western societies a milieu, which he terms "cultic," where much that is rejected by the dominant culture accumulates—alternative therapies, alternative beliefs, and to some extent alternative lifestyles. Both ideas and people usually belong more to the milieu than to any specific group within it. Individuals easily shift their allegiances from group to group and idea to idea, and ideas and groups are themselves linked to each other by a shared network of publications and venues.[49] Wilson was describing the final third of the twentieth century when he developed his now famous concept, but his model applies equally well to the late nineteenth century.

The original objectives of the Independent Group for Esoteric Studies were not forgotten, and Guénon seems to have taken them seriously, even if the later Encausse himself seems not to have done so. These objectives had been defined as the discovery of the Perennial Philosophy, which Encausse called the "original light." Ignoring the work of Casaubon on the dating of the *Corpus*

Hermeticus, Encausse and his more serious followers believed that the Perennial Philosophy had been transmitted by Hermes from Ancient Egyptian sources, and they saw in this transmission the source of initiation. Encausse also followed Blavatsky and even Burrow in turning to the Hindus, regarding "the Indian tradition" as "the longest lasting historical example of continuity of religious exoterism." The task of his Independent Group for Esoteric Studies, then, was to "reassemble these exoteric debris" of Hinduism "in the light of unceasingly transmitted tradition"—the initiatic tradition of Hermes.[50] Guénon accordingly immersed himself in the study of Hinduism and in the separate but complementary search for an uninterrupted initiatic tradition. He was the first of many Traditionalists to follow this route.

A mystery that has occupied Guénon's various Traditionalist biographers is the source of his knowledge of Hinduism. Given Traditionalism's later emphasis on "authentic" transmission from master to disciple, Traditionalists have searched for Guénon's Hindu masters and failed to find anything very substantial. There is a general supposition that he must have been "initiated" by "some Hindus" in Paris. It seems likely, though it cannot be definitively established, that there were no such masters, and that Guénon's understanding of Hinduism derived exclusively from his reading of texts and studies then available in Paris.[51] Nowhere did Guénon claim that this was not the case, and he never visited India. Though such a conclusion may seem unacceptable to later Traditionalists, there is no particular reason why the Guénon of the time should not have considered himself entitled to write about Hinduism without firsthand experience of it. In so doing, he would only have been following the example of many eminent early Orientalists, who also worked almost exclusively from texts. Guénon did, however, occasionally rely on texts generally considered by scholars to be spurious.[52]

It was Guénon's search for initiation that first led him into conflict with Encausse. Guénon evidently despaired of Martinist initiation and after two years found a better initiation independently—from the long-dead Jacques de Molay (1243–1314), the last grand master of the Order of Knights Templar, an order of crusading knights that many supposed was the recipient of initiatic secrets acquired in and around Jerusalem.

The instructions of Jacques de Molay, communicated to Guénon during a seance in 1908, were for the reestablishment of the Order of the Temple. Guénon proceeded to establish an Ordre du temple rénovée (Renewed Order of the Temple) with the help of five other Martinists, one of whom encouraged Guénon to help himself to the Martinist mailing list. Two of these other Martinists became close followers of Guénon, remaining with him through the 1920s and being among the main contributors to his journal *Le Voile d'Isis/Etudes traditionnelles* during and after the 1920s. They were Georges-Auguste Thomas, an important figure in the early history of Traditionalism and a marine engineer who had earlier left the Theosophical Society in disgust,[53] and

Patrice Genty, a member of Encausse's irregular Masonic lodge Humanidad.
. The eccentric Genty was an employee of the city gas company. He spent his
mornings reading gas meters and his afternoons in the National Library, and
he lived in a small apartment so full of books that there was hardly room for
visitors.[54]

The Renewed Order of the Temple met on the premises of the Free School
of Hermetic Sciences under the guise of a Society for Higher Religious and
Philosophical Studies. Exactly what happened during these meetings is uncertain; the episode of the Renewed Order of the Temple was one that in later
years Guénon found embarrassing and avoided discussing.[55]

Unsurprisingly, when Encausse learned of these activities and of the loss
of his mailing list, he saw them as a threat to his own authority. He must have
recalled the effect that the foundation of his own Martinist Order had had on
French Theosophy. Guénon and some others (including Thomas and Genty)
were accordingly expelled from the Martinist Order and from Humanidad. The
remaining neo-Templars were reintegrated under Encausse's authority.
Guénon's Renewed Order of the Temple seems to have ceased to function,
though it was not formally dissolved until 1911.[56]

Other Perennialists

Traditionalism has its earliest direct origins in Martinism and Theosophy, but
it was to develop very differently. Whereas Martinism and Theosophy were
both highly successful mass organizations whose popularity derived partly
from their all-inclusiveness, Traditionalism was never all-inclusive and never
aspired to a mass following, though it was to attempt to influence the masses.
Another important difference between Traditionalism and its nineteenth-
century origins was its total lack of their evolutionary optimism. Blavatsky
believed that "we have finished the descending arc and have begun our return
to Deity, both the globe and the human family on it. Exiles from God, prodigal
sons in a far country, we have set out on our homeward journey."[57] Similarly,
Emerson differs from Guénon in including two important aspects, both deriving from the Romantic movement: the spirituality of nature, and reverence for
originality, placed in opposition to tradition (which Emerson understood in a
more general sense than did Guénon). Echoes of the former may be found in
later Traditionalism, but the latter is the very antithesis of Traditionalism. In
1836, Emerson wrote:

> . The foregoing generations beheld God and nature face to face; we,
> through their eyes, why should not we also enjoy an original relation
> to the universe? Why should not we have a poetry and philosophy of
> insight and not of tradition, and a religious revelation to us, and not

the history of theirs? . . . In the woods is perpetual youth. Within
these plantations of God . . . I become a transparent eye ball; I am
nothing; I see all; the currents of the Universal Being circulate
through me; I am part or parcel of God.[58]

Guénon would be altogether more pessimistic.

These, then, were the origins of Guénon's Perennialism. I will now briefly
consider the origins of the Perennialism of Guénon's collaborator, Ananda
Coomaraswamy. Despite his name, Coomaraswamy was English. His father,
Mutu, came from Ceylon's Tamil Indian community but was a very Anglicized
Tamil who often traveled to England. The first Indian to become a British
barrister (he was called to the Bar of Lincoln's Inn in the 1860s), Mutu was
knighted in 1874 and was married to an Englishwoman by the archbishop of
Canterbury in 1876. Ananda Coomaraswamy was born in Ceylon, but when
Ananda was two, Sir Mutu decided to move to England to stand for election
to the British Parliament, a plan encouraged by the British prime minister,
Benjamin Disraeli. Sir Mutu, however, died before reaching England, and Ananda was brought up in Kent by his mother's family.[59] He can have had no
memory of his father or of Ceylon.

Coomaraswamy's upbringing and education were, so far as is known, entirely English, though one would expect that the probable reactions to his surname and complexion by other boys at Wycliffe College, the English boarding
school he attended, would have left him feeling less English than he had felt
as a young child. At university, he studied geology and botany, and in 1903 he
was appointed to an assistant professorship ("Fellowship") at University College, London. In 1902 he married Ethel Partridge, and in 1905 he inherited a
considerable fortune.[60]

The journey from wealthy English geologist to American art historian and
Traditionalist was a long one, passing through anti-colonial nationalism.
Shortly after his marriage, Coomaraswamy applied for the post of director of
the Ceylon Mineralogical Survey, which he occupied from 1903. In later years
he often spoke of one morning in 1904 when, while having breakfast in a
remote village, he saw a Ceylonese woman with her child, both dressed in
"filthy and bedraggled" Western-style clothes, which implied conversion to
Christianity. "They were the local converts to a foreign religion and a foreign
dress," he reflected, "equally unnatural and equally misunderstood." Two years
later he addressed a Ceylonese audience in Jaffa along the same lines: "It is
difficult for any of us, who have not actually been brought up in England, to
realize the hopeless inadequacy of our attempts at imitation; to Englishmen
the absurdity is obvious, but to us it is not revealed."[61] The absurdity had
evidently been revealed to Coomaraswamy, and it looks rather as if a very
English embarrassment at his father's people's poor imitation of English ways
had a lot to do with Coomaraswamy's conversion to Ceylonese nationalism.

Another factor, probably, was the influence of his cousins Ponnambalam Ramanathan and Sir Ponnambalam Arunachalan, both of whom were active in the nationalist movement.[62]

In 1906 Coomaraswamy founded the Ceylon Social Reform Society, whose objective was a cultural and national revival. That morning in 1904 remained with him: adopting "a veneer of Western habits and customs, while the real elements of superiority in Western culture have been almost entirely neglected," had led to "neglect of the elements of superiority in the culture and civilization of the East," a neglect which Coomaraswamy wished to remedy. Among the Ceylon Social Reform Society's specific aims were uniting "the Eastern races of Ceylon," education in local languages rather than English, "the revival of native arts and sciences," and, finally, "the protection of ancient buildings and works of art."[63]

Little more is heard of the Ceylon Social Reform Society, and Coomaraswamy began to concentrate his efforts on ancient buildings and works of art; his attention had probably been drawn to this area partly by his wife, Ethel, a photographer, whose brother, Fred Partridge, was involved in William Morris's Arts and Crafts Movement. In 1906 Coomaraswamy arranged an exhibition of handicrafts in Ceylon. In 1907 he returned to England, where in 1908 he published a book on *Mediæval Sinhalese* (Ceylonese) *Art*[64] and presented a paper on "The Relation of Art and Religion in India" to the Third International Congress for the History of Religion. In 1910 he became involved in a very public controversy, played out in the correspondence columns of *The Times* and elsewhere, on the status of Indian art. This had started when Sir George Birdwood, while chairing the Indian Section of the annual meeting of the Royal Society of Arts, had announced that there was no "fine art" in India and had somewhat unwisely responded to the suggestion that a particular statue of the Buddha was an example of fine art: "This senseless similitude, in its immemorial fixed pose, is nothing more than an uninspired brazen image. . . . A boiled suet pudding would serve equally well as a symbol of passionless purity and serenity of soul." This controversy culminated in the foundation of the India Society, later the Royal India Society, to combat the views of the Birdwoods of this world. Coomaraswamy played a major part in this endeavor.[65]

Despite his shift from geology and Ceylonese nationalism to the study of art, Coomaraswamy remained interested in politics. When the First World War started in 1914, he publicly opposed Indian participation on the British side, and when conscription (to which he would have been subject) was introduced, he left England for America. In 1916 he was appointed curator of the Department of Indian Art at the Boston Museum of Fine Arts at the behest of a trustee who bought Coomaraswamy's substantial collection of Indian and Ceylonese art and donated it to the museum. It was presumably this purchase that led Coomaraswamy to live in America rather than India, where he had failed to find a sponsor for a project to use his own collection as the basis of a national museum of Indian art.[66]

During these events, Coomaraswamy followed an intellectual journey that had by 1914 transformed him into a Perennialist. The earliest intellectual influence on him was William Morris's Arts and Crafts Movement. Coomaraswamy's enthusiasm for Morris led Coomaraswamy to learn Icelandic (Morris was a devotee of Nordic literature),[67] and on his return to England in 1907 Coomaraswamy had spent considerable sums in support of Charles Asbee's Guild and School of Handicraft. *Medieval Sinhalese Art* was even printed on the Kelmscott press, the press that Morris had created to print his edition of Chaucer, which Coomaraswamy had bought from Asbee.[68] Morris prepared Coomaraswamy for the anti-modernist elements in Traditionalism.

The most important preparation for Traditionalism, though, doubtless came from Coomaraswamy's reading of William Blake, the great English poet and painter of the late eighteenth and early nineteenth centuries, who knew the original Renaissance Perennialism of Ficino and others through a contemporary, the English neo-Platonist, Thomas Taylor.[69] Before his departure for America, Coomaraswamy was a friend of William Butler Yeats, the Irish poet, occultist, and student of Blake.

Coomaraswamy had clearly discovered Perennialism by 1914, the year in which, in an article on "The Religious Foundations of Life and Art," he wrote that Blake's work contained "the essentials of religion, already written in hieroglyphics and Vedas, already taught by Christ and Orpheus and Krishna, Lao-Tse and Eckhart and Rumi."[70] Coomaraswamy in 1914 was a Perennialist but not yet a Traditionalist. In the same article he wrote confidently that "the religion of the future will announce as the objects, duties and meaning of life, liberty both of body and mind to exercise the divine arts of imagination."[71] Here he sounds close to Emerson (whom he had also been reading).[72] He was perhaps moving in the direction of Aleister Crowley's occultist group, the Golden Dawn, with which he was connected through Yeats. There was also another connection to Aleister Crowley: Coomaraswamy's wife, Ethel, is said to have become pregnant by Crowley in 1916. Coomaraswamy and Ethel subsequently divorced.[73] This incident presumably helped to diminish Coomaraswamy's enthusiasm for occultism, making him more receptive to Guénon's Traditionalism and to the idea that what mattered was not the religion of the future but the tradition of the past. Coomaraswamy, however, retained something of his earlier views even after he became a Traditionalist, and it is this fact that allowed him to make a distinctive contribution to the Traditionalist philosophy: introducing to Traditionalism an emphasis on the esthetic that derives ultimately from Blake and Morris.

3

Gnostics, Taoists, and Sufis

Separated from his first master, Gérard Encausse, after the episode of the Order of the Temple, Guénon was not yet fully prepared to steer an independent course. In 1909 he joined the Universal Gnostic Church, an organization closely related to the occultist milieu. It was here that Guénon met a central figure in the early development of Traditionalism, Count Albert-Eugène Puyou de Pouvourville, a Taoist. Guénon derived from de Pouvourville the second basic element in the Traditionalist philosophy, inversion, which at first expressed itself as hostility to contemporary Catholicism. Guénon's first journal, *La Gnose*, was affiliated with the Universal Gnostic Church; it was in *La Gnose* that the first recognizably Traditionalist writings were published, by Guénon and by another follower of de Pouvourville, the Sufi Ivan Aguéli, an important figure in the history of Western Sufism.

Neo-Gnosticism

The Universal Gnostic Church was established around 1888 by Jules-Benoît Doinel, an archivist in Orléans. Doinel's Church was inspired by references to Gnosticism in two texts of the second century A.D. (the *Philosophoumena* of Hippolytus and the *Adversos Haereses* of Bishop Irenaeus of Lyons), and by various visions, and differed significantly from genuine second-century Gnosticism. This had been a theological tendency (later condemned as the Gnostic Heresy) within the early Christian Church, mostly in Egypt, rather

than a defined group. Second-century Gnostics believed in a form of continuing revelation and in the availability of a direct, personal experience of God
to a gnostic (knowing) elite. They differed in many other ways from what
developed into the Catholic Church, but these differences were not known until
the discovery of the third-century Coptic Nag Hammadi texts in 1945.[1] In the
nineteenth century the Gnostics were known principally from hostile references in the writings of their opponents, the Church Fathers, among which
were the two texts used by Doinel. With no sources for Gnostic ritual, Doinel
adapted rites taken from the Cathars and other sources which he believed
derived from original Gnosticism.[2] Having obtained a consecration from three
Cathar bishops and a genuine Catholic bishop in Utrecht, Doinel established
the Universal Gnostic Church, of which he was patriarch (as Valentine II).[3]

Doinel was introduced to Theosophical and Martinist circles, and his
Church was joined by various early Martinists, including Encausse himself
and Léonce Fabre des Essarts, a poet who was at that time working with Encausse on *L'initiation* and was employed at the French ministry of education.[4]
In 1891 the Holy Office in Rome formally condemned the revival of the Gnostic
Heresy and at the same time put Encausse's *L'initiation* on the Index of Prohibited Books.[5] The Universal Gnostic Church underwent a crisis in 1894,
when—as a result of a vision in which Saint Stanislas Kostka appeared to
him—Doinel abandoned Gnosticism and returned to the Catholic Church. As
an act of contrition he then wrote a book, *Lucifer démasqué* [Lucifer Unmasked],
denouncing the Universal Gnostic Church, Martinism, and Freemasonry as
the work of Satan.[6] Doinel's book was one of a number of similar exposés
published at that time,[7] a genre to which Guénon's *Théosophisme* and *L'erreur
spirite* later contributed.

At this point the Universal Gnostic Church split into two, with a Martinist
group forming a Catholic Gnostic Church and Fabre des Essarts taking over
the original Universal Gnostic Church as Patriarch Synésius and moving away
from Encausse.[8] It was Fabre des Essarts who in 1909 consecrated René
Guénon as Palingenius, bishop of Alexandria, and also consecrated Guénon's
faithful associates from the Order of the Temple, Georges-Auguste Thomas
and Patrice Genty.[9] This, then, was Guénon's third "initiation," coming after
the Martinists and the neo-Templars.

De Pouvourville

Another member of the Universal Gnostic Church that Guénon joined in 1909
was Count Albert de Pouvourville, who Guénon was still acknowledging as
"one of my Masters" in 1918.[10] Born into an aristocratic military family, de
Pouvourville had been sent to the elite military academy at Saint Cyr but had
rebelled against the well-worn path mapped out before him and in 1884 re-

signed his commission in the French army. He enlisted in the Foreign Legion, was sent to French Indochina, and saw action in France's colonial wars there. Somewhere in South Vietnam he deserted from the Legion, and it was probably as a fugitive that he joined two Triads (secret societies), the T'ien-ti hui and the Bac Lieu. The Triads were in general strongly opposed to the French occupation, a factor that may have made them sympathetic to a deserter.

Like all Triads, the T'ien-ti hui was of Chinese origin. It arrived in Vietnam in the eighteenth century and from 1875 was joined by large numbers of Vietnamese (the origin of the Bac Lieu is unknown).[11] Vietnamese Triads at this time were less philosophical and text-based than their Chinese prototypes, serving economic and social purposes as well as religious ones, with a resemblance to Masonry that fascinated the first Western scholars to study them. Their rites, including elaborate initiation rites, were drawn from Taoist, Buddhist, and to a lesser extent Confucian sources but were described merely as "Taoist" by Vietnamese and foreigners alike.[12] De Pouvourville thus described his membership in the Triads as a "Taoist initiation."

De Pouvourville was rescued from the possible negative consequences of his desertion from the Foreign Legion by the intervention of his father, a senior officer with good connections. Having learned Vietnamese, the younger de Pouvourville was assigned to special duties, first as an interpreter and then as an inspector under the Ministry of Foreign Affairs. After being wounded during the Tonkin campaign (1890–91), he returned to France and published his first book, *Le Tonkin actuel* [Tonkin Today].[13] This was a violent condemnation of French colonial policy in which he attacked the colonists' ignorance of local languages and of the true state of affairs.[14] After a mission that took him back to Indochina in 1892 under the auspices of the Ministry of Fine Arts, de Pouvourville began his second career, as a writer and journalist in Paris. He wrote on colonial topics in journals such as the *Journal des sciences militaires, La dépêche coloniale,* and *Le courrier de Saïgon.* His output was prodigious: in addition to his journalism, from 1894 to 1911 de Pouvourville published approximately one book a year, initially on Chinese art and Indochinese history.[15] The most successful of his books, *De l'autre côté du mur: récits chinois des guerres de 1883* [From the Other Side of the Wall: Chinese Accounts of the Wars of 1883], went through 45 editions between 1887 and 1935.[16] In 1898 he was made a member of the French Colonial Institute and then president of the Foreign Legion Veterans' Association,[17] his youthful desertion from the ranks either forgotten or never known.

Beginning in the 1890s de Pouvourville wrote increasingly on spiritual subjects and published translations of Lao-Tzu's *Tao Te Ching.*[18] Like Guénon, he spent some time in Encausse's circle, publishing in *L'initiation,* but then (like Guénon) he broke with Encausse. In 1904 de Pouvourville launched a journal of his own in competition with Encausse's and joined the (non-Martinist) Universal Gnostic Church.[19] In three books published between 1904 and 1907[20] he showed himself to be an anti-Catholic Perennialist. He distinguished between "religion" and "religions" ("love religion, and distrust the religions") and argued that the Church Fathers had destroyed the teachings they had received,[21] an indirect justification of the Universal Gnostic Church, which drew on a Christian tradition earlier than the Church Fathers.

One of Guénon's earliest articles, "La religion et les religions" of 1910, not only takes its title from the distinction made by de Pouvourville, but specifically acknowledges de Pouvourville (described as "our master and collaborator") as the originator of the idea that "the primordial doctrine" can only be one and that "parasitic vegetation must not be confused with the very Tree of Tradition." Despite this acknowledgment, there were (as we have seen) other and more important sources for Guénon's Perennialism. What Guénon took principally from de Pouvourville was not Perennialism but an emphasis on the avoidance of "parasitic vegetation," the Catholic Church.[22] This is one, indirect origin of the concept of "inversion" in the Traditionalist philosophy.

De Pouvourville was also the source of another important conviction of Guénon, that the West was under threat. De Pouvourville was preoccupied by the need to the defend of the "white races" against the "yellow race," then seen to be waking from its slumber. The need for this defense was made clear by the deplorable Russo-Japanese War of 1905 (which the Russians had lost with embarrassing rapidity), and by the extraordinary and little-known philosophical and sociological achievements of the "yellow race."[23] The defense of the "white races" was to have two prongs. One was Franco-German entente, promoted by de Pouvourville in a bilingual French-German monthly, Le continent, started in 1906 and edited jointly by de Pouvourville and an unidentified Dr. Hans Richter in Berlin.[24] The other was to secure Western control of Chinese philosophical and sociological resources, much as some later imperialists wanted to secure Western control of Arab oil. This was probably not de Pouvourville's motivation when he first joined the Triads as a deserter from the Legion, but it had become his objective by 1906.

Interestingly though less importantly, de Pouvourville evidently considered opium to be among the Chinese resources that the West should make use of. One of his works was L'opium, sa pratique [The Practice of Opium],[25] a subject on which he also wrote in his Franco-German Le Continent in 1906 and lectured at the School of Higher Commercial Studies in 1908 (the text of this lecture was later published by the Committee of French Colonial Congresses). According to de Pouvourville's nephew, he even succeeded in persuading the minister for the colonies, Albert Sarraut, to smoke opium with him (it was not until after the First World War that European countries began to restrict and finally criminalize the use of opiates). It seems likely, then, that it was from de Pouvourville that Guénon learned to use opium.[26]

Ivan Aguéli

The group around de Pouvourville and *La Gnose* included one further important follower of de Pouvourville's version of Perennialism, the Swedish painter
Ivan Aguéli.[27] Aguéli joined de Pouvourville and Guénon in 1910, after meeting
Georges-August Thomas in an esoteric bookstore he helped run, La Librairie
du Merveilleux. Thomas was one of the Martinists who had followed Guénon
through the Order of the Temple to the Gnostic Church. Aguéli joined the
Universal Gnostic Church, and began to write in *La Gnose*.[28]

La Gnose described itself as the official journal of the Universal Gnostic
Church and was established and jointly edited by Guénon and Thomas. It was
in *La Gnose* that Guénon's "La religion et les religions," discussed earlier, was
published. *La Gnose* was really Guénon's own journal, and for some time he
used it as a platform to conduct a personal vendetta against Encausse, rather
as the younger Encausse had used *Le voile d'Isis* for his polemic against Blavatsky. It then became the platform for a series of articles that contained the
essentials of what would become Traditionalism. The articles that would later
become Guénon's first book, the *Introduction générale*, were first published in
La Gnose. Most were on Hinduism written by Guénon, but Aguéli also wrote
a series of articles on Sufism and Islam. Twenty years later both Sufism and
Islam would became of primary importance for Guénon and many other Traditionalists. When this happened, Aguéli's Sufism would assume an importance it did not have in 1910.

La Gnose was not the only periodical in which Guénon was writing at this
time. In 1909 he, Thomas, and one other ex-Martinist wrote a joint letter
attacking Encausse to Abel Clarin de la Rive, editor of *La France chrétienne*
[Christian France]. This was a Catholic journal that had started a campaign
against Encausse and Martinism in 1894–95 under a previous editor, Léo
Taxil.[29] When Guénon published an article in *La Gnose* criticizing the illogi-
cality of the then standard Masonic system of high grades ("Les hauts grades
maçonniques" [Masonic high grades]), Clarin de la Rive was very happy to
reprint it in *La France chrétienne* the following year. Clarin de la Rive also
accepted an invitation from Guénon to attend a Universal Gnostic ceremony,
which evidently impressed him. He and Guénon became friends, and *La
France chrétienne* began to attack Encausse's Gnostic Catholic Church—but not
the Universal Gnostic Church to which Guénon belonged. Guénon became a
regular contributor of letters and then articles to Clarin de la Rive's journal,
which by 1913 had changed its name to the more accurate *La France anti-
maçonnique* [Anti-Masonic France].[30] Guénon's participation in *La France chré-
tienne/La France anti-maçonnique* does not mean that he had himself become
Catholic or anti-Masonic—as we will see, he was a practicing member of a
Masonic lodge during this period and retained a low opinion of the Catholic

Church—but rather means that he found Clarin de la Rive's journal useful as a platform against Martinists, atheist Masons, and others who, he was convinced, spread a dangerously wrong view of spirituality and religion.

In 1911 Guénon was initiated by de Pouvourville into his Triad, possibly along with other members of this group. Guénon and another Gnostic, Leon Champrenaud, were also initiated by Aguéli into the Shadhiliyya Arabiyya Sufi Order (discussed later), taking the Muslim names Abd al-Wahid and Abd al-Haq. These events were not (as they have sometimes been portrayed) conversions in the normal sense of the word. There is absolutely nothing to suggest that Guénon, for example, practiced Islam or followed the precepts of Taoism or Buddhism in 1911, or indeed until his arrival in Egypt in 1930.[31]

Given the importance of Sufism and of Islam for Guénon after 1930, and then for Traditionalism as a whole, I will now consider how Aguéli came to be in a position to admit people into a Sufi order and then discuss the nature of Aguéli's Islam, as well as that of two other contemporary Western Sufis.

Though Aguéli was a Swede, he spent most of his adult life in France and Egypt, having left his native country at the age of 21 for artistic reasons—and perhaps personal reasons as well; he had been dismissed from three different schools in Sala, the small central Swedish town of his birth, and his parents opposed his chosen career as a painter.[32] During the "Belle Epoque," Paris was almost the only possible destination for a serious artist, and that is where Aguéli went in 1890. He studied and painted in the atelier of Emile Bernard, a talented painter and sculptor who helped launch the careers of Paul Gauguin and Paul Cézanne. Aguéli also involved himself in many of the other interests permeating the Parisian artistic and alternative milieu, notably anarchism, feminism, and Theosophy—to which he was introduced by Bernard in 1891 and which he never fully rejected.[33]

Soon after joining the Theosophical Society, Aguéli became closely involved with a married French Theosophist somewhat older than himself, Marie Huot. She was an anarchist, a vegetarian, and an animal rights activist—on one occasion she disrupted a demonstration by Louis Pasteur at the Sorbonne and was saved from the anger of Pasteur's supporters only by the intervention of Ferdinand de Lesseps. She was also secretary of the Popular League against Vivisection and founded France's first hospice for animals.[34] In addition, she was a poet, but in retrospect a mediocre one at best.[35] It is unclear whether or not Aguéli's close relationship with Huot was a romantic one, but it was to last for many years.

Huot was indirectly responsible for introducing Aguéli to Sufism. It was his connection with anarchists, through her, that led to a short term of imprisonment in 1894 during which he began to read the Koran, and it was Huot's husband who paid for Aguéli's boat ticket to Egypt on his release.[36] It is unclear why Aguéli chose Egypt as his destination; North Africa would have been a more obvious destination for a Parisian interested in Islam, for both

geographical and linguistic reasons. Perhaps Aguéli was considering continuing toward India because of an interest in Hinduism; the standard route from
Europe to India then passed through Egypt.[37]

After a first visit to Egypt in 1894–95, Aguéli abandoned painting for some
years and returned to Paris to study Arabic at the leading French institution
for such purposes, the Ecole des Langues Orientales, and to study Sanskrit
with Sylvain Lévi, the Indologist who later rejected Guénon's thesis. Aguéli
also became Muslim and returned to Egypt.[38] He became briefly famous in
France during a return visit in 1900, as a result of Huot's determination to
resist the introduction into France of Spanish-style bullfighting (in which the
bull is killed, which does not happen in French-style bullfighting). Aguéli accompanied Huot to the bullring and shot the matador. This was the first instance of what might be called Traditionalist (or proto-Traditionalist) terrorist
activity, and was motivated less by theoretical considerations than by Aguéli's
relationship with Huot. The matador survived, and because of public sympathy
for Huot's cause, Aguéli received only a suspended sentence. The promoters
of Spanish-style bullfighting abandoned their attempt to introduce it in
France.[39]

Back in Cairo in 1902 Aguéli involved himself in anti-colonial politics,
working closely with an Italian, Enrico Insabato. Insabato, like Aguéli, had an
anarchist background; he was also a Mason but not, so far as is known, a
Theosophist. Insabato was also the private agent of Giovanni Giolitti, Italian
prime minister from 1903 to 1905, with whom he corresponded directly; he
had no supporters in the Foreign Ministry or the Italian Legation in Cairo,
where he was detested. His objective was to unite nascent Italian imperialism
with Islam.[40] Like de Pouvourville's Franco-German entente, this objective was
never realized, and all hope of it was lost in the Italo-Ottoman War of 1911–12.
Before this disaster, Insabato's successful projects included establishing a *riwaq*
(college) for Tripolitanians at Cairo's Al Azhar university, and an Italian-
sponsored mosque in Cairo named in honor of King Umberto 1, completed in
1906.[41] More important for Traditionalism, he published a bilingual Italian-
Arabic Islamist periodical, *Al nadi / Il Convito*, for which Aguéli and Insabato's
principal Egyptian supporter, Abd al-Rahman Illaysh, both wrote.

Abd al-Rahman Illaysh was the son of a distinguished scholar, Muhammad
Illaysh, from 1854 the Maliki mufti, one of the dozen most important offices
in the Egyptian Islamic hierarchy. Abd al-Rahman fled Egypt for Damascus
after his father's death in prison (where he was put for political reasons),[42] and
there he became a close associate of the Amir Abd al-Qadir, the Algerian resistance leader who had spent his closing years honored by the French for his
statesmanship and by Syrian Muslims for his knowledge of the great medieval
Sufi theorist Muhyi al-Din ibn al-Arabi.[43] Abd al-Rahman's association with
Insabato, then, may be seen as a continuation of his father's anti-British activities; it is also possible that Insabato's Masonry played some role, since Abd

al-Qadir was himself a Mason.[44] Illaysh evidently later became disenchanted with Insabato. He refused Insabato's offer to arrange his appointment as Shaykh al-Islam (doyen of Islamic scholars) of Ethiopia, and in 1909 he abandoned Insabato's plans, turning his energies instead to an attempted Franco-Islamic rapprochement.[45]

Illaysh introduced an emphasis on Ibn al-Arabi into the pages of *Al nadi / Il Convito*, which announced the formation of a Society for the Study of Ibn al-Arabi in Italy and the Orient;[46] nothing more is known of this project, however. He also fostered Aguéli's interest in Ibn al-Arabi, whose teachings Aguéli was later to see as yielding the secret or essential doctrine of Islam. Ibn al-Arabi is important to Sufis in the Islamic world; for most Traditionalists, who followed Aguéli's lead, he was to become overwhelmingly significant. The later Traditionalist emphasis on Ibn al-Arabi, then, derives ultimately from the Amir Abd al-Qadir.

Aguéli also entered a Sufi order at Illaysh's hands, the Shadhiliyya Arabiyya. Hundreds of such orders then existed in Egypt, some doing little more than providing a sympathetic context for the religious practice of pious Muslims, but some taking small numbers of believers far along the path toward the mystic experience of God. Islam, like Traditionalism, distinguishes between exoterism (*zahir*) and esoterism (*batin*), and Sufis sometimes describe the relationship between Sufism and non-Sufi, mainstream Islam in these terms. Mainstream Islam attends to the *zahir*, the exoteric; Sufism gives access to the esoteric *batin*, to pure spirituality. The Sufi path, it is stressed, is a path *within* Islam: the scrupulous practice of mainstream Islam is a precondition for access to the *batin*.

Illaysh's Sufi order, the Shadhiliyya Arabiyya, dated from the seventeenth century and had flourished in the late eighteenth century. Its leadership had been inherited by Illaysh's father, Muhammad, on his own father's death, but by then the order was already in decline. It was not uncommon for a scholar to combine offices such as that of mufti with the leadership of a Sufi order as Muhammad Illaysh did, but for him the predominant role was clearly that of scholar and political player, not of Sufi. During the lifetime of Muhammad Illaysh's son Abd al-Rahman, the Shadhiliyya Arabiyya seems to have ceased to have any active membership.[47] In Sufi terms, it did not matter that the Shadhiliyya Arabiyya no longer had any organizational existence: it is perfectly correct to "give" to another any order one has taken, so long as one has been given permission—an *ijaza*—for that purpose, whether or not one has any active followers. Of course, an order without followers can hardly be described as an important or successful one. Illaysh not only gave Aguéli the Shadhiliyya Arabiyya, but also an *ijaza* to give that order himself.

In 1909 Aguéli returned to Paris, where he became known for extravagant behavior. Quick tempered and given to making lengthy speeches on unpopular subjects such as the excellences of anarchism, he frequently wore a turban or

Arab dress.[48] Such behavior was almost expected of Belle Epoque artists, who had "developed a systematic technique of scandal in order to keep their ideas before the public." Aguéli's more famous contemporary, the playwright Alfred Jarry, author of the seminal *Ubu Roi*, walked the streets of Paris dressed as a bicycle racer and carrying pistols in his belt.[49] It was at this point that Aguéli met de Pouvourville and used his *ijaza* from Illaysh to give the Shadhiliyya Arabiyya to Guénon and Leon Champrenaud.

Aguéli was not the only Western Sufi of the early twentieth century, though he is the first Westerner known to have established a genuine branch of a Sufi order, however small, in Europe. Perhaps the best-known Western Sufi of the time was Isabelle Eberhardt, a French journalist and novelist born in Geneva of Russian parents (her surname was German because her maternal grandmother had been German, and both she and her mother were illegitimate).[50] Eberhardt's writings presented a romantic view of the desert and of Arab life that proved very popular in France; they were the Algerian equivalent of Pierre Loti's enormously popular romantic novels of Ottoman Turkish life. Eberhardt's own life is also often interpreted romantically, and the picture of the intrepid Frenchwoman braving danger and colonial disapproval in the clothes of an Arab man has a lasting appeal. Eberhardt has as a consequence become something of a feminist (and, to a lesser extent, an anti-colonial) icon.[51]

Eberhardt's father, Alexander Trofimovsky, was born a serf, and had been employed as tutor by Eberhardt's mother's first husband, an army officer. Trofimovsky, Eberhardt's mother, and her first three children left Russia together for Switzerland, where Eberhardt herself was born. Trofimovsky was a radical socialist and an atheist, following Tolstoy and Bakunin. His education of his daughter, Isabelle, was similarly radical and nonconformist; not only did he teach her Latin and Greek (then more commonly taught only to boys) but he also encouraged her to dress as a boy.[52] Eberhardt also learned Arabic, possibly from her father, who was an enthusiast of Islam as an anti-colonial force. Among her father's friends was James Sanua, an Egyptian Jew of Italian origin, who had moved to Paris in 1878.[53] Sanua became a close friend of Eberhardt, mostly through a correspondence started in 1896, and introduced her to various Tunisians, one of whom she corresponded with on religious matters.[54]

The Trofimovsky household collapsed, and the 20-year-old Eberhardt and her mother moved to Algeria in 1897. One of Eberhardt's half-siblings remained in Switzerland; the other two returned to Russia, where they both later committed suicide. In Algeria, Eberhardt supported herself and her mother through her journalism, which was to some extent modeled on the writing of Pierre Loti. She meanwhile shocked local French colonial sentiment with her behavior—dressing not only as a man but as an Arab man, smoking hashish, appearing drunk in public, and sleeping with large numbers of Algerian men. She also shocked the French by describing herself as a Muslim and a Sufi.[55]

It is unclear how or when Eberhardt became Muslim; it seems that her father converted to Islam before his death, probably more out of political sympathy than spiritual conviction,[56] and Eberhardt may well have become Muslim in Europe before leaving for Algeria. Conversion to Islam is, technically, an easy process: there is no need for any period of instruction or any real formalities. All that is required is to pronounce in front of two witnesses—who must themselves be adults, Muslim, and sane—the Confession of Faith, the words (in Arabic): "I bear witness that there is no god but God, and I bear witness that Muhammad is His Prophet." The person who says these words is then Muslim, and as such is obliged to abide by the Sharia, the code of Islam—which among other things proscribes dressing in the clothes of the opposite sex, discourages the smoking of hashish, forbids the consumption of alcohol, and prohibits sex outside marriage. Eberhardt, then, does not seem to have been a very good Muslim, or—put differently—her understanding of what it meant to be Muslim did not include carefully observing the prohibitions of the Sharia.

It is not clear whether Eberhardt observed the Sharia in other respects. The Sharia does not only consist of prohibitions, but also specifies the religious practices required or encouraged by Islam—ritual prayer, periodic fasting, almsgiving, and the like. Almsgiving was probably not an issue, since what is known of Eberhardt's often desperate financial situation suggests that she would have been exempted from this duty on grounds of poverty, but prayer and fasting are required of all. Many born Muslims do not pray regularly, of course, though nearly all fast Ramadan; unfortunately, there are no reliable reports of whether or not Eberhardt prayed and fasted.

Eberhardt was, however, serious about aspects of Sufi practice, even if not about the prohibitions of the Sharia. She was in contact with two different Sufi orders, the Qadiriyya and the Rahmaniyya.[57] She joined the Qadiriyya in 1899 or 1900, two years after her arrival in Algeria, and in 1901 went into retreat (khalwa), a Sufi practice which differs little from its Catholic equivalent. In 1902 she made the difficult journey to Bu Sada in the south of Algeria to meet a Rahmani shaykh (leader of a Sufi order), Zaynab bint Muhammad ibn Abi'l-Qasim. Zaynab was remarkable as the successor of one of the most celebrated Algerian shaykhs of the nineteenth century, Muhammad ibn Abi'l-Qasim, her father, and also for being a female shaykh (which was and is very rare).[58] In 1903 Eberhardt again traveled south to see Zaynab, and in 1904 she went into a second retreat, this time with a Qadiri shaykh at Kenadsa, again in the south. These visits are what one would expect of a regular Algerian Sufi; the two retreats would, in an Algerian, indicate real dedication to the Sufi path.

Shortly after her second retreat, late in 1904, Eberhardt was killed (along with many others) in a flood—aged only 27, but suffering from malaria and possibly syphilis, and having lost all her teeth. Despite her anti-colonial stance, she was at the time supplying sensitive intelligence on the Algerian resistance to French commander General Hubert Lyautey, with whom she may have also been conducting a love affair.[59]

As a convert to Islam who ignored much of the Sharia yet visited Sufi shaykhs and went into retreat, Eberhardt was a special kind of Muslim—more of a Sufi than a Muslim, it might seem. During the twentieth century the view of Sufism as something separate from Islam became widespread in the West, but it is essential to appreciate that this view is a purely Western one and that the variety of non-Islamic neo-Sufism that has come into being in Europe and America is a purely Western phenomenon.[60] In Algeria and elsewhere in the Islamic world, Islam and Sufism were and are inseparable. Sufis are by definition Muslim, and the religious practices of a Sufi are based on the careful observance of the Sharia. Eberhardt's approach to religion would have been incomprehensible to most Muslims, though perhaps it was not to her shaykh, since great shaykhs are specialists in the many ways of the human heart.

The real nature of Eberhardt's conversion to Islam will remain unknown, but it may have been less a religious act than a means of identification with the Algerian world she clearly loved, and rejection of the French world she clearly detested. It is also possible that she found spiritual solace in Sufi Islam but was unwilling or unable to abandon those elements of her lifestyle that were incompatible with the Sufi path.

A third Western Sufi of the same period was Rudolf Freiherr von Sebottendorf (born Adam Glauer), whose Sufism was, like Eberhardt's, partial, but, like Aguéli's, seems to have been based in Western occultism. Von Sebottendorf is a notable figure in the history of Western Sufism. His spiritual interests were primarily in alchemy and Masonry, and he evidently subscribed to a somewhat Emersonian form of Perennialism and held a Blavatskian and Emersonian conviction of the usefulness of Oriental spirituality for the materialist West.[61]

Von Sebottendorf was the son of a German railroad engineer and obtained the name Sebottendorf and his title of nobility (Freiherr von) in controversial circumstances.[62] After dropping out of high school, he went to sea to earn his living. He jumped ship in the cosmopolitan Greek-Egyptian port city of Alexandria and found employment as an engineer with a local landowner who was (like many of the higher Egyptian aristocracy of the time) an Ottoman Turk and who took von Sebottendorf with him to Turkey. Von Sebottendorf spent most of the rest of his life in Turkey, taking Ottoman citizenship in 1911.[63] While in Turkey he studied first the Kabbala (the Jewish esoteric tradition) with a Jewish Kabbalist in Brussa, who introduced him to a Masonic lodge in that city in the 1890s.[64] He went on to study an unusual variety of Sufism with some Bektashi Sufis who were also Masons.[65] From them von Sebottendorf learned more numerology (a spiritual science in which Bektashis had always been prominent) than Sufism.[66]

So far as is known, von Sebottendorf did not actually follow a Sufi path as Eberhardt at least partly did, though he probably became Muslim.[67] Instead, he tried to blend all that he had learned into a single system. After many years, by 1910 von Sebottendorf had succeeded in his objective, at least in his own estimation. Having found what he conceived of as "the key to spiritual realization," von Sebottendorf decided to impart his discovery to those who needed it—not Muslims (for whom Sufism was already available and sufficient) or even believing Christians, but rather materialists who could no longer believe in anything, principally those found in Germany.[68] Thus in 1913 von Sebottendorf returned to his native land, where after some years and many disappointments he published his discovery in 1924, as *Die Praxis der alten Türkischen Freimauerei* [The Practice of Ancient Turkish Freemasonry]. This short book gives detailed instructions for a set of numerological meditation exercises that bear little resemblance to either Sufism or Masonry; they seem not to have impressed those who attempted them, however, and were it not for von Sebottendorf's later involvement in politics he would have been as forgotten as was his 1924 book.

Von Sebottendorf, like Eberhardt and Aguéli (to judge from his paintings), had a definite romantic attachment to his country of adoption, though of a somewhat different variety. Eberhardt's stories reveal a love of the desert and its inhabitants; von Sebottendorf portrays Ottoman Muslim civilization as one that did rather better than Germany itself in and after the First World War.[69] For both, a rejection of Western bourgeois civilization, or at least of their own understanding of that civilization, was one motive for their embrace of an Eastern alternative. This romantic motivation is absent from Guénon. In letters home from Sétif in Algeria (where he was teaching philosophy at the lycée) in 1917, Guénon complained of the Algerian climate, of having to work too hard at the lycée, of ungifted pupils, and, above all, of "the absence of any intellectual milieu."[70] Eberhardt would not have approved. Guénon was later a Western Sufi integrated into the Arab and Islamic world, but in 1917 his reaction to Algeria was most unenthusiastic.

Eberhardt's religious experience of Sufism must remain a matter of conjecture. Von Sebottendorf's approach to Sufi practice is clearer: it had almost nothing to do with what most Sufis would consider Sufism and everything to do with his previous experience of Masonry and European occultism. It is hard to say what Aguéli's approach was. His conversion to Islam seems to have had little impact on his daily life. He continued to paint the human figure and to sketch female nudes, infringements of the Sharia that a pious Sufi would normally avoid (though far less severe than those of Eberhardt). On the other hand, to judge from his writings, his understandings of Islam, Sufism, and Arabic were all excellent—and, at least in comparison to von Sebottendorf's, entirely orthodox.[71]

Aguéli appears as the most serious and most orthodox of these three West-

ern Sufis, but even so his conversion to Islam, like Eberhardt's and von Sebottendorf's, was a special kind of conversion, not found before the nineteenth
century. Other Westerners had from time to time become Muslim since the
rise of Islam, and various Ottoman pashas were of Western European origin.
These converts abandoned their Christian and European identities and names
for Muslim identities, merging themselves into the Muslim populations of the
areas they inhabited, as do some converts to Islam to this day. Though romantically attached to their adopted countries (Egypt, Algeria, and Turkey) and
committed to nationalist or anti-colonial politics, Aguéli and the other Western
Sufis remained Westerners, retaining their original connections and much of
their original identities. The same was true of Blavatsky and Olcott, both of
whom also "converted"—Blavatsky to Hinduism and Olcott to Buddhism, or
at least to their own versions of these religions.

The First World War

In 1912 Guénon received his sixth and final initiation, into the regular Masonic
lodge Thébah. He was introduced to this lodge by Oswald Wirth,[72] a central
figure in the history of Masonic Traditionalism. Wirth, the single most important figure in twentieth-century French Masonry, had earlier made the same
journey from occultism to respectability that Guénon would make under Catholic auspices. Initially associated with Encausse and others in occultist circles[73]
from whom (like Guénon) he had derived his basic objectives, during the 1890s
Wirth had turned his attentions to regular Masonry and distanced himself from
his earlier associates.[74] Wirth and the Masonic aspect of Traditionalism are
discussed later.

Guénon's introduction to regular Masonry was the last significant event
of the first phase of his adult life, the occultist phase. Although it was the First
World War that finally put an end to the activities I have been discussing, which
were quintessentially of the Belle Epoque, there was a preparatory lull in 1913.
La Gnose had ceased publication in 1912,[75] probably because of lack of money
and readers—most occultist periodicals were short-lived for these reasons. Another possible explanation is that Guénon had other things on his mind, for
in 1912 he married Berthe Loury, an assistant schoolteacher who at 29 was
three years older than he was, and whom he had met through his aunt during
a visit to his native Blois the previous year. It was at this point that Guénon
gave up using opium and hashish.[76] As required by French law, the first marriage ceremony was a civil one; the next week, they went through a Catholic
marriage ceremony in Blois (as was noted earlier, Guénon's new wife was a
devout Catholic).[77]

The First World War completed the dispersal of the group around de Pouvourville. Fabre des Essarts, patriarch of the Universal Gnostic Church, died

in 1917. Genty asked Guénon to become the new patriarch, but Guénon refused, and so Genty assumed the patriarchate himself. Since few other Gnostics recognized him, however, the Universal Gnostic Church split and declined.[78]

Aguéli, like des Essarts, did not live to see the armistice of 1918. He started painting again in 1911 and returned to Cairo in 1914. As a result of his contacts with pro-Ottoman Egyptians, however, he was expelled as a subversive alien in 1915[79] and moved to neutral Barcelona. There, penniless, he was run over by a train in 1917; there was some suspicion of suicide.[80] Aguéli's talent as a painter had by then been spotted by the brother of the king of Sweden, Prince Eugène, who was also a painter, but his gift of money arrived only after Aguéli's death. Prince Eugène rescued Aguéli's canvasses,[81] however, and appreciation of Aguéli's work grew in Sweden until he finally came to be seen as one of the leading Swedish painters of the period, honored by numerous exhibitions and biographies, a museum, a set of postage stamps, and in 1981 by a best-selling novel, which for the first time drew Swedes' attention to the fact that Aguéli had been a Muslim.[82]

De Pouvourville survived the war but was changed by it. The actual conflict with Germany replaced a possible conflict with the "yellow race," and the one-time proponent of Franco-German entente turned his pen to patriotic propaganda, publishing in 1916 *Jusqu'au Rhin, les terres meurtries et les terres promises* [To the Rhine: Bruised Lands and Promised Lands], which went through six editions by 1917.[83] His postwar writing was devoted to increasingly popular journalism of this sort, culminating in *Alerte sur Paris, le mur de lumière* [Alert over Paris: The Wall of Light] (1934), and then five brochures on *La guerre prochaine* [The Coming War] followed by 25 brochures on *L'héroïque aventure* [Heroic Adventures], sold at 1 franc each in 1935 and 1936.[84] There seems to have been no contact between him and Guénon during these years. After contributing much to Traditionalism, de Pouvourville disappears from the story.

De Pouvourville's later works suggest financial difficulties, a problem certainly faced by Guénon as a consequence of the war. Although excused from military service on medical grounds, Guénon found that he could no longer live off his investments—perhaps also because of the need to provide for his wife. In 1914 he returned to formal education, preparatory to getting his first job.

The war also marked the end of the Martinism that had been Guénon's first field of activity. Encausse was mobilized into the French army as a physician with the rank of major in 1914, and in 1916 he died of pulmonary disease contracted in the trenches.[85] He was succeeded as master of the Martinist Order by Charles Détré, a journalist who had lived for some years in England and who had run the irregular Masonic lodge Humanidad,[86] but Détré died in 1918. The order then split into several sections, each following different claimants, and declined quickly. An attempt by Encausse's son Philippe to revive Martinism in 1952 (after a career in medicine and sporting journalism) met with no success.[87]

The First World War, then, cleared the stage for the emergence first of the Traditionalist philosophy, and then (in the 1930s) of the Traditionalist movement. The war's horrors also destroyed much of the general faith in modernity that had underlain the Belle Epoque. The war thus produced circumstances that were conducive to the favorable reception of Traditionalism's anti-modernism.

PART II

Traditionalism in Practice

4

Cairo, Mostaganem, and Basel

In the late 1920s, just as Traditionalism was beginning to become an established philosophy, Guénon's life in Paris was shattered by a number of blows. As a consequence, he moved from Paris to Cairo in 1930, beginning the third and final phase of his adult life. This was also the longest phase, during which Traditionalism first became a movement, made up of loosely allied groups that either followed a distinctive religious practice or engaged in political activity. The religious aspects of the early Traditionalist movement are considered in this chapter, and the political ones in chapter 5.

At the start of 1927 Guénon was 40 years old, married, and reasonably comfortable. His career as a philosophy teacher could not be described as successful: he was at that point teaching in a private girls' school, then about as low as one could go in the French academic hierarchy. His books were increasingly appreciated, however, at least in restricted circles, and the number of his admirers was growing. He and his wife, Berthe, had had no children, but since 1918 they had been bringing up a niece, Françoise (then aged six), with the help of Guénon's favorite aunt, Madame Duru,[1] through whom he had met Berthe in 1911.

Within two years Guénon lost everything except his admirers. In 1927 Berthe died on the operating table during an appendectomy, at only 44, and Guénon lost his job at the girls' school. In 1928 Madame Duru died. The next year after some unpleasantness between Guénon and Françoise's mother (Berthe's sister), Françoise—then 16 or 17—was taken away from her uncle.[2]

This series of disasters resulted in the first sign of mild paranoia on Guénon's part. In March 1929 he wrote to Charbonneau-Lassay, who as well as being a friend from *Regnabit* knew Berthe's family, that Françoise "had been playing a double game"—telling him she wanted to stay with him and telling her mother that she wanted to be with her. Guénon also suspected her of letting people into the apartment while he was out. "I can really say that I fed a viper," wrote Guénon. He was surrounded "by a real net of spying and treason," he claimed. "The main objective of the people who caused all this," continued Guénon in another letter to Charbonneau-Lassay, "is precisely to make it impossible for me to . . . continue [my work]."[3] It was never entirely clear who "the people who caused all this" were, but Guénon seems to be referring to the "unsuspected low powers" mentioned in *Orient et Occident*: counterinitiatic organizations, including the surviving Martinists. In fact, Françoise was likely removed from her widower uncle's care because his lifestyle hardly provided the ideal environment for a young lady, whom one can imagine sitting alone in an empty apartment as Guénon went off to discuss tradition with his admirers.[4] Guénon and Françoise, who later became a Catholic nun, almost certainly never met again.[5]

Guénon's work had to continue, and it did. He busied himself with *Le voile d'Isis* and kept up his contacts with his admirers. It was in Paul Chacornac's bookshop that in 1929 he met Dina Shillito (born Mary Shillito), a wealthy American widow with a strong interest in the occult, and a convert to Islam. Guénon and Shillito seem to have established an immediate rapport and may even have become lovers.[6] They planned a series of Traditionalist books, to be edited by Guénon and financed by Shillito. After spending two months in Alsace for unknown purposes, they sailed for Egypt in 1930 to spend three months collecting texts for their series. The idea must have been Shillito's, since Guénon had never previously shown any great interest in foreign travel or in actual contact with the traditional Orient about which he wrote. The choice of destination was also probably Shillito's; her husband had been Egyptian and she would still have had contacts in Egypt.[7] Guénon's meeting with Shillito, then, was of the utmost importance for the subsequent history of Traditionalism, which became increasingly dominated by Islam. Without Shillito it is hard to see how this development could have happened.

Three months after the pair left France for Egypt, Shillito returned to France alone. Guénon and she had, for whatever reason, broken off relations. The planned series of Traditionalist books never materialized, and Shillito had no further contact with the Traditionalists.

Guénon the Egyptian

Even after Shillito's departure, Guénon at first intended to spend only a few more months in Egypt, but his return to France was delayed, then postponed, and in the end never happened. At first Guénon's only source of income was the royalties from his publications, which proved inadequate. Guénon sent a desperate letter to Reyor (who in 1932 became editor of *Le Voile d'Isis/Etudes traditionnelles* and so one of Guénon's main points of contact with France) asking him to extract some royalties overdue from Chacornac. In response, a wealthy admirer of Guénon traveled from Paris to Cairo to visit him and found him living "in a single miserable room, visibly undernourished." A number of Guénon's admirers then began to remit money in the guise of royalties (which had not, in fact, been earned),[8] but Guénon was never rich. In 1939 John Levy, a wealthy English Traditionalist who had been converted by Guénon's works from Judaism to Islam and who was visiting Guénon in Cairo, bought the house that Guénon had been renting and gave it to him as a gift,[9] thus to a large extent ensuring his financial future.

His economic situation somewhat stabilized by gifts from France, in 1934 Guénon married Fatima Muhammad Ibrahim, a devout Egyptian woman of modest social background.[10] The following year he arranged for his Paris apartment to be vacated, and over the coming years he and his Egyptian wife had the family he had never had in France—two daughters, one son, and a second son who would be born posthumously. In 1948 Guénon took Egyptian citizenship in order to pass it on to his children.[11]

Four reasons can be identified for Guénon's decision to stay in Egypt, and they do not include his marriage, which was arranged by his wife's father and so was a consequence rather than a cause of his decision to remain in Cairo. The first likely reason was that he felt he had nothing to return to in Paris. The second was that he could live more cheaply in Cairo than in Paris. The third was his fear of "unsuspected low powers" in France. The fourth and most important reason was that in Egypt, for the first time, Guénon found Islam and living tradition.[12]

Cairo in 1930 could not be described as a traditional city, nor even as a particularly Islamic one, but among its inhabitants were many pious Muslims whose lives had still been little touched by modernity and Westernization. This was the class into which Guénon married and among which he lived, at first in the working-class area around the ancient Husayn mosque and later in the middle-class suburb of Doqqi. That Guénon always dressed in a *gallabiyya* robe suggests that he avoided areas where Europeans normally lived out of choice. In Egyptian terms, wearing a *gallabiyya* was not so much traditional as archaic—the educated middle and upper classes had long abandoned this and many other of the usages that Guénon now adopted, replacing them with dress and customs of French origin. Guénon did retain some French customs, however, ending the day-long Ramadan fast not by eating a meal, as is normal in Egypt, but by smoking a cigarette and drinking a coffee.[13]

In Cairo Guénon lived as a pious Muslim and a Sufi. All reports indicate that he scrupulously followed not only the requirements of the Sharia, but also the recommendations of the *sunna*, the voluntary practices of Islam; for example, he knew by heart the prayers recommended for use when bidding farewell to someone about to leave on a journey.[14] Guénon at this time differed, then, from all three of the Western Sufis considered earlier, none of whom followed the Sharia at all scrupulously, and perhaps barely followed it at all. There was, however, one departure from the Islamic practice that one would expect of a pious Sufi: Guénon never made the Hajj pilgrimage to Mecca. Technically he was not obliged to make the Hajj because he was still supporting a young family, but the Hajj is not just a question of obligation; it is something that almost any pious Muslim yearns to do, and it is hard to conceive of any pious Muslim turning down the opportunity to make the Hajj if it was offered. In Guénon's case the opportunity was offered in some form, since his wife, Fatima, made the Hajj in 1946,[15] and Guénon turned down the opportunity to accompany her.[16]

As well as observing the Sharia, Guénon followed a Sufi order. The last traces of the Arabiyya Shadhiliyya order that Aguéli had taken from Abd al-Rahman Illaysh seem to have vanished with the death of Illaysh in 1929, and Guénon instead joined the Hamdiyya Shadhiliyya order.[17] This was an order of recent origin, then still led by its founder, Salama al-Radi, one of the most prominent Sufi shaykhs of his time. It was presumably because of al-Radi's prominence that Guénon selected the Hamdiyya Shadhiliyya, but al-Radi is in some ways a slightly curious choice of shaykh for a Traditionalist.

Sufi shaykhs can in general be divided into three categories: "the routine," "the charismatic," and "the specialist." Most shaykhs are routine shaykhs, men such as Illaysh, who have inherited an order from their fathers and who maintain what is really an extension of the day-to-day religious practice of pious Muslims. A few shaykhs, like al-Radi, are charismatic, men who gather large and enthusiastic followings who regard them as saints; they are often the starting point of a new order. A charismatic shaykh is often the past follower of a specialist shaykh, that is, a man who leads a small circle of dedicated followers far along the Sufi path, often finally to the experience of mystic union with God. A specialist shaykh would normally be the choice of a Muslim who was devoting his entire life to religion, so Guénon might have been expected to follow a specialist. Al-Radi, however, was a charismatic shaykh.[18] Perhaps Guénon did not follow al-Radi as a spiritual guide but merely attended periodic communal *dhikr*. His opinion of the orders in general was not high. "All are initiatic in principle and origin," he wrote to a follower two years after arriving in Cairo, "but unfortunately there are those that have lost a lot spiritually, either through having been too widely spread, or above all through the intrusion of political influences."[19] The "political influences" to which Guénon referred were, presumably, the engagement of many orders in the anti-colonial nationalist movement.[20]

Though a pious Muslim in his religious practice, Guénon remained a confirmed Perennialist in his beliefs. He said that he had not converted to Islam but "moved into" it: "whoever understands the unity of traditions . . . ," he wrote, "is necessarily . . . 'unconvertible' to anything."[21] Of his "moving into" Islam Guénon also wrote: "There is in it nothing that implies the superiority of one traditional form—in itself—over another, but merely what one could call reasons of spiritual convenience."[22]

Guénon remained not only a universalist in his beliefs, but a Traditionalist rather than a Muslim in his writings. There are few references to Islam in his work before 1930, and despite a slight increase in references after 1930, Islam never became an important source for him. Nor was it an important element of his reading: his private library contained some 3,000 volumes at the time of his death, but four times as many on Hinduism as on Islam, and few or perhaps none in Arabic.[23] When Guénon wanted to refer to the works of the great Sufi theorist Ibn al-Arabi, he wrote for references to a follower in Paris who knew Ibn al-Arabi well.[24] In fact, it is likely that Guénon did not read Arabic. He is often described as fluent in Arabic, and he would certainly have been fluent in the Egyptian dialect (the only language his wife spoke), but fluency in an Arabic dialect does not imply any ability to read the classical form of the language in which religious books are written. It takes years of hard work for a Westerner to learn to read classical Arabic with any fluency, and by the time Guénon settled in Cairo, he probably had neither the time nor the inclination for such study.[25] He was in his fifties; he had done his learning, and now he was teaching.

In Cairo Guénon continued to read and to write books and articles and conduct an extensive correspondence just as he had in Paris, retiring from his study to play with his children or to sit in an armchair and stroke his cats. His correspondence took him hours every day, especially in later years; he answered all letters equally carefully, irrespective of their source and subject.[26] This correspondence now constituted the focal point for the organization of his Western "elite" and stretched from India to Brazil.[27]

Guénon also received the occasional visitor from Europe, but often reluctantly, as his paranoia increased. An illness in late 1937 confined Guénon to his bed for some months and was, he thought, the result of a magical attack by a European visitor, whom he believed to have been sent by counterinitiatic circles in France.[28] There were also rumors that Guénon's first wife, Berthe, had been killed by magic,[29] rumors that may have originated with Guénon himself. After his 1937 illness Guénon not only took precautions of a ritual nature, but also kept his address secret, routing his correspondence through post office boxes. He agreed to meet only those Europeans of whose identity he was certain, and in later years he rarely left his house.[30]

Guénon does not seem to have had many friends in Cairo—certainly nothing like the circle he had had in Paris. His oldest friend was Countess Valentine de Saint-Point, a Frenchwoman who had been in Cairo even longer than he had. She had converted to Islam in Morocco in 1918, some seven years after the end of a successful career as a poet and novelist in Belle Epoque Paris. An early feminist, she was the first woman to cross the Atlantic in an airplane, and she had modeled naked for the sculptor Auguste Rodin. She moved to Cairo in 1924, where she supported the nationalist movement, as had Aguéli, while experimenting with acupuncture. Guénon had been given an introduction to her for his arrival in Cairo.[31]

Guénon's other friends in Cairo seem to have been of the same type (though with less spectacular pasts): Western converts to Islam, and cosmopolitans such as the young Najm al-Din Bammate. Of Daghestani origin, Bammate was the son of the Afghan ambassador in Paris; he studied in Switzerland and spent his later years teaching at a French university, becoming an important figure among French Traditionalist Muslims in the 1970s and 1980s.[32] There were also some Westernized Egyptians such as Muin al-Arab, a retired diplomat who had converted to Buddhism and married an Englishwoman (who herself converted to Islam).[33]

Just as Islam is little visible in his writings, Guénon seems to have had few contacts with Islamic scholars in Cairo. One exception is Abd al-Halim Mahmud, a Sufi and from 1973 to 1978 shaykh of Al Azhar, the most senior position in the Egyptian Islamic hierarchy.[34] Mahmud devoted much energy to defending Sufism in a period during which it was becoming distinctly unfashionable among educated Egyptians, and he was later frequently presented in Traditionalist circles as a close associate of Guénon and even as a Traditionalist. The evidence for Mahmud's Traditionalism is unconvincing, however,[35] and indeed Mahmud on one occasion admitted that he had never read any of Guénon's books (which he could have done had he wanted to: his Ph.D. was from Paris).[36] Mahmud, who first met Guénon while delivering a book sent by a mutual acquaintance in France, did write one long article praising Guénon, but his praise was not for Guénon's writing but rather for his piety, the unspoken message being that if this brilliant Frenchman could become a Sufi, then there could be little wrong with Sufism.[37] Another exception to his lack of contact with Islamic scholars was Guénon's participation in Al-marifa (Illumination), a mainstream Islamic journal of Sufi inclination, shortly after his arrival in Cairo. For unknown reasons, this participation was short-lived.[38]

Guénon's influence on Egyptian Islam seems to have been negligible; a few of his articles were translated into Arabic, but he left no other traces. This is so perhaps because in Egypt there was no real equivalent to Guénon's audience in France. Egyptians have a voracious appetite for religious books but favor modern and ancient titles about Islam, not about Hinduism. Indeed, almost any pious Egyptian would have been scandalized by the suggestion that his religion could have anything to do with Hinduism, commonly seen as a variety of pagan idol worship. Guénon's Perennialism would have been poorly received: the standard view of Islam (to which there are, however, some very occasional exceptions) is that all other religions were superseded by the reve-lation of Islam and can now be followed only out of ignorance or perversity. Previous revelations were only partial and preparatory revelations of God's will and were then distorted by their followers, as, for example, by those Christians who invented the impossible lie that God had children. The gulf, then, between Guénon's interests and those of "traditional" Egyptian Muslims was simply too large for any real communication.

The gulf between Guénon and Egypt's intellectuals was even larger. Muin al-Arab once took Guénon to meet Taha Husayn, the leading Egyptian intel-lectual of the early twentieth century. A secular modernist, Taha Husayn was married to a Frenchwoman. Apart from their having in common a cross-cultural marriage, it is hard to imagine why Muin al-Arab thought there was any reason to introduce the two. As might have been predicted given Taha Husayn's own agenda, his reaction to Guénon's Traditionalism was immediate and very visible hostility.[39] "It is not true," wrote Taha Husayn on another occasion, "that 'the West is materialistic' . . . ; its material triumphs are the product of its intellect and spirit, and even its atheists are willing to die for their beliefs."[40]

Though Guénon may have learned little or nothing from Muslim scholars present or past while in Cairo, he did learn something from his years in Egypt. His experience of the realities of life in the East made his view of it more realistic and so completed the transition from the idealization of the East found in Eberhardt and Aguéli to the idealization of tradition as a concept indepen-dent of location. This transition is reflected in the appendix Guénon added for the new 1948 edition of Orient et Occident, in which he distinguished between the "mystic Orient" (tradition) and the "geographical Orient"[41]—Egypt and other places, where not all is traditional and where not everyone is a pious Sufi. Despite this change of views, Guénon's early idealized (and unrealistic) picture of the East remained influential for many later Traditionalists who—like Guénon before 1930—often had little or no direct experience of it.

A more important consequence of Guénon's direct experience of how pi-ous Muslims lived and worshipped was his growing appreciation of the im-portance of religious practice,[42] an appreciation that was especially Islamic in the sense that Islam stresses daily practice more than do many other religions. This appreciation was soon reflected in Guénon's writings. In general the ar-ticles Guénon wrote in Cairo are adjustments of the Traditionalist philosophy, and his books from this period are edited compilations of earlier articles from 1910 to 1915. The one really new area on which he wrote was initiation, to which he devoted a whole series of articles from 1932 until 1939, when the Second World War cut off communications between Egypt and Europe. These articles, later collected and published as Aperçus sur l'initiation [Views on Ini-tiation] (1946), stress the need for personal initiation into an orthodox religious tradition.[43]

These articles led to a stream of letters to Guénon in Cairo. Dismayed Traditionalists who had thought they were engaged in a primarily intellectual quest joined more enthusiastic newer readers of Guénon's works in asking much the same question: what initiation should they take? Guénon never recommended any particular initiation in print, though he excluded organizations he saw as devoid of initiatic validity—the Catholic Church, various neo-Hindu groups in the West, and of course anything counterinitiatic. He also pointed out the practical difficulties that anyone not born a Hindu would have in following any form of Hinduism. By implication, that left only two choices: Freemasonry (discussed later) or Guénon's own personal choice, the Sufi path within Islam. Guénon did not always recommend Islam to his correspondents, however, and not always immediately. In *Orient et Occident* he had hoped to avoid or at least moderate the "assimilation" of the West by the East, and his objective was never anything so simple as the Islamization of the West. He always retained an interest in the possibility of surviving Western forms of initiation. He was also for some time much interested in the possibilities apparently represented by a surviving Western initiatic organization, the Fraternity of the Cavaliers of the Divine Paraclete.

The Fraternity of the Cavaliers of the Divine Paraclete

The Fraternité des Chevaliers du divin Paraclet (Fraternity of the Cavaliers of the Divine Paraclete) was discovered by Reyor in France after Guénon's departure for Egypt. Reyor, editor of *Etudes traditionnelles* and one of Guénon's leading admirers in Paris, was most reluctant to become Muslim and had little taste for Masonry. He thus recalled with interest occasional references to an unspecified medieval Christian order he had seen in articles written by Charbonneau-Lassay.[44] Reyor's interest was not only for himself: as editor of *Etudes traditionnelles,* he received frequent inquiries from readers concerning what initiation they should take. He therefore contacted Charbonneau-Lassay, who told him that the references were to L'estoile éternelle (The eternal star), a Catholic order formed in the fifteenth century which had barely survived the French Revolution but still existed, consisting of twelve persons, Some years before, one of its members, Canon Benjamin-Théophile Barbot, had contacted Charbonneau-Lassay in response to his published work on Christian symbolism to offer him access to their archives.

Reyor was interested, but the Estoile éternelle was not the answer to his problem. It would initiate a new member only when one of its number died, and there were far more than one or two Traditionalists looking for initiation.[45]

Under pressure, Charbonneau-Lassay admitted that there was also another order, the Fraternité des Chevaliers du divin Paraclet. The Divine Paraclete (from the Greek *parakletos,* intercessor) is generally understood in Catholic theology as the abiding presence of the Holy Spirit in the absence of Christ. The Fraternité des Chevaliers du divin Paraclet, said Charbonneau-Lassay, had operated from the sixteenth century. Though it was disbanded in 1668, its initiation had been kept alive within the Estoile éternelle and had been passed to Charbonneau-Lassay by Canon Barbot. Charbonneau-Lassay was at first reluctant to revive the Fraternité, but when Reyor pointed out to him that if he did not do this then various Traditionalists would be obliged to convert to Islam, Charbonneau-Lassay consented.[46] In 1938 the Fraternité des Chevaliers du divin Paraclet was formally reconstituted by Charbonneau-Lassay, Reyor, and Georges-Auguste Thomas—the same ex-Martinist who had been a member of Guénon's early Order of the Temple. A few more Traditionalists joined the Fraternité in 1939.[47] Soon afterwards, the start of the Second World War interrupted activities.

Guénon had followed matters with interest from Cairo and concluded that though the Fraternité des Chevaliers du divin Paraclet itself seemed orthodox, there were "lacunae" that rendered it of little use—that is, there were no traces whatsoever of any spiritual practice. Reyor suggested that a practice might be reconstructed, perhaps by parallels to Sufi practice, but Guénon seems to have rejected this possibility. In 1943, in German-occupied Paris, the still reluctant Reyor left the Fraternité and became Muslim.[48] In about 1946, however, Charbonneau-Lassay told Thomas (who succeeded him as master of the Fraternité) that he had remembered a detailed set of daily practices that Barbot had told him about, the importance of which it had unfortunately taken him almost twenty years to see. Thomas passed these practices on to his successors.[49]

Charbonneau-Lassay's sudden recollection of the practices of the Fraternité des Chevaliers du divin Paraclet is simply too convenient to be credible, as is the detail in which they were remembered. Some believed that they had been dreamed up by Thomas,[50] but it seems more likely that they were dreamed up by Charbonneau-Lassay. Thomas had no reason for deliberately deceiving his successors in the Fraternité, but Charbonneau-Lassay did: to save souls from damnation. Despite his earlier collaboration with Guénon on *Regnabit*, Charbonneau-Lassay had once been a lay brother and remained a pious Catholic; he had concluded that although Guénon's work was interesting and sometimes right, his books could be "dangerous" and often had "deplorable results": conversion to "a superreligion reserved for an elite of initiates who may pass, without the slightest difficulty, from one form of worship to another according to the regions that they may successively inhabit,"[51] a dismayed paraphrase of Guénon's own comments on his "moving in" to Islam. Charbonneau-Lassay would thus have had every reason to dream up almost anything in good conscience, if it would keep Traditionalists within the Catholic Church.

In fact, Charbonneau-Lassay might well have dreamed up the Fraternité itself in the first place. The four people he named as its sixteenth-century founders all existed, but there is no evidence to link them except Charbonneau-Lassay's undocumented account of the Fraternité[52] Charbonneau-Lassay was an antiquarian, and it would not have been very hard for him to come up with four plausible names and other plausible details. Indeed, it seems suspicious that all four sixteenth-century names are names that could be identified in the twentieth century. It might have looked more convincing if at least one of the founders had left no other traces.

If the Fraternité des Chevaliers du divin Paraclet was an entirely bogus organization, dreamed up by a believing Catholic in order to prevent apostasy to Islam—which must remain a hypothesis but seems a very plausible one—it would be the first instance of what Guénon had in 1924 termed "deviations." It would not be the last.

Freemasonry

Though the Fraternité des Chevaliers du divin Paraclet was a disappointment, Masonry provided initiatic possibilities which continued to interest Guénon until his death.[53] Indeed, Reyor—with Guénon's agreement—at one point routinely recommended Masonry to those who wrote asking for an initiatic path, recommending Sufism only when Masonry was rejected (as, according to Reyor, it usually was).[54]

As we have seen, Guénon's principal Masonic associate was Oswald Wirth, who had introduced him to the lodge Thébah. Wirth and Guénon were never quite collaborators, and indeed are said to have quarreled;[55] Guénon does not seem to have attended the meetings of Thébah after 1914. However, their views remained sufficiently in tune for Traditionalism to participate in the reform and revival of French Masonry with which Wirth is in large part credited.

By the early twentieth century French Masonry was in one sense the victim of its own success. Masonry had almost died out during the French Revolution but revived under Napoleon. The Grand Orient (the main French Obedience) attracted so much official favor[56] that it later easily became part of the republican establishment, of those opposed to monarchical and other nonliberal alternatives to the republic. By 1900 half the members of the Chamber of Deputies (as the French National Assembly was known until 1946) were Masons, and Masonry was known jokingly as "the Church of the Republic." Social and political activities had eclipsed most others—or, as Wirth put it, "essential matters were more and more neglected for the sake of developments of a profane order," and the level of instruction in spiritual matters in most lodges "would have been appropriate in a primary school."[57] When the survival of the republic and of republicanism was no longer in serious question, both a republican movement and the Church of the Republic became somewhat superfluous.

Wirth's objective was to return Masonry to essentials, reforming both ritual and the general understanding of its significance and purpose. His own understanding of the function of Masonic ritual was little different from some understandings of the purpose of religious practice, though he stressed that the objective was this-worldly rather than other-worldly.[58] Properly understood, he maintained, the objective of Masonic ritual was the individual's moral and ethical improvement, through the control of the will over the animal passions. The rituals in the lodge were symbolic representations of means that could and should be used to this end outside the lodge. They would work only to the extent that their symbolism was properly understood and to the extent that they were purified of all irrelevant and confusing accretions that had accumulated during the nineteenth century.[59] To this end, Wirth founded a journal, Le Symbolisme, and wrote a number of enduringly popular books on Masonry. His work was generally appreciated by senior Masons in the French Grand Lodge, an Obedience rivaling the Grand Orient that had been set up in 1880 and was less political than the Grand Orient. Wirth's work even came to be appreciated by some in the Grand Orient, which itself became somewhat less political during the second half of the twentieth century. Wirth did achieve something of the reform of French Masonry for which he hoped.[60]

Although their overall frameworks were very different,[61] Wirth's understanding of Masonic ritual was close enough to Guénon's understanding of esoteric practice for a certain alliance to develop. During Wirth's lifetime Guénon sometimes wrote in Wirth's Le Symbolisme,[62] and Wirth's successor as editor of that journal was open about the debt he owed to Guénon's work,[63] though he could not otherwise be described as a Traditionalist. Traditionalist work on symbolism blew new life into the rituals of many lodges, causing a minor Masonic renaissance. The Traditionalist philosophy later came to be well known in French Masonic circles, and to a lesser extent among Italian and Spanish Masons. Traditionalism's contribution to Masonic reform was reflected in the existence at the end of the twentieth century of a number of Masonic lodges with Traditionalist emphases, including a Swiss lodge called "René Guénon." Traditionalism had much less impact on American and British Masonry, which are somewhat removed from continental Masonry, though by the end of the twentieth century it was far from unknown even there. These developments, however, took place after the Second World War, and so must wait until a later chapter.

Schuon and the Alawis

It was not the Fraternité des Chevaliers du divin Paraclet or a Masonic lodge that was to be the main Traditionalist religious organization, but a Sufi order, the Alawiyya, later known as the Maryamiyya. This, like the Fraternité des

Chevaliers du divin Paraclet, was established in the early 1930s in response to Guénon's new emphasis on initiation and religious practice. Two Swiss in their mid twenties were responsible for its creation: Titus Burckhardt and Frithjof Schuon. The two men had first become friends at school in the city of Basel in German-speaking Switzerland. They were from somewhat different backgrounds, although both were artistic. Burckhardt was born in Florence, the son of a sculptor, but brought up mostly in Switzerland.[64] He was from one of Basel's oldest and most distinguished families and was the great-nephew of Jakob Burckhardt, whose *Die Kultur der Renaissance in Italien* [Culture of the Renaissance in Italy] (1860) is the classic expression of the view of the Renaissance as a triumph of the human spirit and the birth of a glorious modernity—a view decisively rejected by Guénon. Schuon, in contrast, was the son of immigrants. His father was a German violinist and his mother a Frenchwoman from Alsace, so Schuon's nationality at birth was not Swiss but German.[65]

Little is known of Burckhardt's life before his encounter with Traditionalism, but Schuon's early life is known in some detail as a result of his autobiographical *Erinnerungen und Betrachtungen* [Memories and Reflections] (1974). This is an astonishingly frank work and an invaluable resource for the historian.[66]

Schuon was 16 when he first read Guénon's *Orient et Occident*, which was given to him by Lucy von Dechend, a German childhood friend who knew of his interest in Vedanta, an interest he derived from books in his father's library.[67] Schuon's immediate reaction was enthusiastic.[68] In 1931, while doing his military service, he wrote to Guénon.[69] His initial reaction to Guénon's recommendation of Sufism was the same as Reyor's had been: extreme reluctance. As he expressed it in a letter to a friend: "How can you think that I want to reach God 'via Mecca,' and thus betray Christ and the Vedanta?"[70] After some agonizing, one day in Paris in 1932 Schuon prayed to God to grant him a sign. Shortly afterwards, he went out into the street and saw the unusual spectacle of a detachment of North African cavalry trotting past. Taking this as the sign he had prayed for, Schuon became Muslim and wrote to Guénon asking him to recommend a shaykh.[71]

Periodic signs and visions such as this were to play a crucial part in Schuon's life, and thus in the lives of many others who followed him. Even his birth, he was told, had been attended by a sign: the hospital in which he was born had been struck by lightning and all the clocks had stopped. To some, this might not have seemed a good start, especially for someone whose first name literally meant "thief of peace." (It was a Norwegian rather than a Swiss or German name, chosen by his father, who had Norwegian friends.)[72]

In his autobiography, Schuon himself lays great emphasis on his childhood, which clearly marked him for the rest of his life. His happiness was shattered by the sudden death of his father when he was 13.[73] Up to that point he had lived in reasonable comfort in a relaxed and artistic ambience; he was unsure whether he wanted to be a painter or a poet, but he was sure it would be one or the other. His father's death, however, left the family in a difficult financial situation, and in 1920 his mother took Schuon and his slightly older brother, Erich, away from Basel to live with her own mother in Mulhouse, some 25 miles across the French border in Alsace. Schuon was miserable in Alsace. He not only missed his father and early home, but was treated with general hostility as a German—one consequence of the First World War was that to be a German in France in the 1920s was to be a pariah. Financial considerations meant also that neither poetry nor painting was possible; Schuon was obliged to leave school at 16 and take a job in a factory, as an apprentice textile designer, to support his family.[74] Meanwhile his relations with his mother were very poor, and with his grandmother nonexistent. His mother wanted him to be a good French bourgeois, to which end she had her Protestant, free-thinking children baptized as Catholics shortly after their arrival in France.[75] Schuon, in contrast, wanted to retain what he could of the artistic milieu of his earlier childhood.[76] In 1923 Erich left home for a seminary; he later became a Cistercian ("Trappist") monk.[77] Writing in his diary, Schuon expressed his desolation at being deprived of all that he held dear: his father and brother, his home and his country, his "spiritual and social caste."[78]

The young Schuon spent his free time reading philosophy and books about the East. He detested modernity for its "pettiness, meanness and ugliness," and he would wander the streets of Mulhouse, dreaming of "nobility, greatness and beauty."[79]

Even at this stage Schuon had intimations that his own greatness would be religious. In 1923 or 1924, when he was 17, he wrote in his diary of an expectation that one day he would be summoned as *parakletos*.[80] The meaning of this passage is not entirely clear; *parakletos*, as we saw in the context of the Fraternité des Chevaliers du divin Paraclet, is a Christian term, usually taken as referring to the Holy Spirit. For Schuon it must have had some other meaning; there is nothing else to indicate that at 17 Schuon supposed himself part of the Divinity.[81]

As soon as he could leave Mulhouse, Schuon did so, going to Paris in 1929 and taking a job as a textile designer. By now he was somewhat happier than he had been in Mulhouse. In 1932, however, he lost his job as a result of the Great Depression, and in despair he decided to leave France for the East. It was shortly after this that he prayed for and received his sign, became Muslim, and then went back to Switzerland, where he found a young Iranian mullah who taught him the Fatiha (the opening chapter of the Koran and the central text of the ritual prayer).[82] He also paid a number of visits to a small group in Basel which was by then meeting regularly to discuss Guénon's work.[83]

Schuon briefly rented a cheap attic room in Lausanne, in French-speaking Switzerland. An unidentified schoolfriend who was living in that city took pity on him and visited him every morning in his attic, bringing him some break-fast. One day when the schoolfriend was busy, he sent his 17-year-old sister instead. This was Madeleine (surname not known). Schuon was immediately struck by her beauty.[84]

From Lausanne, Schuon proceeded to the French Mediterranean port of Marseilles, where he met his friend von Dechend. He had not yet received a reply to his letter to Guénon asking him to recommend a shaykh. In Marseilles, Schuon and von Dechend met some Algerian (or perhaps Yemeni) sailors who talked to Schuon of Shaykh Ahmad al-Alawi.

Ahmad al-Alawi was an Algerian and one of the most celebrated Sufi shaykhs of the early twentieth century. A shaykh of the charismatic type, al-Alawi had traveled to Morocco, where for fifteen years he had followed a spe-cialist shaykh of the Darqawi Order, Muhammad Bu Zidi. On his return to his birthplace, the port of Mostaganem, he established his own order, called the Alawiyya in honor of Ali (alawi is the Arabic adjective formed from Ali), the son-in-law of the Prophet, who appeared to him in a vision and gave him that name for his new order (he also adopted the surname "al-Alawi").[85] Schuon, of course, was not the only recipient of signs and visions, which have always been a normal part of the spiritual life of most Sufis. Al-Alawi's career is typical of that of a shaykh of his type, as is the time he spent in Morocco; Sufism has from the beginning ignored national boundaries.

The Alawiyya Order spread far and fast, aided by al-Alawi's following among sailors. One Yemeni sailor, for example, settled in Cardiff in 1925 and established a British branch of the Alawiyya that soon dominated the religious life of the Yemeni community in Britain.[86]

Living in French Algeria, al-Alawi was well aware of the importance of good relations with the Europeans. The French authorities at this time regarded Sufism with great suspicion, since most of the early resistance movements against the French occupation of North Africa had been led by Sufis.[87] The Amir Abd al-Qadir, the associate of Illaysh mentioned earlier, was the most famous of many Sufi resistance leaders. The fight against the French had now clearly been lost, however, and al-Alawi adopted a conciliatory approach. He understood French well, though he was reluctant to speak it, and when dealing with Europeans he emphasized the points that Sufism and Christianity had in common rather than their differences. As a result, he was well regarded by many French, and it was he who was asked to lead the first communal prayer to inaugurate the new Paris Mosque in 1926. He also had a small number of European followers, including Probst Biraben, one of Guénon's early admirers in Paris.[88]

The Algerians whom Schuon had met in Marseilles perhaps arranged a free passage for him to Oran in Algeria,[89] but not for von Dechend (perhaps because she was not Muslim), and she returned to Basel.[90] In late 1932 Schuon arrived at the zawiya (mosque complex) of the Alawiyya in Mostaganem.[91]

Some time after his arrival, Schuon received a letter from Guénon, which had been forwarded, recommending a shaykh: Ahmad al-Alawi.[92] This coincidence is easily explained: Schuon spoke French and German and probably only a little Arabic, and al-Alawi was the most celebrated French-speaking shaykh then alive.

By 1932 al-Alawi was an old and ill man, and Schuon saw little of him, though in early 1933 he was taken to al-Alawi for the short ceremony that admitted him to the Alawiyya Order.[93] Instead he spent his time talking with other Alawis, especially Adda Bentounès, one of al-Alawi's *muqaddams* (deputies). A shaykh with a large following (such as al-Alawi) commonly appoints a number of *muqaddams*, primarily to run subsidiary *zawiyas* in outlying areas, and sometimes to assist in the running the main *zawiya*. A *muqaddam* is normally given an *ijaza* (permit), which allows him to admit others into the order.

Schuon spent three months in this way, living in a room in the *zawiya* furnished only with a straw mat, a mattress, and a blanket. In addition to talking to other Alawis, he spent time walking on the beach, and after the ritual prayer at sunset would stand in the courtyard outside the mosque to admire the poignant beauty of the scene.[94] This routine is fairly normal for a new arrival in a Sufi order, who in this way becomes part of the community centered around the shaykh, learning from that community by example as well as through casual conversation, taking time to digest and internalize the whole experience. At the end of three months Schuon left Mostaganem, partly because the local French authorities had become curious about his presence there, and returned to Europe.[95]

Schuon's Traditionalist friends in Basel were astonished; he seemed "a changed man."[96] Burckhardt met Schuon again at this point, not having seen him since their early teens, and immediately wanted to go to Mostaganem himself, though he was dissuaded by reports of al-Alawi's declining health and the difficulties that Schuon had had with the French authorities. He decided instead to go to Morocco.[97]

Changed though he was, Schuon retained his Traditionalist Perennialism. Even in the *zawiya* in Mostaganem he had spent some time writing an article for *Le voile d'Isis* on "L'aspect ternaire de la tradition monothéiste" (The threefold appearance of the monotheist tradition), that is, the fundamental unity of Christianity, Islam, and Judaism.[98] He had also had an argument with another Alawi, a Moroccan who had much upset Schuon by maintaining that Christians could not go to heaven—a view that al-Alawi himself may or may not have held[99] but that in any event a view he would certainly have been tactful enough not to announce to a recent convert whose brother was known to be a Christian monk.[100]

Burckhardt, in contrast to Schuon, seems to have become more Islamic and somewhat less Perennialist. He went to Fez, where he spent the winter learning Arabic, and became Muslim. In the spring of 1934 he met some Sufis of the Darqawiyya Order in Salé, and later he entered that order at the hands of Ali ibn Tayyib al-Darqawi of Fez[101]—but only after a strange experience at the Darqawi *zawiya* in Salé. Burckhardt was taken into a room where many other Darqawis were waiting, and on entering he felt that he was being welcomed by a small crowd of multiple Schuons.[102]

At about the same time, back in Paris, Schuon had his first vision while reading the Bhagavad Gita: "The All-Highest Name [Allah] sounded in me and continued vibrating powerfully in me. I could do nothing but give myself to this vibration." Schuon put down his book and left the house, walking for a long time along the *quais* in something of a trance, repeating the All-Highest Name.[103]

A few days after this experience, Schuon learned that he had had his vision on the day of al-Alawi's death. He decided that the meaning of the vision was that al-Alawi had given him permission to use the All-Highest Name in his personal litany,[104] a permission normally given only to those well advanced on the Sufi path. Schuon's awareness of the All-Highest Name would, however, come and go over the next few years, and this consciousness of it seems to have become for Schuon the mark of his own spiritual progress.

Shortly after this event Schuon returned to Mostaganem, where he was received by Adda Bentounès, once al-Alawi's *muqaddam* and then his successor as shaykh. After about a week Bentounès sent Schuon into *khalwa* (retreat), a standard element in Sufi spiritual training, during which state Schuon saw not only some of the prophets but also Japanese golden images of the Amida (Buddha)[105]—the latter, presumably, evoked by the Japanese statues of the Buddha in the Basel Ethnographic Museum that Schuon had much loved as a small child.[106]

At the end of the *khalwa*, according to Schuon in *Erinnerungen und Betrachtungen*, Bentounès appointed him an Alawi *muqaddam*.[107] This appointment was later to become the subject of much dispute. Some later Alawis confirmed Schuon's appointment, while some denied it;[108] it is clear that once Schuon began to act as a *muqaddam*, he was for a while accepted as such by Bentounès,[109] but that does not mean that this was Bentounès's original intention. Some of Schuon's later followers have copies of the text of an undated *ijaza* signed by Bentounès, and the accompanying but later French translation is titled "Moqaddem Diploma," but this document merely adds to the confusion. There is no mention of accepting people into the Alawiyya. The crucial sentence reads: "[Schuon] has been authorized to spread the Call to Islam . . . [and] accept the words of Unity, 'La illaha ila Allah, Muhammadan rasul Allah'." The "words of Unity," more commonly called in English the confession of faith (There is no divinity save God, [and] Muhammad is the Prophet of God), are those that must be pronounced by a non-Muslim in order to become Muslim. On the face of it, then, Schuon's *ijaza* permits him to proselytize for Islam and to accept conversions. No special permission is required, however, for what Schuon's *ijaza* permits him to do: it is the duty of any Muslim to proselytize for Islam, and any sane adult Muslim can witness (and so accept) a conversion.

The most likely explanation of this unusual text is that Schuon, aware of the need to provide the Traditionalist elite with a valid initiation into an ortho-dox tradition, had suggested to Bentounès that an *ijaza* might be useful for him in Europe, rather as Reyor had asked Charbonneau-Lassay to revive the Fraternité des Chevaliers du divin Paraclet, and that Bentounès wanted neither to grant the implied request nor to turn it down outright, and so he gave Schuon a form of *ijaza* that did not actually give him permission to accept people into the Alawiyya but was a sort of consolation prize.

Although Schuon's *ijaza* has attracted dispute, what matters even more than the document itself is what lay behind it. An *ijaza* is both an administra-tive technique and an honor. As an administrative technique, it is a way of delegating some of a shaykh's powers and responsibilities, to be exercised on a shaykh's behalf. Schuon was never to act on al-Alawi's behalf. As an honor, it may be a certificate of achievement. In mainstream Sufi terms, Schuon's achievement at this time was that he had completed the first stage of his train-ing as a Sufi. That he had hardly completed all this training is suggested by a comparison between the length of time he had spent at the Alawi *zawiya* (a few months) and the time al-Alawi had spent with his own shaykh (fifteen years).

Though there were later doubts about Schuon's *ijaza*, there were none in Basel in the 1930s, and Schuon himself had no doubts about his ability to admit people into the Alawiyya.[110] At first he admitted several of the Basel Traditionalists—including Burckhardt and Harald von Meyenburg, a friend of Burckhardt and later Burckhardt's brother-in-law—all of whom had previously become Muslim. They began to meet from time to time to pray and do silent *dhikr* (repetitive prayer) together, and then Schuon started a regular weekly meeting for loud *dhikr*, held by Burckhardt (who was more often in Basel) in an apartment rented for that purpose in one of Basel's less smart districts, "with communists on the floor below and hookers underneath that."[111]

The normal length of a loud *dhikr* is about one hour, during which Sufis sit in a circle or stand in rows (depending on the order) and together repeat short prayers, usually moving their upper bodies to the rhythm of the prayer. The Basel *dhikr* sessions, however, started at 8 P.M. and often went on until 1 A.M. or 2 A.M. The movements accompanying the prayers were so enthusiastic that some other tenants once came upstairs to complain that their light bulbs were going out and the pictures on their walls were shaking. On another oc-casion the Traditionalists' ceiling collapsed on them; after a pause of about three seconds, Burckhardt continued the *dhikr* amid the rubble.[112]

Some time later the building was condemned and demolished, and the *dhikr* sessions were briefly discontinued until von Meyenburg found a new *zawiya*, a small two-storied building on the edge of the Rhine, with one large room on each floor. Here Schuon imposed order and moderated the participants' enthusiastic behavior. The *dhikr* was reduced to a more normal length, its form regularized, and its participants told to wear "traditional" clothes: Arab dress and a turban. Even at this early stage, Schuon was attentive to the details of how things were staged.

That Schuon was able to take control of the Basel group of Traditionalists so easily must have been partly a matter of personality, partly because of his *ijaza*, and partly because of Burckhardt's experience in Salé, where he sensed a crowd of Schuons at the *zawiya*. Burckhardt's Arabic was good—probably better than that of any Westerner mentioned so far since Aguéli—and so were his understandings of Islam and of Moroccan culture. Furthermore, Schuon had spent less time with Ahmad al-Alawi than Burckhardt had with his shaykh, and he was less knowledgeable in terms of both his Arabic and his Islam. It was Schuon rather than Burckhardt, however, who quickly became the group's acknowledged leader.

While imposing moderation on the enthusiastic brethren of Basel, Schuon also instructed them to perform only the *fard* (obligatory) ritual prayers, and to omit the *sunna* (customary, recommended) prayers.[113] While many Muslims in the Islamic world do habitually omit the *sunna* prayers, and while what is classified as *sunna* is by definition not required, most Sufis in the Islamic world are careful to perform *sunna* acts whenever possible, and it is almost unheard of for a Sufi shaykh to *instruct* anyone to omit such an act. Schuon's instruction reflected a conviction that the *dhikr* was what mattered, not the ritual prayer. *Dhikr* was the means to "the truly initiatic path," to "[mystic] union with God." "There is a certain incompatibility," wrote Schuon in 1939, "between the practice of this supreme means . . . and the indefinite multiplication of secondary ritual prescriptions, the aim of which is individual salvation rather than fana (mystical union) in Allah. That is why we . . . must restrict ourselves to what is indispensable in what concerns devotional ritual, *the strict necessity of which we nevertheless recognize.*"[114]

Almost no Sunni Muslim in the Islamic world would concur with this view, or with the unusual interpretation of Koran 29:45 that many of Schuon's followers use to support it.[115] This "deviation" from the standard practice of the Islamic world was to be the first of many over the next fifty years and seems ultimately to have emerged from Schuon's conviction that Islam was not so much an end in itself as means to an end, that end being the Perennial Philosophy or the *religio perennis* (perennial religion).

At this point Schuon again met Madeleine, the girl who had once brought breakfast to his Lausanne attic. Madeleine's brother arranged a meeting between her and Schuon by Lake Leman, the spectacular lake on which the city lies, and for a while the two met occasionally, sometimes going for walks in the woods just outside Lausanne. On one occasion Schuon watched Madeleine dancing, either in the woods or in his room. And then, for reasons Schuon does not explain, Madeleine ended the relationship.[116]

Schuon had fallen in love with Madeleine, and his "unhappy love" for the woman he referred to as his *Freundin* (a German word literally meaning a "female friend" but normally meaning girlfriend in contemporary usage, that will here be translated as "beloved") took on monumental proportions. Schuon wrote numerous poems to his beloved (a selection of which he would later have printed),[117] and went frequently to a chapel near the lake where they had met, to pray for her to change her mind about him.[118] He even abandoned his use of the All-Highest Name in his daily litany because he was distracted by his "earthly love."[119] Schuon required that his followers in the Alawiyya join him in this "unhappy love." "Whoever does not love Madeleine is not of the order!" he would often say.[120]

"Beauty," he later wrote, "indeed all that we love, belongs to Heaven; all that is good comes from God and belongs to God. Earthly beauty is good if it gives us a key to the love of God, if it is the frame of our prayer or our meditation."[121] Schuon clearly felt that Madeleine had given him the key to the love of God, and he wished to share it with his followers. This incident is of importance, since beauty and love, and the love of beautiful women, will recur in the later history of Schuon's order.

Developments were reported to Guénon in Cairo, though it is not known whether these reports included the extra-Islamic details in Schuon's visions.[122] Guénon was immediately enthusiastic: here was the initiatic basis for his elite.[123] Soon both he and Reyor in Paris (on Guénon's instructions) began referring Traditionalists to Schuon, and the Alawiyya grew.[124] It also acquired members from the Swiss social circle of Schuon and Burckhardt. Louis Caudron, a Traditionalist in Amiens, France, gave Schuon a job in the textile factory he owned there, and a second Alawi *zawiya* opened in Amiens; another was soon opened in Paris, and then one in Lausanne, where Burckhardt moved from Basel to work for a publisher. After Schuon took a better-paying job in Thann (Alsace), Caudron became Schuon's first *muqaddam*, for Amiens. By 1939 the *dhikr* at the Basel *zawiya*, to which Schuon traveled every week from Alsace, was attended by thirty or forty Traditionalists.[125] Von Meyenburg later described this time as "the golden age," with an "extraordinary spiritual intensity."

From the start, the existence of the Alawiyya was largely secret. This is in striking contrast to Sufi orders in the Islamic World, which are always public organizations,[126] though sometimes they may meet privately. There seem to have been several reasons for this secrecy, some Traditionalist and some practical. First, all the other religious groups discussed so far since the Theosophical Society were in some way secret—Masonic lodges, the Order of the Temple, the Fraternité des Chevaliers du divin Paraclet. Secrecy is a part of the Western or occultist conception of initiation, though it plays no part in the Sufi conception. Second, in *Orient et Occident* Guénon had warned of the need to act with discretion to avoid the hostility of "unsuspected . . . powers," though it is not known to what extent this concern influenced Schuon's emphasis on secrecy. Third, Islam was a means to an end rather than an end in itself. When von Meyenburg—the third person to join Schuon's Alawiyya—was asked about secrecy during an interview, his initial reaction was one of surprise: how could it have been otherwise? What would have happened to their jobs if people had discovered they had become Muslim? In fact, he added, his employers (a major Swiss chemicals concern) had discovered, and in the event nothing had happened. Another consideration at that time, according to von Meyenburg, was that there was little to be gained by coming out as Muslims—there was almost no other Muslim community in Switzerland at that time, and no mosque where anyone could pray the Friday Prayer, for example.

In 1937 Schuon had his second vision, during which the consciousness of the All-Highest Name returned to him: "I woke with the certainty that I had become the shaykh; I felt I was gliding as I went out into the street." Shortly after, he "received" in a manner unspecified "Six Themes of Meditation"— "Death and Life," "Repose and Action," and "Knowledge and Being."[127] The two visions mark the formal separation of Schuon's Alawiyya from the Algerian Alawiyya: if Schuon was the shaykh, then he was no longer a *muqaddam* and was answerable to nobody but God. The Six Themes of Meditation were introduced into the practice of the Schuonian Alawiyya (as precisely that: themes for meditation exercises), formalizing the separation: the Schuonian Alawiyya now had its own distinct practice.

In the aftermath of these visions, Schuon found himself having doubts, both about himself and about the West as the appropriate frame for his activities.[128] These doubts became well known to Schuon's followers,[129] but Schuon overcame them.

In 1938 Schuon met Guénon for the first time, traveling to Cairo for this purpose. Other than saying that he visited Guénon almost every day and found his conversation somewhat disappointing, Schuon is silent about this visit, which lasted only a week.[130] Guénon however now seems to have been convinced that Schuon had been right to separate himself from Mostaganem. In 1936 Guénon was expressing slight concern that Schuon was going too fast and had separated himself too soon,[131] but in 1938 he agreed that changes since the death of al-Alawi were "far from satisfactory. Everything is being sacrificed to propagandist and exoteric tendencies which we can in no way approve."[132]

In 1939 the activities of Schuon's Alawiyya—like those of Reyor's Fraternité des Chevaliers du divin Paraclet—were interrupted by the start of the Second World War. Schuon arrived in Bombay just as war was declared, and almost immediately he took a ship back to Europe, carrying with him a copy of the Sanskrit text of the Bhagavad Gita, not to read but because of the "power of its blessing."[133] His traveling companion, the John Levy who had recently bought Guénon's house for him, remained in India, joined the British army, and subsequently converted to Hinduism,[134] becoming the first Traditionalist Muslim known to have left Islam.

Mobilized into the French army, Schuon participated in the catastrophic defeat of France in 1940 without seeing action. The German victory brought a new danger for him. Germany had annexed the disputed French province of Alsace to the Reich and was proceeding to draft Alsatians into the German army. Not only was Schuon's mother from Alsace, but his father had been a German. Not wishing to serve in the German army, Schuon fled over the Swiss border. As was then normal, on his arrival he was interned by the Swiss.

Schuon, who had influential friends among his Swiss followers, applied for Swiss nationality (on the basis of his birth in Switzerland), which was granted in 1941, thanks especially to the assistance of Jacques-Albert Cuttat, a follower of Schuon who was the son of a Bern banker and a rising star in the Swiss diplomatic service.[135] So as not to risk prejudicing his naturalization application, Schuon ordered the Basel *zawiya* of the Alawiyya to discontinue operations. Although it would slowly start up again, Basel would never again be the center of Traditionalist Sufism.[136]

Schuon's Swiss followers apparently looked after him financially.[137] He rented a small apartment in Lausanne, where Burckhardt and Schuon's beloved Madeleine lived, but Schuon discovered that she was now married. In 1943 they met, and she showed him her baby. As a result of this meeting, "the whole environment became my beloved." This change was permanent: thereafter, Schuon felt that he had "so to speak entered into the cosmic body of the beloved, I was in her as in mother-love."[138]

Shortly before this event Schuon went shopping to furnish his new apartment. In a shop window he saw an antique statuette of the Virgin Mary and was struck by its beauty and the incongruity of its surroundings. Despite its high price and his relative poverty, Schuon bought the statuette, took it home, and installed it in a place of honor. Statues in general are forbidden to Muslims by the Sharia, and statues of the Virgin are commonly associated with Catholic churches; mindful of this restriction, Schuon later explained: "I was always painstaking in questions of holy rules, but on the other hand I stood above all on the ground of the Religio Perennis and did not allow myself to be imprisoned by forms that for myself could have no validity—for myself, since I would not allow another to break the same rules."[139]

This statement neatly summarizes the status of the Alawiyya at the end of the 1930s: a Traditionalist Sufi order whose members followed Islam and the Sharia, but whose shaykh privately stood on more universalist ground and included among his most prized possessions a copy of the Bhagavad Gita and a statuette of the Virgin Mary.[140] The full implications of Schuon's purchase of this statuette, however, would become clear only later, as Schuon's purchase combined with the mother-love that he experienced on seeing Madeleine's baby. This issue will be discussed in a later chapter.

5

Fascism

Before the start of the Second World War, the lives of Guénon, Schuon, Burckhardt, Reyor, and Thomas were little affected by the rise of Fascism in Europe, living as they were in Egypt, Switzerland, and France. The development of Traditionalism in Italy and Romania, however, took place against a very different political background. Fascist regimes[1] were installed in Italy in 1922 (with Mussolini's March on Rome), in Germany in 1933 (with Hitler's election victory), and in Romania in 1940–41 (with the entry into the Romanian government of Horia Sima). Occultist groups were involved in, though far from central to, the early stages of the development of the Fascist regimes in all three countries. In Italy and Romania Traditionalism became involved with politics in a way that it did not in France or Switzerland.

The Origins of the Nazi Party

The origins of the German Nazi Party demonstrate the earliest connections between occultism and a Fascist regime. In 1913 von Sebottendorf, a neo-Sufi occultist of German origin and Ottoman nationality, returned to Germany after almost a quarter of a century in Turkey, hoping to spread among the materialist Germans the "key to spiritual realization" that he thought he had found and that they were so much in need of.

Von Sebottendorf was disappointed by his reception. After trying out various occultist and spiritualist groups as possible vehicles for spreading his message, he retired discouraged. Excused military service during the First World War as a result of his Ottoman nationality plus a wound he received while fighting for the Ottomans in the Balkan War of 1912, he spent the early war years fairly aimlessly, acquiring but one follower—a young worker whose pregnant sister-in-law he had helped rescue when she went into labor on a mountain walk. In 1916, however, while visiting his lawyer, he saw a newspaper advertisement illustrated with runes, advertising a then unknown group, the Germanen-Orden (Germanic Order). Ever hopeful, von Sebottendorf contacted the group's leaders and to his delight thought he had at last found the appropriate vehicle for his spiritual plans. It was explained to him that the order was working for the inner rebirth of the Germans and against the Jews and their influence; von Sebottendorf replied that he would help, since "you in Germany lack the unity of faith. You must therefore bring out another unity, that of race, if you want to achieve anything."[2]

What the Germanen-Orden thought of von Sebottendorf's key to spiritual realization is unknown. The Germanen-Orden was loosely related to the Hoher Armanen-Orden (Higher Armanen Order), an occultist group that drew on Theosophy and Masonry. The Hoher Armanen-Orden claimed descent from the Templars, who had once interested Guénon, and wished to reestablish the science of runes and the worship of Wotan as well as an Aryan-dominated empire loosely based on the Teutonic Knights. The interests of the Germanen-Orden, however, were primarily racial,[3] and it is likely that its leaders were more interested in von Sebottendorf's offer to assist with his time and—no doubt even more welcome—his money than in his key to spiritual realization.

Von Sebottendorf was appointed *Ordensmeister* (local master of the order) in Munich, Bavaria, where the Germanen-Orden operated under the name of Thulegesellschaft [Thule Society]. Von Sebottendorf lectured the members of the Thulegesellschaft on "astrology, symbolism, and rune-lore" and established a periodical, *Die Runen* [The Runes]. The leadership of the Germanen-Orden was disappointed, however, and called for action of a more political nature, so von Sebottendorf purchased a local weekly newspaper, the *Münchner Beobachter* [Munich Observer]. After changing its title to *Münchner Beobachter und Sportblatt* [Munich Observer and Sports Paper] in the hope of improving its circulation, he began to edit it along the desired lines. At this point von Sebottendorf reflected in wonder that he, who had never wanted to be involved in politics and believed in the "human rights of all men," should end up editing an anti-Semitic political newspaper.[4] Von Sebottendorf also instructed a sports journalist belonging to the Thulegesellschaft, Karl Harrer, to set up a political group aimed at ordinary workers. This group, at first called the Deutsche Arbeiterverein (German Workers' Union), was soon renamed the Deutsche Arbeiterpartei (German Workers' Party).[5]

Von Sebottendorf left the Thulegesellschaft in the aftermath of the demise of the short-lived Soviet Republic of Bavaria. During a brief armed struggle in

1919 between the Bavarian Soviet regime and its opponents, in which a detachment drawn from the Thulegesellschaft played a significant part, ten hostages were shot by the Soviet government of Bavaria, seven of them members of the Thulegesellschaft. The Bavarian Soviets had somehow come into possession of the Thulegesellschaft membership lists; for this—and for the consequent choice of hostages and so for their deaths—von Sebottendorf was blamed by others, and by himself. He accordingly left Munich, first for Freiburg, then the Harz Mountains, and then in 1922 for Turkey.[6]

As is well known, in 1919 Adolf Hitler joined the Deutsche Arbeiterpartei, and in 1920 he pushed out the sports journalist Harrer and established his own control. He later added the adjective "Nationalsozialistische" to the name, making it the Nationalsozialistische Deutsche Arbeiterpartei, or the Nazi Partei for short. The *Münchner Beobachter und Sportblatt* was renamed the *Völkische Beobachter* and subsequently became the Nazi equivalent of *Pravda*. No trace of von Sebottendorf's teachings are to be found in the Nazi Party, however; Hitler himself had no sympathy for occultism of any variety. His minor interest in Wotan and Teutonic times derived purely from Wagner.[7]

Von Sebottendorf played no further part in the events leading to the Nazi victory in 1933. He did, however, return to Germany in 1933, publishing *Bevor Hitler kam: Urkundlichen aus der Frühzeit der nationalsozialistischen Bewegung* [Before Hitler Came: Documents from the Early Days of the National Socialist Movement], recalling his own role in the events of 1918 and 1919.[8] The first printing of this book sold well, but it came to the attention of Hitler, who— unsurprisingly—was unenthusiastic. The second printing was confiscated, and von Sebottendorf himself was arrested and sent to a concentration camp.[9]

Von Sebottendorf evidently retained some goodwill in important places from his Munich days. He was released from the concentration camp and allowed to return to Turkey, where he even came to receive a small pension in the form of occasional payments from German Military Intelligence for services rendered. Herbert Rittlinger, the German intelligence officer who took over the running of von Sebottendorf during the Second World War, later wrote that "as an agent, he was a disaster [eine Null]." Despite this, Rittlinger turned the occasional payments to von Sebottendorf into a reasonably generous retainer, partly to ensure loyalty and partly because he felt pity for this strange, by then penniless man, whose history he did not know, who pretended enthusiasm for the Nazi cause and admiration for the SS but who in reality seemed little interested in either, much preferring to talk about Tibetans.[10]

Shortly after Germany's defeat in 1945, von Sebottendorf's body was found floating in the Bosporus, presumably as the result of suicide.[11]

Von Sebottendorf bears no responsibility for the Nazi Party. Had the Deutsche Arbeiterpartei that von Sebottendorf initially controlled not existed, Hitler would have taken over a different party, and had the *Münchner Beobachter und Sportblatt* not existed, Hitler would have found or established some other news-

paper. One can even perhaps believe von Sebottendorf's occasional protestations that he was not particularly political or anti-Semitic, since they were made
long before such protestations would have been in his best interests. It took
extraordinary political naivete to suppose that the Germanen-Orden could be
used for the propagation of a key to spiritual realization. Von Sebottendorf,
however, was not the only person to attempt to turn nationalist and rightist
political organizations to their own spiritual ends, as we will see.

Evola, Mussolini, and the SS

An identical attempt was made, first in Italy and then in Germany, by Julius
Evola. Evola's name later came to be linked by many with Guénon's own as a
co-founder of Traditionalism, and Evola was arguably Guénon's most important collaborator, ultimately more important than Coomaraswamy. Evola's Traditionalism, like Coomaraswamy's, shows the influence of his earlier intellectual influences, only more so. While Coomaraswamy principally fleshed out
Traditionalism, Evola took it in new directions.[12]

Evola was introduced to Traditionalism in about 1927 by Arturo Reghini,
an Italian mathematician and mason who was a correspondent of Guénon.
Evola and Reghini were at that time producing a somewhat occultist journal
called Ur. Evola already knew Guénon's Introduction générale but had not been
much impressed by it. It was not until about 1930, when Evola and Reghini
were no longer on speaking terms, that Evola came to see the importance of
the work of Guénon, whom he later described as "the unequaled master of our
epoch."[13]

Evola's most important Traditionalist work was his Rivolta contro il mondo
moderno [Revolt against the Modern World] (1934),[14] which joins Guénon's
Crise du monde moderne in inspiring the title of this book. The difference between the two titles is the key to the difference between the two authors: while
Guénon wished principally to explain the crisis he saw, Evola was keenly aware
of what the Surrealist sympathizer of Traditionalism, René Daumal, had called
"that law . . . that necessarily pushes that which there is in us of man towards
revolt." Daumal and Evola had something in common, as avant-garde painters
interested in philosophy—Spinoza in the case of Daumal, Nietzsche in the
case of Evola. As Daumal experimented with carbon tetrachloride, so Evola
experimented with ether.[15]

Evola's career as an avant-garde painter (with fingernails painted violet)
started after the First World War, during which he saw action as an artillery
officer. He evidently had an adequate private income, since he seems never to
have been obliged to take any form of employment. After the war he contributed to the Dadaist journal Revue bleu and mounted two Dadaist exhibitions—
the first in Italy, the second in Berlin. He also wrote two Dadaist books, pub-

lished in Switzerland in 1920 by the leading Dadaist, Tristan Tzara. One was poetic and theoretical (*Arte astratta* [Abstract Art]) and the other purely poetic (*La parole obscure du paysage intérieur* [The Obscure Speech of the Interior Landscape]).[16] Like Aguéli before him, however, Evola began to take an interest in Theosophy, and like Aguéli, he ended up abandoning painting for spiritual pursuits. Unlike Aguéli, though, Evola never started painting again, and as a painter he is little known, except to art historians interested in Dadaism.

Evola first joined the Independent Theosophical League, which had been established in Italy by Reghini and Decio Calvari. Through this league and through Calvari, Evola discovered oriental religion.[17] Through Reghini he encountered Western esotericism of almost every variety. Reghini's interests were varied, including—in addition to Masonry—Pythagoras, the Cathars, Roman paganism, and magic.[18] All this and more was to be found in the pages of *Ur*, for which Reghini wrote, and which Evola edited for its short life (1927–29). In addition to carrying translations of Tantric, Buddhist, and Hermetic texts, *Ur* moved in a new direction, neo-paganism, publishing a translation of a Mithraic ritual.[19] Roman paganism was also an interest of another Traditionalist admirer of Guénon with whom Evola was in contact, Guido de Giorgio.

The Evola of this period was immortalized in a work of fiction, *Amo, dunque sono* [I Love, Therefore I Am] (1927) by Sibilla Aleramo, whom he met in 1925 and who was his lover, although he was twenty-two years younger than she. Evola is the basis for the character of Bruno Tellegra, a magician inhabiting an old castle in Calabria.[20] Given Evola's subsequent political career, it is interesting to note that Aleramo—a feminist famed for her many lovers, and the friend of Maxim Gorki, Auguste Rodin, and Guillaume Apollinaire—was also a lifelong Communist.[21]

As Evola later explained, two philosophers other than Guénon were of importance to the Traditionalism he developed in *Rivolta contro il mondo moderno*. These were Friedrich Nietzsche and Johann Jakob Bachofen. From the former Evola took the Nietzschean *Übermensch* (superman), and from the latter a less well-known binary typology of uranic and telluric civilizations.[22]

What initially appealed most to Evola in Nietzsche's work, even as an adolescent, was his attacks on bourgeois Christian values—appropriately for a future Dadaist, since Dada set out to shock the bourgeoisie. What most interested Evola was the superman, the "absolute individual," an interest reflected in his first post-Dada work, *Teoria dell'individuo assoluto* [The Theory of the Absolute Individual], which he wrote in 1924. At this point Evola had abandoned painting and was evidently contemplating the possibility of a career in mainstream philosophy, since he wrote *Teoria dell'individuo assoluto* "with the necessary learned apparatus and in the appropriate academic jargon." He could not find a publisher for the book, however,[23] and seems at this point to have dropped any idea of an academic career, as Guénon did after the rejection of his doctoral thesis. Though the book was in fact published later, in 1927,[24] by then Evola's interests had moved on. Despite his loss of interest in the academic world, most of Evola's subsequent works came closer than Guénon's to normal scholarly standards in style, footnoting, and quality of sources.

Bachofen, Evola's other philosopher, had been professor of Roman law at the University of Basel and was an early philosopher of history. He was interested in the cultural factors that he believed were as important as political and economic ones in determining both history and legal systems, and, on the basis of his study of ancient mythology, he developed an evolutionary theory of human history. According to Bachofen, human society had progressed from early, matriarchal, "basely sensuous" civilizations to "spiritually pure" patriarchal civilizations (such as his own).[25] This typology was the basis not only of Evola's telluric/uranic pair, but of Nietzsche's Apollonian/Dionysian pair. Interestingly, Nietzsche's connection with Bachofen was through Jakob Burckhardt, the Basel historian from whom Schuon's collaborator descended, whom Nietzsche much admired. Bachofen was also appreciated by late nineteenth-century anthropologists and by Friedrich Engels (who quotes him while discussing the origin of the family), but by 1900 his fundamental thesis of matriarchy as the original form of human society had been discredited, and his work has since been largely forgotten.[26]

As a Traditionalist, Evola of course reversed Bachofen's evolutionary thesis. Although in theory (female) telluric qualities and (male) uranic ones are for Evola a dynamic pair of opposites, in practice he posits decline from uranic to telluric. As a Nietzschean, he emphasized action, which he saw as a uranic quality, associated in Hindu terms with the *kshatriya* or warrior caste. Guénon, in *Autorité spirituelle et pouvoir temporel* (1929), maintained that in the primordial Traditional state, spiritual authority was superior to temporal authority, that is, that the *brahmin* was superior to the *kshatriya*.[27] Evola, however, refused to subordinate action in this fashion. He instead maintained that the *brahmin* and *kshatriya* castes were originally one and that they became disassociated only in the course of the decline from primordial Tradition. This decline, according to Evola, produced the "desacralization of existence: individualism and rationalism at first, then collectivism, materialism and mechanism, finally opening to forces belonging not to that which is above man but to that which is below him." Simultaneously, what Evola called "the law of the regression of castes" operated, with power passing from the priestly and military caste to the merchant caste (as in the bourgeois democracies) and finally to the serf caste (proletariat), as in the Soviet Union. The primordial sacral caste was uranic and pre-Christian; Catholicism, with its allegedly nontraditional conception of a personal God, was telluric and characteristic of modernity.[28]

Evola's analysis of modernity is recognizably a variation on the established Traditionalist philosophy. Where Evola differs most from Guénon is in his prescription. For Guénon, the transformation of the individual through initiation was the means of the transformation of the West as a whole through the influence of the elite. Evola was never explicit about his own prescription, perhaps intentionally, but called for self-realization through the reintegration of man into a state of centrality as the Absolute Individual, this to be achieved through uranic action.[29] This precept has been interpreted in various fashions.

To judge from Evola's own actions, however, the transformation of the individual was to be not so much the means as the *consequence* of the transformation of society. Although even at the end of his life Evola was uncertain about the means to *individual* self-realization, his views on the transformation of society seem to have been definite from the start. These views are manifest in the 1920s, in his engagement with the Fascist regime that governed Italy. In this engagement Evola followed the example of Reghini, who had hoped for the spiritual education of the new political elite.[30]

Evola wrote that in the late 1920s he had sympathized with Mussolini as he would have sympathized with anyone who opposed the post–First World War democratic regime and the political Left, though he disliked the dubious origins of the Black Shirts and also disliked the Fascists' nationalism. However, he forgave Mussolini his "socialist and proletarian origins" when Mussolini spoke of the "ideal of the Roman State and Imperium" and of "giving birth to a new type of Italian, disciplined, virile, and combative."[31] For "a new type of Italian" one might read "the Absolute Individual," and for "virile" one might read "uranic."

Evola's first known activity on becoming a Traditionalist was to attempt to guide Fascist society toward Traditionalism. This was a less absurd initiative than von Sebottendorf's involvement with the Germanen-Orden, but an older Evola later admitted that it demonstrated a lack of tactical sense, indeed of common sense.[32]

In 1929 *Ur* ceased publication in the wake of a row between Evola and Reghini—Evola had accused Reghini of trying to misuse *Ur* for Masonic ends, and Reghini had accused Evola of stealing his ideas for his *Imperialismo pagano*, which Evola published in 1928, and which is discussed later.[33] Both complaints were justified.[34] In 1930 Evola started a new journal, *La Torre* [The Tower], subtitled "A Paper for the Various Expressions of the One Tradition." In some respects, this journal resembled *Etudes traditionnelles*. Reghini did not participate, but Evola's main collaborator was closer to Guénon than to Reghini: Guido de Giorgio, who had spent time with Sufis in Tunisia.[35] In other respects, Evola's *La Torre* differed radically from Guénon's journal. In the first issue of *La Torre*—which Evola said was "not a refuge for more or less mystic escape, but a post of resistance, of combat and of superior realism"—Evola called for tradition to enter all realms of life. "To the extent that Fascism follows and defends these [Traditionalist] principles," he declared, "in that measure we may consider ourselves Fascists. That is all." In a later issue Evola went further, calling for "a more radical, more intrepid Fascism, a really absolute Fascism, made of pure force, inaccessible to compromise"[36]—that is to say, a Fascism more in line with Evola's own views. The compromise that Evola most regretted, and that he felt Italian Fascism had made, was with the bourgeoisie.

This was not the first time that Evola had attempted to participate in Fascist discourse. His previous attempt was in 1926 or 1927, before he modified his own views under the influence of Traditionalism. In a series of articles in *Critica Fascista*, one of the Fascist Party's more intellectual journals, Evola argued that Roman paganism rather than Christianity was the proper basis for Fascism. This was a view to which the Vatican and many others objected strongly, appearing as it did in a quasi-official publication, that Evola was soon dropped from the pages of *Critica Fascista*. Undiscouraged, he then wrote *Imperialismo pagano. Il fascismo dinnanzi al pericolo euro-cristiano* [Pagan Imperialism: Fascism Face to Face with the Euro-Christian Danger], a 160-page book that took his argument even further. Evola was now recommending that the Catholic Church be deprived of all her authority and subordinated to the Fascist state. *Imperialismo pagano*, unlike Evola's articles in *Critica Fascista*, carried no implication of any official endorsement, and when it appeared in 1928 it was greeted with little interest.[37] In 1929 Mussolini signed a Concordat with the Catholic Church.

The Fascist Party received Evola's Traditionalist proposals of 1930 even less favorably than his pagan proposals of 1928. The first issue of *La Torre* was greeted with condemnation in the established Fascist press, threats against Evola's life, and a suggestion from the police that it would be a good idea to suspend publication. Evola ignored this suggestion, but after the fifth issue— the one in which he called for "a more radical, more intrepid Fascism"—the police forbade Evola's printers to produce any more copies of *La Torre*. Evola appealed to the Ministry of Interior, but the ministry declined to help, and *La Torre* ceased publication.[38]

Evola briefly retired from politics, starting work on what he describes as his first Traditionalist book, *La tradizione ermetica* [The Hermetic Tradition] (1931).[39] De Giorgio, whom Evola described as a manic-depressive, retired more permanently, to a ruined presbytery in the Alps, where he lived for most of the rest of his life. He spent much of the Second World War there, working on *La Tradizione romana* [The Roman Tradition], a book in which he attempted to reconcile Roman religion with Christianity, Vedanta, and aspects of Islam. This book was still unpublished when, in 1959, de Giorgio hanged himself. It was published posthumously in 1973.[40]

In 1932 Evola published another Traditionalist work, *Maschera e volto dello spiritualismo contemporaneo. Analisi critica delle principali correnti moderne verso il "sovrannaturale"* [Masks and Faces of Contemporary Spiritualism: A Critical Analysis of the Principal Modern Currents of "Supernaturalism"].[41] This book was based on Guénon's two anti-occultist books—*Théosophisme* and *Erreur spirite*—but it extended Guénon's attack on Theosophy to cover Rudolf Steiner's Anthroposophy, and also Guénon's attack on other "counterinitiatic" groups to cover Krishnamurti. Evola also added a new section in which he attacked Freudian psychoanalysis, which he saw as an inversion that falsely privileged "the sub-personal and irrational base of the human being."[42] That Freudianism can hardly be described as supernaturalism is perhaps why, in the next edition (1949), "sovrannaturale" was changed to "sovrasensibile" (Supersensiblism) in the subtitle.

Maschera e volto dello spiritualismo is most interesting for Evola's treatment of what we have been calling occultism—he actually defined *occultismo* as "a mania for obscure language." This is a far narrower definition than Guénon's. Evola made a distinction between two forms of magic, one which he called "degenerate" and which he condemned, and one which he did not condemn— because, it is fair to deduce, he himself practiced it. "Degenerate" magic, according to Evola, was characterized by excessive "ceremonialism" and by "using rites and formulas with an almost realist objectification of entities and powers."[43]

The question of Evola's own personal spiritual practice is not as important as that of Guénon's, since Guénon's practice was an example to other Traditionalists whereas Evola's practice was not. It is, nevertheless, still of some interest. It almost certainly included Hermetic elements, which are probably principally what Evola was contrasting with "degenerate" magic. The Hermetic practice that most interested Evola was alchemy, which, he maintained, was not the "infantile" stage of chemistry, for which it was often mistaken, but "an initiatic science explained under a metallurgic-chemical disguise."[44] This interpretation of alchemy was later to be popularized by the widely read Brazilian writer Paulo Coelho in his novel *Alquimista* [The Alchemist].[45]

To alchemy can almost certainly be added some form of neo-paganism, and also sexual magic (the techniques of managing states arising during sexual intercourse in order to manipulate various energies). Before becoming a Traditionalist, Evola had led a secret group based around the journal *Ur*, consisting of twelve to fifteen persons. These included Maria de Naglowska, a novelist of Russian and Polish-Jewish origin who later moved to Paris, where in the 1930s she led an occultist group and became known for her practice of sexual magic.[46] It thus seems likely that Evola's own practice (at least before the end of the Second World War) included sexual magic.[47] In addition, it would be strange if the author of *Imperialismo pagano* had never been involved in any pagan practices, though he later dismissed Roman paganism as a "purely political and juridical reality, with a cover of superstitious practices and cults."[48]

In 1967, toward the end of Evola's life, a French Muslim Traditionalist named Henry Hartung (discussed later), who was interested in the unanswered question of Evola's own practice, asked Evola how he believed that self-realization was to be achieved. Evola replied that initiation was one possibility, "but which, and under what circumstances?"[49] Elsewhere he indicated that he believed that Guénon's personal path "offered very little" to people who "don't want to turn themselves into Muslims and Orientals,"[50] something Evola evidently did not want to do. In this he cut himself off from the central strand of Traditionalist spiritual practice. In conversation with Hartung, he listed six practices as alternatives to initiation: learning, loyalty (defined as "interior neutrality, the opposite of hypocrisy"), withdrawal, "virile energy," "symbolic visualization," and "interior concentration."[51] We can safely assume that at some point in his life Evola had tried all of these.

Evola's importance lies not so much in his personal spiritual practice as in his writing and political activity. In 1933 he returned to his doomed attempt to guide Italian Fascism along Traditionalist lines when he was given a page on "Spiritual Problems in Fascist Ethics" to edit in the major Fascist newspaper, *Regime Fascista*, which was edited by one of the few old Fascists who, in Evola's view, had resisted the general tendency of servility toward Mussolini. Almost every day until the fall of the Fascist regime in 1943 a contributor chosen by Evola—sometimes Guénon himself—addressed the Italian public from Evola's page. The reaction, when there was one, was generally negative, however, and Evola became progressively more disillusioned with the possibilities of Italian Fascism.[52] He later wrote: "Some say that Fascism ruined the Italians. I would say the opposite . . . that it was the Italians who ruined Fascism, to the extent that Italy seems to have been incapable of providing adequate and suitable human material for the superior possibilities of Fascism . . . to be properly developed, and the negative possibilities neutralized."[53]

Though Evola had to abandon hope of traditionalizing Italy through Fascism, he for some time hoped that he might do better in Germany. In 1933, the year in which Hitler came to power, a German version of *Imperialismo pagano*—*Heidnische Imperialismus*—was published in Leipzig.[54] *Heidnische Imperialismus* was not just a translation of *Imperialismo pagano* but a revised and expanded—one might say, Traditionalized—edition, sufficiently different to be translated back into Italian in 1991.[55] *Heidnische Imperialismus* was very well received in Germany, favorably reviewed in newspapers from *Die Literarische Welt* [The Literary World] to *Völkische Kultur* [The People's Culture].[56] Evola later admitted that part of the interest in it derived from the mistaken belief in Germany that he was the leading representative of an interesting trend in Italian Fascism—they did not realize that Evola was, in his own words, "a captain without any troops."[57] Whatever its origin, the interest was real, and Evola was invited to Germany. His principal host was Ludwig Roselius, a wealthy industrialist (the son of the founder of the HAG coffee firm, makers of the caffeine-free Kaffee-HAG that is still well known in Europe).[58]

Evola arrived in Germany in 1934 full of hopes. He thought that Germany was a country in which the "law of the regression of castes" was less advanced, where the military caste (represented by the Prussian military tradition, the Junker class, and the surviving political power of the nobility) was better preserved than elsewhere in Europe.[59] He attended a Nordic-pagan meeting organized by his host, Roselius, the second Nordic Thing—*thing* being an Old Norse word for an assembly.[60] He then addressed the Herrenklub (Gentlemen's Club) in Berlin, an important political group of ultra-Conservative inclination, to which belonged industrialists such as Fritz Thyssen and Friedrich Flick, and politicians such as Hjalmar Schacht (Hitler's talented minister of finance) and Franz von Papen, chancellor of Germany from 1932 to 1934, who presided over and assisted Hitler's rise to power. The Nordic Thing proved a disappointment, both to Evola, who found it too political and insufficiently spiritual, and to the mainstream German Nordic Movement, which described it as a mistake not to be repeated. The Herrenklub, however, delighted Evola: "there I was to find my natural milieu."[61]

In 1935 a German translation of Evola's central work, *Rivolta contro il mondo moderno*, was published as *Erhebung wider der moderne Welt*. This was also favorably reviewed, though Hermann Hesse, in a private letter to his publisher, described it as "really dangerous." In 1936 Evola returned to the Germanic world, this time Vienna, to address the Kulturbund (Cultural Union) of Prince Karl Anton von Rohan. This was the Viennese counterpart of the Berlin Herrenklub, though with a more Catholic emphasis and an enthusiasm for pan-European nationalism. It included among its members a rare early Austrian Traditionalist, Walter Heinrich.[62] Under the sponsorship of members of this Kulturbund, Evola then traveled on to Hungary and to Romania, where he met with the leader of the Legion of the Archangel Michael (discussed later).

In addition to these visits, Evola and his German and Austrian friends were publishing each other's works, with German and Austrian ultra-Conservatives appearing in *Regime Fascista*, and Evola appearing in Prince von Rohan's *Europäische Revue* [European Review].[63] Although many details are unclear, Evola had evidently allied himself with a political movement of potential importance that was proving far more receptive to his ideas than had been the Italian Fascist Party—as is confirmed by the opposition to these contacts within Italian Fascist circles, which almost resulted in the withdrawal of Evola's passport.[64]

While there is no direct evidence of what Evola was trying to achieve through this alliance, we may deduce it from a book he published in 1937 (his next book after *Rivolta contro il mondo moderno*, which he was therefore presumably working on at the time of his German and Austrian contacts). This was *Il mistero del Graal e la tradizione ghibellina dell'Impero* [The Mystery of the Grail and the Ghibelline Tradition of the Empire],[65] which (though not translated into German until 1955)[66] must have mirrored Evola's thinking in those years.

Il mistero del Graal was an extended treatment of a subject first considered in *Rivolta contro il mondo moderno*. The Grail was the Holy Grail, though Evola does not use the word "Holy," seeing the Christian elements in the Grail myth as later additions, to be discarded. The Grail, he maintained, "symbolizes the

principle of an immortalizing and transcendent force connected to the primordial state and remaining present in the very period of . . . involution or
decadence. . . . The mystery of the Grail is the mystery of a warrior initiation."
The Ghibellines would have been better known to an Italian than to an English-
speaking audience; they were one of two loose alliances (the other being the
Guelfs) in a bitter struggle for control of central and northern Italy during the
thirteenth century. The Ghibellines were the partisans of the Holy Roman
emperor and were predominantly feudal lords, while the Guelfs were predominantly merchants and partisans of the papacy.[67] Evola saw the final Guelf
victory as an incident in the regression of castes, with the merchant caste taking
over from the warrior caste. The Ghibellines, as opponents of the Catholic
Church, were taken as representing "the opposite tradition"—the surviving
pre-Christian Celtic and Nordic initiatic traditions represented in the Grail
myth.[68]

Evola, then, was at this point contemplating an Italian-German (or Roman-
Teutonic) alliance as prefigured in the Ghibellines, represented in an order that
was to be the recipient of a Nordic initiation. This is reminiscent of the objectives of the Hoher Armanen-Orden from which von Sebottendorf's Germanen-
Orden grew, but there is no known connection between the two.

Evola was to be disappointed. Although the Nazi Party had maintained
cordial relations with his new friends during its rise to power, once established
in power the Nazis lost interest in such alliances—just as Evola must have
thought he was finally really getting somewhere. In 1934 Chancellor von Papen
gave a speech at Marburg in Hessen most of which was written by von Papen's
private secretary and speechwriter, Edgar Julius Jung, a close contact of Evola
from the Herrenklub. This speech contained references to the Ghibellines and
to an "Empire of the Holy Ghost" as a sort of new Holy Roman Empire, which
could have had their origin only in Evola. The speech is remembered principally, however, for the chancellor's objection to growing Nazi totalitarianism.
It was one of the direct causes of the Night of the Long Knives, which consol-
idated the Nazi grip on power, forcing von Papen to resign the chancellorship.
Another casualty of the Night of the Long Knives was von Papen's speechwriter
Jung, who was killed. The Herrenklub survived as an institution only by changing itself into a Deutsche Klub (German club), and its importance declined.
Evola's Viennese friends, including the Traditionalist Heinrich, were arrested
immediately after the Anschluss of 1938. In 1939 von Papen was exiled as
German ambassador to Turkey. By 1944, relations between Evola's 1934–36
associates and the Nazis were such that twelve former members of the Herrenklub were among those executed in the aftermath of the failed July 20 plot
against Hitler.[69]

Despite these reverses, Evola did not give up. He apparently now switched
his attention to the SS, and in 1938 probably spoke at Wewelsburg, the SS
Ordensburg (SS castle, ceremonial headquarters) in Westphalia, proposing a

secret order to work for a Roman-Teutonic Empire. No details of this proposal are known directly,[70] except that the secret order was to publish a newspaper, but Evola's objectives were evidently much the same as before. SS Führer Heinrich Himmler commissioned an investigation of Evola's ideas from SS Oberführer Karl Maria Wiligut, a personal favorite of Himmler in the SS Rasse und Siedlungshauptamt (SS race and settlements department) and one of the few senior Nazis with an occultist background. It was Wiligut who had designed the SS lightning flash—actually rune—and death's head symbols.[71]

Wiligut's report was not favorable. He concluded that "Evola works from a basic Aryan concept but is quite ignorant of prehistoric Germanic institutions and their meaning,"[72] and recommended rejecting Evola's "utopian" proposal. This rejection was approved at a meeting attended by Himmler himself, where it was also decided to prevent further access by Evola to "leading cadres [führenden Dienststellen] of the Party and State" and to put an end to his activities in Germany, though, fortunately for Evola, "without any special measures."[73] Ironically, Wiligut himself also lost access to the SS the following year when it became widely known that he had spent the years 1924–27 in a Salzburg mental asylum while suffering from delusions (he had then believed himself the heir of a long line of German kings descended from God).[74]

Within ten years, then, Evola attempted to influence three separate groups along Traditionalist lines. The two most important—the Italian Fascist Party and the SS—had rejected his ideas. Only one had accepted him (though it is not known on what terms), the ultra-Conservatives, and they had been disbanded by the Nazis.

Evola seems then to have turned his attention to a new strategy: the infiltration not of a group but of an issue. The issue he chose was a topical one, race. Evola had already published articles and short pamphlets on this issue, as well as a historical account (commissioned by a Milan publisher) of the development of racial theory during the nineteenth and twentieth centuries. In 1941 he published a major work on the subject, *Sintesi di dottrina della razza* [Synthesis of Racial Doctrine].[75] Although superficially in accordance with the racial theory then prevalent in Germany and Italy, *Sintesi di dottrina* was actually a radical attack on it, arguing for a spiritual definition of race. In general Evola went along with the familiar condemnations of the Jews, but at the same time he argued that the root cause of the problem was spiritual rather than ethnic. "Aryan" or "Jew" should not be understood in biological terms, he said, but as denoting "typical attitudes which were not necessarily present in all individuals of Aryan or Jewish blood." The real enemy was not Jews biologically defined, but "global subversion and anti-tradition."[76]

Evola had finally found his way in. Mussolini read his book and liked it enough to call Evola to meet him (in 1942). *Sintesi di dottrina della razza*, he told Evola, offered a way of aligning Italian racialism with German racialism while maintaining a distinctive difference, the concept of spiritual race. He also liked the suggestion, made elsewhere in the book, that there was an "Aryo-Roman" race of Nordic descent. On Mussolini's instructions, it was suggested to various editors that *Sintesi di dottrina della razza* be publicized. "There was a deluge of reviews, starting with the pompous *Corriere della Sera* and other major newspapers which had never [previously] deigned to concern themselves with my books," recalled Evola. Surprisingly, given the distance between Evola's conceptions and those of the Nazis, there was even a German translation—though with the somewhat more cautious title of *Grundrisse der faschistischen Rassenlehre* [Essentials of Fascist (i.e., Italian, not German) Racialism] (1943).[77]

Evola took advantage of his access to Mussolini to talk of his German contacts and to suggest an Italian-German dual-language periodical, to be called *Blood and Spirit*. A detailed proposal was worked out between Evola and senior officials at the Ministry of Popular Culture, approved by Mussolini, and Evola left for Berlin—at last in reality what he had mistakenly been taken for in 1935, the representative of an interesting current within Italian Fascism.[78] Traveling under official Italian auspices, Evola had overcome his 1938 rejection by the SS.

But then everything went wrong again. Partly because the real difference between Evola's views and his own had been made clear to Mussolini, and partly because of alarm at speeches Evola was making in Berlin, reportedly saying that Italians could be classified racially as either Nordic or Mediterranean, the Italian Foreign Ministry ordered Evola home prematurely. On his return, his passport was revoked.[79] At this point Evola seems to have finally given up. He started work on a book on Buddhism.[80]

A year later the Fascist regime in Italy fell, and Evola fled to Germany, along with many leading Fascists. He returned to Rome during the German occupation of that city and left again shortly before Rome fell to the Allies. The year 1945 found him in Vienna, where he had been helping the SS recruit international volunteers. He was caught in a blast shortly before the Russian army took the city, and paralyzed from the waist down. He spent the rest of his life in a wheelchair.[81]

In the end, Traditionalism played no significant role in either Italian Fascism or German Nazism, despite Evola's efforts. This was so partly because the later Mussolini was little interested in ideology, and Hitler was his own ideologist; neither they nor their regimes had any need of Evola. A more basic reason was that Evola's elitist conceptions were hardly compatible with the mass character which the Fascist and Nazi regimes assumed in practice, if not always in theory.

That Evola's Traditionalism was an unfashionable minority strand within Italian Fascism, however, meant that when the majority strand had been discredited with the collapse of Mussolini's and Hitler's states, Evola's view dominated what ground there was left to dominate, as we shall see.

Evola is often described as having been a Fascist, but this characterization is hardly accurate—at least in the original, precise sense of the word "Fascist." He never belonged to the Fascist Party and could hardly be described as a follower of the Fascist line. Nor were he or his views approved of by the Fascists or the Nazis, except in the brief period of favor in 1942 that ended with the revocation of his passport.

Evola's activities under Fascism fall into two periods, the first from his first articles on paganism in 1926 to his visit to von Rohan's Viennese Kulturbund ten years later, and the second from his probable contacts with the SS in 1938 to his official visit to Berlin as an Italian racialist in 1942. We know almost nothing of his activities between 1943 and 1945, but it is possible that in those chaotic years he was concerned principally with his own survival. The first period appears relatively innocent in comparison with the second. During the second period Evola voluntarily entered the two darkest areas of twentieth-century West European history. In 1938 the SS had not yet begun the murderous activities for which it would be remembered as a rare human embodiment of pure evil. There is no evidence that Evola guessed at what was to follow, and indeed it is possible that he never even visited Wewelsburg—that visit is my reconstruction. The benefit of the doubt is vanishing fast by 1942, however. Is it possible that anyone involved in official racialism in Berlin in that year, in any capacity, could have had no idea of what was implied?

Romania

For the last development of Traditionalism under Fascism we have to return to the period after the First World War, and attempt to ignore what happened later, in order to understand events of the 1920s and 1930s in terms appropriate to those decades, rather than in terms of later associations.

Romanian Traditionalism derived not from Paris or Cairo but from Rome. The earliest identifiable Romanian Traditionalist, Mircea Eliade, was in 1927 a distant follower of Evola'a and Arturo Reghini's *Ur* group and was introduced to the work of Guénon by Reghini, as Evola himself had been.[82] Eliade became a central figure in the history of Traditionalism. It is unclear how he got in touch with Reghini and the *Ur* group, but the contact was presumably a consequence of Eliade's youthful interest in occultism: he was reading Theosophical works at the age of 16, as well as Louis-Claude de Saint-Martin (the eighteenth-century Perennialist Mason after whom Encausse's Martinism was named).[83]

After reading the Theosophists, Eliade recorded in his diary his desire to read the Sanskrit originals,[84] rather as Aguéli had determined to learn Sanskrit in 1895. The study of Sanskrit was less advanced in Romania than in France, and when in 1925 Eliade went to the University of Bucharest, it was to read philosophy, under Nae Ionescu, whose many interests included religion. Then in 1928 Eliade went to Calcutta to study Sanskrit and Hinduism, funded by a grant from the maharaja of Kassimbazar. Eliade had a close relationship with Evola in these years, to judge by his reactions recorded in his diary on learning of Evola's death in 1974: "Today I learn of the death of Julius Evola, . . . Memories surge up in me, those of my years at university, the books we had discovered together, the letters I received from him in Calcutta."[85]

In 1931 Eliade returned to Romania, and in 1933 he successfully defended his doctoral thesis. He began to teach at Bucharest University[86] and quickly became a figure familiar in small countries such as Romania, a general intellectual—scholar, cultural critic, journalist, and novelist.

By about 1933 an informal group of Romanian Traditionalists had come into being. It was led not by Eliade but by the more committed Vasile Lovinescu, who may or may not have encountered Traditionalism through Eliade.[87] Lovinescu is the central figure in the history of Romanian Traditionalism. There were at least a dozen Bucharest Traditionalists, making them the largest such group outside France and Switzerland. One was a student of Eliade from Bucharest University, Michel Vâlsan, also later an important figure in the history of Traditionalism.[88]

The activities of this group were inspired by both Evola and Guénon. The Evolian inspiration is visible in the Eliade's and Lovinescu's engagement with the Legion of the Archangel Michael, and the Guénonian inspiration is visible in the search for a valid initiation carried out by Lovinescu and Vâlsan, and probably others—but not, as far as is known, by Eliade, which suggests that he was then more of an Evolian than a Guénonian. Some members of the group also engaged in the Traditionalist research project based around *Etudes traditionnelles*. After a 1934 article on the Holy Grail (the subject of a 1937 book of Eliade), Lovinescu wrote a series of articles on "hyperborean Dacia," published in *Etudes traditionnelles* in 1936 and 1937.[89] These articles argued that Dacia (the Roman province from which Romanians consider themselves to be descended) was the location of a supreme spiritual center, making Romania a repository of primordial tradition—an idea similar to one popularized earlier in the century by Vasile Parvan, a non-Traditionalist neo-pagan favored by some members of the Legion of the Archangel Michael and similar movements.[90] The Bucharest Traditionalists also established their own journal in 1934, *Studii de tradiţie ezoterică* [Studies in Esoteric Tradition], edited by Marcel Avramescu, a convert from Judaism to Orthodox Christianity.[91] This journal lasted only two years; it was the second imitator of *Etudes traditionnelles* after Evola's *La Torre*.[92]

Eliade wrote not for *Etudes traditionnelles* (though he may have written for *Studii de tradiţie*) but for mainstream journals, notably the newspaper *Vremea* [The Times]. He also published scholarly books and best-selling novels. That he was addressing a general audience had several important consequences for his work. One was that Traditionalist authors were rarely cited, at least after some very early work,[93] even when they should have been. Two entire chapters of *Mitul reintegrârii* [The Myth of Reintegration] (1942), for example, are taken almost word for word, and without acknowledgment, from a 1935 article by Coomaraswamy, "Angel and Titan."[94] In 1951, after reading a new edition of Eliade's important *Traité d'histoire des religions* [Treatise on the History of Religions] (1948), Evola wrote to Eliade saying that he quite understood that Eliade had to base himself on "official academic literature," but—though he hoped Eliade would not be offended at his saying this—"one finds not one word, not just about Guénon, but also about the other authors whose thought and work it is that enables you to deal so easily with your material."[95]

Eliade's reply does not survive, but in his diary he noted:

> One day I received a rather bitter letter from [Evola] in which he reproached me for never citing him, no more than I did Guénon. I answered him as best I could, and I must one day give the reasons and explanations that that response called for. My argument couldn't have been simple. The books I write are intended for today's audience, and not for initiates [Traditionalists]. Unlike Guénon and his emulators, I believe I have nothing to write that would be intended especially for them [potential and actual initiates].[96]

Eliade seems to be saying that he is writing for the general public, not the pages of *Etudes traditionnelles*, and that overt Traditionalism would lose him readers.[97] Guénon had already come to a similar conclusion about Eliade's motivation independently, even if Evola had not.[98]

If this was Eliade's view, he was right. As we will see, there is a general rule that "soft" Traditionalist works—works in which Traditionalism is not overt—can often become popular, while "hard" Traditionalism—what Guénon and Evola and "his emulators" wrote in *Etudes traditionnelles* and elsewhere—never reaches beyond a fairly small audience. Eliade, then, is a "soft" Traditionalist, in the sense that the Traditionalism in his work is not overt. He is also a "soft" Traditionalist in that he himself was not committed to Traditionalism in the way that Lovinescu and Vâlsan were. For them, Guénon was the most important writer of the age, and Traditionalism was the all-encompassing explanation of everything that really mattered. For Eliade even more than Evola, other sources were important, and Eliade was happy on occasion to dissent from established Traditionalist views, as in his evident acceptance of Christianity.

Eliade had other reasons for avoiding mention of Traditionalists in his work. By 1943 at least he was well aware of the problem that academics commonly point to: that Traditionalists sometimes denied "the evidence of history and completely ignored the factual data gathered by researchers."[99] Eliade here echoes Sylvain Lévi on Guénon's thesis and the *Harvard Journal of Asiatic Studies* review of Coomaraswamy's *Hinduism and Buddhism*—though Eliade did not include the work of Coomaraswamy in his criticism, calling him "one of the most learned and creative scholars of the century."[100] It seems clear that Eliade realized that if he was to make a career as an academic he could not admit a debt to authors who were—at least in academic terms—not serious. Coomaraswamy was fairly open about his Traditionalism, but then Coomaraswamy by 1933 (when he published his first Traditionalist book) was 56 years old and in an established—indeed unassailable—position. Scholars in his position can get away with far worse than that. Eliade, as a young scholar, had to tread much more carefully.

To excavate the Traditionalism in the work of a "soft" Traditionalist is more difficult than to survey the thought of a "hard" Traditionalist such as Guénon, and in the case of a writer as prolific and at times as subtle as Eliade it is exceedingly difficult. It seems, though, that Eliade's Traditionalism is to be found not so much in the detail (though Traditionalist influence has been found there too)[101] but in his objectives, and thus also in his method.[102]

Rather than trying to reassemble primordial truth from the debris so as to assist an elite in averting the implosion of the West or its assimilation by the East, Eliade's project was the construction of a general model of human religiosity, as expressed in universally valid myth and symbol, and defined as "the foundation of constituted consciousness and being"—a model that might aid human self-understanding and so "provide the means for cultural renewal," a renewal all the more necessary because of "the historical age into which we are entering and in which we will not only be surrounded but also dominated by 'foreigners,' the non-Occidentals."[103] This is really very close to what Guénon wrote in *Orient et Occident*. Eliade himself made the connection between the study of symbolism and the Traditionalist project in 1937, when he described the work of the major Traditionalists in academically respectable terms: Guénon, Evola, and Coomaraswamy, he said, "are trying to stabilize the unity of the traditions and symbols which are at the base of the ancient Oriental, Amerindian and Western civilizations and also of 'ethnographic culture.' "[104]

Eliade's general model of human religiosity is in effect the Perennial Philosophy dressed up in secular clothes. His hope for cultural renewal through the understanding of religious myth and symbolism was entirely acceptable in the 1960s, better than renewal through the understanding of esoteric spirituality, and infinitely better than religious renewal. Once assembled, a general model of human religiosity would differ little from the Perennial Philosophy.

What Eliade did over his entire career was to pursue the standard Traditionalist research project of "reassembl[ing] . . . debris" under other names and by more scholarly methods. His subject material was much the same as that found in *Etudes traditionnelles*, but instead of calling it "tradition" he called it "archaic religion" (though he does sometimes use the word "traditional" as well).[105] A regular Traditionalist would study various traditions as a believer in them all as expressions of the Perennial Philosophy; Eliade instead studied archaic religions *as if* a believer, "on their own plane of reference." To what extent Eliade actually believed that the "archaic religions" he worked on were aspects of a Perennial Philosophy is impossible to say, but to the extent that he did believe this, it must have made it easier for him to place himself in the position of a believer in one religion after another.

Eliade found a justification for his almost exclusive emphasis on archaic religion in a somewhat shaky theory about views of time: that the modern view of time as linear was atypical in comparison to the far more general archaic view of time as cyclical, and so nonarchaic religion was also atypical. This principle relieved him of any need to refer to the *kali yuga* (the "fourth age" of terminal decline, discussed in chapter 1), fortunately since by 1957 he found that the concept was actually a rather late addition to Hindu thought.[106] It enabled him, however, to dismiss modernity as firmly as Guénon had—though only in its religious aspect, which is what he wanted. A little before 1978 Eliade said that what it was about Guénon's work that "irritated me [was] his excessively polemical side, and his brutal rejection of the whole of modern Western culture, as if it were enough to teach at the Sorbonne to lose all possibility of understanding anything."[107]

That Traditionalist Perennialism informed even Eliade's later work is suggested by the later experience of one of his former students trying to establish an independent scholarly identity. The student, by then himself a professor of religion, read the proofs of a book he had written on early Taoism with dismay: "Every other paragraph seemed to use the word 'primordial' or some classic Eliadean variant. I went through the proofs in a frenzy to purge myself once and for all of the contamination of primordiality!"[108] A de-primordialized book was accordingly published in 1983.

It is not clear whether or not Lovinescu and Eliade were members of the Legion of the Archangel Michael, but both supported it and were in contact with its leader, Corneliu Zelea Codreanu.[109] The Legion (also known as the Iron Guard) had been established in 1927 by Codreanu, previously a follower of Alexandru C. Cuza, a political economist at the University of Bucharest who had established a League of National Christian Defense in 1923. Cuza's League was violently—in the words of one later historian, "monomaniacally"—anti-Semitic, and it was over the question of anti-Semitism that Codreanu broke with Cuza. This rift occurred not because Codreanu was not himself an anti-Semite—he was, though arguably "[not] to a degree notably more extreme than, or markedly at odds with, Romanian society"—but because he felt that blaming the Jews for everything was not enough. The objective of his Legion was not just the purification of Romanian life from Jewish influence but also the "moral rejuvenation" of Romania on a Christian as well as a national basis, including the elimination of (then pervasive) corruption from public life.[110]

The Legion was very different from Cuza's League, especially after 1932, the year Cuza opened relations with the rising Nazi Party, declared that the

Romanians were of Aryan origin, and adopted the swastika as the symbol of his League. Cuza's League also had a paramilitary movement, the Lancieri (Lancers), comparable to the early Nazi SA (the "Brown Shirts"]. The green-shirted rank and file of Codreanu's Legion were guilty of various excesses, but in comparison to Cuza's Lancieri they appear a model of good behavior.[111]

In 1933 Eliade's former teacher and then boss at the university, Nae Io-nescu, joined the Legion, in which he was followed by many of his students,[112] including—it would seem—Eliade. There is no record of Eliade's membership, but he clearly supported the Legion, writing not especially subtle propaganda for it. Thus in 1937 he wrote an article in *Vremea*, "Comentariu la un juramint" [Commentary on an Oath], in which he said of the Legionary oath: "The sig-nificance of this oath is overwhelming. The extent to which it will be fulfilled and made fruitful will prove Romania's capacity for spiritual renewal. . . . The meaning of the revolution to which Mr. Corneliu Codreanu aspires is so pro-foundly mystical that its success will signify once more the triumph of the Christian spirit in Europe."[113]

That same year Eliade wrote elsewhere that he "believe[d] in the victory of the Legionary Movement" because it was a part of the divine and historical destiny of the Romanian people and would not only save Romania but also "bring forth a new type of man." The Legionary Movement, according to Eliade, was distinct from all others in being spiritual rather than political. Whereas Communism acted in the name of economics, Fascism in the name of the state, and Nazism in the name of race, the Legionary Movement acted in the name of Christianity.[114] Not that Eliade dismissed race altogether—on at least two occasions he wrote in *Vremea* on the need to purify the Romanian race of Jewish and Hungarian influences, once in an article titled "Bucuresti Centru Viril" [Bucharest, a Virile Center].[115] The influence of Evola's concept of uranic action may be discerned in this article, as in Eliade's whole involvement with the Legion.

Though there is no evidence to this effect, it is possible that Eliade was also trying to influence the Legion from within, like Evola in Italy and Ger-many. When Evola visited Romania in about 1937,[116] it was Eliade and Lovi-nescu who introduced him to Codreanu, whom Evola found "one of the wor-thiest and spiritually best orientated figures that I ever met in the nationalist movements of the time."[117] Evola and Eliade then proceeded to lunch at the house of Nae Ionescu.[118]

There were, however, Guénonian activities in Bucharest as well as Evolian ones. In 1935 Lovinescu visited the celebrated Greek Orthodox monastery on Mount Athos in search of initiation. He reported his experiences to Guénon, who concluded that either there had never been anything there or it was no longer there, and he introduced Lovinescu to Schuon. In 1936 Lovinescu trav-eled to Basel and, after "preparation" by Burckhardt, went to Amiens and en-tered Schuon's Alawiyya.[119]

Eliade's ex-student Vâlsan made the same trip with the same consequences in the same year. In 1935 Vâlsan had been among the thousands of Romanians who traveled to Maglavit (a small town on the Romanian side of the Danube) to visit Petrache Lupu, whose visions and miraculous cures unleashed "a wave of religious exaltation [that] swept over the whole country"—and who was adopted by Cuza's League of National Christian Defense after he cured a Cuzaist journalist of "uncontrollable blinking."[120] As Lovinescu had reported to Guénon on Mount Athos, so Vâlsan reported to Guénon on Lupu, until Guénon again concluded that there was nothing of interest there and sent Vâlsan to the Alawiyya. Lupu's effect on Vâlsan was almost the opposite of that on the Cuzaist journalist he cured: Vâlsan felt haunted by Lupu, and Reyor—who met Vâlsan in Paris on his way to Schuon—described him as a man "visibly in terror." The Alawiyya, and the act of throwing into the Seine a watch that Lupu had blessed, restored Vâlsan to equilibrium, but the memory of Lupu was to remain with him in later years.[121]

With Vâlsan's help, Lovinescu established a Bucharest branch of the Alawiyya, but no further details are known of it. There is no evidence that Eliade ever belonged to it, nor that he ever embarked on the search for an initiation. Many years later he suggested that the rediscovery of a "sacred text" by a "competent reader" could substitute for initiation through an initiatic chain.[122] This seems to have been the "initiation" Eliade chose for himself.

After 1938 much of Romanian Traditionalism vanished under the pressure of the storm then gathering over Europe. King Carol II of Romania, who had established a form of personal rule on his accession in 1930, decided in 1938 to take control of the Legion and had Codreanu and many other Legionaries arrested—including Eliade and his friend Nae Ionescu. Codreanu and twelve of his principal supporters were strangled in prison ("shot while attempting to escape"), but the others were later released.[123] Leadership of the Legion then passed to Horia Sima, who shared Cuza's Nazi orientation and who transformed it into the Iron Guard, which became familiar to the Allies during the Second World War as a Romanian equivalent of the Nazi Party. Vâlsan had meanwhile succeeded in getting himself posted to the Romanian legation in Paris (where Lovinescu had previously served), and in 1939 Eliade obtained a posting to the Romanian legation in London.[124]

In 1940 Germany forced Romania to cede large amounts of territory to Hungary, a German ally, and King Carol abdicated. The new king, Michael, appointed a government of which Germany would approve, led by the generally respected Marshal Ion Antonescu and including, in addition to the (less respected) new Iron Guard leader Sima, Eliade's friend Nae Ionescu. Ionescu, however, died of natural causes in the same year.[125] In 1941 Romania joined the Axis, and Eliade transferred from enemy London to the Romanian legation in neutral Portugal. Both he and Vâlsan remained in their diplomatic posts until the end of the war. Lovinescu stayed in Romania, where he was briefly *sindaco* (mayor) of his native town, Falticeni.[126] Romania had been assigned to the Soviet Union at Yalta, and although she did not formally become a People's Republic until 1947, it was already clear in 1945 which way the wind was blowing, and Vâlsan and Eliade both decided to remain abroad.

Vâlsan remained in France after returning to Romania briefly in 1945, and Eliade moved from Portugal to France and then later to America. Their subsequent histories will be discussed later, but I will mention here a charge brought against Eliade toward the end of his life by philosopher Kelley Ross: that "the kind of theory of religion represented by Eliade" which privileges archaic and "morally unschematized" religions "leads logically and directly to the neo-pagan amoralism of the Nazis, and furthermore that Eliade directly promoted such a thing in Romania during or before World War II."[127]

Variations on this charge were behind the more heated criticisms leveled at Eliade toward the end of the twentieth century and can be answered on two bases: that to recognize and study "the nonrational and nonmoral" does not have to encourage nonmoral and nonrational activities (and may well do the reverse), and that Eliade passes Ross's "recognition of evil test":

> Eliade can justly be accused of political naiveté. If it was *merely* naiveté, that would be a kind of defense—a kind of defense that is often offered for Heidegger and Werner Heisenberg. The problem is whether foolish or ignorant views are vicious or merely well-meaning but uninformed. The proof is whether the views become *disillusioned* in the face of conspicuous demonstrations of evil. If there is no disillusionment in such circumstances, then we must ask whether such evils really *follow* from the views and so whether the views are really naive or in fact informed, deliberate, and actually pernicious.[128]

Eliade showed disillusionment when he left Romania for London. In comparison, neither von Sebottendorf nor (especially) Evola did recognize evil, and, as has been suggested, von Sebottendorf had more excuse than Evola.

Romanian Traditionalism survived the People's Republic of Romania, but with little contact with Traditionalism elsewhere. Its later history will therefore be quickly reviewed here. Lovinescu's Alawiyya continued functioning in some form until the 1970s with seven or eight followers, and in 1958 Lovinescu established a separate Traditionalist study circle, the Brotherhood of Hyperion, consisting of about ten people who met weekly and which might have been related to an Orthodox initiatic order. Lovinescu started writing in 1964, and in 1981 he published his first book, *A patrulea hagialîc* [The Fourth Pilgrimage].[129]

Traditionalism enjoyed renewed popularity in Romania after the fall of Ceauşescu in 1989. Hyperion expanded into a more formal organization and began publishing Lovinescu's works, while other Traditionalists were translated and published by a major mainstream publisher; Traditionalism even became the subject of a weekly radio broadcast.[130] The concentration of Romanian Traditionalists in the Foreign Ministry in the 1930s was repeated in the 1990s, with Traditionalists serving as foreign minister, as ambassador to Paris, and also as ambassador to Tunisia. The embassy to Tunisia was given as an honorable exile to a man who was briefly vice-president of the Council of Ministers after serving on the tribunal that condemned Ceauşescu to death.[131] For purely practical reasons, however, any detailed examination of contemporary Romanian Traditionalism falls beyond the scope of this book.

6

Fragmentation

The Second World War was a period of intense activity for Evola but was otherwise a time of inactivity for Traditionalism. Guénon was in Egypt, which was occupied by British troops, while most Traditionalists were in France, which was occupied by German troops. Schuon was in neutral Switzerland and had appointed Michel Vâlsan as his *muqaddam* in Paris. The correspondence which had previously united these and other Traditionalists around the world was interrupted by the war, although the diplomatic bag of neutral Brazil allowed some communication until 1942.[1] *Etudes traditionnelles* suspended publication, and Guénon's works were not available in France. All varieties of Masonic activity ceased, and French Masons were persecuted.[2]

Even during the war years, however, Guénon found some new followers, most important among them Martin Lings, a young Englishman who by the end of the twentieth century would become one of the most important Traditionalist Sufis. Lings, who had joined the Alawiyya in 1938 after reading Guénon while teaching English in the Baltic States, was in Egypt visiting Guénon at the start of the war. Unable to return to Lithuania, he took a job in the English Department at Cairo University, and during the war became Guénon's closest associate, though never exactly an intimate.[3]

Guénon also acquired some new readers during the war, including Alain Daniélou, a French musician and convert to Hinduism then living in Benares, India, who began the translation of some of Guénon's works into Hindi. His elder brother, Jean Daniélou, who at the end of his life was a Catholic cardinal and member of the

Académie française, became interested enough in Traditionalism to write occasional articles on the subject.[4] The most celebrated of Guénon's new readers, however, was the French novelist André Gide. Gide spent much of the war in Morocco, where in 1943 a French Sufi Traditionalist lent him some of Guénon's books. "What would have become of me if I had found them at the time of my youth?" wondered Gide in his diary. By 1943 it was too late to change: "my sclerotic spirit bends . . . with difficulty," wrote Gide, and the books instead reminded him of what he called his "occidentality," of why he was with Descartes and Bacon.[5] Even so, Gide could not quite dismiss the challenge of Traditionalism, as is shown by a conversation at about this time recorded by Henri Bosco (discussed previously), who was also in Morocco during the war and had recently been introduced to Gide. After saying to Bosco and a group of others much of what he had written about Guénon in his diary, Gide added:

"If Guénon is right, well, all my oeuvre falls. . . ."

To which someone replied: "But then others fall with it, and not the least; that of Montaigne, for example. . . ."

[GIDE]:   "There is nothing, absolutely nothing, to object to in what Guénon wrote. It's irrefutable."

[Another silence, then]: "The chips are down, I am too old." [Adds]: "I love life passionately—multiple life. I cannot agree to deprive mine of the pleasure it takes in the marvelous diversity of the world, and why? to sacrifice to an abstraction—to Unity, indefinable Unity! . . . Limited beings, perishable creatures, only they interest me and elicit my love, not the Being, the Eternal Being, the Unlimited Being."[6]

Gide is clearly worried that Guénon was right and that he has been wrong. He seems to be trying to justify to himself his failure to take action, to follow the example of the man who had given him Guénon's books and become a Sufi, abandoning the world for God. Gide, of course, never became a Sufi, but his reflections show something of how Guénon's books and indeed the personal example of Sufi Traditionalists can appear to others: as a challenge, a powerful call to some variety of religious vocation.

Revival

Traditionalist activity in France revived quickly after the end of the war, and soon it proceeded in new directions. The first of these was Masonic. Shortly after the end of the war a Russian Traditionalist living in Paris, Alexandre Mordiof, wrote to the French Grand Lodge. The grand master, Michel Dumesnil de Gramont, and some other senior Masons evidently appreciated the work

of Guénon as they had that of Wirth, and in 1947 they authorized the founding
of a new lodge on Traditionalist lines, La Grande Triade [The Great Triad]—
the name came from Guénon's book on Masonic initiation, *La grande Triade*
(1946).[7] This required special permission because there was then a general
prohibition against establishing new lodges; Masonry had barely survived the
occupation, and the number of Masons attached to the French Grand Lodge
had fallen from about 124,000 in 1939 to a mere 3,000 in 1945.[8] There was a
pressing need to revive old lodges, not to start new ones.

The experiment of reviving "traditional" Masonic ritual by excising later
additions, as argued for by Wirth and under the guidance of Guénon's work,
attracted much interest in Masonic circles. In addition to a number of Traditionalists (including Mordiof), the eleven first members of the Grande Triade
included the then Grand Master of the Obedience (de Gramont) and a future
grand master,[9] and the number of visitors to the lodge was at first so great that
there was often no room left to sit.[10] One visitor in 1948 recorded his favorable
impression of both the rituals and the discussions that followed them (the two
complementary parts of every Masonic meeting):

> The Venerable Ivan Cerf directed the Works with mastery. . . . From
> the moment he took his place at his table, everything in his attitude
> changed to take an appearance that can only be described as hier-
> atic, without any affectation. . . . The rites were executed punctually
> and intelligently, the circumambulations carried out correctly, in the
> direction and with the rhythm that was appropriate. . . . The quality
> of the Works was on par with that of the ritual. The average intellec-
> tual level of the members was certainly higher than that in most
> lodges. Many Brothers had a vast and genuine wisdom. The subjects
> dealt with were also almost always intelligently treated, and the de-
> bates that followed were pertinent and courteous, thanks also to the
> perfect discipline that was observed.[11]

As the return of peace made possible new initiatives such as this, it also allowed
individual Traditionalists to return to interrupted business. One of these was
Henri Hartung, an important figure in the history of Traditionalism. Hartung,
a member of France's small but often important Protestant minority and the
son of a commandant of the Ecole militaire, had been introduced to the work
of Guénon in 1938 by Olivier de Carfort, the father of a friend, Francis de
Carfort. He had stayed up all night reading the book he had been given (the
Introduction générale), and found his life "transformed" as a consequence. The
war, however, had delayed the consequences of this transformation. After finishing his university education, Hartung joined the Resistance in 1942, fled to
Switzerland with his friend Francis de Carfort in 1943, and in 1944 returned
to France to join the Free French army. After being wounded in Alsace and
decorated for valor, Hartung was appointed an aide to President de Gaulle. It

was only then that, while on a mission to India in 1945, Hartung could return
to his Traditionalist search.[12]

In southern India again in 1947, Hartung spent ten days at Tiruvanna-
malai, the *ashram* (*zawiya*) of Ramana Maharshi, one of the most celebrated
Hindu gurus or sages of the century. This visit was the decisive spiritual experience of Hartung's life—he described Ramana Maharshi as "the living incarnation of the divine reality which is in every human being, but which he
had rediscovered"[13]—but it did not satisfy his search for initiation. Back in
Paris, where he completed a Ph.D. in geography after leaving the army,[14] Hartung met Vâlsan, and in February 1949 he entered into correspondence with
Guénon. At first they discussed Ramana Maharshi and other contemporary
Hindu gurus, as well as a translation of a work of Ramana Maharshi that
Hartung was hoping to publish in *Etudes traditionnelles*. Encouraged by Vâlsan,
in May Hartung wrote to Guénon—in the excessively formal tones a young
man felt appropriate for using with such a sage—that given the difficulties the
practice of Hinduism presented to a Westerner, "would it not . . . be possible
for me to turn towards an exoteric framework to which I aspire profoundly and
which might—although so far I have known Islam much less well than India—
bring me influences and a framework better adapted to the development of
the spiritual life of a Westerner?" A fortnight later Guénon replied that he
"altogether approve[d] of this intention," and in June or early July 1949 Hartung
and his wife became Muslim and joined the Alawiyya.[15]

The Alawiyya too was moving in new directions. Its practices were becoming more elaborate, with candles and incense being used during *dhikr* ceremonies, part of what a hostile source referred to as a general preoccupation
with "staging" (*mise en scène*).[16] The aftermath of a *dhikr* of about 1947 was
described as follows:

> After a simple meal—rye bread, cheese, fruit and tea—taken in si-
> lence, the Shaykh would speak of doctrine and the spiritual life and
> would answer questions. On these occasions I would invariably feel
> a powerful breath of benediction coming out of his mouth; it was
> almost as if I could see rays of light emanating from him. He was
> seated on his divan in Moroccan dress, as were also his disciples
> who were sitting on the floor in a half-circle, the women in the rear.
> The traditional garment, which the Shaykh insisted upon, gave dig-
> nity to each one. Two Moroccan lamps of finely chiseled copper cast
> delicate lace patterns on the ceilings and the walls, and while we
> were performing the rites, incense filled the air. All was sacred
> beauty and peace, and I would walk home after these evenings as if
> drunk with the wine of truth.[17]

Schuon's preoccupation with ambience is visible even today in the houses of
Schuon's followers, which are almost all beautifully decorated in a "tradi-

tional" style that may in part be traced back to Coomaraswamy, and are invariably equipped with a prayer room furnished with Koran and candle, and usually a dagger.[18] Beauty was always an important means of access to God for Schuon and his followers.

A second new direction for the Alawiyya resulted from Schuon's long-standing interest in Native Americans, which he himself traced to stories told to him as a child by his paternal grandmother, who had spent some time in America in her youth.[19] This interest became more serious in 1946, when Schuon wrote to various followers and admirers asking to be put in touch with a Native American "elder." In response, Joseph Epes Brown, an anthropologist at the University of Indiana and already an Alawi, sent Schuon John Neihardt's *Black Elk Speaks* (1932).[20] This was a best-selling first-person account—now known to have been heavily edited—of the life of Black Elk, a Lakota-speaking Oglala Sioux leader and *wichasha wakan* (holy man) who had taken part in the battles of Little Big Horn and Wounded Knee.[21] *Black Elk Speaks* much impressed Schuon; in 1948 it was one of the first books that he gave to Catherine Feer, a recent arrival in the Alawiyya, later to become his wife.[22] After reading this book, Schuon began to discuss Native American spirituality in his correspondence with Guénon, and he also recommended that Brown contact Black Elk; Brown did so, spending a year with him around 1947-48.[23] The results of that year's research were published in 1953, simultaneously in English and in French, as *The Sacred Pipe: Black Elk's Account of the Seven Rites of the Oglala Sioux*, and *Les rites secrets des Indiens sioux* [The Secret Rites of the Sioux Indians].[24]

The Sacred Pipe for many years joined Neihardt's *Black Elk Speaks* as a basic source text for the study of Native American religion, though it never achieved the extraordinary popularity that Neihardt's book had.[25] *The Sacred Pipe* was written largely in Lausanne over a period of six months, with the benefit of Schuon's Traditionalist understandings made available during a weekly review by Schuon of Brown's draft as it developed.[26] *The Sacred Pipe*, then, resulted in the generally unsuspected passage of "soft" Traditionalism into mainstream academia.

Dissension

This resumption of Traditionalist activities was interrupted in 1948 by an increasingly public dispute between Guénon and Schuon. It centered on the validity of Christian initiation. Schuon had for some time maintained privately that the Christian sacraments of baptism and confirmation retained a form of validity as esoteric initiations, a view expressed in the July–August 1948 issue of *Etudes traditionnelles* in an article, "Mystères christiques" [Christic Mysteries]. Guénon was evidently less concerned about the views Schuon expressed in "Mystères christiques"—views with which he was already somewhat familiar, though he disagreed firmly—than he was angry that the article had been published in what he still saw very much as his own journal.[27] The idea that Schuon was mounting a challenge to Guénon's authority would have been encouraged by reports reaching Cairo from Reyor, who in 1948 complained to Guénon that Schuon's followers were trying to take control of the Grande Triade and that many had canceled their subscriptions to Etudes traditionnelles and were only ordering back copies containing articles by Schuon.[28]

There is no evidence of any attempt by Schuon to take over the Grande Triade, but some challenge to Guénon's authority by Schuon might have been expected. There is a general pattern of such challenges: Guénon had himself rejected the authority of the older Encausse, as Encausse when young had once rejected the authority of Blavatsky. Schuon's rejection of Guénon's authority at this point was even more likely due to the interruption of communications during the war, as a result of which Schuon's followers became more independent of Guénon, just as Vâlsan's followers had become more independent of Schuon.

The dispute between Guénon and Schuon in 1948 was not only about authority; it was also about the proper nature of a Traditionalist Sufi order. Guénon's position was clear: not only must esoteric practice take place in an orthodox exoteric framework, but the two must coincide. A Traditionalist Sufi order in Europe should not differ from a Sufi order in the Islamic world, and the exoteric Islam of its followers should not differ from orthodox Islam.[29] Anything else would be "the mixture of traditional forms," syncretism. Schuon's view was more permissive: he believed that esoteric practice was what really mattered and that its exoteric framework was less important.

This was not just a theoretical concern. Schuon's view was reflected in relaxations of the Sharia that he permitted some of his followers in Lausanne, probably starting during the late war years. There is no indication of such relaxations before the war, other than omitting the sunna prayers. The first reports of relaxations reached Guénon in 1948 from Reyor, according to whom Schuon's followers were no longer fasting Ramadan.[30] By 1950 this report was being repeated independently by both Vâlsan and Hartung, according to whom it was for individual followers that Schuon had relaxed the Sharia, not for all,[31] which seems to have been the case.[32] In Basel, von Meyenburg and others kept the Ramadan fast as they always had.[33]

This and other departures from the Sharia by Schuon's followers were justified by Schuon, according to Vâlsan, as departures from "exoteric formalities," needed to "adapt . . . to the conditions of life in the West," a justification that Vâlsan himself clearly rejected.[34] Vâlsan's understanding was more or less accurate: in a later document Schuon wrote of "simplifications" of the Sharia "legitimate under the particular conditions, not only of life in dar al-harb (non-Islamic lands) in general, but also and above all of current cyclical conditions."[35]

In the words of a contemporary Schuonian, "Some required religious prescriptions were intended to be accomplished with the outward support of the entire
traditional civilization. . . . Insistence upon certain more exoteric prescriptions
risks compromising the original intention of the religion because under the
unusual conditions of the modern world, these prescriptions may in fact become a burden rather than a support for the inner spiritual life."[36]

In addition to the failure to observe the Ramadan fast, Vâlsan also regretted
the performance of the ritual prayer at irregular times and improper ablutions
before prayer.[37] These require some explanation as well as comment. The essentials of Islamic practice are described as its five "pillars," of which the first
is the Confession of Faith. The second is the ritual prayer, to be performed five
times a day during specified periods—between dawn and sunrise, between
noon and halfway from noon to sunset, and so on. For the ritual prayer, a
Muslim must be in a state of ritual purity, achieved through washing the ex-
tremities of the body, forearms, mouth, and some other parts in a specified
order and fashion. An alternative to these ablutions, tayammum—the performance of limited symbolic ablutions using not water but sand or dust—is
permitted when no water is available. According to Vâlsan, Schuon's followers
were using it even when water was available. The third pillar is fasting from
food, drink, tobacco, and so on, from dawn to dusk during the lunar month
of Ramadan.

Schuon had some reason to want to "simplify" (as he later put it) these
pillars. The second and third pillars of Islam are easy enough to perform in
the Islamic world if one wants to—mosques have ablution areas, and it is
expected that someone's attention will begin to wander toward the end of the
day during Ramadan. In the West, however, they present certain difficulties
even today, and these difficulties were even greater during the 1940s, when
immigration had not yet made Muslims somewhat familiar in the West. There
were no mosques to pray in, and people who started washing their forearms
and feet in a public bathroom would have attracted unwelcome attention.
Someone who fell asleep at his or her desk during a Ramadan afternoon would
not have been treated with understanding. In addition, in the 1940s Ramadan
fell in the summer, and though the weather in Switzerland in August is normally cooler than it is in Cairo, the sun rises a lot earlier and sets a lot later,
making the period of fasting much longer—though there are ways of dealing
with this difficulty without abandoning the fast altogether.[38] One can see, then,
why Schuon might permit some departures from the Sharia in these areas,
though it is not entirely clear why he would want to permit tayammum when
water was available.[39]

Although Vâlsan clearly did not sympathize with Schuon's "simplifications" and Guénon seems not to have sympathized either, it is interesting to
note that, as Islam became more widespread in the West toward the end of the
twentieth century, it became common for Western converts to Islam to be

permitted some relaxations of the Sharia on purely pragmatic grounds[40]—it is foolish to push anyone to the breaking point. There is, however, a subtle but important difference between allowing a convert to Islam to delay a ritual prayer in order not to lose a job,[41] and allowing such a delay because of "current cyclical conditions" or because the time of the prayer is only an "exoteric" formality that can be "essentialized."[42] Most Muslims aware of conditions in the West would sympathize in the case of the former situation. The second reason was rejected by Guénon and Vâlsan and would scandalize almost any Muslim. In some cases it would bring to mind the well-known story of the shaykh traveling through the desert with his exhausted followers during Ramadan. Suddenly, an oasis with a cool, clear pool and date palms laden with ripe dates appears from nowhere. "Help yourselves!" says the voice of God. "You are so dedicated to My way that you no longer need worry about formalities." "I take refuge in God from Satan the accursed!" replies the shaykh. "How did you know it was me?" asks Satan (for indeed it was him). "Partly because of the way your voice sounded," replies the shaykh, "and partly because I know that God never releases anybody from observing the Sharia."

One other departure from the Sharia reported by Vâlsan requires comment. This was permitting Alawis to drink beer during family or business dinners,[43] evidently in order to allay suspicions that they were Muslim. Some parallels exist to Schuon's other relaxations of the Sharia elsewhere, but there is no known parallel to this one.[44] The Sharia does permit Muslims to deny their faith in order to avoid death (though it is better to die a martyr if you can), and recent converts are sometimes advised not to tell everybody of their conversion until they feel ready to cope with the reactions. No other shaykh, however, is known ever to have authorized forbidden acts in order to reinforce a fiction. Besides, some Alawis soon came to drink beer privately as well as in public.[45]

Schuon had not abandoned the Sharia entirely, however, and would never do so, though there would be additional departures over the coming years. Schuon still insisted on the Sharia enough to remind his followers that "sexual relations outside marriage *are absolutely forbidden*" [original emphasis],[46] and to refuse admittance to the Alawiyya to an old French friend of Guénon, Roger Maridort. Maridort, like others of his generation, had encountered the work of Guénon in 1927–28, and in the 1930s he visited Guénon in Cairo several times—he may have been the wealthy follower who rescued Guénon from hunger during the latter's first years in Egypt. Referred by Reyor to Vâlsan, he had sought a Sufi initiation, as did others, Vâlsan refused Maridort, however, because he was living with a married woman who could not divorce her husband. Schuon also refused him for the same reason. Guénon was evidently more sympathetic toward Maridort's predicament, and it was with Guénon's approval that Maridort traveled to Morocco and entered the Darqawiyya, the same order that Burckhardt had entered, though at the hands of a different shaykh, Muhammad al-Tadili. Al-Tadili later gave Maridort an *ijaza* to give the Darqawiyya, and so a second Traditionalist Sufi order became established.[47]

The counterpart to Schuon's emphasis on esoteric practice and disregard of elements of the exoteric Sharia was his readiness to regard the Christian sacraments as initiatic, and so to accept followers who were Christian. He never allowed non-Muslims to join the Alawiyya itself but did allow them to attend (though not actively participate in) the Alawi *dhikr* ceremony.[48] By 1950 Guénon took seriously reports that Schuon had Christian followers, notably a Catholic priest who had been initiated into the Fraternity of Cavaliers of the Divine Paraclete. After the death of Charbonneau-Lassay control of this body had passed in 1946 to Guénon's old associate from the Order of the Temple, Thomas.[49] Though the history of the Paraclete between 1946 and its being "put to sleep" in 1951 is obscure, it seems that the reports reaching Guénon were accurate, since the priest used Schuon's meditation exercises—on the Six Themes—until the mid-1960s, when he is reported to have visited Lausanne for the first time, disliked what he saw, and broken with Schuon.[50]

Guénon was concerned not only about Schuon and the Fraternity of the Cavaliers of the Divine Paraclete, but also about the Grande Triade. The popularity of this lodge had started to bring its own problems. No lodge may formally restrict membership to any particular group (though it may decide on its own rituals within limits), and the Grande Triade was soon faced with the problem of Masons who were not much interested in Traditionalism and who disputed the need for exoteric practice to accompany the esoteric practice of the lodge, and also Traditionalists who were not much interested in Masonry creating complementary difficulties. The lodge was also obliged to operate within the structures established by the French Grand Lodge, which, according to some, limited its possibilities. By 1949 Guénon was beginning to express doubts, although he continued to take a keen interest in the development of the lodge's ritual until his death.[51] In 1950 Reyor, who on Guénon's instructions had joined the Grande Triade shortly after its foundation, caused uproar and dismay by using his turn as orator in the lodge to launch a condemnation of the lodge for failing to achieve its objectives. Reyor was asked to leave the lodge, and did so.[52]

A second Traditionalist attempt at establishing a Masonic esoteric practice was made at this point (or perhaps slightly earlier) by Reyor and another Traditionalist correspondent of Guénon, Jean Tourniac.[53] Reyor and Tourniac together founded the Trois Anneaux [Three Rings], a "wild" lodge (one not answering to any Obedience). As a wild lodge, it was less restricted in its activities than the Grande Triade was under the French Grand Lodge, and it derived its rituals this time from the "operative" Masonic rituals of Clement Stratton, an English Mason who claimed to have rediscovered the original (pre-eighteenth-century) rituals of Masonry—a claim that Guénon had in part accepted, though he identified parts of Stratton's rituals as being modern insertions. Its rituals may also have included repetitive prayer similar to the Sufi *dhikr*.[54] Though freer than the Grande Triade, the Trois Anneaux aroused much less interest. It is said to have attracted few recruits and to have suffered from tensions between its Muslim and Christian members. These tensions must have had more to do with personalities than with religions, since Muslims belonged to the Grande Triade without difficulties, and Christians and Muslims often shared the same (non-Traditionalist) lodges in the Middle East.

Difficulties with Guénon's Masonic projects were not his worst problem. During 1950, relations with Schuon deteriorated further, and Guénon and Reyor (acting on Guénon's instructions) started to refer seekers after initiation not to Schuon, but directly to Vâlsan in Paris, or to Maridort. Schuon, attempting to avert a breach, sent Jacques-Albert Cuttat (by profession a diplomat) to Reyor to suggest that Schuon might go to Cairo to see Guénon in person. Guénon, however, announced that if Schuon came to Cairo he would refuse to meet him.[55] He had by then decided that Schuon's followers were spying on him—showing the same mild paranoia that was visible when he lost his niece, Françoise, in Paris—and that Lings was reading his correspondence on Schuon's behalf, a charge that Lings always denied.[56] It was Lings's task to receive Guénon's mail and deliver it to Guénon's house, and letters were showing signs of having been tampered with. If Guénon's mail had indeed been opened, however, it was almost certainly opened not by Lings but by the Egyptian censorship, intrigued by the Masonic symbols in many of Guénon's letters.[57] Guénon and Schuon never met again.

By mid-1950 Schuon was suffering his first defections. Among them were Cuttat, his earlier emissary to Reyor, and Cuttat's friend Hartung, who had joined the Alawiyya only a year before. By July 1950 both men were objecting to Schuon's "de-Islamization" of the order (according to Hartung's notes), to his abandonment of parts of the Sharia, and to his introduction of elements of practice "which are in reality no more than [the fruits of Schuon's] imagination without any traditional value whatsoever."[58] This complaint presumably refers to the Six Themes of Mediation discussed in chapter 4: Reyor had already complained to Guénon in 1948 that Schuon had introduced meditations on subjects outside of Islam.[59]

Cuttat and Hartung left the Alawiyya together but followed different paths thereafter. Cuttat, whose wife left the Alawiyya with him, began to take instruction from an Orthodox Christian priest in 1951. In 1955 (while serving as Swiss ambassador in Colombia) he and his wife entered the Catholic Church. He retained an interest in Traditionalism, however, lecturing on Guénon at the Sorbonne in 1957.[60] As Swiss ambassador to India in the early 1960s, he went to considerable lengths to facilitate Switzerland's acceptance of Tibetan Buddhist refugees fleeing the Chinese.[61] Hartung, on the other hand, left his wife in the Alawiyya (though that was not the only reason for their subsequent divorce) but remained a scrupulously practicing Muslim until his death in

1988. His entry into the Alawiyya had been secret, and his Islam remained secret (except to his immediate family) until almost the end of his life—and even then it was not announced, though it might have been deduced from the prayers said at his burial by some non-Schuonian Alawis.[62]

Finally, in September 1950, Guénon encouraged Vâlsan to write a short letter to Schuon, separating the Paris Alawiyya that Vâlsan had been leading since 1940 from Schuon's original Alawiyya.[63] Guénon gave his reasons in a letter written in October: "At Lausanne, ritual practices have been reduced to the strict minimum, and most no longer even fast during Ramadan." Guénon believed the Alawiyya was turning from a Sufi order into "a vague 'universalist' organization."[64] The same points were made by Vâlsan at much greater length in November, in a highly critical, 25-page open letter to Schuon the tone of which was extremely harsh, at times even sarcastic. Vâlsan charged Schuon with moving from Islam toward "a superficial and facile universalism," assigning to himself a "universal role outside Islam," ignoring the need for "genuine Muhammadan faith," and replacing the Islamic character of the Alawiyya with a "universalist" one.[65] The distinction between Perennialism and "universalism," a distinction I will myself adopt in this book, is that the former finds unity in the primordial Perennial Philosophy, while the later lumps religions together indistinctly.

Cuttat and Hartung had also criticized Schuon in July for "the divinization of a man,"[66] presumably of Schuon himself. This charge, and the "universal role outside Islam" alleged by Vâlsan, present a chronological puzzle. As we will see, according to his *Erinnerungen und Betrachtungen*, Schuon came to see himself as being charged with a universal role only in the mid-1960s, and he seems to have come to regard himself as a variety of divine manifestation only during the 1980s and 1990s. Cuttat's, Hartung's, and Vâlsan's charges in this respect seem, then, to come too early. Perhaps they had detected the first signs of a later development. Reyor evidently did detect such signs in 1947, when he reported to Guénon that one of Schuon's followers had described Schuon as "my divine master" and that another had said, "Is it not highly significant that the man who today best understands Christianity carries the name of Jesus?" (Isa, the Arabic form of Jesus, was Schuon's Muslim name.) Of course Reyor is referring not to Schuon's own view of himself, but to the views of Schuon's followers. It happens, though not often, that Sufis in the Islamic world develop ideas such as these about the status of their shaykhs. There are some cases of Sufi shaykhs even in the Islamic world coming to accept their followers' valuations of themselves, and something of the sort may ultimately have happened to Schuon.

The breach with Schuon and other difficulties took their toll on Guénon. His oldest friend in Cairo, Valentine de Saint-Point, wrote afterwards of letters "which tortured him, reporting ridiculous gossip which made him believe in persecution, [and] shortened his life.... The smiling, happy, peaceful and pleasant writer gave way to a nervous, edgy man who, despite his smile, was visibly unhappy."[68]

De Saint-Point was evidently not exaggerating. Guénon's health had deteriorated, to the extent that in 1950 a visiting journalist—the first known to have met him—noted that his face was emaciated and his hands "diaphanous" (but took these features for a sign of "great spirituality").[69] In the late fall of 1950, at about the same time that Vâlsan wrote his 25-page open letter to Schuon, Guénon caught from his children what was probably one of the many varieties of influenza that trouble Cairo's inhabitants at that time of year, and he took to his bed. His health never recovered, and late in the evening of January 7, 1951, he died, at the age of only 64. He was buried the next day (as is the Muslim practice) in Cairo's vast and ancient Southern Cemetery, attended by Lings and by an American Alawi, Whitall Perry, who had been living in Cairo since 1946.[70]

Guénon left a son, two daughters, and a pregnant wife. Fortunately for his family, the French community in Cairo was alerted by Guénon's death to something they had not previously appreciated, that a notable Frenchman had been living in Cairo, and the Franco-Egyptian Lycée in the wealthy suburb of Heliopolis offered to educate Guénon's children free of charge.[71] They all grew up bilingual in French and Arabic; the eldest son, Ahmad, later emigrated to France, where he became a doctor, while the other three children remained in Cairo, living more or less the normal lives of the Egyptian middle class.[72]

Shortly before his death, Guénon had asked his wife to leave his study untouched, saying that he would then be able to see his widow and children after his death, even though they would not be able to see him.[73] His wishes were respected (except for an unsuccessful attempt by his widow to sell his library in 1953), and at the end of the twentieth century his study remained as he had left it, though with the addition of a television.[74]

Traditionalism in Cairo did not last long after Guénon's death. Lings was obliged to leave Egypt for England after the 1952 Revolution, when British citizens were dismissed en masse from Cairo University.[75] The Perrys had decided shortly before the revolution that there was little point in remaining in Egypt in a visibly deteriorating political situation without Guénon; they moved to Lausanne.[76] Guénon's Egyptian associate Muin al-Arab, never really a Traditionalist anyway, became a dedicated follower of the Hindu guru Krishna Menon, to whose work he was been introduced by S. Katz, the doctor who attended Guénon's final illness. Krishna Menon was also the guru of John Levy, the Jewish convert to Islam who had bought Guénon his house and was traveling with Schuon at the start of the Second World War; Katz, also of Jewish origin, was an acquaintance of Lings.[77] Even though Menon acquired a number of Traditionalist followers, he does not seem to have been in any way a Traditionalist, but was rather a modernist.

The French community that awoke late to Guénon's presence in Cairo during his life commemorated the first anniversary of his death with a meeting in Guénon's house that featured a second secretary from the French Embassy, readings from the Koran, and speeches given mostly by people who had barely met Guénon. On the second anniversary of his death, much the same people established an Association of the Friends of René Guénon in Egypt, but little was to come of this organization, since the French community in Egypt was then in its last days.[78] Some seem to have seen the Association of the Friends of René Guénon as a way of improving Franco-Egyptian relations after the 1952 Revolution,[79] but if so, they misunderstood the nature of the revolution.[80]

Except among a very few French-educated Egyptians, Guénon was soon forgotten in Egypt. In contrast, the teachings of Krishna Menon—disseminated at first by al-Arab—were to attract a following there that would continue into the twenty-first century.

Traditionalism was Guénon's achievement, in the sense that without him and his writings the movement would never have existed—none of his early associates produced anything that would have attracted people like Coomaraswamy, Evola, Eliade, and Schuon. His achievement was based not only on his work but also on the deep seriousness with which he dedicated himself to his task, especially to his correspondence. Such seriousness and dedication remained characteristic of the Traditionalist movement. Traditionalism, however, also inherited two problematic characteristics from Guénon: his secrecy and his isolation. Guénon wrote on Hinduism without having any known contact with Hinduism as it was lived and practiced in India, and similarly wrote on Islam without any significant contact with living Islamic scholarship. His work, and Traditionalism as a whole, suffered as a consequence.

Independent Orders

At Guénon's death, there were three independent Traditionalist Sufi orders: Schuon's Alawiyya, Vâlsan's Alawiyya, and Maridort's Darqawiyya. A fourth, established by Abd al-Wahid Pallavicini, came into being in the late 1970s, a branch of the Ahmadiyya order in Milan; chronological order will be disturbed to consider it in this chapter for the sake of completeness. All four developed in different directions. Schuon's (which will be discussed in the next two chapters) was by far the most important and became increasingly universalist. Vâlsan's order became increasingly Islamic, and Maridort's Darqawiyya increasingly Guénonian. Pallavicini's order became the most publicly visible Traditionalist order in the West.

Maridort's Darqawiyya

Maridort was an established Traditionalist, an old friend of Guénon who was a member of the Grande Triade, and he took his Masonry seriously—he once told a close friend in the lodge that it was his Masonic practice that gave him the strength to continue his Islamic practice. For some in France, Maridort seemed to have inherited Guénon's mantle. Therefore it was to Maridort that Reyor referred a sizable group of Italian Traditionalists in search of an esoteric initiation during the 1950s, and it was to Maridort that Chacornac turned for a new editor for *Etudes traditionnelles* after he dismissed Reyor from this post in 1960. Maridort declined, however, and suggested Vâlsan, who then edited *Etudes traditionnelles* from 1961 until his death in 1974.[81]

Chacornac had dismissed Reyor because he discovered that he had been diverting monies from *Etudes traditionnelles* to his own use—Reyor is said often to have been short of money as a result of having no regular job and also having to support several wives and a number of illegitimate children. His Traditionalist career is a sad one: one of Guénon's first admirers in 1928, he was happier with the original Traditionalist philosophy than with the later Traditionalist movement and its emphasis on initiation. He participated in all the major French Traditionalist projects—*Etudes traditionnelles*, the Fraternity of the Paraclete, the Alawiyya, the Grande Triade, and the Trois Anneaux—but mostly reluctantly, and without contributing significantly to any of them, and spent the last twenty years of his life largely forgotten by the Traditionalist movement.[82]

Finding that he had more Italian than French followers, Maridort by 1961 had moved from France to Italy and established his Darqawiyya in Turin. There he and his followers launched an Italian equivalent of *Etudes traditionnelles*, called *Rivista di Studi tradizionali* [Review of Traditional Studies], and an Italian equivalent of Editions traditionnels (as Chacornac's publishing business was now known), Edizioni Studi tradizionali. Over the years, Edizioni Studi tradizionali published Italian translations of nearly all Guénon's work, while the *Rivista di Studi tradizionali* published shorter translations of classic Traditionalist and Islamic texts—Aguéli as well as Guénon, al-Tadili (Maridort's own shaykh), and Ibn al-Arabi. It also remained true to Guénon's original interests, publishing translations of various Hindu texts.

The Turin Darqawiyya in time came to see itself as the sole defender of Guénon's original Traditionalism, faithful to a degree described by some French Traditionalists as "Guénolatry." Its later writings not only imitate Guénon's prose style but also his paranoia: there are references to "the objective . . . of demolishing the work of René Guénon" explaining the actions of "forces among the strongest in our world." As well as being defensive, Darqawi writings are at times offensive. For example, one non-Darqawi Traditionalist, identified as "the individual of whom we have already spoken too much," is accused of acting only "to display his pretended knowledge of initiatic techniques, in a hopeless attempt to pass himself off as that which he is not." All other Traditionalists are generally assumed to be acting in bad faith. Thus not only is Schuon accused of "manifest hate" for Guénon, but Vâlsan is accused of "underhand and even more dangerous falsity."[83]

This tone may derive in part from a lengthy and acrimonious dispute involving Maridort and others, including Vâlsan, concerning the copyright to Guénon's work, which was owned by Guénon's children. In dispute was not who would receive royalties but who would have editorial control of Guénon's writings. The origin of this dispute, which even included some litigation, was that Ahmad Guénon—René's oldest son—married a follower of Maridort, transferred his share in his father's copyright to Maridort, and was then killed in a car crash; the dispute had still not been settled to the satisfaction of all parties in the 1990s.[84] Whatever its cause, one consequence of Darqawi hostility is that little is known in wider Traditionalist circles about the later history of the Darqawiyya. When I attempted to contact the Darqawiyya, I was told politely but firmly that what mattered was metaphysics, and that biographies were of no account. No more, then, can be said about the Darqawiyya.

Vâlsan's Alawiyya

The Paris Alawiyya of Vâlsan, in contrast, moved ever closer to mainstream Sufi Islam. Vâlsan is, tellingly, the only Traditionalist shaykh who, from later descriptions, emerges as does a Sufi shaykh in the Islamic world—as a sort of saint. All that is missing are the miracle stories that commonly collect around the memory of a great shaykh in the Arab world. He is also the first Traditionalist shaykh to be openly Muslim and integrated into a general Islamic milieu. From the start of his years in Paris he regularly attended the Paris Mosque, establishing good relations with the imam, a Tunisian, whose daughter he married. He became a regular visitor to a saintly Tunisian Sufi in Tunis, and various Arab Sufis visited his *dhikr*, though none actually joined his order.[85]

Vâlsan was, in Islamic terms, both orthodox and pious. In addition to praying the Friday Prayer at the mosque and carefully observing the ritual prayers and fasts, he spent hours every day in supplementary prayer, and twice he performed the pilgrimage to Mecca (the Hajj in 1965 and an *umra* pilgrimage in 1974). He followed the strictest possible interpretation of the Sharia, ensuring that his children prayed from the age of 7; his son Muhammad fasted Ramadan for the first time at the age of 5. His children were not even allowed to draw—a somewhat astonishing prohibition, since even in the Islamic world the Sharia's condemnation of making images is generally interpreted fairly loosely, even by the most pious.

In addition to his piety, Vâlsan was both modest and ascetic. He refused to act the shaykh, dressing in normal Western clothing rather than "fancy dress" (a sarcastic reference to Schuon's "staging"), never making public speeches despite various invitations, and living extremely simply. As a Romanian diplomat during the Second World War he had lived in comfort; after abandoning the diplomatic service, he was reduced to "the greatest poverty," to which he seems not to have objected, living first in cheap hotels and finally in a public housing project. His first wife found it difficult to adapt to this new lifestyle and left him; for some years Vâlsan brought up his first child, Ahmad, alone and in poverty. He then remarried, again rather as a shaykh in the Islamic world might: his second wife was Khadija, the young daughter of his closest follower, René Roty, and with her Vâlsan had twelve more children. In later years his main source of income was *allocations familiales* (family allowances), payments made in proportion to family size by the French social security administration. These were supplemented by a small income from *Etudes traditionnelles* and occasional small gifts from some of his followers.

Vâlsan also followed the standard Islamic pattern in being an accomplished scholar. He had worked hard on his Arabic, which has been reliably described as excellent,[86] and immersed himself in the study of the texts of Ibn al-Arabi. He accumulated a considerable collection of Ibn al-Arabi manuscripts, on whose writings he based most of his teachings.[87] He also edited and published various texts of Ibn al-Arabi in French translation.[88]

Vâlsan's order followed his example—pious and orthodox, with some emphasis on scholarship for those who were capable of it. No departures from the Sharia were permitted, and most of his followers attended a *dhikr* once or even twice a week.[89] In 1951, when he split from Schuon, Vâlsan had only a dozen or so followers, but by his death in 1974 he had perhaps 100 followers,[90] a respectable number, only rarely exceeded by shaykhs in the Islamic world.[91]

Some of Vâlsan's earliest followers had originally entered the Alawiyya at the hand of Schuon, both from Paris and from the Amiens *zawiya* once run by Schuon's ex-employer, Louis Caudron (who left Islam in the wake of the split between Schuon and Guénon). Roty was one such Traditionalist of the prewar generation. He became Muslim at Guénon's urging in 1932 and, like many other Traditionalists, was from an artistic background. A craft potter, he was the grandson of the celebrated nineteenth-century engraver Oscar Roty, whose *Semeuse* [Girl Sowing] had become one of the modern world's most successful symbols—it was the female figure of the Republic that appeared on most French coins from 1897 to 2002.[92]

Among other early followers of Vâlsan were a penniless marquis of the pre-Napoleonic nobility and a young French student named Michel Chodkiewicz.[93] The son of a magistrate, Chodkiewicz read Guénon's *Crise du monde moderne* at 18 while doing his military service at Tours airbase, and then the rest of Guénon's work, and became Muslim in 1950 after being introduced to Vâlsan by the nephew of the penniless marquis. Chodkiewicz was the first French Traditionalist to begin what may be called the revenge of Traditionalism against the Sorbonne. His initial project of a Ph.D. thesis on Ibn al-Arabi had to be abandoned in the face of resistance from Louis Massignon, who dominated French Islamic studies in the 1950s and who had no sympathy for Ibn al-Arabi, and also in the face of the need to support a young family. Chodkiewicz followed his shaykh in many things, but not in his spartan lifestyle. He got a job with the major French publisher Editions du Seuil and remained there until his retirement in 1989, by then du Seuil's president. Despite this career, he continued work on Ibn al-Arabi, publishing various high-quality translations of and studies on his work, and also on his later follower, the Amir Abd al-Qadir (in whose Damascus circle Aguéli's shaykh Illaysh had once been). Chodkiewicz's work received the academic recognition it deserved, and beginning in 1982 he taught as an adjunct professor at the Sorbonne[94] while also running du Seuil. After his retirement from du Seuil he was appointed to a full professorship, from which he retired in 1994, generally accepted as one of the leading figures in the French study of Islam.

Other such figures emerged from Vâlsan's order. One was Charles-André Gilis, a Belgian academic and Traditionalist. Another was Denis Gril, who had become a Muslim at the age of 6, when his parents joined Vâlsan's Alawiyya. He completed his undergraduate studies in Mecca; he then began a distinguished career in French Islamic scholarship, becoming professor of Arabic and Islamology at the University of Provence, France's preeminent center for the study of Islam. Gril followed Vâlsan and Chodkiewicz in focusing his work on the texts of Ibn al-Arabi.

Late twentieth-century Western Islam, like Islam in the Middle East itself, is dominated not by Sufism but by the movement that replaced Sufism during the nineteenth century as the dominant influence—Salafism, the modernist reformist movement that ultimately gave rise to Islamism. There is, however, a strong Sufi countertrend in Europe, for which Vâlsan's order is in part responsible. It is striking that there are more classic Sufi texts generally available in French translation than in English, many of them the work of Vâlsan, Chodkiewicz, Gillis, and Gril; the influence of Chodkiewicz, Gillis, and Gril in French academia has pushed this trend further.[95] Vâlsan's influence is also visible beyond academia—Roty's son Yaqub, for example, taught at the Paris Mosque and published a number of successful children's books on Islam.[96] To this extent, Vâlsan's order proved to have something of the effect on France that Guénon had predicted for his elite in Orient et Occident in 1924.

Though as close to a regular Sufi shaykh as is possible in the West, Vâlsan remained a Traditionalist. Under his editorship Etudes traditionnelles developed a marked Islamic emphasis, but it continued to publish on other religions. Vâlsan himself retained an interest in Masonry, though he was not himself a Mason.[97] According to his son Muhammad, his primary motivation was always the esoteric path on which he had started in Romania in the 1930s, but his practice was entirely founded on the example of the Prophet Muhammad and the works of Ibn al-Arabi—to the extent that he developed the theory that the work of Guénon was also founded on Ibn al-Arabi[98] (which, as we have seen, was not actually the case). He made a clear distinction between religion and metaphysics: "The esoteric unity of traditional forms . . . ," he wrote, "concerns only universal principles . . . [and] is only real for the very highest aspect of metaphysics."[99] This approach, as we will see, is very different from that of Schuon.

The explanation of why Vâlsan—and so also Vâlsan's followers—differed so much from other Traditionalist Sufis probably lies in Vâlsan's earliest experiences, especially his time with Petrache Lupu in Romania. Lupu's movement was, in Traditionalist terms, a clear instance of "counterinitiation" and evidently gave Vâlsan a lifelong aversion to anything that even smacked of the unorthodox. This explains his aversion to Schuon's approach, and his experience of Schuon—in the words again of his son Muhammad—"vaccinated" him against any temptation toward anything other than the strictest orthodoxy.

The fate of Vâlsan's following after his death, however, casts some doubt on the stability of his mixture of Traditionalism and Islam. As often happens with newly established Sufi orders in the Islamic world after the death of the founding shaykh, Vâlsan's following split into a number of groups. One was led by Roty until his own death, and others by other followers; one was later led by Vâlsan's second son, Muhammad. By the end of the twentieth century, three of these groups survived in various parts of France, and the leaders of all three had attached themselves and their followers to regular Sufi orders in the Arab world: one to a branch of the Alawiyya in Damascus, another to the largest Syrian order of the time (the branch of the Naqshbandiyya led by the Mufti of Damascus), and the third to a North African branch of the Darqawiyya.[100] In the study of one of these successors to Vâlsan, the walls are lined with books in Arabic and books by Western scholars of Islam. The works of Guénon are relegated to an inaccessible space behind a sofa.

Pallavicini's Ahmadiyya

Guénon and Traditionalism are much more important for the Ahmadiyya in Milan, though not to the extent of "Guénolatry." This most visible of all Traditionalist orders was established, like Vâlsan's Alawiyya, by a former follower of Schuon, Abd al-Wahid Pallavicini, an Italian.

Like Maridort, Pallavicini came of a wealthy family. He read Guénon in Italian translation as a young man during the Second World War, and after the war he contacted Evola (who was Guénon's Italian translator). Evola told him that his interests were more in power than in spirituality and referred him to Burckhardt. Pallavicini traveled to Lausanne and entered Schuon's Alawiyya in 1951.[101]

Little is known of Pallavicini's years as a Schuonian Alawi except that he traveled extensively in the East and eventually married a Japanese practitioner of Zen. Pallavicini himself later described these years as "the life of a vagabond." In the mid-1960s, however, Pallavicini left Schuon's order, which he had come to see as too remote from the real Orient and as "romanticized" Islam—evidently a reference to Schuon's passion for "staging." In later years Pallavicini also cited Schuon's earlier stance against Guénon on the question of the validity of the Christian sacraments as a reason for his break with Schuon—somewhat strangely, given Pallavicini's own later association with Christians, and also given the time elapsed between the original controversy and Pallavicini's taking sides in it. There are also suggestions that Pallavicini may have had personal reasons, which in no way reflect badly on him, for separating himself from Lausanne.[102]

Like Hartung, Pallavicini remained a Muslim and a Traditionalist after leaving the Alawiyya. He spent some years without a Sufi order of his own— but still searching. In 1971, while working as a piano player in Singapore, Pallavicini was told of Abd al-Rashid ibn Muhammad Said, the most prominent shaykh of that time in Singapore. He visited his *zawiya* and entered his Sufi order—the Ahmadiyya. This was an order of Arab origin; the family of Shaykh Abd al-Rashid, a Malay, had played an important part in spreading it. It has no connection at all with the controversial movement of the same name that originated in British India.[103]

Pallavicini spent some time in Singapore with the Ahmadiyya, more with one of Shaykh Abd al-Rashid's two *muqaddams,* who spoke fluent English, than with the shaykh himself, who spoke only Arabic and Malay (which Pallavicini did not know) and who was anyhow busy with many other concerns. Pallavicini would have received a good grounding in Sufism despite this lack of contact; the *muqaddam,* a Singaporean of Malay origin, was (although not interested in Traditionalism) well versed both in Sufism and in the dilemmas of modernity and multiculturalism—Singapore is a very modern place, and the Muslims there are a minority. Like Schuon before him, however, Pallavicini completed only the first stage of Sufi (or at least Ahmadi) training.

Only one problem marred this period: a dispute over the transcendent unity of religions, Schuon's version of Perennialism. This was the same characteristically Traditionalist doctrine that led to problems during Schuon's own stay at Mostaganem. Pallavicini refused to accept the standard Islamic position that his shaykh taught, even after the shaykh obtained a *fatwa* (the authoritative though not binding view of a senior scholar) from Al Azhar in Cairo, as close as Islam comes to a preeminent body.[104]

Despite this dispute, Shaykh Abd al-Rashid gave Pallavicini an *ijaza* to give the Ahmadiyya before Pallavicini left Singapore for Italy. The existence of this *ijaza* has since been questioned, but sources in the Ahmadiyya in Singapore and Malaysia confirm it. The same sources report that Shaykh Abd al-Rashid was later "very angry" with Pallavicini, but they cannot say why.[105] The cause may have been related to Pallavicini's Perennialism.

Pallavicini returned to Italy with no intention of founding an order of his own. This did not happen until the 1980s, and was an accidental consequence of Pallavicini's involvement in Islamo-Christian dialogue during the 1970s. This dialogue resulted from the Second Vatican Council of 1962-65, which recognized that the Holy Spirit might operate outside the structures of the Church and that all religions contained *semina Verbi* (seeds of the Word). The Vatican established a Secretariat for non-Christians, later the Secretariat for Ecumenical Activities, which approached the principal Islamic organization in Rome at that time, the Centro Culturale Islamico d'Italia. This had a grand-seeming council, composed of the ambassadors of various Islamic countries, but few active participants—sometimes no more than five or six persons attended the Friday prayer. Among them was Pallavicini, and given his excellent knowledge of Italian, of Christianity, and of European culture, it was Pallavicini who was asked to respond to the Vatican's overture.[106]

Pallavicini responded enthusiastically, seeing the possibility for a common front against what he later called "the desacralization of life, reduced to merely material well-being"[107]—that is, against modernity and materialism. And what better basis could there be for ecumenism than the theory of transcendent unity? The response of the Catholic Church was, however, disappointing. The hierarchy displayed no interest in discussing metaphysics with Pallavicini, and the Vatican soon stopped inviting him. The Milan diocese (Pallavicini had residences in both Rome and Milan) displayed no interest either and never responded to his proposal to construct a "little Jerusalem" on part of Pallavicini's Milan property. This structure was to be a living example of faith in a dark age, a *zawiya* built next to a Catholic chapel and perhaps a synagogue. One rabbi did attend one meeting, but the project was abandoned and replaced by a Centro Studi Metafisici "René Guénon," a metaphysical studies center to act as "a forum for fraternal exchange open to all who want to deepen their understanding of traditional metaphysical doctrines," Christian as well as Muslim.[108]

Though the Catholic hierarchy was not interested in Pallavicini, various Catholic organizations were. Pallavicini was frequently invited by the Catholic University to speak in Rome, and by groups such as the Catholic Association of Italian Workers, and he was published in such journals as *Sacro e Profano* [Sacred and Profane], the organ of a Catholic "friendship association" in Sicily.[109] A number of individual Catholics also attended meetings at Pallavicini's Metaphysical Studies Center. There they were given Guénon to read, and as a result some converted to Islam and joined the Ahmadiyya. In 1980 Pallavicini held the first Ahmadi *dhikr* ceremony in Milan.

By the mid-1990s the Milan Ahmadiyya had some 30 or 40 followers, nearly all in their late 20s or early 30s, most of them Italian but some French. All were of backgrounds similar to Pallavicini's—well educated, cultured people. These Ahmadis formed a tight community; some worked together in businesses established by Pallavicini, including a design studio and a small publishing house. Those living in Milan met every week, and those from outside Milan every month, for activities that symbolized the dual nature of the Ahmadiyya as Sufi and Traditionalist. Every Friday the Ahmadis prayed the Friday Prayer together at noon and then went for lunch at a neighborhood pizzeria, the owner of which in 2000 described them to a newspaper reporter as "great guys [brava gente] and excellent customers."[110] In the evening they met for "traditional discussions," that is, discussions of Traditionalism. These were followed immediately by a *dhikr* ceremony, which was much the same as the *dhikr* held by the Ahmadiyya in Singapore.[111]

Though Traditionalist, the Ahmadiyya was also Muslim. Pallavicini avoided Schuon's universalism or anything suggesting syncretism, though less scrupulously than Vâlsan, and he and his followers carefully observed the Sharia. Except in their Perennialism, the Ahmadiyya is not known to have departed in any way from the Islam that is found in the Islamic world.[112] Pallavicini, like Vâlsan but unlike Schuon or even Guénon himself, has performed the Hajj pilgrimage to Mecca, no less than three times.[113]

Though Muslim, the Ahmadiyya remained Traditionalist—hoping for the recovery of traditional esotericism by Catholicism, and in some cases appearing to be Muslim more because of Traditionalism than because they regarded Islam as the true religion of mankind. The Ahmadiyya is also Traditionalist in that it proselytizes for Traditionalism much more than for Islam. In Pallavicini's lectures, it is not the Koran that is appealed to as the ultimate authority, but Guénon.[114]

A considerable amount of Ahmadis' time and energy is spent in a more direct type of proselytization than found anywhere else in the Traditionalist movement. Pallavicini's followers make no secret of their Islam—Pallavicini himself has a large beard and dresses imposingly in a *gallabiyya* robe—and they attend almost every forum where they might hope for an audience, from Catholic organizations to academic conferences, from public lectures where they may respond to requests for questions from the floor by giving Traditionalist speeches to—at least on one occasion—a fashionable Milan disco.[115]

The effects of these activities are mixed. Some Italian academics, for example, wish that they could have conferences without Traditionalist interruptions.[116] Much more effective in spreading the Traditionalist message have been Pallavicini's frequent appearances in the Italian press. These started in 1986, when Pallavicini attended a Day of Prayer for Peace in Assisi—organized by Pope John Paul II—in one of several Islamic delegations. The Assisi meeting started as a meeting of the twelve religions that were invited, but in the face of mounting criticism, the Pope shifted the emphasis onto peace rather than ecumenism.[117] Despite this change, Pallavicini issued to the press a statement on the meeting of religions and was interviewed by several Italian newspapers.

The Italian press liked Pallavicini. His tone was conciliatory, especially toward Catholicism. He spoke well, and many appreciated what *Il Giornale* called his "spiritually and intellectually very elevated" views.[118] An Italian running a Sufi order was also newsworthy, though the *Corriere della Sera*, one of the country's leading serious newspapers, went too far in describing him as leader of "one of the most important *sufi* brotherhoods."[119] As the interest of the Italian public in Islam mounted in the early 1990s in response to the Gulf War and to the first arrival in Italy of significant numbers of immigrants from Islamic countries, interest in Pallavicini increased further. In 1991 and 1992 Pallavicini was the single most interviewed Muslim in Italy.[120]

The arrival of large numbers of Muslim immigrants in Italy that produced the public interest in Islam from which Pallavicini benefited was also the source of his first major difficulties. When he started his Islamo-Christian dialogue in the 1970s, there was no significant Muslim community in Italy. In the 1990s there was, and many of its leaders objected strongly to what Pallavicini was saying, and to Pallavicini himself. These leaders were not averse to Pallavicini as an Italian—some of them were also Italian converts to Islam. Pallavicini's offenses, in their eyes, were to present Sufism as Islam and to present Traditionalism as Islam. He was guilty on both counts. From a historical point of view, he was quite justified in his presentation of Sufism: though many contemporary Muslims, the product of Salafi or Wahhabi educations, may reject Sufism as un-Islamic, it cannot be disputed that for at least a thousand years it was an integral part of Islam. From any point of view but a Traditionalist one, however, Pallavicini's presentation of Traditionalist positions as Islam, and most important, Perennialist ones, cannot be regarded as accurate.

As early as 1986 Pallavicini was accused in print of "filling the gaps in [his knowledge of Islamic] doctrine with his own personal theories, the pronouncing of which is a clear form of *kufr* (apostasy)."[121] By the 1990s hostility toward Pallavicini became so pronounced that he was once physically ejected from Milan's most important Islamic center, and on another occasion a demonstration was organized outside a bookshop in Rome where he was speaking.[122]

Pallavicini responded in kind, accusing the converts among his opponents of "inciting revolt and terrorism . . . [and] seem[ing] to want to cut off their Christian past, perhaps not so much because it was Christian as because it was their past."[123] It was in fact two converts who did most damage to Pallavicini, circulating a newsletter that reproduced a letter from Shaykh Abd al-Rashid denying that Pallavicini had received an *ijaza* from him.[124] This letter was almost certainly a forgery,[125] but it has received wide credence nevertheless.

At the height of this animosity, in 1992, Pallavicini wrote: "If in the churches they have almost given up talking of God and speak instead of peace, in the mosques they only talk of war. On the one hand, the Muslims seem to have forgotten even their Confession of Faith, which affirms that 'there is no god save God' to idolize their own religion, almost reaching the point of saying that there is no god, and no truth, save in Islam."[126] This statement encapsulates the problem neatly. On the one hand, there is no "almost" about it: nearly all non-Traditionalist Muslims would assert unhesitatingly that there was no proper access to God, and no final truth, except in Islam. On the other hand, there was a real dispute between Pallavicini and his opponents over the place of war in Islam. Pallavicini had for years been at pains to present Islam to Italians as a religion, not a warlike political creed. Many of his opponents, however, were radical Islamists, for whom it was little more than a lie to suggest that Islam could possibly exclude the political.

Relations between Pallavicini and the wider Muslim community in Italy became very bad, but two of his followers with better diplomatic skills, his son Yahya and a French astrophysicist and polymath, Bruno Guiderdoni, fared better. Both came to enjoy reasonable relations with the wider Muslim community in Europe and were successful in the difficult task of presenting Islam to the Western public in a favorable light.[127] Guiderdoni for many years even presented French television's single Islamic program, "Connaître l'Islam," and in the 1990s became increasingly prominent as a speaker on Islam, welcomed by both Muslims and non-Muslims, in France and abroad.

Despite his difficulties with other Muslims in Italy, Pallavicini enjoyed good relations with official Muslim organizations abroad and was routinely invited to state-sponsored Islamic conferences, introduced to government ministers, and so on.[128] Partly in response to these conflicts and contacts, some of Pallavicini's objectives began to change during the 1990s. Abandoning Islamo-Christian dialogue at any official level, Pallavicini concentrated more on Islam, replacing the project for building a "little Jerusalem" with a project for building a mosque on the plot of land he owned in Milan. The Center for Metaphysical Studies became the Italian Association for Information on Islam, and finally, in 1997, the Comunità Religiosa Islamica (Islamic Religious Community), or CoReIs.

CoReIs entered the overcrowded competition to sign an *intesa* (agreement) with the Italian Republic. To balance the concordat between Italy and the Vatican, the republic had embarked on a series of lesser agreements with other religious groups, granting various privileges, including state funding for certain purposes. It was clear who should negotiate for and benefit from the *intesa* for Judaism, for example, and also for various hierarchically organized non-Catholic Christian churches, but far less clear who could claim to represent Islam. Although Muslims can and do organize themselves in various ways for various purposes, Islam as a religion has absolutely no organizational structure. Therefore, almost every Islamic organization in Italy wanted to sign an *intesa*, leading many observers to speculate that no *intesa* with Islam would ever be signed. That Pallavicini, directly representing no more than a few dozen individuals, should hope to represent Islam to the Italian Republic struck many as extraordinary. Pallavicini's logic was that CoReIs alone could claim to represent purely Italian Islam, as well as Islam as a religion rather than as a political ideology.[129] It was the mosque project which had replaced the "little Jerusalem" project that returned Pallavicini to national prominence in 2001. Pallavicini applied for the municipal permits required to change the use of his plot of land to "mosque." An uproar resulted. Although by then there were thousands of what were in effect mosques scattered all over Italy, all but one were officially designated as something else—usually cultural centers. The single exception was the highly official Rome Mosque, planned since 1963 and finally inaugurated in 1995. Pallavicini thus seemed to be applying for permission to build *the* Milan mosque, the second in the country. His application received much publicity and unleashed anti-immigrant feeling. "Yes to freedom of religion," read one banner in a street demonstration, "no to ghettoization of the quarter!"[130] That Pallavicini and the Ahmadiyya, as Italians, were hardly able to turn their quarter of Milan into an immigrant ghetto either escaped the demonstrators or did not concern them. The *Corriere della Sera* did remark that such a threat hardly seemed to be presented by "these gentlemen in jackets and ties, with the appearance of lawyers or executives."[131] But the battle lines were drawn. The right wing Lega Nord party organized a "referendum" against the mosque, collecting votes outside churches on a Sunday. The cardinal archbishop of Milan, who had failed to respond to Pallavicini's overtures in the days of Islamo-Christian dialogue, signed an Appeal to the City calling for tolerance. The Lega Nord denied having organized the picket of a previously unknown "Citizen's Front" outside the Ahmadi *zawiya*. Riot police arrived to separate them from a counter-picket organized by an anarchist group. Finally, Pallavicini won the necessary vote in the city council, and the controversy and the pickets vanished, at least for a while.[132] It is not clear at the time of writing, however, that Pallavicini has managed to secure the necessary funding for building his mosque.

Masonic Traditionalism

For the sake of completeness, I will briefly review the various Traditionalist lodges that, like the Sufi orders just considered, proceeded independently after Guénon's death. The earliest of these, the Grande Triade, was still operating at the end of the twentieth century under a Traditionalist venerable master (a nuclear physicist) and with Traditionalist members, but it had long ceased to be at the forefront of attempts to restore tradition to the West.

When the death of Guénon removed a stabilizing influence, the other early Traditionalist lodge, the Trois Anneaux, collapsed in 1953 as Tourniac (Catholic) and Reyor (Muslim) had a falling out. This marked the end of Reyor's participation in Masonry, but Tourniac continued as the major figure in Traditionalist Masonry, bringing it closer to the heart of the Grand National Lodge of France. The Grand National Lodge of France was a third Obedience (distinct from the French Grand Lodge) established in 1918 by Masons who left the Grand Orient, and it required belief in the Grand Architect of the Universe. It was a smaller body than either of the other two: unlike them, it was officially recognized by the English Grand Lodge.

Tourniac occupied various official positions in the Grand National Lodge of France beginning in 1960, becoming in 1977 grand prior, an official junior only to the grand master.[133] Part of the authority he had in these years derived from his known association with Guénon in the 1940s; by extension, his Traditionalism gave more prominence to Traditionalism in general, as did his books.[134] He also revived the Trois Anneaux under another name in the mid 1970s,[135] this time with only Christian and Jewish members—Tourniac was especially interested in Judeo-Christian concordance. By the end of the twentieth century this "wild" lodge had given rise to several other Traditionalist lodges in various parts of France,[136] answering to Tourniac as a variety of grand master (though the term was not used). An unidentified Traditionalist Mason succeeded him on his death.

In addition to these activities, Tourniac was involved in an ambitious Traditionalist project to restore good relations between Masonry and the Catholic Church. This project was principally the work of a Jesuit priest, Michel Riquet, and of Jean Baylot, who was a Mason, a parliamentary deputy, and the Paris chief of police. Both were convinced—on partly but not exclusively Traditionalist grounds—of the complementarity of Catholic exoteric practice and Masonic esoteric practice, as was Tourniac.[137] Their activities to this end were reflected in both publications and organizations. All three wrote books and articles arguing for the compatibility of Masonry and Catholicism,[138] and in the late 1960s or early 1970s Riquet and Baylot together established the Fraternité d'Abraham (Fraternity of Abraham)[139] as a prototype for Catholic-Masonic cooperation—not a lodge but a *commanderie* (command—the term used for the principal divisions of Medieval orders such as the Knights of Malta) under Masonic auspices.

It is not known what part these activities played in the closest the Catholic Church has yet come to a reconciliation with Masonry, a private letter issued by Cardinal Fanjo Seper, prefect of the Congregation for the Doctrine of the Faith, to the effect that it was permissible for a Catholic to belong to a lodge under the Grand National Lodge of France, the Obedience to which Tourniac and Baylot belonged. This ruling was overturned after 1983, however, by a subsequent ruling from a later prefect, Cardinal Ratzinger.[140]

The most lasting impact of this group of Traditionalist Masons was perhaps to achieve rapprochement between Traditionalist Masonry and French academia. In 1964 Baylot established a research lodge named after the early thirteenth-century architect Villard de Honnecourt (a research lodge, as its title suggests, engages not in ritual but in research), which held lectures and published a scholarly journal devoted to Masonic and Traditionalist questions. The keynote speaker at its opening meeting was Mircea Eliade, and its journal has since achieved general respect. In addition to publishing many articles by Tourniac, it also publishes the work of a number of French religious studies scholars with Traditionalist interests, some of whom are themselves Masons.[141]

Traditionalist Masonry continues to flourish. A further Traditionalist lodge under the French Grand Lodge was established in the 1990s, the Règle d'Abraham (Rule of Abraham), dedicated not only to ends similar to those of Tourniac, Baylot, and Riquet, but to understanding among the three Abrahamic religions (not just Judaism and Christianity but also Islam), based especially on the work of Ibn al-Arabi.[142] The Masonic expression of Traditionalism is notably different from all other expressions of Traditionalism in operating with the full blessing of the relevant authorities. This is true perhaps because Masonry is closer than any other expression of Traditionalism to the milieu in which Traditionalism had its origins.

PART III

Traditionalism at Large

7

The Maryamiyya

After Guénon's death in 1951, Schuon's Alawiyya (which changed its name during the 1960s to "Maryamiyya" for reasons that will be explained later) developed independently of the rest of the Traditionalist movement.

For his followers, Schuon had replaced Guénon as the father of Traditionalism. While a few older Maryamis such as Lings would never forget Guénon, for most of those who will now be discussed Guénon was a remote figure. Schuon himself soon began to minimize his own debt to Guénon, crediting him with little more than his understanding of Vedanta and of metaphysics. Guénon, he said, was "a mathematician, a Freemason and an occultist," which was not enough.[1]

Two tendencies emerged from the 1960s to the 1990s. On the one hand, the Maryamiyya—as I will now call it—and Schuon's non-Muslim following grew in size and importance, exceeding in both respects all the other Traditionalist orders considered so far. On the other hand, Schuon's own universalism also developed, as did his ideas about his own function. Developments in Schuon's views were sooner or later reflected in changes in the group he led, but there was always a time lag, and some Maryamis did not become aware of some developments until the very end.

Schuon's following soon developed into the premier Traditionalist group. The majority of those Westerners whose reading of Traditionalist works inspired them to embark on a personal spiritual voyage, and who were in search of an orthodox master in a valid initiatic spiritual tradition, turned to Schuon for guidance. They did so partly because of the lack of easily available alternatives (at least outside Paris, Turin, and Milan) and partly because of Schuon's increasingly central position in the networks of Traditionalist writers and journals. To some extent this trend was also due to the recruiting of carefully identified individuals who might be suitable members of the elite.

The Virgin Mary

Schuon's "unhappy love" for Madeleine came to an end in Lausanne in 1943, or rather was transformed into "the cosmic love of the beloved." Five years later, at the somewhat advanced age of 42, Schuon married for the first time. His wife, Catherine Feer, then aged 25, was the follower to whom he had given *Black Elk Speaks* in 1948. According to an unconfirmed account, Schuon decided to marry her after receiving a sign, just as he had become Muslim in Paris after a sign.

The daughter of a diplomat, who had grown up mostly in Swiss embassies in Argentina and Algeria, Catherine Schuon had larger ideas than her husband. In the words of a sympathetic observer, "an artist by temperament and a painstaking organizer, she helped give the growing community [in Lausanne] a minimum of basic rules."[2] In the view of others, who later clearly resented both her influence and her activities, she was overly ambitious, both for herself and for her husband, and her "organization" of the community was most unwelcome. One of her first actions was to organize Schuon's followers to support their shaykh in better style, moving him and her first to a larger apartment and then, in 1953, installing him in a decent house with a proper *zawiya*. These were built by general subscription in the pleasant commune of Pully, just outside Lausanne.[3] In addition to taking charge of the collection of alms (*zakat*), she soon began to involve herself in aspects of Schuon's followers' lives that many felt were beyond her competence, however artistic her temperament.[4] Soon after the arrival in Lausanne of Whitall Perry (the wealthy American who had attended Guénon's funeral along with Lings) and Perry's wife, Catherine Schuon suggested that the Perrys buy and build on a plot adjoining her own house, and she arranged for Perry to act as Schuon's chauffeur, in his own words a "privilege" which he enjoyed for 25 years.[5]

In addition to organizing Schuon's entourage in this way, Catherine Schuon joined her husband in an activity that was to become increasingly significant: painting. After his marriage, Schuon began to paint seriously, abandoning for some years the writing of poetry. One of his first paintings was of two Native Americans, one of whom was naked, symbolizing the exoteric (clothed) and the esoteric (naked).[6]

Schuon's interest in Native American spirituality continued to grow, and in 1959 the Schuons visited America for the first time, at the invitation of

Thomas Yellowtail, a Native American whom they had first met in Paris in 1953 and who would become prominent. They went first to the Sioux reservation at Pine Ridge, South Dakota, once the home of Black Elk, and then to Sheridan, Montana, where Yellowtail lived—taking with them a Schuon painting of the White Buffalo Woman, a prominent figure from Lakota myth.[7] One of Frithjof Schuon's purposes in making this visit was to help save the Native American tradition from modernity.[8] As it happened, however, Native American religion had more impact on Frithjof Schuon than the other way round.[9]

Schuon had first discovered the divine qualities of nature almost ten years before, when shortly after his marriage his wife took him to the Swiss mountains. There he experienced a "liberation" he had previously felt only at the Alawi *zawiya* at Mostaganem; in a borrowed mountain log cabin he learned to enjoy "days totally close to nature and in some ways medieval days."[10] Like the mountains of Switzerland, the landscape around Sheridan, Wyoming, reminded Schuon of Mostaganem."[11] What Mostaganem, the Swiss mountains, and the plains of Wyoming all have in common, of course, is that the modern world is far away.

In addition to meeting many Native Americans, the Schuons participated in a number of Native American dances, initially as spectators but becoming increasingly engaged. The highlight of their trip was witnessing the Sun Dance at Fort Hall, Idaho. The Sun Dance is the crowning rite of the Oglala Sioux and the Shoshone-Crow, a complex three- or four-day-long ceremony performed around a "sacred tree" erected for the purpose, during which the participants aim to offer expiation through sacrifice and in a sense unite themselves with the Greater Sacred (sometimes controversially glossed as "God"). Not only do the participants fast for one or more days, but they also offer other forms of ordeal, such as staring at the sun during sunrise or cutting a strip of flesh from the upper arm.[12] For Schuon, the opening ceremonies of the Sun Dance were extraordinarily moving, "unification with the One."[13] On the second day he and his wife fasted with the participants, though they otherwise remained spectators. On a later visit to the (deserted) Sun Dance Place, Catherine Schuon danced there alone.[14]

Before the Schuons returned to Switzerland, they were adopted into the Sioux, receiving the names of Wicahpi Wiyakpa (Bright Star) and Wowan Winyan (Artist Woman). For Schuon, the experience was decisive, and, as he wrote later, it allowed him to recover from the "spiritual wounds of [his] youth." The Schuons returned to America in 1963 for a similar, three-month-long visit.[15]

Despite this experience, by 1965 Schuon had fallen into a state of depression, exacerbated by asthma.[16] In this state he received another vision, the most dramatic yet: a visitation from the Virgin Mary. On a boat from Europe to Tangier, Morocco, in 1965, Schuon was sitting alone in his cabin: "Suddenly I was overcome by Divine mercy in a special way. It came to me internally in a female form that I cannot describe, and from it I knew that it was the Holy

Virgin." As a result, Schuon "felt better and found [him]self in an ecstasy of love and joy."[17]

Frithjof Schuon initially had doubts. On the road from Tangier to Tetuan he began to return to his earlier state, and when he and his party stopped for the night in a hotel in Tetuan he felt too weak to go out with the others. Alone in his hotel room, however, the state produced by his vision returned, lasting until the party reached their destination, Fez. In Fez he began to worry and doubt again, but "in the night there came over me again that heavenly comfort that gushed from the essential feminine [Urweibliche]," and this time the state lasted until his return to Switzerland.[18]

These experiences brought together the two themes of 1942–43: the "cosmic love of the beloved . . . as in mother-love" that Schuon had experienced on seeing Madeleine's baby, and the attraction to the Virgin that he had felt on seeing a statuette of her in a Lausanne shop window. Schuon had in fact been occasionally aware of the Virgin's presence between 1942 and 1965, first during the break with Guénon in about 1949, when he "felt her blessing," and once while doing *dhikr* at home on his own in about 1953. On that second occasion he had sensed a "powerful presence" that he immediately identified with the Virgin.[19]

Schuon was not sure at first how to interpret his experiences of 1965. The first question was whether they amounted to a true or a false vision. A true vision, Schuon decided, could be distinguished from a false one by the beneficial effect it had on its recipient, and this vision had the beneficial effect of freeing him from the love of books, newspapers, and the theater, in which he found he could no longer lose himself.[20] Schuon did not consider, in this context, another effect of his vision: the "almost irresistible need to be naked like her baby." For some time thereafter, Schuon took off his clothes whenever he was at home alone.[21]

Once Schuon decided that his experiences were a true vision, the next question was how to interpret them. His final conclusion was that the vision marked the coming of "a special relationship with Heaven." The exact nature of this special relationship is not made clear, but since the Virgin Mary is "the incarnation of Divine mercy and at the same time of the Religio Perennis,"[22] it seems clear that Schuon took it as a change in his role from being shaykh of the Alawiyya (the position given him in his earlier vision of 1937) to a more universal role, above and beyond Islam.

Before I consider the consequences of this conclusion for the Maryamis, I will briefly consider an even more dramatic vision of the Virgin Mary that Schuon had the following year, 1966, also in Morocco. Schuon imagined his statuette of the Virgin, which "began to quiver and stir slightly, and I knew, as fear seized me and at the same time love overwhelmed me: this is no longer a dream, this is reality." The Virgin appeared, Schuon wrote, "but it is not fitting for me to say any more."[23] The reason Schuon did not feel it fitting to say more in writing was, according to numerous reports, that the Virgin Mary was naked. ⎤ ʸᵉˢ!

Schuon's nakedness and the possible nakedness of the Virgin have caused some non-Maryamis to ascribe a Satanic origin to these visions, but Schuon himself clearly excluded such an explanation—though not immediately, since he did ask himself whether his 1965 vision was a true one or not. Mainstream Islam tends to see nakedness in exclusively negative terms, but Christian images of the Virgin often show a naked breast. Perennialists are usually familiar with Hinduism, in which nakedness is an established element of certain religious practices. Henri Hartung's Ramana Maharshi, for example, went naked from the age of 17, though not entirely so—he wore a *kaupina*, a narrow band that conceals the genitals.[24]

The main consequence of these visions for Schuon seems to have been that he decided he had a universal mission, since it was at about this point that the emphasis shifted from the Maryamiyya to perennial religion in the widest sense. Schuon also decided that he had a special relationship with the Virgin,[25] as well as with God. His painting changed, and from this point he and his wife concentrated on the figure of the Virgin Mary. Frithjof Schuon's images of the Virgin Mary sometimes showed her naked or partially naked, with visible breasts, "a reference," it was explained, "to the unveiling of truth in the sense of gnosis, and to liberating mercy."[26] Schuon saw his earlier pictures of the White Buffalo Woman as a "presentiment" of these pictures of the Virgin Mary,[27] a significant development—Schuon had connected his experiences in America in 1959 with his experiences in Morocco in 1965. His adoption by the Sioux came to be seen as "join[ing him] to the last link [of the initiatic chain] of a genuinely primordial religion,"[28] though he never referred to it as "initiation" but rather as "adoption."[29] By the late 1960s, then, Schuon was a Traditionalist with two esoteric initiations. He was a Muslim with a Sufi initiation from the Alawiyya, appointed shaykh of a Sufi order in a vision, but he was also a universalist with a primordial initiation from the Sioux, appointed to a universal mission by the Virgin Mary in another vision. That primordial mission would from then on gradually replace Schuon's original role as a Sufi shaykh.

The immediate result of all this for Schuon's followers was not so dramatic as the later consequences would be. For many years Schuon continued to present an essentially Islamic face to the world. All that happened in the 1960s was that the name of his order was changed, as was some of its daily practice. A short prayer to the Virgin was added to the daily litany, and Schuon's paintings were added to the Six Themes as a very informal focus for the meditation of his followers.[30] The date of this second change is not certain, but the late 1960s seems the likely period.

The name of the order was changed to "Alawiyya Maryamiyya," generally shortened to "Maryamiyya," the adjectival form of Maryam, which is the Arabic form of Mary. It does not seem likely that many Maryamis knew the full details of the visions that led to these changes. The new focus on Maryam was justified primarily in terms of its symbolism—the Virgin Mary was a figure in whom were united the three monotheistic religions, as "a Jewish princess of the house of David," "mother of the founder of Christianity," who "occupies, in Islam, the summit of the hierarchy of women." The Virgin Mary "loves the three religions, and religion in general, as do we [Maryamis]."[31] Schuon's devotion to the Virgin Mary was not syncretism, explained one Traditionalist, since "Mary is often venerated in Islam with much fervor, as one can see at Ephesus," where "Muslims as well as Christians" pray at a shrine called the Meryemana Evi (the House of Mary).[32] The point is not so much whether these explanations are justified (which, from an Islamic standpoint, they are not),[33] but that this is how many Maryamis justified to themselves their emphasis on the Virgin Mary.

The use of Schuon's paintings as an informal focus for meditation was explained in part as follows: "No one is forced to be interested in them," wrote a senior Maryami in the 1980s, "but everybody is obliged to respect them since they emanate from the Shaykh and reflect aspects of his personality and experience."[34] That Schuon "was always convinced that everything he did had a sacral character," in the words of one of his earliest followers, incidentally explains the remarkable frankness of his *Erinnerungen und Betrachtungen*: details that seem to us private and very human evidently seemed to him to be of more than merely personal significance.

At about this time, Schuon's following began to formulate its own canonical texts. These were short compositions of a page or two by Schuon, the earliest of which dated from the 1930s but most of which were written after 1951, addressing a wide variety of potential spiritual problems or issues, later collected into a *Livre des Clefs* [Book of Keys].[35] These were numbered for ease of reference, so that a Maryami might advise a junior colleague to "read text number 258." Though they followed Islamic practice in starting with "In the name of God the merciful, the compassionate," these texts usually dealt with the problem at hand in Traditionalist much more than in Islamic terms and drew on Hindu sources as much as the Koran and *hadith*. The central texts of Schuon's following, then, were Traditionalist rather than Islamic.[36]

A further relaxation of the Sharia also occurred at this time. When in 1965 Schuon took a second wife (allowed by the Sharia, if not by Swiss law), the marriage was arranged on Traditionalist rather than Islamic lines. The new wife, a follower of Schuon, was already married to another of his followers. While the Sharia would require her to divorce her first husband and then wait some months before remarrying, Schuon allowed her to remain married to and live with her original husband and to marry him [Schuon] "vertically." The distinction between the vertical (that which links people to God) and the horizontal (that which is purely of this world) derives not from the Sharia but from

Western metaphysics and was used in Guénon's *Symbolisme de la croix*. Schuon's "vertical marriage"—referred to by some later followers as a "spiritual marriage"—was, in the words of Catherine Schuon, an "arrangement [that] satisfied Western Law and social necessity . . . [and was] prefaced by unmistakable celestial signs allowing and blessing" it. It was also endorsed—reluctantly—by Burckhardt and Lings.[37]

The existence of this "marriage," which it would be impossible to justify in purely Islamic terms, did not become widely known until the late 1980s. Burckhardt is said to have been deeply troubled by it as well as by similar episodes involving women,[38] but to have concluded after some internal struggle that his duty of loyalty to his shaykh came before all else. Sufism in general stresses absolute loyalty to one's shaykh and strongly discourages judging him. There is, for example, a well-known story of a shaykh abandoned by his faithless followers after they saw him kissing a strange woman; the followers subsequently discovered, to their embarrassment, that the woman was their shaykh's younger sister.

In 1957 Burckhardt reminded another Maryami that the followers of a shaykh should judge their master not by their understanding of their master's actions but by his teachings and method.

> It is in trusting to that [teachings and method] that we "obligate" God toward us: God does not deceive us; He does not require us to analyze the personal actions of the master. . . . If a master teaches errors or a method contrary to the Revelation, leave him, but if he appears to commit immoral actions, distrust your own distrust. . . . A spiritual master is like a mirror that shows us our true mature; a fault of *niyah*—of inner orientation—is enough for us to project our faults onto it, and the devil will hurry to make us attribute them to the mirror.[39]

The Imperial Iranian Academy of Philosophy

It was at the time the Maryamiyya was beginning to move away from Islam that it acquired its first and most important follower who was Muslim by birth, Seyyed Hossein Nasr, an Iranian, later a central figure in the history of Traditionalism. Nasr's nationality is significant, since in various ways Iran is closer to the West than is the Arab world, and during the late nineteenth and early twentieth centuries sections of the Iranian elite had become increasingly Westernized. Nasr was born into this elite: he was a Sayyid, a descendant of the Prophet, and his father (Dr. Wali Allah Nasr) was a national political and intellectual figure, a former dean of the Faculty of Humanities at Tehran University, and also at one point the Iranian minister of education.[40]

Much of the young Nasr's intellectual universe was Western. His father's library contained Montesquieu and Voltaire as well as Persian classics, and he was sent to high school in New Jersey at the age of 12, for reasons that are not entirely clear.[41] From New Jersey he proceeded to the Massachusetts Institute of Technology, majoring in geology and geophysics. In his second year at MIT Nasr experienced what he later described as "a full-blown spiritual and intellectual crisis" as he began to feel the limitations of natural science as an explanation of reality. With his faith in physics eroded by lectures on the Manhattan Project by Robert Oppenheimer (who quoted from Hindu texts) and a discussion with Bertrand Russell, Nasr turned to philosophy, though he completed his degree in science. Giorgio de Santillana, the philosopher of science who was then teaching at MIT, introduced Nasr to a wide range of influences, from Plotinus to Jacques Maritain (once Guénon's sponsor at the Catholic Institute in Paris), as well as Guénon himself. Nasr also met some former students of Coomaraswamy, who introduced him to Coomaraswamy's widow, and in Coomaraswamy's library Nasr found the early works of Schuon. Guénon, Schuon, and Burckhardt "settled the crisis." "Henceforth I knew with certitude," wrote Nasr many years later, "that there was such a thing as the Truth and that it could be attained through knowledge gained by means of the heart-intellect and also through revelation."[42]

Though Nasr was Muslim by birth, his readings of the Traditionalist awakened an interest in Hinduism rather than in Islam,[43] just as they had for Schuon and many others who were born Christian. The Islamic works of Burckhardt and Schuon, however, redirected this interest:

> The writings of Sufi masters and Islamic philosophers began to regain the profoundest meaning for me. . . . But this newly gained meaning was no longer simple imitation or repetition of things inherited. It was based upon personal rediscovery after long search and one might add suffering. . . . Islamic wisdom became a most intense living reality, not because I had happened to be born and educated as a Muslim, but because I had been guided by the grace of Heaven to the eternal sophia [approximately, Perennial Philosophy] of which Islamic wisdom is one of the most universal and vital embodiments.[44]

Nasr, though closer to the religion to which he was to devote his career than Coomaraswamy had been to his, approached it—again like Coomaraswamy—from an essentially Western and Traditionalist perspective. Unlike Coomaraswamy, he also devoted himself to the practice of that religion. His search for initiation ended when he joined the Maryamiyya, probably on a visit to Morocco in 1957.[45]

Traditionalism turned Nasr's interests from natural science to the philosophy of science and to what is sometimes called "Islamic philosophy." This is a school of intellectual esotericism that is especially strong in Nasr's native Iran and is represented most famously by Sadra al-Din Muhammad Shirazi (seventeenth century) and Shihab al-Din Yahya Suhrawardi (twelfth century).[46] Nasr completed a Ph.D. on the philosophy of science at Harvard[47] and studied in Iran under the two leading teachers of Islamic philosophy there, Muhammad Husayn Tabataba'i and Abu'l-Hasan Raf'i Qazwini,[48] He then embarked on a career devoted to Islamic science and Islamic philosophy, understood in an essentially but not explicitly Traditionalist framework.

Nasr's career falls into two halves, the first at Tehran University until the Islamic Revolution of 1979, discussed later, and the second in America after the Revolution. During both halves he was influential through his writings, though his most important books were written in Iran (in English). Some of these books are addressed to a general audience—most notably *Ideals and Realities of Islam, The Encounter of Man and Nature: The Spiritual Crisis of Modern Man*, and *Sufi Essays*[49]—and may be described as Islamic Traditionalism; others are addressed to more specialized audiences and deal with the work of Islamic philosophers and with the relationship between Islam and science.[50] Nearly all have been translated into various languages, both Western and Islamic—especially Persian, Turkish, and Malay.

During the Iranian half of his career, Nasr taught philosophy of science and Islamic philosophy at Tehran University and also set up the most important Traditionalist institution of the twentieth century, the Anjoman-e Shahanshahi-ye Falsafahi-e Iran (Imperial Iranian Academy of Philosophy). Established in 1974, this was was an independent body under a board headed by the academy's patron, the Empress Farah, with whom Nasr enjoyed good relations. It was also generously financed by the imperial Iranian court.[51] It was to be a school for the study and spread of the traditional sciences, especially Islamic philosophy, and for the training of a small elite to carry this work forward in other institutions, both in and beyond Iran. The idea was to give about ten scholarships at a time to outstanding graduate students, who after a minimum of three years at the academy would go on to teach at universities in Iran and abroad. Some would already have Ph.D.s, and some might prepare Ph.D.theses for submission to universities abroad while at the academy (the academy itself did not award any sort of degree).[52]

As Nasr announced in the first issue of the academy's journal, published in Persian and in English under the titles *Javidan Kherad* and *Sophia Perennis*:

> The goals of the Academy are the revival of the traditional intellectual life of Islamic Persia; the publication of texts and studies pertaining to both Islamic and pre-Islamic Persia; making the intellectual treasures of Persia in the fields of philosophy, mysticism and the like known to the outside world; making possible extensive research in comparative philosophy; making Persians aware of the in-

tellectual traditions of other civilizations in both East and West; encouraging intellectual confrontation with the modern world; and
finally, discussing from the point of view of tradition various problems facing modern man.[53]

The reference to pre-Islamic Persia was probably included for the benefit of
Nasr's imperial sponsors: the shah especially was far more interested in Iran's
pre-Islamic than its Islamic past.[54] So far as is known, the academy never
concerned itself with pre-Islamic Persia.

The goals of the academy are a good example of how Traditionalism can
remain almost invisible. Read by anyone not familiar with Traditionalism, they
appear normal, but read in a more informed way, they are thoroughly Traditionalist and might almost have come out of an advertisement for a new series
of *Etudes traditionnelles*.

The academy established itself in a pleasant and substantial house which
it had received as a gift, on the same street as the French embassy. It decorated
this house in "traditional" style, with specially commissioned furniture from
Isfahan and liberal use of blue tiling, blue being chosen as the color of eternity.
The new building contained a library, a lecture hall, administrative offices, and
offices for visiting researchers and scholars. The original premises were soon
extended by the purchase of two adjoining buildings. Under imperial sponsorship, the academy had the financial resources to fill them with students and
teachers. Nasr himself taught at the academy once a week in "traditional" fashion, gathering the other members of the academy in a circle around him while
he read and commented on a text by an author such as Suhrawardi.

The academy's key personnel were in general Maryamis, belonging to an
Iranian branch of the Maryamiyya that was established and headed by Nasr,
or in some cases were Traditionalists following other Sufi orders,[55] but many
of its members were partisans of the classical school of Iranian mystical philosophy without any interest in Traditionalism. Two of its most eminent members were Ayatollah Jalal al-Din Ashtiyani and Professor Henry Corbin. Ashtiyani, who became the leading Iranian authority on Islamic philosophy,[56] knew
no languages other than Persian and Arabic, and while he had doubtless heard
of Guénon, he neither read him nor ever referred to him.[57]

Corbin, one of the most eminent French Orientalists of the century,[58] who
for some years spent every summer in Iran as the guest of the academy, was
likewise not a Traditionalist. In the same year that Nasr established his academy
in Tehran, Corbin established in Paris an International Center for Comparative
Spiritual Research, also known as the University of Saint John of Jerusalem;
its objectives were (in the words of Eliade, who was a participant) "the restoration of traditional sciences and studies in the West." Corbin's Center was to
provide "a forum for those advanced sciences, the abandonment and forgetting
of which is both the cause and the symptom of the crisis of our [Western]

civilization," and to "assure the vocation of spiritual chivalry." By "spiritual chivalry" (*chevalerie spirituelle*) Corbin meant, according to Eliade, "Western medieval myths, symbols, initiatory patterns, and secret organizations." Eliade thus sees the late Corbin as part of the "resurgence of a certain esoteric tradition among a number of European scholars and thinkers," a group in which he includes Coomaraswamy.[59]

Despite the similarities between Corbin's body and Traditionalism, however, Corbin and many of his associates were traveling a different path. Their path in places lay parallel to Traditionalism, but they were not themselves Traditionalists. In the view of a French scholar who had discussed these matters with him, Corbin was interested in the common aspects of Islam, Christianity, and Judaism, including esoteric aspects. He had no interest, however, in primordial religion, transcendent unity, or anything to do with Hinduism or any nonmonotheistic religion.[60] In Nasr's words, Corbin "had an aversion to the teachings of the main representatives of the traditionalist school, especially Guénon."[61]

Similarly, although all the carefully selected graduate students who studied at the academy were exposed to Traditionalism, not all became Traditionalists. Most came to occupy important positions, however. Among them were Gholam-Reza Aʿavani, brought by Nasr from the American University in Beirut, and an American, William Chittick.[62] Aʿavani became director of the academy after the Revolution, and Chittick went on to a distinguished career in American academia as the country's leading authority on Ibn al-Arabi. A friend of Nasr's who would never enter the academy's buildings, given its imperial title, Ayatollah Mortada Motahhari nevertheless sent to the Academy Haddad ʿAdil, who later became professor of philosophy at Tehran University and was an influential figure in the Islamic Republic. Corbin brought Pierre Lory, who was later to succeed him at the Sorbonne in Paris. Lory has read Traditionalist writers and retains an interest in their work and activities but is in no sense influenced by them in his own work or life.[63]

The importance of the academy outside Iran was that it gave Traditionalism a highly respectable base, which was sometimes used to invite distinguished visitors and sometimes used as a platform for participation in international events. The 1975 annual meeting of the Institut international de philosophie, for example, was held in Tehran on the theme of relations between religion, philosophy, and science,[64] a theme dear to Nasr and other Traditionalists. The English section of the academy's journal carried many Traditionalist articles, reaching a readership far wider than that of *Etudes traditionnelles*.

The academy was even more influential in Iran than abroad. In addition to introducing small numbers of Iranian intellectuals to Traditionalism, it contributed significantly to a general growth of interest in Islamic philosophy, which was also partly the result of Nasr's activities elsewhere. Traditionalism itself never reached far beyond restricted intellectual circles,[65] and probably was not intended to. Although the Persian section of *Javidan Kherad* contained a few overtly Traditionalist articles, including occasional translations of Schuon, and although Nasr arranged for the first publication of a work of Guénon in a non-Western language (the *Crise du monde moderne*, published in Persian by Tehran University Press in 1970), the main thrust of Nasr's activities in Persia was toward tradition, not Traditionalism. His purely Traditionalist activities were directed beyond Iran.[66]

It was not only at the Academy that Nasr worked for the recovery of tradition in Iran. He was appointed to Tehran University on his return from America to teach philosophy and the history of science, "philosophy" then being generally understood in the Faculty of Letters to mean Western philosophy—Tehran University had been established on standard American lines, both in its structure and in its syllabi. Nasr introduced the teaching of Islamic philosophy and successfully worked with his friend Ayatollah Motahhari (who introduced Islamic philosophy into the Department of Theology at about the same time) to spread understanding of, and interest in, Islamic philosophers both within and outside of Tehran University. Both Nasr and Motahhari also lectured on these subjects to more general audiences at the Husayniyya-ye Irshad, a celebrated institution of the time.

The academy added its own lectures to the activities of Nasr and Motahhari, and also edited and published many classic texts of Islamic philosophy. In its first year of existence it published fifteen books, including three works of bibliography and nine translations into English of Islamic philosophers;[67] the Persian section of the academy's journal, *Javidan Kherad*, also published many texts by, or articles about, Islamic philosophers.[68]

The ultimate impact of these activities was unexpected. In the unanimous opinion of Iranian philosophers and clergy interviewed for this book, Nasr and his academy made a definite contribution to the Islamic revolution. The growth of interest in Islamic philosophy contributed to the growth of interest in Islam among Iranian students, a significant factor in the revolution's success. Nasr's teacher Tabataba'i was explicit about the role of Islamic philosophy: he defended his teaching of it on the grounds that students came to him with their heads full of Western and Marxist ideas and that Islamic philosophy could be used to replace these ideas.[69] Further, Nasr's speeches for tradition and against modernity in practice joined the general stream of agitation for Islam and against Western decadence, and so by implication against the shah's regime.

Nasr's (and so Traditionalism's) contribution to the revolution was definitely in the second rank, far behind the contributions of Ayatollah Khomeini, Ayatollah Motahhari (the principal ideologue of Islamic sovereignty), and Ali Shariati, a sociologist whose highly original blend of Islam and socialism did more than anything else to turn Iran's students toward Islam in the years before the Revolution (and, incidentally, an appreciative occasional reader of Guénon, though in no way a Traditionalist).[70]

Nasr's contribution to the revolution was not only accidental, but furthermore one that he himself had no desire to make. Throughout his career in Iran he was a staunch supporter of the shah's regime. There were personal reasons for this position: he was connected with the court as his father had been before him, and his imperial connections certainly did not hinder his distinguished academic career. This included spells as dean of the Faculty of Letters at Tehran University and as vice-chancellor (in American terms, president) of Aryamehr University, a technical university in Tehran. More important, however, were reasons of principle: Nasr seems to have regarded monarchy as a traditional form of government, preferable, despite its many manifest failings, to what was likely to succeed it. He especially disliked Shariati's blend of Islam and socialism, which he saw as distinctly anti-traditional.[71]

As the revolution approached and Iranian life became increasingl politicized, Nasr's close association with the court became more and more of a liability. The case of a young Iranian who was later to become one of Iran's most prominent intellectuals, Abd al-Karim Soroush, serves as an example. Soroush had read Guénon while studying philosophy of science at the University of London under a pupil of Karl Popper, and on his return to Iran he was at first attracted by Nasr, but soon he concluded that Nasr's views were irrelevant to the issues of the time and that Nasr was even guilty of hypocrisy in identifying himself with both Islam and the court, in remaining silent while injustices were committed. Like many others, Soroush turned to Shariati, and later he suggested that the rise of Shariati marked the eclipse of Nasr.[72]

As individuals and organizations began to distance themselves from Nasr and from the Imperial Academy, some suggested to Nasr that he should distance himself from the increasingly detested shah and even change the name of the academy. Nasr refused, and if anything, his relations with the court became closer. When he translated Tabataba'i's *Shi'ite Islam* into English, Nasr omitted the condemnations of monarchy in the book,[73] and by 1977 he accepted appointment as Empress Farah's principal private secretary and began to undertake special diplomatic missions overseas.[74] Nasr remained true to his principles and allegiances. The revolution of 1979 caught him in London on his way to Japan and, on the telephoned advice of the empress, he remained abroad.[75] As of 2003 he had not returned to Iran, although, as we shall see, some figures associated with the revolution came to wish that he would.

To what extent the revolution advanced the objectives of Traditionalism and to what extent it represented the disguised triumph of a particular form of modernity is hard to determine, and certainly lies beyond the scope of this book.

8

America

Maryami Traditionalism flourished during the 1960s and 1970s not only in Iran but also in Europe and America. By 1979, Maryami *zawiyas* existed in several European countries (three in Switzerland, at least two in France, and at least one in England), in at least one Latin American country (Argentina), and also in America.[1] There were also *zawiyas* in a number of places in the Islamic world. In addition to these, there was a wider community around Schuon, including a number of non-Muslim Traditionalists. One of these, Jean Borella, a professor of philosophy at the University of Nancy in France, led a subsidiary group of perhaps fifty Catholic Traditionalists. Rama Coomaraswamy, the son of Ananda Coomaraswamy, led another Catholic group in America. According to one source, Rama Coomaraswamy's group (and so probably Borella's as well) integrated Schuonian Traditionalism into their religious practice by means of repetitive prayer similar to the Sufi *dhikr*, but using Christian terms and concepts.[2] None of these Christians were actually members of the Maryamiyya, but they followed Schuon personally as a Maryami would. The term "Schuonians" is used in this chapter to denote both Maryamis and non-Muslim followers such as these.

Of the three known American *zawiyas*, the most important was the one centered around Indiana University in Bloomington. It was established in 1967 by Victor Danner, a professor of religious studies. Danner had written to Schuon after reading his books, much as people once wrote to Guénon. He was put in touch with Joseph Epes Brown, the author of *The Sacred Pipe*, who had also once taught at Indiana. Having joined the Maryamiyya himself, Danner proceeded to assign some Traditionalist works to his students—Nasr on the main reading list, Schuon as a supplementary text. "It was done very subtly," recalled an ex-student who later joined the Maryamiyya through Danner. Danner did not, of course, mention the Maryamiyya, then a secret organization, nor the fact that he was Muslim, which was also kept secret, following the Maryami norm. Some of Brown's and then Danner's students, however, became sufficiently interested in what they were reading to want to proceed further.[3] By 1979, there were perhaps fifty Maryamis in Bloomington, most of them ex-students of Brown, Danner, or another Maryami professor at Indiana University.

The case of Danner provides one example of how the Maryamiyya spread. It is probably a fairly typical example, since several other Maryami and Schuonian professors at American and European universities have been identified.[4] Followers of Schuon in such positions aided recruitment and the formation of the "elite." In addition, there were what look like targeted recruitments to the Maryamiyya, though it is not clear to what extent this was a deliberate policy and to what extent individual Maryamis just decided that a particular person was suitable to be given copies of books by Schuon, and then perhaps told a little about the Maryamiyya.

One such recruitment has been studied in detail: that of Thomas Merton, the Cistercian (Trappist) monk who was—in America, at least—the best-known Catholic mystic of the twentieth century. Merton never became a Maryami, but he seems to have been on the brink of becoming a Schuonian at the time of his sudden death in Thailand at the age of 53.

Merton was an unusual monk, a convert to Catholicism from a background similar to that of many who became Traditionalists. His mother was an American, and his father, a New Zealand painter, brought him up partly in the artistic milieu of Paris.[5] Merton was a gifted writer from an early age. It was not the works of Traditionalists that the young Merton encountered during the early stages of his spiritual quest in the late 1930s, however, probably because he was living in England rather than in France, but instead the books of William Blake and Aldous Huxley (both Perennialists) as well as Jacques Maritain. Merton's spiritual quest led him in 1942 to the Cistercian monastery of Our Lady of Gethsemani in Kentucky. He became famous shortly afterward with the publication of his spiritual autobiography, *The Seven Storey Mountain* (1946), a book that sold more than a million copies.[6]

It is unclear why a leading Schuonian, Marco Pallis, decided to begin a correspondence with Merton in 1963; it may have been in response to Merton's 1961 book, *Mystics and Zen Masters*.[7] The moment was, in any event, well judged. Merton was in a disturbed period of his life in the 1960s. He had always borne ecclesiastical discipline badly, making numerous requests to move to other monasteries, orders, and even countries, all of which had been firmly rejected by his abbot. Once Merton appealed directly to Pope John XXIII, who could hardly ignore the appeal of such a famous Catholic; he sent Merton a personal emissary bearing as a gift the stole that the pope had worn at his coronation—and a firm refusal of Merton's request.[8] Merton reconciled himself to staying at Gethsemani but became involved in a variety of activities unusual for a monk, including active engagement in the (anti–Vietnam War) Peace Movement from 1961, and a platonic relationship with a female nurse in Louisville (the city neighboring the monastery) from 1966. He also became increasingly interested in interfaith dialogue, which had not yet come into fashion among Catholics. One of the earliest mentions of this activity is in his diary in 1957: "If I can unite *in myself* the thought and the devotion of Eastern and Western Christendom, . . . I can prepare in myself the reunion of divided Christians."[9] Merton's interests soon expanded to include non-Christian religions, especially Taoism and Zen Buddhism, but also Islam and Sufism. In 1959 he began a correspondence—largely about the great tenth-century Sufi Hallaj—with the leading French scholar of Islam, Louis Massignon.[10]

In 1963, Pallis sent Merton a selection of Traditionalist books, one by himself, others by Guénon, Schuon, and Lings; Merton liked best Lings's classic *A Moslem Saint of the Twentieth Century* (1961).[11] The Muslim saint—described as a "Sufi Saint" in the title of later editions, a change that improved sales considerably—was Ahmad al-Alawi, the shaykh from whom Schuon had taken the Alawiyya. "I am immensely impressed by him," wrote Merton, "and by the purity of the Sufi tradition as represented in him."[12] It is unclear by what standard Merton judged "purity," but it would have been unsurprising if he found similarities between Lings's conceptions and those of, for example, Blake.[13]

Merton and Pallis corresponded for about two years, discussing tradition and modernity, Islam, Buddhism, and Christianity, a correspondence that Merton seems to have excluded from the censorship that was a standard part of the Cistercian rule.[14] Then in 1966 Pallis sent a gift of an ancient Greek icon ("I have never received such a precious and magnificent gift from anyone in my life," said Merton in his thank you letter) followed by a letter in which he disclosed the existence of the Maryamiyya—"we all feel you should be fully in the know." The Maryamiyya was described as a Sufi order with "a small number of adherents of other traditions."[15] The letter in which Pallis issued Schuon's invitation to Merton is missing, but Merton noted in his diary in June 1966:

Another letter, and an important one, came: a message from a Moslem Shaikh (Spiritual master)—actually a European, but formed by one of the great Moslem saints and mystics of the age (Ahmad al-'Alawî). That I can be accepted in a personal and confidential relationship, not exactly as a disciple but at any rate as one of those who are entitled to consult him directly and personally. This is a matter of great importance to me, because in the light of their traditional ideas it puts me in contact with the spirit and teaching of Ahmad al-'Alawî in a way that is inaccessible just to the scholar or the student. It means I can have a living place in a living and sacred tradition. It can have tremendous effects. I see that already."[16]

Merton's understanding of the relationship between Schuon and al-Alawi is hardly accurate—Schuon had been "formed" by Guénon much more than by al-Alawi—and his understanding of the likely relationship between himself and Schuon raises difficult questions as well. In Catholic terms Merton already had a "place in a living and sacred tradition" as a Cistercian, and he hardly needed a new one. In Schuonian terms Merton already had a valid initiation and again did not need a new one. How, then, could a "personal and confidential relationship" with Schuon give Merton special "contact with the spirit and teaching" of al-Alawi and a new place in a new tradition unless Merton were to become Muslim and a Maryami, which he seems not to be considering ("not exactly as a disciple")?

This question may never be answered. In December 1966 Merton wrote to Pallis: "I have not yet written to M. Schuon as I intended." Unfortunately, the rest of the Merton-Pallis correspondence is missing, lost or destroyed, with the exception of a single postcard of June 1968 which confirms that the correspondence did continue.[17]

In late 1968 Merton left America on a world tour. One of his later stops was to be a visit to Nasr in Tehran,[18] where his taking further steps toward Schuon and the Maryamiyya would have been far from impossible, to judge from some of the things he was saying on his tour. In Calcutta he attended a multifaith "Spiritual Summit Conference," where some of the address he gave sounded distinctly Traditionalist: "The deepest level of communication is not communication, but communion. . . . We discover an older unity. My dear brothers, we are already one. But we imagine that we are not. What we have to recover is our original unity." Merton's "original unity" seems little different from the Perennial Philosophy. From Calcutta, Merton proceeded to the Himalayas, among whose peaks a lama taught him a mantra, and where he met the Dalai Lama. That night he dreamed of himself wearing not Cistercian robes but rather the clothes of a lama. From the Himalayas he went on to tell a Catholic audience in Darjeeling much what Guénon had once told Catholics in Paris: that "we [in the West] need the religious genius of Asia and Asian culture to inject a fresh dimension of depth into our aimless thrashing about."[19]

Merton, however, never reached Tehran. From India he flew to Thailand, stopping first in Sri Lanka, then traveling north to visit the ancient Buddha figures at Polonnaruwa. In Thailand he delivered a paper on "Marxism and Monastic Perspectives" to a Conference of Benedictine and Cistercian Abbots at a conference center near Bangkok, then retired to his room. There he died,

according to the Thai police, electrocuted by a faulty electric fan. The sudden-
ness of his death inevitably aroused suspicions—some even believed that he
had been assassinated by the CIA because of his activities in the peace movement—but there is no evidence that his death was anything but an accident.[20]

Another well-known American religious writer did, however, reach Tehran
and the Maryamiyya. This was Huston Smith, a Methodist minister and the
author of *The Religions of Man* (1958), later retitled *The World's Religions,* which
joined Merton's *Seven Storey Mountain* as one of the most widely read American religious books of the twentieth century, with sales of over 1.5 million
copies.[21] The success of Smith's book owes much to his great skills as a communicator, but also much to its universalist perspective, the emphasis on what
seven major religions have in common that gives the book its unity. This perspective derived not from Traditionalism but from Smith's readings of Aldous
Huxley and Gerald Heard while a graduate student.[22] It left Smith with a problem, however, which he called "the problem of the one and the many." Smith
knew what different religions had in common, "but I had no real idea what to
do with their differences." He was thus searching for "an absolute I could live
by." "I knew that such an Absolute couldn't be slapped together from pieces
gleaned here and there," he wrote. This would have "made about as much
sense as hoping to create a great work of art by pasting together pieces from
my favorite paintings." He also excluded the alternative of trying "to find a
single thread that runs *through* the various religions. . . . Who is to say what
the common essence of the world's religions is, and how could any account of
it escape the signature of its proponent's language and perspective?"[23]

Smith followed a variety of religious practices while waiting for the solution to this problem. He continued to attend Methodist churches but while
teaching at Washington University in St. Louis, he also studied Vedanta under
a swami to whom he had been referred by Heard.[24] Vedanta was replaced by
Buddhist practice when Smith moved to MIT in 1958 (this was after Nasr had
left MIT for Harvard).[25]

In 1969 Traditionalism provided the solution to Smith's problem. In that
year went on a world tour of religions not unlike Merton's, and took with him
to Japan Schuon's *In the Tracks of Buddhism* (1968). He had already read
Guénon but found him excessively pessimistic; he had also started Schuon's
Transcendent Unity of Religions but had abandoned it unfinished. As he read *In
the Tracks of Buddhism,* however, "the Way of the Gods opened before me." In
India he bought Schuon's *Language of the Self,* an Indian reprint of an article
on Vedanta and gnosis that Schuon had published in *Etudes traditionnelles* in
1956, and found that "a decade's tutelage under a swami . . . had familiarized
me with Vedanta's basic outlook, but Schuon took off from there as from base
camp." In Tehran Nasr gave him *Understanding Islam* (1961), Schuon's second
most important book.[26]

Smith divided Traditionalism into two constituent parts, Perennialism and what he called "Traditionalism." Perennialism solved the problem of what to do about "the relation between religions," "the problem of the one and the many." The solution was easy enough: "Don't search for a single essence that pervades the world's religions. Recognize them as multiple expressions of the Absolute which is indescribable."²⁷ What Smith called "Traditionalism"—what I have been calling the Traditionalist understanding of modernity—complemented the views that Smith had already been developing, especially at MIT, where he seems to have seen his real job as being the strong, if small, voice of philosophy and religion against what he called "scientism."²⁸ Postmodernists, he wrote, were right to "see through scientism"—but wrong because "the question of our time is no longer how to take things apart, but how to work responsibly at reassembling them."²⁹

Smith's personal religious journey had been somewhat public, and although he made no public mention of the Maryamiyya or ever said in so many words that he had become Muslim, he has told the press that he has fasted Ramadan "more than once" and that he "for 26 years has prayed five times a day in Arabic" (the two quotes are from two different newspaper profiles of Smith).³⁰ Smith also continued to practice yoga and attend his local Methodist church, even though he announced that the Methodists were "theologically . . . all washed-out."³¹

Smith has clearly contributed to the spread of the Traditionalist philosophy in America. He did his best to promote the new 1975 edition of Schuon's *Transcendent Unity* in a glowing introduction that warned that the book was difficult and that even Smith had been unable to finish it the first time, but that strongly indicated that it was very worthwhile finishing. His 1991 reedition of his by then classic work *The Religions of Man* (as *The World's Religions*) was slightly more Traditionalist than the original 1958 edition, and contained more on Sufism and Native American religion. Traditionalism was also visible—to those who would recognize it—in his 1989 plenary address to the American Academy of Religion (AAR, the largest American learned society for the study of religion).³²

Smith published two Traditionalist works: *Forgotten Truth: The Primordial Tradition* (1976) on tradition and modernity, and *Beyond the Post-Modern Mind* (1982) against "scientism."³³ Neither one enjoyed the success of *The Religions of Man*, perhaps because they were too overtly Traditionalist, despite Smith's generally ultra-accessible style. Even Smith could not make the Traditionalist philosophy comprehensible to everybody, let alone interesting or entertaining. Both were widely read, however, even though they did not sell millions of copies. *Beyond the Post-Modern Mind* was the subject of the first of a three-part PBS series for "Thinking Allowed" in 1998, and "The Primordial Tradition" was the last of these three parts. These programs are good examples of "soft" Traditionalism: the arguments made are simple, there is no mention of Guénon, and between the first and last parts came an even softer center, with no Traditionalism at all—"Psychology of Religious Experience," dealing mostly with Smith's own investigations into psychotropic drugs in the early 1960s.[34] Some of Smith's "soft" Traditionalism raises the difficult question of at what point Traditionalism becomes so soft that it is no longer Traditionalism but merely a vague stand against materialism.

Smith's Traditionalist works were just a few among many produced by Schuonians. In the period 1950–99 Schuon and 23 other identified followers published some 220 books. Eighty of these were well enough received to be translated into other languages (135 translations in total) or to go into new editions. Thirty were major works—none with sales as impressive as Merton's *Seven Storey Mountain* or Smith's *Religions of Man*, but all going through multiple editions with several publishers and in various languages.[35]

Some of these books were "hard" Traditionalism, often published by overtly Traditionalist publishers—still sometimes by Editions traditionnelles in Paris, as the Chacornac Brothers' business was now called, or more important, by the Schuonians' own World Wisdom Books in Bloomington. Some were published by specialized publishers such as Archè, a French-language publisher in Milan. These "hard" Traditionalist books continued the development of the Traditionalist philosophy and addressed principally the existing Traditionalists and those engaged in a serious spiritual quest. Only a few of these books achieved significant sales.

More important were books aimed at a more general public, "soft" Traditionalism—books dealing with spirituality or religion in general, or with aspects of Islam, Christianity, Buddhism, and American Indian religion—rarely Hinduism or Judaism any more.[36] Many of these came from mainstream publishers such as Penguin and Routledge, the Harvard, Princeton, and Oxford University Presses, or Gallimard in France.[37] Some were also published or reprinted by what might be called "soft" Traditionalist publishers; the three important ones were all started by or with the involvement of the same person—Gray Henry.

In addition to writing herself and broadcasting on Islam—for example, on the BBC World Service—Henry established two publishing houses in England (Quinta Essentia in 1979, and the Islamic Texts Society in 1981) before returning to her native America and setting up another publisher, Fons Vitae, in Kentucky in 1997. All three of these followed much the same formula. Relatively short lists of important texts contained both "hard" and "soft" Traditionalism but were dominated by translations of classic traditional texts, all of the highest quality, both from a scholarly point of view and in terms of design and production. The great late eleventh-century Sufi author Muhammad al-Ghazali, for example, was previously available in English only in editions that were from every point of view of dreadful quality, often printed on cheap paper in Pakistan and full of spelling mistakes, not to mention major errors in translation. The Islamic Texts Society began the process of bringing out al-Ghazali's work volume by volume, beautifully produced and painstakingly translated by scholars who, though not always Schuonians or Maryamis, were often English or American converts to Islam. In the same way that Nasr assisted a renaissance of classic mystic texts in Iran, and Vâlsan and his followers helped make similar texts available in French, Henry did in English.[38]

This short account of some of Henry's activities suggests remarkable talent, dedication, and energy. Similar qualities are also visible in the World of Islam Festival, an event organized in London in 1976 which involved everyone from Queen Elizabeth II (who opened the festival) to the archbishop of Canterbury, who received Abd al-Halim Mahmud, the Egyptian shaykh of Al Azhar who had written admiringly of Guénon without reading any of his books.[39] The festival was financed mostly by the newly oil-rich United Arab Emirates and was administered by a trust (foundation) dominated by prominent Englishmen—six of the eight trustees had titles, and the trust's chair was Sir Harold Beeley, an academic historian and diplomat who had twice made a success of the difficult task of being British ambassador to Cairo under Nasser.[40] Despite this broad support, Traditionalist views of Islam—and Maryamis—predominated at the festival.[41] Nasr organized the exhibition of Islamic science and technology at the Science Museum, Lings oversaw the exhibition of Islamic manuscripts and calligraphy at the British Library, and there also seems to have been some Maryami input in other exhibitions.[42] Books by Traditionalists in general and Maryamis in particular featured prominently in the output of the World of Islam Festival Publishing Company Limited, and reviews of their books appeared in the special issue of *The Times Literary Supplement*.[43]

The festival generated considerable favorable publicity for "traditional" Islam, to judge from the British newspapers of the time, but its impact was soon lost in the general reaction to the Islamic revolution in Iran, a reaction that did not focus on Ayatollah Khomeini's mystical leanings and poetry.[44] The impact of the Maryamiyya's other activities on the general public in the West is harder to assess. It is probably true to say that any Westerner who has read widely about Islam during the late twentieth century (out of spiritual interest rather than academic specialization) has encountered the Maryamiyya, usually without realizing it.

Schuonian authors are usually acknowledged experts in some field, which may be one related to the religion they are dealing with—for example, some aspect of Islamic art and architecture, but also possibly Greek poetry or Renaissance music.[45] Their books are well written and never harangue the reader but instead present religion in a way that does not put off even the most agnostic reader. Maryami spokespersons for Islam, in contrast to most Muslims who try to present Islam to the Western public,[46] come across as intellectuals of quality who are advancing a genuine alternative in which they themselves are entirely confident, having solid grounds for dismissing the obvious counterarguments. Whether or not one feels any personal attraction toward that alternative is another question.

Schuonian books generally present the esoteric tradition within the religion or religions with which they are dealing as the most important expression of it, in effect downplaying any differences between esoteric and exoteric forms[47]—Schuon's *Understanding Islam* and Nasr's *Ideals and Realities of Islam* are really more about Sufism than about Islam. They also emphasize artistic expressions of religion, as in Burckhardt's *Fez: City of Islam* (English translation 1992). Finally, they tend to present the esoteric tradition of any given religion as an expression of an absolute truth of immemorial origin, accessible only to those who can suspend rationalism and scientism, which are—it is implied—among the ills of modernity.

Only someone who knows the Traditionalist philosophy and is looking for it will recognize its presence in these books; Traditionalist interpretations are never presented as such, but rather are given as the simple truth. There need be no dishonesty in this practice: we all present things in the way we see them, without feeling obliged to explain precisely how we have come to see them in that way. Readers who are sufficiently interested will, however, find the occasional reference to "hard" Traditionalist works, which some pursue.

In the late 1980s Nasr edited two volumes entitled *Islamic Spirituality* in the excellent Crossroad series on world spiritualities. Almost every contributor to these two volumes is a Maryami. Despite its title, the work deals exclusively with Sufi spirituality. That much is clear to any reader, who can make his or her own judgment as to whether spirituality is really not to be found anywhere else in Islam. What most readers will be unable to distinguish between is Sufi spirituality and Maryami, or Traditionalist, spirituality. To a specialist in Sufism who is familiar with Traditionalism, almost every essay contains interpretations that are clearly Traditionalist but are never signaled as such. Many of these interpretations are open to dispute, to say the least. To the nonspecialist reader, however, neither the origin nor the questionable nature of the interpretations is evident.[48]

Not everyone is happy when they discover Traditionalism behind these books. One Scandinavian scientist who had converted to Islam reacted with dismay on reading an article of mine which identified Traditionalist writers that she and others she knew, had read unawares: " 'Traditionalist' books are everywhere, . . ." she wrote. "Perhaps most scary is the subtle penetration of 'traditionalist' thinking without references. . . . People pick up these ideas because they are appealing and then pass them on . . . [This] is something that affects everyone who depends on non-Arabic (non-Urdu, non-Turkish, etc.) literature."[49] This "subtle penetration" of Traditionalism also struck another observer, James W. Morris, who found it more ironic than sinister. "One rarely encounters academic specialists in the spiritual dimensions of religious studies who have not in fact read several of the works of Schuon," wrote Morris, but "this wide-ranging influence is rarely mentioned publicly" because of "the peculiar processes of academic 'canonization.' "[50]

The Feathered Sun

Beginning in the late 1970s Schuon and a segment of his following began to move further away from Islam toward a form of universalism that placed increasing emphasis on Schuon himself. *Erinnerungen und Betrachtungen* ends in 1973, and so Schuon's own understanding of his role during this period is not known. *Erinnerungen und Betrachtungen* does, however report a further vision of Schuon, in 1973, about which he is less explicit than he was about earlier visions. He reports only that "this mystery" (presumably the Virgin) returned to him, "in connection with the overwhelming consciousness that I am not as other men."[51] According to one possible interpretation, Schuon at this stage may have been wondering whether he was perhaps the prophet Elijah returned at the end of time, or alternatively a manifestation of the Hindu goddess Kali.[52]

It is unlikely that this was Schuon's last vision—their frequency had begun to accelerate—and subsequent visions of which we have no details may have contributed to his apparent conviction, implied in a 1980 letter, that he was "the human instrument for the manifestation of the *Religio Perennis* at the end of time."[53] By the time of Schuon's death in 1998, one group of Schuon's followers had left Islam behind and taken on the characteristics not of a Sufi order but of what scholars of religion term a "new religious movement."

Schuon began to distance himself publicly from Islam in 1978—perhaps in reaction to events in Iran—with a number of reflections in an article on "Paradoxical Aspects of Sufism" which were almost anti-Islamic in tone.[54] In 1981 he wrote to a follower that "our point of departure is the quest after esotericism and not after a particular religion," and in 1989 he explained to another followert: "Our point of departure is the Advaita Vedanta and not a moralist, individualist and voluntarist anthropology with which ordinary Sufism is undeniably identified—however much this may displease those who would like our orthodoxy to consist of feigning or falling in love with an Arab-Semitic mentality."[55] Some contemporary Schuonians contend that these statements simply reflect what had always been Schuon's position from the beginning.[56] To some extent that is clearly the case, but the force with which the point is made is not found before the late 1970s.

In addition to distancing himself from Islam, Schuon also distanced himself further from Guénon: in 1984 he published in Paris an article accusing Guénon of overestimating the Orient and underestimating the Occident—the traditional rather than the modern Occident, of course.[57] This particular criticism was not new either, and it might have passed without comment, but

Schuon's general tone regarding Guénon in this article could not. Schuon wrote, for example, "One of the most astonishing things is the astonishment of Guénon on points that any child should be able to understand."[58] This article caused a furor among non-Schuonian Traditionalists, who demanded that Schuonians be excluded from the pages of *Etudes traditionnelles;* French Schuonians responded by starting a journal of their own, *Connaissance des religions* [Knowledge of Religions], a well-edited and excellently designed publication that quickly achieved a greater circulation than the by then distinctly old-fashioned *Etudes traditionnelles.* In 1992 *Etudes traditionnelles* finally ceased publication, after slightly more than a century.[59] What had been Chacornac's publishing house and bookstore (Editions traditionnelles), however, continued into the twenty-first century as a general esoteric bookstore with a specialization in Traditionalism, continuing to reprint those Guénon works to which it had the copyright.[60]

In 1981 Schuon moved from his native Switzerland to Indiana, where a new Schuonian community was established at Inverness Farms, a former housing project on the edge of a forest, about three miles from Bloomington. The Inverness Farms community in Indiana consisted of some 60 or 70 persons—American, Swiss, and Latin American—who were permanent residents around Schuon's house in Inverness Farms, or in nearby locations.[61] Schuon's house had been built on a plot adjoining that of a Maryami who had given Schuon the land and whose own house contained the *zawiya*, "a largish room . . . [with] three arches at one end and a polished wooden floor," which the builder had been told would be a dance floor.[62]

Schuon's immigration to America, a remarkable move for a man of 73, was in response to a sign from heaven, the details of which are unknown.[63] In one letter to a follower Schuon implied that the reason for his move from Europe to America was to establish a primordial community, though the reason usually given by Schuonians was Schuon's desire to be closer to Native American religion.[64] The two are connected: the later Schuon wrote often of the primordial nature of Native American religion and of his own primordial role. The Inverness Farms community adopted as its symbol a Plains Indian symbol, the "feathered sun"; it later became the logo of World Wisdom Books, Schuon's publishing house in Bloomington. By the late 1980s Schuon was seen by many at Inverness Farms as the "Master of the Religio Perennis," above Islam as he was above—because he was at the center of—all individual traditions. The Inverness Farms community was considered a " 'direct' manifestation of the Primordial Tradition in its 'purest' state, whereas all other esoteric organizations were only 'indirect' manifestations of it."[65]

The Inverness Farms community was grafted onto the Bloomington Maryamiyya established in 1967 by Professor Victor Danner, and although Danner himself was soon excluded from any role in directing the new community, something of the older Maryamiyya remained until the end. The emphasis, however, was on the "inner circle" of Primordialists, the new Schuonians, not on the outer circle of more Islamic Maryamis, generally described as "Muslim Muslims," who were looked down on by the Primordialists for their excessive attachment to the exoteric formalities of Islam. Many older Maryamis were increasingly absent or excluded. Burckhardt, who had been ill for some time, did not follow Schuon to America; he died in 1984.[66] Danner died in 1990, not having met with Schuon since 1985.[67] Nasr visited Inverness Farms only occasionally (about once a year), and according to some sources there was a deliberate attempt to hide from him some of what was going on there. Lings also visited only once a year, but he too was perhaps not allowed to see everything and was regarded by some or even many Primordialists as a pedant, tolerated only with difficulty.[68]

Schuon, approaching his eighties, became increasingly inaccessible. In later years he attended the *dhikr* only occasionally, and rarely spoke in public—he was not comfortable in English (though he knew the language well), preferring to speak in French and use an interpreter.[69] The direction of the Inverness Farms community passed into the hands of his *muqaddam* and other Primordialists, most prominent among whom was Catherine Schuon, who regulated access to her husband. A young American, Patricia Estelle (pseudonym), also became important, joining Schuon in his painting and, according to some, encouraging the view of him as more than merely human. She also became his third "vertical" or "spiritual" wife, though, unlike his other two "vertical" wives, she had no other husband at the time of her "marriage" to Schuon.[70]

Most of the Inverness Farms community was at least nominally Muslim and Maryami, and the rites of Islam and Sufism continued to be practiced, though interest in Islam as a religion was little encouraged—it was too exoteric. One English Maryami who expressed an interest in learning Arabic was advised to learn French instead so that he could read Schuon's works in the original. Fasting Ramadan was voluntary—a Maryami who was busy at work was allowed "to make alternative sacrifices," so long as he or she fasted at least three days of that month and concentrated even more than usual on *dhikr*.[71] The old authorization to drink beer to disguise one's Islam remained in force.[72]

Non-Islamic terminology began to replace Islamic terminology, with Schuon being frequently described not as a *qutb* (the highest rank that Islamic Sufis normally give their beloved shaykh) but as *pneumatikos*. Views as to the proper interpretation of this Greek term differ. For some Traditionalists, it merely indicates a person with an especially spiritual temperament, a gnostic who has reached the end of the spiritual path in God, while for others it indicates a person in whom the divine spirit—rather than a merely human soul—predominates. It is likely that both interpretations were present. Some Schuonians came to see Schuon as an *avatar*, a Hindu term for a divine incarnation.[73] Stories began to circulate of Schuon's spiritual rank being recognized by lions and elephants, and of his future rank being acknowledged by the archbishop of Strasbourg when Schuon was a child in Mulhouse. There were even stories of people who treated Schuon disrespectfully in the street being frozen to the spot as a result.[74]

Schuon attempted to divert the growing attention paid to him, but in somewhat equivocal terms. In 1981 he wrote: "I do not wish my person to be made the object of symbolist and mystical speculations which—apart from their possibly problematical character—create supplementary preoccupations and divert the mind from that which alone matters: to follow my teachings without adding anything thereto."[75] Such statements do not seem to have had much effect.

Various "primordial" practices were introduced. The weekly *dhikr* was followed not only by a brief lesson (written by Schuon and read aloud) and sometimes Arabic poetry, as is normal in Sufi circles, but also by a "a sort of Red Indian chant or song, performed by [the *muqaddam*] while beating a drum."[76] "Indian Days" (also known as "pow-wows") were also instituted, taking place about once a month during the summer and featuring dances and ceremonies sometimes led by Yellowtail, with the *muqaddam* leading the drumming and chanting.[77] For these Indian Days, a form of Native American dress was adopted, which in the case of women sometimes amounted to ornamented bikinis. Schuon would appear on these occasions dressed as a Native American chief, bearing a feathered staff.[78]

In addition to the Indian Days, there are also reports of secret "primordial gatherings" attended only by Schuon and a small number of his closest followers—according to one report five or six women and three men, and according to another report ten to fifteen of each sex. A source close to Schuon described one such occasion in this way:

> The women were naked except for me & [another woman]. We preferred to be somewhat dressed because we were getting older—so we wore transparent-like saris. The men wore loin cloths except for the Shaykh [Schuon] who wore a "free" loin cloth—that is, there was nothing under it so one could often see him naked. After a good, simple dinner, [a woman] did some lovely Hindu like dancing—or American Indian—or Balinese with headdress & flowers. It was celestial, formal & very, very beautiful. . . . The Shaykh would do the Primordial Dance while we'd watch—and [one woman] would sometimes try to pull his loin cloth off! [The other 'older' woman] sometimes did flamenco dancing too and occasionally [three further women] would do a charming dance together.[79]

Schuon, it will be remembered, saw beauty as affording access to the divine. As he wrote around this time:

Given the spiritual degeneration of mankind, the highest possible degree of beauty, that of the human body, plays no role in ordinary piety; but this theophany may be a support in esoteric spirituality. . . . Nudity means inwardness, essentiality, primordiality and thus universality. . . . Nudity means glory, radiation of spiritual substance or energy; the body is the form of the essence and thus the essence of the form. But there is not visual beauty only; poetry, music and dance are likewise means of interiorization; not in themselves, but combined with the remembrance of the Sovereign Good.[80]

Contemporary Schuonians argue that how an observer sees nakedness— as spiritual or as sexual—is a function of the spiritual state and status of the observer. In Schuon's words, "Earthly beauties . . . lead the spiritual man to God. They lead the vulgar man merely to himself."[81]

If these secret gatherings existed, only the most inner of the "inner circle" knew of them, but many "Muslim Muslims" (and even some of the more recent recruits to the Maryamiyya) were unhappy with the Indian Days, with what they saw as fancy dress and affectation, with the claims made for Schuon, and with "the human ambience"—which according to one participant was characterized by "backbiting, intrigue, spying and petty power struggles that seemed to be going on constantly in and around the 'inner circle'—not to speak of the common gossip." Despite this situation, "fear of being ostracized oneself or even of being regarded as a 'peripheral' disciple was an effective way of keeping everyone 'in line.' "[82]

Not everyone could be kept in line, however. There were sufficient objections to the role played by Catherine Schuon for Frithjof Schuon to be obliged to write that "No one has the right to believe that the Shaykh's wife concerns herself with matters beyond her competence, because if they were, she would not concern herself with them."[83] This circular argument did not convince everyone. In the late 1980s the number of people leaving the Maryamiyya was increasing, especially after 1988, when Alawi al-Alawi of the Algerian Alawiyya visited New York and reportedly denied the validity of Schuon's claim to an Alawi *ijaza*.[84] In addition, it gradually became generally known that Schuon had "vertical" wives.[85]

Disaster finally struck Inverness Farms in 1991 when Mark Koslow, who had for some time been close to the inner circle and was also in a romantic relationship with one of Schuon's "vertical" wives, Rose Connor (pseudonym), broke with Schuon after permission for him and Connor to continue their relationship was refused. Koslow went to the police with stories of "primordial gatherings" and other activities at Inverness Farms. He and some others alleged that, at the end of both the Indian Days and the "primordial gatherings," Schuon would embrace the women present, including some under the age of

16, in such a way that their genitals might briefly touch.[86] Koslow clearly associated nakedness with sex rather than spirituality, as did the police.

A police investigation was started, and after some months it led to Schuon's indictment by a grand jury for child molesting and sexual battery. The basis of the first charge was that women under 16 had allegedly been present at the alleged "gatherings" and had allegedly been embraced by Schuon along with the other women, and the basis of the second charge was that the women who had allegedly allowed Schuon to press himself against their bodies did so as a result of "undue cult influences and cult pressures."[87]

These charges were later dropped by the prosecutor because there was "insufficient evidence to support a criminal prosecution on these charges." The prosecutor told the press, "Insofar as [Schuon] has been labeled, a miscarriage has occurred."[88] Most of the Inverness Farms community had been solid in Schuon's defense.[89] The existence of secret "primordial gatherings" was denied, as were sexual embraces by Schuon in general and embraces of minors in particular.[90] According to an Inverness Farms spokesperson, some of the under-age girls who had allegedly been embraced were in fact elsewhere on the dates in question.[91] Even had the embraces occurred and been admitted, Schuon would arguably not have been guilty of any offense under the laws of Indiana, since both offenses require "the intent to arouse or satisfy . . . sexual desires";[92] there is no suggestion that this was the case. Even Koslow now accepts that Schuon's intentions "were not primarily about sex, but about . . . [Schuon's] pursuit of absurd delusions of power."[93]

Although Schuon had been exonerated in the eyes of the law, of most of his followers, and of the Indiana press, the case still had repercussions. The assistant prosecutor on the case was found not to have given the grand jury "appropriate guidance on the legal criteria [required] to substantiate such charges," and he resigned.[94] Connor brought a civil action against Koslow for possession of the house she had bought him. A former Maryami who had sided with Koslow against Schuon, Aldo Vidali, was sued by another Maryami for the alleged fraudulent altering of a marine contract, and was also sued by his own son for allegedly selling a sailboat in which his son allegedly had a one-third share.[95]

Away from Indiana, an established opponent of Nasr's views—Ziauddin Sardar—published a review of a number of Nasr's books in *Insight International*. It began by quoting Nasr's most effusive praise of Schuon and then went on to describe, with evident glee and in the most hostile tones, the charges against Schuon.[96] Rumors of events at Inverness Farms began to spread across the Traditionalist community in Europe, and into Western and Islamic Sufi circles beyond Traditionalism. Members of the Inverness Farms community attempted to prevent this spread, for example by obtaining (on grounds of copyright) a court order preventing Aldo Vidali from distributing apparently compromising photographs of Schuon, and then by bringing a further action against him when he distributed drawings of a photograph instead.[97] The damage, however, had been done.

Schuon, now an old and evidently also a troubled man, wrote to his principal *muqaddams* announcing that he was retiring from directing the Maryamiyya and that they should proceed independently. Lings, Nasr, and the Maryami *muqaddam* for Switzerland protested their loyalty to Schuon, but in practice they began to proceed independently of him.[98] They have since continued the Maryamiyya without reference to Schuon's later primordialism, meeting annually in Cairo to coordinate activities. These sections of the Maryamiyya had always emphasized Islam and since the early 1990s have become even more Islamic. Schuon spent the last years of his life writing—including some 3,000 poems in his native German—and died in 1998.[99] The Inverness Farms community still exists, and reports suggest that it continues to function with an emphasis on primordialism. It has grown little in recent years, with most increase resulting from the admission of members' children on coming of age.[100] Since Schuon's death, it has become much less secretive; although Inverness Farms is surrounded by a high security fence that keeps out prying eyes, the Maryamiyya itself is now openly discussed.[101]

The reactions of other Maryamis to these events and revelations varied. The innermost circle at Inverness Farms was unmoved by the details of Koslow's accusations, though not by the events themselves. If the accusations were unfounded, they knew them to be so. If the accusations were based on fact, they had endorsed the practices by participating in them, and they saw nothing wrong in them. Either way, their view is best expressed by Catherine Schuon, writing in a more general context: "The presence of the sacred can . . . generate hatred. Thus the Shaykh had to suffer the painful experience of people who rebelled against him and heaped false accusations upon him."[102]

Others outside Inverness Farms averted their gaze: strange things had evidently been happening, but these were probably the fault of elements in Schuon's entourage there rather than of Schuon himself, and it was neither right nor useful to inquire too deeply into what was in the nature of things impossible. As Burckhardt had written thirteen years before in response to earlier suggestions of impropriety on Schuon's part: "Do you believe that God could disappoint men who, for more than forty years, have followed the Path quite properly putting their trust in God in the person of their master . . . do you believe that God could wish to reward them with a scandalous disillusionment?" "Is it conceivable that a man whose very nature is intellectual incorruptibility . . . would succumb to banal temptation?"[103]

Some people, however, left the Maryamiyya for other Sufi orders such as the original Algerian Alawiyya, and some left Islam for other religions or for none; most of these found their lives dislocated to a greater or lesser degree, and some experienced real suffering and personal tragedy.[104] Others took themselves as far as possible from what one American Maryami, resident in the Arab world, described as "the darkness underneath the lantern," they followed the example of Danner, who had privately disassociated himself from Schuon but maintained that Schuon was the authentic shaykh of an authentic Sufi order but was (in the words of a Maryami who expressed his doubts to Danner) "surrounded by mediocre and even wicked people, whose faults Schuon himself was largely blind to."[105] When this Maryami told Danner of his departure from the Maryamiyya for the Alawiyya, Danner wrote to him kindly that "attachment to another Shaykh is one of the solutions to the numerous problems posed by [Schuon]," but he advised him "not to hold any recrimination against [Schuon] or any of his followers here. . . . Otherwise, the thought of him might darken your mind."[106]

For many longer-standing Maryamis, the way in which the Maryamiyya developed at Inverness Farms was a deeply confusing tragedy. Some suggest various explanations ranging from the impact of the American environment to the influence of Estelle. The most frequent explanation among thoughtful ex-Maryami Traditionalists, however, is that Schuon confused the accurate, Perennialist observation of the transcendent unity of religions with a foolish and impossible attempt to recreate a single unified religion on earth. Schuon had lost sight of the fact that "the *religio perennis* is in no sense the advance revelation of the universal religion that is to come [at the end of time], or the remanifestation of the spiritual form of the primordial golden age."[107] The result of "endow[ing] [the primordial state] with a sensible form composed of elements drawn from Islam, North American shamanism, . . . and Christian Orthodox iconography" was to "substitute a fantasy for genuine esotericism."[108] As we have seen, Huston Smith asked rhetorically in another context: "Who is to say what the common essence of the world's religions is, and how could any account of it escape the signature of its proponent's language and perspective?"[109] According to this view, Schuon had tried to answer the question, and his answer had indeed borne a personal signature.

9

Terror in Italy

Julius Evola and Frithjof Schuon were the longest surviving Traditionalists of the first generation. Before Evola died, in 1974, he was to play an important role in Italian postwar history, becoming the Traditionalist whose name was best known to the public—a name that came to be generally reviled.

The events of the Second World War thoroughly discredited Fascism in Italy, but Italy did not experience an equivalent of the de-Nazification program which the victorious Allies imposed on Germany, and as a result extreme right politics resurfaced sooner in Italy than in Germany. When this happened, the marginality of Evola during the war (and so his innocence of any responsibility for the debacle of Mussolini's Fascism) placed him in an advantageous position.

Postwar Italian extreme right politics can be divided into two periods, one linked in certain ways to Mussolini's Fascism, and the other to the new radicalism which derived from the social and political turmoil of 1968. In both periods, the activities of the chief rightist political party, the Movimento Sociale Italiano (Italian Social Movement) or MSI, were supplemented by a number of groups without parliamentary ambitions. For many of these groups, though not for the MSI itself, Evola's works were of central importance.

Evola's first involvement was with the Fasci di Azione Rivoluzionaria (Fasces of Revolutionary Action) or FAR, the earliest postwar rightist group, though the nature of this involvement is unclear. The FAR were established in late 1946, and soon divided into two groups, one revolutionary and one "utopian." In 1949 Evola had published in *Imperium*, the journal of an MSI youth group, an article called "Due intransigenze" [Two Intransigences], presumably addressed to the utopian wing of the FAR, arguing for the primacy of spiritual revolution. This article was the basis of an important 1950 pamphlet, *Orientamenti* [Orientations].[1] At this stage, Evola was still thinking in terms of an initiatic, uranic order of the sort encountered in chapter 5, if not any longer of the Italo-German order he had pursued during the Second World War. According to one source, he supported the aims and activities of Junio Valerio Borghese, an aristocrat, a Fascist, and Second World War military hero.[2]

In 1951 the Italian police arrested some thirty members of the FAR and charged them with plotting to reestablish Fascism. Evola was among those arrested, though not a member of the FAR. He was accused of inspiring the FAR by his writings—an accusation that could not be made to stick in court, and Evola was acquitted.[3] The publicity surrounding this trial, however, helped launch Evola on his postwar career. He expanded *Orientamenti* into a book published in 1961, *Cavalcare la Tigre: Orientamenti esistenziali per un'epoca della dissoluzione* [Riding the Tiger: Existential Orientations for a Period of Dissolution]. *Cavalcare la Tigre* later became the central text for the Italian extreme right. This book also marks the end of Evola's interest in initiatic and uranic orders.[4]

The most important extreme right organization of the first period of postwar Italian history was Ordine Nuovo (New Order), an MSI splinter group established by Pino Rauti in 1956.[5] Rauti was a dedicated follower of Evola, or at least of Evola's published work, and Ordine Nuovo was publicly committed to the defense of "all that of the traditional that has been saved and has found a 'pole.'" It launched a journal, *Ordine Nuovo*, and offered courses and seminars based around Evola's (and sometimes Guénon's) works, including Evola's *Orientamenti*.[6] One small group from within Ordine Nuovo even followed Evola's earliest interest, ceremonial magic and Roman neo-Paganism, establishing I Dioscuri (Greek *Dioskouroi*, sons of Zeus) in Rome in the late 1960s. Little is known of the activities of this group, except that it ran into difficulties of some sort that led to the suicide of many of its members. There were rumors of sacrifices, presumably of animals.[7] By 1975 I Dioscuri had ceased to function in Rome, though a branch in Messina survived.[8]

Most of the activities of Ordine Nuovo, however, were intellectual and political. It and its journal are considered by the Italian sociologist Franco Ferraresi to have served also as a point of reference for a variety of smaller, loosely connected groups, some of which engaged in armed action—bombings and one attempted coup d'état—rather than intellectual activity.

The immediate impetus for violence by Ordine Nuovo groups was not so much Evola as the environment of the early Cold War years and the activities of groups such as the Algerian Front de libération nationale (FLN, National Liberation Front), the armed nationalist movement that ultimately forced the

French out of Algeria. The Italian Communist Party (PCI) was the strongest Communist party in Europe, and concern that Italy might "fall" to the Soviet Union was widespread, in Washington as well as in parts of the Italian government, military, and security services. Circles such as these saw the activities of the FLN in the context of the Cold War rather than of decolonization, and a concept of "revolutionary war" was developed. According to this understanding, the Soviet Union was waging nonconventional, "revolutionary" war on the West through intermediaries such as the FLN and the PCI. It was the right and duty of Western states to respond to revolutionary war as much as to conventional war, using the appropriate weapons: the insurgent and terrorist tactics used with evident success by groups such as the FLN.[9]

Some Evolians associated with Ordine Nuovo were among those who spread the concept of revolutionary war,[10] but they were not at the forefront of this development, which is not connected to Traditionalism in any way. A Rome group deriving from Ordine Nuovo—the Avanguardia Nazionale Giovanile (National Youth Vanguard) of Stefano Delle Chiaie—was, however, at the forefront of the implementation of this theory. With some 500 members, the Avanguardia Nazionale was responsible for at least 15 terrorist attacks between 1962 and 1967, sometimes benefitting from the sympathies (and perhaps even the assistance) of elements within the Italian security apparatus.[11] Its strategy was sometimes direct, sometimes "indirect." A number of Avanguardia Nazionale activists, for example, experienced apparent conversions to the left and then resurfaced, throwing petrol bombs from among groups of leftist students in 1968—actions presumably intended to discredit groups on the opposing side.[12]

The link between the activities of the Avanguardia Nazionale and Traditionalism is unclear. The visible intellectual production of the Avanguardia Nazionale was no more than a little crude anti-Communist propaganda,[13] and so it is impossible to say to what extent Della Chiaie brought Traditionalist ideas with him from Ordine Nuovo. A clearer link is provided in the case of the Udine group of the Ordine Nuovo, run by twin brothers Gaetano and Vincenzo Vinceguerra. When on trial for assassinations and bombings carried out in 1971–72, the Vinceguerra brothers quoted not only Evola but also Guénon in justification of their actions.[14] Another link is provided through the person of Franco Freda, later Evola's most important intellectual disciple— "intellectual" in the sense that intellectual links are very clear whereas there is no information about any personal links. He is a central figure in the history of Italian political Traditionalism.

Freda, a member of Ordine Nuovo from 1966, led a group in Padova which began planting bombs in 1969. The strategy selected was again indirect, as with Avanguardia Nazionale and the Vinceguerra brothers. Freda's followers once planted five bombs in banks in Rome and Milan and then passed information to the police incriminating "22 Marzo" [March 22], an anarchist group. As was intended, the members of 22 Marzo were arrested, and they and other anarchists were subjected to repressive actions by the police, justified by a wave of public outrage. The operation would seem, then, a textbook example of revolutionary war—except that it did not have the desired results. It became gradually clear that 22 Marzo could not have planted the bombs, and the real authors of the attacks became known after a security leak from within Freda's group.[15]

The long-range impact of Freda's operation was the opposite of what was desired. In the immediate aftermath of the bombings, Giuseppe Pinelli, a member of 22 Marzo, fell to his death from the third floor of the Milan police headquarters, where he was being questioned,[16] an incident that was immortalized by Dario Fo, a leftist and later a Nobel laureate, in his play "Morte accidentale di un anarchico" [Accidental Death of an Anarchist] (1974).[17] This play, a withering attack on the stupidity and brutality of the police (and thus by implication of authority in general), was a great success over the following decades, especially on student campuses, and was instrumental in fostering anti-authoritarian attitudes among generations of students throughout Europe. One of the most important consequences of this attempt to put Traditionalism into practice, then, was decidedly "anti-traditional." Attempts to run against the current in any era risk being turned around by the flood and carried along in the direction of the general flow. Something of the kind happened to Nasr's Traditionalist activities in Iran, which contributed to a revolution that Nasr himself was simultaneously working to prevent.

Many other bombings followed. Because of the use of indirect strategies, and because police investigations of many incidents were inconclusive, precise responsibility for the dramatic increase in political violence in Italy at about this time—there were 145 separate terrorist incidents in 1969 alone—has not been finally established.[18] It is clear, however, that activists linked to Ordine Nuovo, who may or may not have been Evolian Traditionalists, were responsible for a significant number of violent attacks on a variety of targets.

The most dramatic incident of this first period was an attempted coup d'état in 1970, aimed against what was perceived as the growing risk of a Communist takeover of Italy. The coup attempt was led by Borghese, whom Evola may or may not have still favored, supported by an assortment of amateur parachutists, trainee Forest Guards, and individuals associated with Ordine Nuovo. The attempt to seize key targets in Rome was abandoned before it was properly launched, and there were so many elements of farce (notably, plotters overloading an elevator on the way to arrest the Rome police chief and therefore being stuck in the elevator all night) that a court refused to charge the plotters with "armed insurrection" on the grounds that they could not be taken seriously as a threat to the Republic.[19]

This first period of rightist violence in Italy ended with the forced dissolution, under court orders, of Ordine Nuovo and of the Avanguardia Nazionale in 1974.[20] Neither Evola nor Traditionalism was responsible for the immediate objectives of this violence (the struggle against Communism) or for the means of these actions—the origins of the concept of revolutionary war lie elsewhere. One contribution of Traditionalism to this period, however, was to provide the vision of a better future which motivated many rightists on an individual level. The other contribution was that Evola's spiritual warrior—the absolute individual—was the model that inspired many participants.

Evola was more important during the second period of rightist terrorism, which started in 1968, as did so much else. It was in this year that sales of Evola's *Cavalcare la Tigre*, previously in the hundreds, took off into the thousands.[21] In *Cavalcare la Tigre*, Evola argues that the late twentieth century is an age of dissolution. There are no states that can claim "inalienable authority"—all are no more than a collection of "'representative' and administrative systems"—but neither are there any "partisan" (anti-state) movements to which one can belong, given the absence of any of the preconditions for successful "rectifying" action, that is, the installation of a legitimate state authority.[22] This analysis represents a reversal of Evola's prewar position; his own activities from the 1920s to the 1940s showed clearly that he then believed in at least the possibility of installing a system that he would have regarded as legitimate.

Despite the impossibility of successful "rectifying" action, Evola observed, some individuals are still "disposed to fight even on lost positions." To them Evola recommended *apoliteia* (separation from the polity), which he defined as "irrevocable interior distance from this society and its 'values'; and the refusal to be tied to it by any moral or spiritual links whatsoever." Evola stressed that he was describing an interior state which need not necessarily have any consequences in the realm of action, but also stressed that it did not require abstention, as from a "conscientious objector."[23]

Exactly what Evola did mean by *apoliteia* in practical terms—in the realm of action—has since been much disputed.[24] What is even more important than what Evola meant, however, is what he was *taken* to mean. Evola's *apoliteia* was developed by Freda into a call for action against the bourgeois state irrespective of effect, a sort of Traditionalist existentialism—and the word "existentialism" is used in the subtitle of *Cavalcare la Tigre*. Freda's development of Evolian Traditionalism was not entirely nihilistic—he also argued for the destruction of the bourgeois state as a necessary preliminary to further developments, which implies belief in the possibility of "rectifying action"—but his call was in effect a call to what Gianfranco de Turris calls "rightist anarchism."[25]

Just as Evola shifted (or was thought to have shifted) the emphasis from the objectives of action to the interior state that gives rise to action, so Freda shifted the emphasis from the objective—which implied some central planning and organization—to the individual. Freda was one of the earliest and most important proponents of the "archipelago solution," the new organizational pattern of Italian extreme right terrorism that emerged in the 1970s—

a solution, by implication, to the problems raised by the dismantling of Ordine Nuovo. This meant the replacement of earlier, relatively large and hierarchical structures by small and fluid groupings, usually forming for a particular operation and then dissolving, and normally acting independently of each other and of any central command.[26]

The archipelago solution presents certain obvious operational advantages. As an extension of the Leninist cell system, it is the ultimate guard against police infiltration: no more than a single operation can ever be compromised. It is, however, more than a defense, since the abandonment of any control over operational groups makes sense only as a corollary to the abandonment of overall strategy. The archipelago solution, then, is the companion of *apoliteia*, at least as Freda understood *apoliteia*. The two together make up *spontaneismo armato* (armed spontaneity), Freda's most destructive discovery, later popularized in his journal, *Quex*.[27] In practice, *spontaneismo armato* differs little from random mayhem.

Despite these developments, there were still stable rightist groups, some of them permanent clandestine units. More interesting were a number of "cultural circles" or "study groups" that were established across Italy, apparently concentrating on studying the works of Evola and other rightist writers. Recruits for operations might be found in these groups and were formed intellectually by them, but none of these groups were themselves operational units.[28]

Freda's replacement of the Communists with the bourgeois state as the rightists' target in 1974 (the year of Evola's death) was mirrored by a shift in the target of leftist violence. Leftists also took on the state (described as "capitalist" rather than "bourgeois") rather than, as in an earlier period, using violence as a form of armed propaganda—such as "executing" industrialists who had been found guilty of exceptionally reprehensible behavior against the interests of the working class. In the same way that rightists adopted the archipelago solution, leftist activists disassociated themselves from political organizations such as the PCI, which had made its compromise with other political forces in Italy. For many leftists, the old division between left and right was no longer of much importance and had been replaced by a divide identified by Asor Rosa as a division between In and Out. Bourgeois industrialists were In, as were unionized workers and the PCI; the unemployed, women, students, and other marginal groups were Out.[29]

During this second period, there were many similarities between rightists and leftists. The single bloodiest terrorist attack of the period, the Bologna railway station bomb of August 2, 1980, killed 85 people; it was for many years unclear whether the bomb was planted by left or right.[30] Not only was the enemy now the same for both, but in both cases the justification for violence became more and more existential as the prospect of immediate political gains receded. Freda even attempted an alliance of left and right on this basis,[31] an alliance that would come into being in post-Soviet Russia, cemented by an ideology derived by a Traditionalist from Traditionalism and other sources.

In Italy the demographic profile of activists of both left and right changed as the police became more successful in infiltrating terrorist groups and arresting their leaders. During the 1980s, with terrorists on both sides becoming younger and younger (often only 15 or 16), organization and strategy vanished altogether replaced by an escalation of increasingly random incidents. Leftists were shooting private security guards, Ministry of Labor employees, and even physicians. Rightists were shooting policemen, and finally even those of their own leaders who remained out of prison. Eventually the police operation succeeded, and by 1983 both leftist and rightist groups were no more.[32]

It is not clear that Evola foresaw or intended the consequences of his writings in this period. It seems likely that he did, however, especially in the light of his earlier involvement with the SS and with 1942 Nazi racial policy. Evola cannot have been ignorant of what was being done in his name, and the only clarification of Cavalcare la Tigre that he ever issued was that it was intended for "traditional" men. Likewise, he wrote some articles condemning the use of violence against "the system," but these seem to be condemning actions that were merely an excess of youthful energies, rather than violent actions per se.[33] In 1971 Evola spoke to Henri Hartung, a Traditionalist of a very different sort who had no sympathy with the political right, of "the Evolian study groups in Genoa, in Palermo, in Calabria." According to Hartung, Evola talked "with a tenderness which it was quite astonishing to see in him . . . of these young men who, rejecting profane degradation, [were] trying to restore a traditional spiritual state. But it was with a withering indifference that he rejected all 'anachronistic' attempts 'at an activism devoid of any serious doctrinal preparation.'"[34]

Evola, then, seems to have approved of what was being done in his name—on condition that it was done with proper spiritual preparation. This does not, however, mean that Evola can be held solely responsible for Italian extreme right terrorism. He was not the only writer whom the terrorists read: Franco Freda established a publishing house, AR, that printed the works not only of Evola but also of Oswald Spengler and Friedrich Nietzsche, as well as Corneliu Codreanu and Muammar Qaddafi.[35] In addition, there were a variety of other important factors—social, economic, and political. Terrorism in the 1960s to 1980s was an Italian, not just a rightist, phenomenon. In the view of Roger Griffin, "1968 created a climate in which if Evola had not existed it would have been necessary to invent him."[36]

The year 1983 saw the end of significant rightist political violence in Western Europe, but not of the right or of Evolian Traditionalism. Evola, and to a lesser extent Guénon, has remained on the reading lists of the New Right, leading to the mistaken idea that both are principally theorists of Fascism.

The most important instance of Evolian Traditionalism at the end of the twentieth century was not in Western Europe but in Russia, and is discussed in a later chapter. There were also Evolian groups in Hungary, Germany, Austria, France, and Argentina, as well as Italy, and possibly in other countries as well.[37] Of these, the most important were the Hungarian and the Italian.

Though the Traditionalist terror in Italy ended in 1983, that was not the end of the Traditionalists who had been involved in it. Some, like Freda's former follower Claudio Mutti[38] (discussed later), operated nonviolently and independently. Others emphasized Evola's thought and writing rather than action, notably those based around the Fondazione Julius Evola (Julius Evola Foundation), established in 1974, which at the end of the twentieth century published books and journals, organized periodic conferences, and maintained an excellent website.[39] A number of Evolian study circles also continued, at least two of which were part of the youth wing of Alleanza Nazionale (National Alliance), a right-wing common front that campaigned with Prime Minister Silvio Berlusconi in the 2001 Italian elections and was rewarded with five ministerial portfolios and a deputy premiership for their leader, Gianfranco Fini.[40]

Freda, rejected by many Evolian Traditionalists and sentenced to 16 years in prison in 1972, reemerged in the late 1980s, and in he 1991 founded the Fronte Nazionali (National Front). Its supporters were predominantly skinheads, and their crusading issue was immigration, not as crude racism but as an attack on multiculturalism in the name of preserving the purity of distinct traditions. Freda and some fifty of his followers were, however, convicted in 1999 of "incitement to racial discrimination," and in 2000 the Fronte Nazionali was dissolved by decree of the minister of the interior and its assets were confiscated.[41] There were rumors, however, that Fronte Nazionali activists, in alliance with members of the Alleanza Nazionale, had helped ferment the violence that shocked Italy during anti-globalization protests at the 2001 G8 summit in Genoa.[42]

Hungarian Traditionalism, like Romanian Traditionalism, became established before the Second World War, survived communism, and resurfaced in the 1990s. Evola's first follower in Hungary had been Béla Hamvas, a librarian and journalist who published works on Traditionalism between 1935 and 1943. After 1945 Hamvas was obliged to work as a night watchman, but he communicated his interest in Traditionalism to András László, a younger dissident philosopher. In 1975 László began to give private lessons in philosophy and Traditionalism to a circle of twenty or thirty fellow dissidents, and this circle developed into open Traditionalism in the 1990s.[43] A Hamvas Béla Kör (Béla Hamvas Circle) was established, as well as an Evolian publishing house (Arkhé), and three Evolian groups.[44]

The most important Hungarian Traditionalist group at the end of the twentieth century was the Kard-Kerezst-Korona Szövetség (Sword-Cross-Crown Alliance) of Tibor Imre Baranyi, based in Debrecen, near the Romanian border.

The size of the Kard-Kerezst-Korona Szövetség's following is unknown but may have been substantial. This group supported a publishing house, a journal, and a church—A Metafizikai Hagyomány Egyháza (The Church of Metaphysical Tradition). This church practiced "an absolutely universal religion . . . on the basis of the primordial and universal spiritual-religious Tradition," but no other details are known.[45]

Post-Communist Hungarian Traditionalism—while based on Evola, Hamvas, and László—shows greater interest in Guénon, Schuon, and religion in general than was the case with postwar Italian Evolian Traditionalism, though the Kard-Kerezst-Korona Szövetség has an obvious political agenda. A similar return to the religious roots of Traditionalism can be seen in Italy. Arx, the Messina branch of the Dioscuri group that had emerged from Ordine Nuovo in the 1960s, revived in the 1980s and held various meetings aiming at reuniting the disparate strands of Roman neo-Paganism. These efforts bore fruit in 1988 with the establishment of a Movimento Tradizionalista Romano (Roman Traditionalist Movement), and in 1992 with the founding of the Curia Romana Patrum (Roman Curia), which standardized neo-Pagan ritual and united the various calendars previously being followed. The Curia Romana Patrum was followed by at least five other neo-Pagan groups in various parts of Italy. It is not known what role Traditionalism plays for these groups; there seems to be little political emphasis, however.[46]

Though Evola remained important to the European extreme right and even parts of the American extreme right at the end of the twentieth century, his work was no longer dominant. For one of the leading writers and publishers of the European New Right, Alain de Benoist, Evola and Guénon were of interest—especially historical interest—but no longer of great importance. De Benoist had read most of their works, and had even written on them, but his own ideas and the ideas explored in the various journals and magazines he controlled were often constructed on bases incompatible with any variety of Traditionalism.[47]

10

Education

During the 1950s and 1960s Mircea Eliade's soft Traditionalism assisted a transformation in the academic study of religion in America. In France, Louis Dumont's Indology, informed by soft Traditionalism, became increasingly influential, while Henri Hartung and his Institut des sciences et techniques humaines (Institute for humane sciences and techniques) began a transformation in the continuing education of adults, and especially of executives. Hartung aimed at the subtle transformation of the general culture, but after some years he concluded in 1968 that his efforts were in vain, and he abandoned the softest of soft Traditionalism for a "hard" Traditionalist broadside—which was indeed in vain. Also in France a leading Jewish educator, Rabbi Léon Askénazi, drew on Traditionalism, but within strict limits that show why Jewish Traditionalism is so rare.

Simultaneously, a venture similar to Hartung's, the Institut scientifique d'instruction et d'éducation (Scientific Institute for Education and Training) of Paul de Séligny, illustrated how far from Guénon's own objectives Traditionalism could lead.

Religious Studies in America

After the end of the Second World War, Mircea Eliade moved from the Romanian legation in Portugal to France, where in 1945 he began to teach religious sciences at the Sorbonne. His work in French established his reputation in the West—his previous work, in Romanian, was largely inaccessible. Though he was briefly involved in Romanian émigré politics, helping to establish the newspaper *Lucea Farul* (Morning Star) with the financial support of a former member of the Legion of the Archangel Michael, he seems soon to have distanced himself from many of his prewar associates, meeting Michel Vâlsan only once, in 1948.[1] He also met Julius Evola once in Rome, probably in 1949, and corresponded with him, but the correspondence seems to have stopped in 1952 or 1953.[2] His prewar activities in Bucharest were generally unknown in France.

During this period Eliade's activities were supported financially by the Bollingen Foundation. This wealthy foundation, established by Paul Mellon (of Gulf Oil), also sponsored an influential series on religion published by the Princeton University Press (the Bollingen Series) as well as the annual Eranos Meetings held from 1933 at Ascona, Switzerland. Eliade was a regular participant at Eranos and was also published in the Bollingen Series, as was Coomaraswamy.[3] Though the Bollingen Foundation contributed to the spread of the new type of religious scholarship exemplified by Eliade and discussed in this chapter, it was not in any way a Traditionalist organization—it was dedicated rather to the work and later memory of C. G. Jung, who dominated Eranos, and of whom Mellon's wife had been a devotee.[4] Jung's and Eliade's interests and work had some elements in common, but more that differed. Jung and Bollingen and Eranos, then, belong to a separate stream of intellectual history from that of Eliade.

Eliade's fame grew, and in 1958 he was appointed to the Chair of History of Religion at the University of Chicago, a post he occupied until his death in 1986. During these years he kept a low profile except as a scholar. Although one graduate student remembers him as an evident Traditionalist, Eliade generally avoided discussion of politics and of his personal religious convictions.[5] This decision to cast a veil over his past was a wise one; when a reaction against his work began shortly before his death, both his Traditionalist and his Legionary connections were rediscovered and "his whimsical smile [was] darkened by whispers of moral and political duplicity."[6]

During the 1960s and 1970s Eliade's influence on American religious studies was enormous, as is suggested by the dedication to him of the 75th anniversary meeting of the American Academy of Religion (AAR, the largest American learned society for the study of religion) two years before his death.[7] The significance of Eliade's work for religious studies lies not in its detail (though his output was prodigious), but in his general approach—that is, in his "soft" Traditionalism. What Eliade did in American—and to some extent also West European—academia was to act as obstetrician for the birth of religious studies as an autonomous field rather than as an adjunct to theology or sociology.

Before Eliade, non-Christian religions had been studied either from a purely Christian point of view, as a more liberal descendant of medieval heresiography, or from a materialist point of view, as by Max Weber and his pupil Joachim Wach, who was Eliade's predecessor at the University of Chicago. What Eliade called "archaic" religions and Guénon called "tradition" had generally been termed "primitive" religion, a term that carried the evolutionary implication that these religions were somehow incomplete precursors of more perfect, later religion. This was the view of Evola's Johann Jakob Bachofen, as well as the standard nineteenth-century view, and was still widespread among scholars in the 1950s, as it is among the general public today.[8]

Eliade's approach was radically different and was the prototype of what has been called the "autonomous" study of religion, the approach that is generally accepted today.[9] As we saw in chapter 5, Eliade dismissed the evolutionary hypothesis on the grounds that the modern way of seeing things was fundamentally different from the archaic and, being atypical, should be disregarded. In so doing, he privileged archaic religion (or tradition) over modernity and superseded both the Christian and the materialist approaches to the study of religion. The Christian approach was superseded for obvious reasons: archaic religion was more important than contemporary Christianity. The materialist approach was superseded because it tended to be evolutionary, and also because Eliade's project required that religions be studied "on their own plane of reference," in the terms in which they made sense to those who believed in them, which were of course not materialist terms.

The "autonomous" study of religion established by Eliade's example implied both a revolution in methodology and a revolution in university structures. The thousands of American scholars who attend the annual meeting of the AAR are in many ways the products of these revolutions. Their departments owe Eliade a great debt for their existence. None of them would think for a second of presenting their research in Christian or in purely materialist terms (though they are, of course, sensitive to the potential impact of material factors on religious phenomena).[10]

The "autonomous" approach that Eliade sponsored derives, at least in part, from Romanian Traditionalism of the 1930s. There were, of course, other factors: not least among them was the fact that the Christian and materialist approaches were beginning to show signs of age. That is why they were so easily replaced. Others came up with similar replacements: theoretical justifications for the "autonomous" approach to the study of religion can easily be found elsewhere. Eliade himself referred to the work of Rudolf Otto, who in his *Das Heilige* [The Holy] (1917) had developed the useful concept of numinosity, which derived ultimately from Kant.[11] That Otto seemed to support Guénon must have been welcome to Eliade, if only because it helped relieve him of the need to cite Guénon.

Eliade's approach to religious studies has not, of course, been immune to criticism. It has been objected, for example, that studying religions "on their own plane of reference" tends to isolate religious studies.[12] This is undoubtedly true, but then the isolation of one discipline from another is a general problem in contemporary academia that has been widely recognized and is to some extent already being addressed by the growing emphasis on interdisciplinary studies. More seriously, Eliade has been charged with "uncritical universal generalization,"[13] and the soft Traditionalist thesis of a general model of human religiosity has come under much attack by those who seek to demonstrate that no general model exists, that myth is *not* universal, and that the lumping together of all archaic peoples and their systems is "aggressively assimilating" and unsound.[14] Eliade's views of cyclical and linear time were among the earliest to be attacked, on the grounds that—it was argued—they were quite simply historically wrong.[15] In both criticisms we can hear echoes of Sylvain Lévi's comments on Guénon's thesis in 1921.

One criticism against which Eliade should be defended is that his project was unscientific because it was a version of the standard Traditionalist research project sailing under false colors. Eliade has recently even been accused of "camouflaging his sources."[16] Although the reconstruction in chapter 5 in part agrees with this judgment, no "duplicity" was involved. The later Eliade certainly did not see himself as a Traditionalist under false colors.[17] The Traditionalist genesis of Eliade's approach does not mean that his work should be dismissed. His scholarship should rather be judged in its own right.

There was one important later attempt to introduce harder Traditionalism into mainstream academic discourse under its own colors. This took the form of a number of sessions at annual meetings of the AAR during the 1980s. The AAR had by then grown so vast that it was divided into a number of "sections," "groups," and "seminars."[18] In 1986 a group—called "Esotericism and Perennialism"—was established for Traditionalism, but it foundered after three years, the victim of the conflicting agendas of the two main groups behind it. One group, composed chiefly of French scholars, wanted to study Traditionalism as a religious phenomenon (rather as it is examined in this book). The other group, composed mostly of American scholars and dominated by Maryamis, wanted to study religion from a Traditionalist viewpoint. The clashes (or "intense debate") between these two incompatible objectives resulted in the group's dismantling, or rather its transformation into a very different seminar for Theosophy and Theosophic Thought.[19]

The approach behind the short-lived AAR group did, however, have one interesting consequence: two articles written by an Indologist, Gene Thursby, who was one of two Traditionalists at the University of Florida. Thursby was first led to Traditionalist works by reading Schumacher's *Guide for the Perplexed*, and then attended a Summer Faculty Seminar held at Berkeley by Huston Smith. Thursby is a Traditionalist in the sense of accepting many Traditionalist premises, but he is not known to belong to any Traditionalist group.[20]

Thursby's two articles recast Traditionalism into the standard terms of twentieth-century scholarship. He explains, for example, that Traditionalism "insists that paths to transcendence and transformation must be situated within traditional contexts. This is so because it is only within such communities that the socializing structures are conditioned by revealed religion."[21] He treats Traditionalism neither as absolute truth—as Nasr and other Traditionalists do—nor as a phenomenon, as the French scholars at the AAR (and this book) do, but as a system, a way of seeing things, a phenomenology (like, for example, Marxism or structuralism).

Thursby's Traditionalism, which he calls "perennial anthropology," thus has the potential to enter mainstream Western intellectual discourse just as Eliade's did, but sailing under its own colors. It has not yet realized this potential, however. Thursby published his articles in scholarly journals,[22] but they failed to elicit much interest. Evidently discouraged by this reception and by the collapse of the AAR group, Thursby has since focused his work elsewhere.

The hostility of most non-Traditionalist scholars to the study of religion from a Traditionalist viewpoint is clear. Wouter Hanegraaff, the first occupant of a chair of esotericism at the University of Amsterdam, advanced as one of the major problems facing the serious study of esotericism that "scholars of Western esoteric currents frequently find themselves scheduled in seminar programs or publication series together with perennialists." Similarly, the German Islamologist Bernd Radtke identified one of the two major problems facing the study of Sufism as being "mystification," the "negative role" played by Traditionalist scholars such as Nasr (the other problem being that too few English-speaking scholars read German).[23]

Sociology and Judaism in France

The career of Louis Dumont in France in some ways parallels that of Eliade in America. Dumont discovered Guénon while a rebellious dropout in artistic circles in Paris in the early 1930s. He then completed his education and also learned Sanskrit while a prisoner of war in Germany between 1939 and 1945. After the war he earned a Ph.D., taught social anthropology for four years at Oxford, and from 1955 until the late 1970s occupied the chair of Indian sociology at the Sorbonne.[24] In this capacity he trained many of France's future sociologists and Indologists. His *Homo hierarchicus* of 1966[25] was, by general agreement, his most important book. In it Dumont developed an altogether Traditionalist conception of Indian society as representing a traditional norm of religiously based hierarchy, a conception that he later contrasted unfavorably with modern individualism in his *Essais sur l'individualisme* [Studies on Individualism].[26] This contrast was further developed by Dumont and a small number of followers who formed a research "team" within France's Centre Nationale de Recherches Scientifiques. This team attempted to found a "French

school of sociology" but achieved only limited recognition;[27] it might be regarded as a rare example of an officially recognized soft traditionalist group in
academia.

Like Eliade, Dumont never cited Guénon, though he did admit in writing
to one other then unfashionable influence on his thought—that of Alexis de
Tocqueville.[28] Guénon's importance for Dumont, however, was known to his
colleagues[29] and was convincingly demonstrated in 1995 in an article by Roland
Lardinois, despite Dumont's plea of "Let's not talk too much of [Guénon's]
influence," made at a conference while Lardinois was preparing his article.[30]
In his article Lardinois also demonstrated certain technical deficiencies in Dumont's work that, he argued, allowed Dumont to reach his quasi-Traditionalist
conclusions.

Dumont and his criticism of modern individualism became popular in the
1970s and 1980s among French writers and intellectuals opposed to the currents that they saw emerging from 1968, notably structuralism and quasi-
Marxist currents in sociology. Those in France calling for a return to "traditional
values" and attacking "modern individualism" frequently drew on Dumont,
often—according to one commentator—without having actually read him.[31]
Few of them could have been aware that they were also drawing on Guénon.

Guénon also appealed to another French educator of a very different type,
Rabbi Léon Askénazi, director of the Gilbert Bloch School at Orsay (just outside
Paris) and a master of the Kabbala, the Jewish mystical tradition.[32] It is not
known how Askénazi encountered the work of Guénon, but it probably happened after his first arrival in France, in 1944, as a 22-year-old chaplain in the
Free French Army. Askénazi was born and brought up in Algeria, where his
father was later the chief rabbi, in both traditional and modern circles. His
parents were from old scholarly families. They spoke informally in Judeo-
Arabic or Judeo-Spanish, formally in classical Hebrew, and publicly in French.
Askénazi himself was educated in Oran's French lycée, and then after his war
service at the Sorbonne in Paris and finally at the Musée de l'homme, where
he studied ethnology and anthropology under Claude Lévy-Strauss.[33]

Askénazi was recruited in about 1945 to teach at the Gilbert Bloch School,[34]
which had been established to train a new generation of French Jewish community leaders to replace those killed during the Holocaust. The school's first
director, Jacob Gordin (a rabbi of Russian origin resident in France since 1933,
and possibly also a reader of Guénon), died in 1947, and Askénazi then directed
the Gilbert Bloch School from 1951. He also ran the Jewish scout movement
in France—the Éclaireurs Israélites de France—and the Union of Jewish Students.

At the Gilbert Bloch School, Askénazi addressed himself especially to
partly secularized students. He saw the school's central mission as being to
"express the Jewish tradition in . . . the vocabulary and terms of the West" or
of "general philosophy."[35] This necessity led him to a wide-ranging study of

contemporary and classical French thought that was by no means restricted to Guénon. What Askénazi took from Guénon was his analysis of tradition and modernity, some of his vocabulary, and his understanding of tradition as intimately related with the esoteric.

Askénazi's original interest in Kabbala as the esoteric aspect of the Jewish tradition, however, derived not from Guénon but from his maternal grandfather, a well-known master of the Kabbala.[36] The Kabbala remained widespread and respected in the North African Jewish circles of Askénazi's origin, even though European Jews mostly rejected it as obscurantist.

The placing of Tradition in opposition to the "modern mentality" proved an effective way of bringing many of Askénazi's students back to their own tradition, just as—in other hands—it would prove effective in bringing Iranian students and Francophone Moroccans back to their religious "roots," as we will see in a later chapter. Askénazi formed almost a whole generation of Francophone Jewry's leaders and imparted an interest in Guénon and in aspects of Traditionalism to many of them.[37] His status and gifts were such that one French scholar, Charles Mopsik, found it necessary to explain why Askénazi did not establish a major sectarian religious group of his own (Mopsik suggests that the reason was partly a question of temperament and partly because Askénazi scrupulously respected the ancient and restrictive rules for the transmission of his Kabbalistic knowledge).[38] Askénazi's successor as director of the Gilbert Bloch School after his emigration to Israel in 1958,[39] André Fraenkel, was also a Traditionalist in Askénazi's mold.[40]

Although Askénazi was influential in spreading a view of Kabbala as a respectable and proper element of the Jewish tradition and of Western modernity as inherently defective, he did not spread Traditionalism proper. He died in 1996. His later followers know Guénon only as one writer among many in whom Askénazi was interested, and they do not attach any particular importance to him.[41] The next generation was educated mostly in orthodox Yeshivot where Guénon was of no interest.[42]

This is almost the only known instance of Jewish Traditionalism, and why this should be so is shown by the ways in which Askénazi's Traditionalism differed from the norm. Although Askénazi is said to have appreciated the writing of Elie Benamozegh, a nineteenth-century rabbi who proposed the Kabbala as a form of primordial religion that could unite both Jews and Christians,[43] he was emphatically not a believer in the transcendent unity of religions. For Askénazi, the primordial tradition of mankind was the Jewish tradition. What was lost to the West with the destruction of the Templars (an event that many Traditionalists emphasize) was not a nondenominational perennial philosophy, but rather the elements of truth that some Westerners had adopted from Judaism. Askénazi followed the Traditionalists in their diagnosis of modernity, seeing it as a final stage in the cycle that led inexorably to the apocalypse, but he differed in his prescription.[44] Although he could sympathize with

Islam more easily than with Christianity—which seemed to him irredeemably polytheistic, even pagan[45]—what astonished him, according to a close follower, was how the other Traditionalists failed to see what was in front of their noses: that the primordial tradition did not need to be recovered but was there, intact and easily available, in Judaism. He supposed that the Traditionalists' lack of interest in Judaism resulted from some form of anti-Semitism, and he even wondered whether Guénon himself might have been of Jewish origin, since "Guénoun" is a common Sephardic surname.[46] Judaism's firm rejection of other religious traditions acts, it would seem, as a bar to the development of full-blown Jewish Traditionalism.

Hartung's Institut des Sciences et Techniques Humaines

After Henri Hartung left Schuon and divorced his first wife (who remained with Schuon), he began a new career as an educator, establishing an up-market night school in Paris, the Ecole supérieure d'orientation [Institute for Education—the French title does not really translate], initially to prepare students for entry to various prestigious institutions of higher education. This was a similar project to the Collège Rollin that Guénon had entered in 1904. The Ecole supérieure d'orientation's philosophy was based on Hartung's observation that many students left high school with plenty of information but little idea of what to do with it. Hartung accordingly taught not just the subjects required for the various entrance examinations, but also *formation générale* (general education) in the "humane sciences"—logic, self-expression, and the like.[47] Though such an approach is widespread today, it was extremely innovative in 1950s France.

In 1956 the Ecole supérieure d'orientation opened a section for the continuing education of executives (*cadres*). This was also a novel concept in France, and Hartung bore much responsibility for spreading it. By 1957 he had IBM France as a client, and the section for executives had proved so successful that it grew into a separate school and finally a major business, the Institut des sciences et techniques humaines (ISTH, Institute for humane sciences and techniques).[48] By 1962 Hartung's clients included Air France, the major bank Crédit Lyonnais, and the petroleum multinational Shell. By 1963, the ISTH employed 66 lecturers, had a journal and its own series of books with the publsher Fayard, and occupied substantial premises in Paris. In 1964 Hartung was lecturing in Japan as part of a high-profile French cultural mission, and in 1966 the opening of an international version of the ISTH in a restored chateau was sponsored by such industrial giants as Simca Aviation and was reported on not just in the French press but in *Time*, the London *Times*, and the *New York Times*.[49] This meteoric success derived partly from the demand for the product that Hartung was offering (executive education with a difference) and partly from Hartung's own qualities as a public speaker: he was an unusually accomplished orator.[50] Hartung also became well known for a series of books and articles on continuing education, and for his part in a campaign which finally produced a 1971 law making continuing education the right of every French citizen, passed by the National Assembly with only one dissenting vote.[51]

Hartung's *Pour une éducation permanente* [For Continuing Education] (1966) was favorably reviewed in France's major newspapers.[52] Hartung had already made what were becoming the standard arguments from necessity in various speeches and articles. Not only were France's economic competitors dangerously more advanced in continuing education, but the modern business world was changing so quickly that executives' adaptability was crucial to economic success. Hartung did not, however, depend on purely economic arguments. Continuing education, he wrote in 1966, "is utilitarian in that it makes possible greater professional efficiency, and at the same time disinterested in facilitating self-realization; collective, its aim being to teach the greatest possible number of men to organize themselves better and work together, it is also personal, since everyone must be alone in their knowledge of themselves and in their understanding of the world."[53]

The need for continuing education thus established, Hartung's *Pour une éducation permanente* discusses its organization and components, underlining the importance of *culture générale* (general culture), essentially general education. Executives should be educated, cultivated persons, trained in logic and self-expression, able to understand contemporary thought and economics. This aspect of continuing education was much emphasized at Hartung's own ISTH and was one of the reasons for its success. In an interview with *Le Figaro Littéraire* in 1962, Hartung had boasted that he had corporate presidents reading Montaigne and Sartre.[54]

Hartung's *culture générale* was not really about Sartre or economics. In chapter 6 of *Pour une éducation permanente*, Hartung finally brings up the need for "self-development," really spiritual realization—and there, well coated in more easily assimilable ideas, is his Traditionalism. Throughout the years Hartung had remained a Traditionalist and a Muslim, though this was a little known fact. He fasted Ramadan in secret and was even in contact with the sole surviving Traditionalist of the first generation, Julius Evola. After first meeting Evola in Rome in 1964, Hartung continued to visit him regularly until Evola's death ten years later,[55] and he carried a photograph of Evola in his pocket until the day of his death (one of half a dozen photographs of his spiritual mentors). This relationship between Hartung—generally seen as a leftist—and Evola the rightist was an unlikely one, as Hartung himself realized: "A resistance veteran, condemned by the Germans, of a social sensibility to say the least different from that of Evola. . . . I find myself in dialogue with him, with this man who calls himself of the Right, who even writes that word with a capital R, who knew Mussolini."[56] It was not Evola's politics that interested Hartung, but his Traditionalism.

In 1924, in *Orient et Occident*, Guénon argued for the revitalization of Western spirituality by an elite formed for that purpose, so as to avert the cataclysmic collapse of Western civilization. In 1966, Hartung argued for spiritual revitalization as a component of cultural growth, and for cultural growth as an element of the continuing education of business executives, and for continuing education on grounds of France's economic competitiveness and also on more humane grounds. On the face of it, Hartung's strategy was a sound one: the danger of lack of economic competitiveness worried far more people in 1966 than did the danger of the cataclysmic collapse of Western civilization. In addition to recasting one of Guénon's central arguments in "soft" terms, Hartung also blended his own form of spiritual revitalization into courses at the ISTH. By 1968 these had been attended by 12,000 French executives and 6,000 other pupils (senior public administrators and the like).[57]

To what extent these 18,000 alumni of the ISTH had absorbed "a cultural base which they seemed very clearly to lack,"[58] let alone a spiritual base, is impossible to say. Hartung himself concluded that he had failed. This conclusion was one consequence of the "events" of May 1968, when a popular revolution at one point seemed about to destroy the French republic. On the evening of May 24, 1968, Henri Hartung went out to walk through the streets of Paris. After watching clashes between student revolutionaries and CRS riot police at the Pont Neuf, he went home and spent the rest of the night pacing the floor of his apartment. That evening was as important a turning point in his life as had been reading Guénon's *Introduction générale* in 1939 or his meeting with Ramana Maharshi in 1947.[59] He realized that he had ended up on the wrong side of the barricades and that "a man can only accept a lie in renouncing his own dignity."[60]

Hartung at first saw the clashes of May 1968 as the "affirm[ation] . . . of interior sovereignty," as "the necessarily violent, liberating, unexpected, and brutal opening towards the future and towards the possible."[61] Hartung later revised this view[62] but still concluded that his "soft" approach was getting nowhere, that he had been co-opted by the system. Evola had asked Hartung in 1966, in response to Hartung's book on continuing education: "What is the use of your readers seeing clearly if, despite this, they accept a 'system' that remains profane?"[63] In May 1968 Hartung broadly accepted Evola's pessimism with regard to the system and traveled to Rome to announce this fact to Evola in person.[64] His efforts had been successful, he thought—but only "on condition that there is no obligation to change, or to share, or to suppress two major abuses: the gulf between interior liberty and everyday life, . . . and the magic of the word that replaces action in an uninterrupted succession of beautiful promises that are not kept."[65] Even the continuing education that became every citizen's right in 1971 was not the type of interior and spiritual education that Hartung had worked for, but rather "an invasion by [the schools], with their hierarchical structure, diplomas, syllabi and pedagogy."[66] This was an objection not to formal learning, but to the continuing triumph of technical training over the education of the whole being.[67]

After May 1968 Hartung abandoned his earlier approach and turned to outspoken criticism of "the system," partly on Traditionalist and partly on leftist grounds. For example, he was invited to address the August 1968 Bilderberg Meeting held at Mont Tremblant, Canada, on two themes: Western-Communist relations and the internationalization of business (what would later be called globalization). This was a considerable compliment. The annual Bilderberg Meeting is more select than the more famous annual meeting of the World Economic Forum at Davos, Switzerland—only about 100 people are invited, as opposed to thousands at Davos. The audience that listened to Hartung in 1968 included assorted luminaries. These meetings and their partici-pants were and are confidential, but the Canadian press spotted Canadian prime minister Pierre Trudeau, the American ambassador to the United Nations, David Rockefeller (president of the Chase Manhattan Bank), and En-och Powell, the British MP then favored by many on the British right as a candidate for premiership and by some as an anti-socialist dictator.[68] Hartung spoke on "The Internationalization of Business: The Social Aspect." By "so-cial," Hartung really meant "spiritual":

> The contemporary economic and social system is apparently only developing on a horizontal plane with no regard to the vertical pro-cess leading towards a transcendency which is denied or, at best, re-jected as scientifically unprovable. . . . The transition of business from the regional and national level to the world-wide level . . . un-less accompanied by parallel research in respect of the inner reality of man . . . can only lead to regression through a return to an even more narrow positivism. . . . By leaving the life of the spirit wholly out of account, the protagonists of the modern world may well be organizing a world of wretchedness in their efforts to abolish the ef-fects of wretchedness.[69]

It is not known how Hartung's audience received this message, but Hartung was not invited to any subsequent Bilderberg meetings.

Hartung's 1968 disenchantment also gave rise to a book published in 1969, *Ces princes du management: le patronat français devant ses responsabilités* [These "Management" Princes: French Bosses and Their Responsibilities]. Hartung wrote this book quickly: in it he said with passion everything he must have wished to say over the preceding 20 years: The triumph of material pro-gress was the triumph of the quantitative over the qualitative, with means inverted into ends, creating a "slave society" (the title of chapter 5). This was "hard" Traditionalism indeed, though with a distinctive leftist twist—Hartung saw the characteristics of commercial life as coloring the life of society as a whole, and conditions of employment as the crucial determinant in the individual's private life.

Hartung's hard Traditionalism met with a very different reception than did his earlier, very soft Traditionalist, books, and initiatives. Former associates wrote to him in sadness and sometimes in hostility. Press reviews of his book were unenthusiastic, dismissing his arguments as nothing new. What most reviewers found interesting was that a man such as Hartung had abandoned his position out of principle, and some even commented on his evident courage.[70] This reception was perhaps precisely due to the passion with which Hartung had written. His book shows an understanding of how commercial life and "the system" really work that is rare among radical critics. This insight might easily be missed by a reader struck by his more extreme positions. At one point Hartung even took the automobile as an example of inversion, of a means becoming an end in itself.[71] While there may be truth in this view, it would strike many readers as faintly ridiculous.

The exceptions to this generally hostile reception are instructive. Only three reviews praised the book. One, in *L'Humanité*, the official organ of the then still powerful French Communist Party, endorsed Hartung's criticisms but—predictably—regretted that his failure to use socialist class analysis doomed his work to "sterility and . . . pessimism."[72] Another, in the conservative Swiss *Tribune de Genève*, recognized that Hartung's position was based in religious faith and wrongly welcomed him as a fellow Catholic.[73] Finally, *Entreprise* [Enterprise], then France's leading business monthly, chose *Ces princes du management* as its book of the week[74]—though whether this choice reflected real interest or self-confident amusement is hard to say.

Two letters of support to Hartung stand out: one from Jacques Maritain, Guénon's one-time sponsor at the Institut Catholique, and the other from Henri d'Orléans, the comte de Paris (legitimate claimant to the French throne), with whom Hartung had had good relations since he had tutored his son in the days of the Ecole supérieure d'orientation. "The struggle you have conducted . . . ," wrote the heir of the Bourbons, "joins with that which for thirty years I have followed in the same spirit."[75]

Though doubtless heartened by such support, Hartung was in general disappointed and hurt by his book's reception, and also was assailed by financial difficulties caused by his abrupt withdrawal from ISTH. Obliged to give up his Paris apartment, he moved to his maternal grandparents' house in Fleurier, Switzerland, which he had inherited. His projects, which will be discussed in the next chapter, were thereafter no longer aimed at the general public.

De Séligny's Institut Scientifique d'Instruction et d'Education

If "deviation" dominated the end of the Maryamiyya in Bloomington, "deviation" was present from the start in one of the strangest independent applications of Traditionalism, that made by Paul de Séligny, a Mauritian of French descent who became a minor 1960s guru—and for some a notorious one. De Séligny had become a Traditionalist in France in the late 1920s or early 1930s, probably in 1927 or 1928 like so many others, and may have visited Guénon in Cairo. He entered the Alawiyya Order in Morocco in 1939 or 1940, though it is not clear exactly how;[76] there was then a small Schuonian group in Morocco, including Jean-Victor Hocquard, with which he was connected. Hocquard, a musicologist who had joined Schuon's Alawiyya in 1938 or 1939, abandoned the Alawiyya and Islam for his original Catholicism in about 1945 and lost contact with de Séligny. Both Hocquard and de Séligny remained in Morocco, however; the former taught at the Lycée in Tangier while the latter became a seed merchant, also in Tangier.[77]

Though Hocquard had left Schuon and Islam, he remained interested in Traditionalism, an interest that he passed on to his son Manuel. In 1960 he renewed contact with de Séligny at the urging of Manuel and of his daughter, Ain Shams, then 18. The Hocquards asked de Séligny to lead them on the Sufi path.

A new Traditionalist branch of the Alawiyya then came into being, led by de Séligny, consisting of Hocquard, his children and other family members, and a few others. It was, however, an unusual branch. De Séligny went even further than the later Schuon did, immediately exempting his followers from the need to follow any aspect of the Sharia and teaching a Perennialism more Hindu than Islamic. His way, he explained, was "an intellectual way, not a mystic way." Its central practice was "the Work" (le travaille), a simplified form of *dhikr* involving the repetition of the Islamic Confession of Faith.[78]

After about a year, de Séligny and his followers left Tangier for Europe and established themselves on the Mediterranean coast in the Principality of Monaco (leaving de Séligny's skeptical wife in Tangier).[79] There the nature of the group changed: it soon became distinctly anti-traditional. In May 1962 de Séligny founded a Centre d'études culturelles (Cultural Studies Center), equipped with a fortnightly newspaper, *Je suis* [I Am]. Early issues of *Je suis* dealt with the (somewhat limited) artistic and literary life of Monaco, and also with fishing and yachting. A "youth page" soon appeared, however. This expanded into a section and displaced fishing and yachting. By the end of 1962, youth issues had taken over the whole newspaper. In February 1963 *Je suis* declared itself to be "entirely edited and published by youth," even though de Séligny, then aged 59, clearly remained in control. "We, youth" had suffered from boredom and alienation (*ennui*) until they met de Séligny; he and *Je suis* changed everything.[80]

The origin of de Séligny's discovery of the issues of youth is unknown but may be related to the affair he had started with Hocquard's daughter Ain Shams, by then 19 or 20. This affair and the financial demands de Séligny was making on his followers—many of whom went hungry to satisfy his tastes for champagne and expensive automobiles—led to disaffection among some of his followers and then to difficulties with Monaco's authorities, and in 1963 de Séligny and his group were expelled from Monaco. *Je suis* also collapsed for lack of subscribers.[81]

De Séligny's group moved further along the Mediterranean coast, reestablishing themselves in Villefranche-sur-Mer outside Nice, where they started an Institut scientifique d'instruction et d'éducation (Scientific Institute for Education and Training), located on a yacht de Séligny had acquired, the *Storm-Bird*. In a less ambitious way than Hartung, de Séligny specialized in the gap between high school and university, and in the children of the French elite. He provided not only the standard curriculum but something more: meditation exercises and a very special milieu. The meditation exercises seem to have been the modified *dhikr* de Séligny had used during his Sufi period, repeating his own "aphorisms" rather than the Confession of Faith.[82] The milieu combined typically 1960s anti-authoritarianism with extreme devotion to de Séligny himself.

One of de Séligny's most devoted later followers was Béatrice Le Mire, the rebellious daughter of a French diplomat. Le Mire was sent to de Séligny's institute by her parents in 1966 after de Séligny had succeeded in transforming her elder brother from an academic disaster who was expelled from his high school into a passable medical student.[83] She later recalled her first private meeting with de Séligny: "For the first time in my life, I had in front of me someone who was not seeking to deceive me with beautiful words, to push me into one way of thinking. . . . He did no more than help me to get to the bottom of my ideas, in such a way that I myself could see the problems, that I could reveal the contradictions."[84] De Séligny wrote: "Everything rests on this fundamental error: we take ourselves for something other than what we actually are."[85] De Séligny, then, assisted his students and followers in a process of self-discovery—or, in the case of Le Mire, the typically 1960s discovery that everything was the fault of her "bourgeois" parents, and the discovery that her hope of salvation lay in de Séligny.[86]

Le Mire was devoted to de Séligny not only as guru but also as lover, a position she shared with Ain Shams. The devotion of others is less easily explicable. Ain Shams's father, Hocquard, was the author of a successful biography of Mozart. He dedicated the revised 1970 edition of this book to de Séligny, "the sage whose works will communicate to the whole world the fundamental wisdom, of a scientific nature, that he has brought to light" (a hope that de Séligny was never to fulfil, since none of his works ever reached the press). De Séligny, wrote Hocquard—then 60 years of age and the official director of the Institut scientifique d'instruction et d'éducation—had helped him to identify "false ideas" by liberating him from "the philosophical, meta-physical and even theological views of which I was prisoner." He had revised his book on Mozart in 1964 to try to remove these "false ideas" and then made an even more thorough revision for the 1970 edition, having "realized the responsibility I bore for having contributed, through my writings, to spreading ideas that only do, and only can do, damage."[87]

In addition to drawing Hocquard into surprising recantations—the writings in question were after all a popular work on Mozart's music—de Séligny inspired such devotion that most of his followers seem to have been happy to subsist on a diet of plain noodles in order to support him, though their hunger was such that the wife of one follower resorted to shoplifting.[88] During the Sufi period some followers sold their furniture;[89] during the period of the Institut scientifique d'instruction et d'éducation Le Mire persuaded her parents to give her an automobile and then immediately sold it to give the proceeds to de Séligny.[90]

The devotion of de Séligny's followers had tragic consequences—broken marriages and abandoned children. They are explicable in terms of de Séligny's possibly unintentional development of standard spiritual techniques. He started as a Sufi shaykh, and the followers of any Sufi shaykh are expected to place the utmost trust in their guide. The community surrounding the shaykh insulates the Sufi from the distractions of the outside world, and ascesis—including fasting—strengthens the will against temptation. In de Séligny's case, his followers came to fear abandonment by "the boss" (patron, as he styled himself) above all else, and the slightest sign of disloyalty or hesitation led either to terrifying indications of de Séligny's displeasure or to the threat of ostracism by his other followers. The community surrounding de Séligny was so tight that it cut individuals off entirely from normal life, and so from the realization that their behavior was increasingly bizarre. The community would also rally round to help any doubting individual through any episode of "weak-ness." The need to confront constant hunger further narrowed the vision, ex-cluding anything that might distract the follower from de Séligny himself. And finally, de Séligny's modified dhikr seemed to work, even to those who were losing confidence in him personally.[91] Something similar seems to have hap-pened, in less extreme fashion, among Schuon's followers at Inverness Farms.

The case of de Séligny also resembled that of Schuon in that he was finally the subject of scandal and legal proceedings relating to sexual behavior. Le Mire's parents discovered that their daughter had dropped out of the University of Nice and was having a relationship with de Séligny. Her mother flew to France to take her home. Le Mire then threatened to kill herself, and her mother consigned her to a psychiatric clinic; the age of majority in France then was 21, so Le Mire was still a minor. Le Mire's father simultaneously used his contacts to have de Séligny, who as a result of his place of birth was a British rather than a French citizen, expelled from France.[92]

In the 1950s this might have been the end of the story, but not in 1970. De Séligny applied to the Nice court for Le Mire's release. More important, a communist weekly, Le Patriote [The Patriot], published a note that Le Mire allegedly smuggled out of her clinic, a note that became famous: "Help, help. They are giving me injection after injection. They're giving me a treatment that is making me crazy. I don't want it. Help." Students at the University of Nice set up a Committee for the Support of Béatrice Le Mire and organized a petition. The dean of the Faculty of Humanities refused to sign the petition, and as a result his office was sacked by students. Le Mire's clinic was picketed by the "Communist-Libertarian Group Spartacus—Nice." In the National Assembly the French minister of the interior was questioned about the expulsion order against de Séligny, the question being put by a Socialist deputy, François Mitterrand (later president of France).[93]

Finally, the Nice court judged that while de Séligny's methods were to say the least dubious, that was not the issue. If Le Mire had been confined in order to prevent her from committing suicide, and if there was no longer any danger of suicide, she should be released. She was accordingly released and was flown by her mother to the Dominican Republic, where her father was then French ambassador. A few months later Le Mire celebrated her coming of age by flying back to France with de Séligny, a return that the French press greeted as a victory for liberty against reaction—Le Mire's family were fine representatives of reaction, since not only was her father an ambassador but her uncle was a retired paratroop colonel.[94]

These events have little to do with Traditionalism. They provide, however, a dramatic example of how influences external to Traditionalism can divert to other destinations what was originally a Traditionalist enterprise.

PART IV

Traditionalism and the Future

11

Europe after 1968

After the deaths of Schuon and Evola, there was no central focus to
Traditionalism in the West. Instead, the last part of the twentieth
century saw the growth of many unconnected Traditionalist groups
and influences. Traditionalism ceased to be the property of individual figures and, especially after the 1960s, gradually mingled with
the mainstream of Western spirituality.

The 1960s were clearly the major cultural and intellectual turning point of the Western twentieth century, perhaps even more than
1914–18. Post-1960s Traditionalism, like the post-1960s West, was
different from what came before it. Just as the Renaissance, which
Traditionalists abhor as the death of the Western esoteric tradition,
saw the birth of the Perennialism that lies at the heart of Traditionalism itself, and just as 1914–18 ushered in Traditionalism at the same
time that the old Europe disappeared, so the cultural revolution of
the 1960s gave new energy to Traditionalism and was the start of
the contemporary Traditionalist movement.

The late twentieth century saw a phenomenal growth in the
public appetite for religious and spiritual alternatives. This appetite
was fed at first by such quintessentially 1960s figures as Alan Watts
in America, and, most importantly, Louis Pauwels in much of Europe. Less important but still influential in France was Raymond
Abellio, who in the 1970s became a popular broadcaster first on radio and then on television.[1]

Pauwels's star began to rise in 1961 with the publication in
Paris of *Le matin des magiciens* [The Morning of the Magicians],[2] a
phenomenally successful mixture of esotericism, scientific populari-

zation, and science fiction. The success of this book led to the foundation in late 1961 of a monthly magazine, *Planète* [Planet], which achieved a circulation of 100,000 within a few months.[3] By 1970 *Planète* claimed to be "the most important magazine in Europe on the basis of the weight of its articles, the number of its illustrations, its circulation and its foreign editions"—it was by then also published in Italian, German, Spanish (in Spain and in Argentina), and Portuguese (in Brazil).[4] In 1970 the original French *Planète* had grown so weighty that it split into three: *Planète-plus* for culture and spirituality, *Planète-action* for politics, and *Le nouveau planète* for everything else. *Planète-action* opened with a special issue on the Vietnamese Communist leader Ho Chi Minh, followed by one on Fidel Castro. *Planète-plus* opened with an issue on the Hindu guru Ramakrishna, followed by one on René Guénon.[5]

Pauwels was not himself a Traditionalist—if anything he was a follower of Gurdjieff—but his interest in Traditionalism is visible in *Le matin des magiciens* as well as in his choice of Guénon as the subject of the second issue of *Planète-plus*. Like Hartung and Abellio, Pauwels was a Resistance veteran and a skilled communicator: before launching *Planète*, he had edited the Resistance journal *Combat* and then the major women's glossy magazine *Marie-France*, and after the *Planète* empire collapsed in the early 1970s (fashion had moved on) he went on to the leading national daily *Le Figaro*, from which in 1978 he launched the *Figaro Magazine*.[6] Though not primarily a Traditionalist, Pauwels was responsible for spreading simplified Traditionalism throughout Latin Europe. The period of *Planète*'s success coincided with a significant increase in sales of Guénon's works.[7]

Alan Watts, an English ex-priest and later the guru of American Zen, knew of Traditionalism, but Traditionalism was not especially important to him. His responsibility for introducing a young American, Eugene Rose (later Seraphim Rose), to Traditionalism was entirely accidental. Rose had met Watts in 1953 while an undergraduate student at Pomona College in Southern California, where Watts was then teaching. He followed Watts to the American Academy of Asian Studies, where he found some of Guénon's books in the library. After a period of immersion in the early San Francisco "counterculture," Rose found that he preferred Guénon to Watts. In the words of Rose's biographer, "While Guénon had attempted to study Eastern religions within their own context, Watts seemed [to Rose] to be trying to make them digestible to Westerners. The 'Buddhism' he espoused as a remedy for the spiritual malaise of the West was thus an unauthentic, synthesized expression of that tradition, streamlined to cater to the modern mentality of self-worship."[8] In other words, Guénon convinced Rose that Watts's informal group, to which he belonged, was "counterinitiatic."

Rose initially followed the familiar path. He read Schuon's *Unité transcendante* and accepted its view. He then looked for an orthodox master in an esoteric Tradition. Rather than encountering the Maryamiyya, however, he se-

lected a Chinese Taoist scholar then teaching at Watts's Academy, and he "resolved to do for the Chinese spiritual tradition what [Guénon] had done for the
Hindu." This intention, however, was soon abandoned. Schuon had interested
Rose in Orthodox Christianity, and after a friend took Rose to some Russian
Orthodox church services, one evening in a San Francisco street Rose experienced the overpowering certainty of Christ's divinity. In 1962 he was received
into the Russian Orthodox Church.[9]

As an Orthodox Christian, and after 1965 as an ordained reader, Rose
concluded that "each tradition possesses truth, beyond doubt, but in varying
measures . . . the 'equality' and 'transcendent unity' of religions is a notion
from the modernist 'simplistic' mentality." Traditionalism was not the full answer: "For all the 'wisdom' of Coomaraswamy, Guénon, and the lesser wise
men of today, we seem near to an even greater collapse. . . . Christ requires us
not to 'understand,' but to suffer, die, and arise to Life in Him."[10] Rose did not,
however, reject Traditionalism entirely. It remained part of his personal philosophy in the 1970s, when he replied to a Traditionalist who had written to
him: "I only pray that you will take what is good from him [Guénon] and not
let his limitations chain you."[11]

What Rose kept for himself from Traditionalism was a devotion to "tra-
ditional" esoteric practice as well as firm opposition to the modern world and
to "counterinitiation," the subject of one of his two books, *Orthodoxy and the
Religion of the Future* (1976). This book was in some ways a revision of
Guénon's *Erreur spirite*, attacking the new religious movements of the time:
Swami Vivekananda, Transcendental Meditation, Hare Krishna, Tantric Yoga,
and even the various UFO movements.[12] Rose's other book, *The Soul after
Death* (1980), was much less Traditionalist.[13]

Rose's devotion to traditional esoteric practice bore fruit in a monastery,
the St. Herman Hermitage, established in 1967 in isolated mountains at Platina, California. The monks at St. Herman lived according to the most traditional rule Rose could find, one he wrote himself on the basis of the principles
of an eighteenth-century saint, the Blessed Paisius Velichovsky. St. Herman
flourished in the late 1970s and 1980s, establishing "missionary parishes" in
California, Oregon, Washington, and Idaho and republishing classic Orthodox
texts in Russian for distribution within what was then still the Soviet Union.
These, and later translations of Rose's own two books, became very popular
in "conservative" Orthodox circles in Russia.[14]

Rose, who after his death in 1982 came to be regarded by many as a saint
(there is no formal canonization procedure in Orthodoxy), is the classic example of how Traditionalism became for many a "stepping-stone"—not a destination in itself in the way that it was for previous Traditionalists, but rather
a decisive encounter during a spiritual search that in the end led to some other
destination. Rose was not alone in turning to Russian Orthodoxy after exposure
to Traditionalism. In 1976 a young Swiss, Jean-François Mayer, was rebaptized

into the Russian Orthodox Church after a spiritual search that had taken him from Opus Dei to the Quakers. Traditionalism, as encountered in *Planète* and then in Guénon's *Crise du monde moderne*, was the stepping-stone.[15]

In most cases the influence of Traditionalism on those who did not subsequently join an identifiable Traditionalist group is invisible. Mayer is an exception because he later became an acclaimed scholar of New Religious Movements (a field in which one might detect a Traditionalist interest in "counterinitiation"), and published an entertaining autobiography, *Confessions d'un chasseur de sectes* [Confessions of a Sect Hunter]. It is impossible to quantify the impact of Traditionalism on all other such individuals, though one journalist investigating the conversion of Christian-born French men and women to Islam reported that the name Guénon came up at some point during most of his interviews.[16] The leader of a major Islamic organization in Italy (not himself a Traditionalist) came to the same conclusion with regard to conversions in that country: Guénon came second only to marriage to a Muslim as the trigger for conversion to Islam.[17]

Some, however, are suspicious of converts from a Traditionalist background. After difficulties involving an Italian who passed from Islam to Russian Orthodoxy and then turned to Buddhism, the abbot of the small Russian Orthodox monastery of St. Serafin of Sarov in Tuscany went so far as to pronounce an anathema against "the impious doctrine of René Guénon and of his followers" that Christianity was "only one of several paths that lead to salvation."[18] Others, of course, remain untouched by Traditionalism. It is clear from his *Foucault's Pendulum*, for example, that Umberto Eco is very familiar with Traditionalism, but it seems to have had no effect on his writings or his life.[19]

Later Traditionalist Groups

The list of late twentieth-century groups incorporating Traditionalism in one way or another could go on and on. Most are located in France and Italy, the two countries where Traditionalism first became established, and in Spain, where Traditionalism became increasingly popular as that country enthusiastically caught up with the rest of the West after the death of General Francisco Franco in 1975. In all these areas and in parts of Latin America Traditionalism spawned study centers, journals, and Masonic orders. Amateur philosophers began to meet to discuss Traditionalism in Guénon's native Blois. An Argentine in Barcelona started a successful "university by mail," with Traditionalism occupying an important place on the syllabus. Small, eccentric groups of Frenchman applied Traditionalism to Royalism and even to homosexuality.[20]

One typical group is considered in the next subsection, followed by a selection of the more interesting recent expressions of Traditionalism.

Hartung's Centre de Rencontres Spirituelles et de Méditation

Typical of later Traditionalism is Henri Hartung's post-1968 project, a Centre de rencontres spirituelles et de méditation (Spiritual meeting and meditation center), established in Fleurier, Switzerland, in 1977. Though modest by the standards of Hartung's earlier projects, the center had its own premises and by the 1980s counted 60 official members, all of whom participated in its administration (Hartung remained a leftist). It ran retreats and lectures, usually attended by several hundred nonmembers, Swiss and French—Fleurier is near the French border, easily accessible by train from Paris. The center's newsletter, *Diagonale*, at one point had a circulation of 500.²¹

[handwritten margin note: These are all very small movements]

Like the ISTH (discussed in the previous chapter), the center was not specifically Traditionalist—the majority of its members had probably never even read Guénon, though most accepted the need for an exoteric practice to accompany an esoteric path, a distinctively Traditionalist stance.²² Hartung on occasion described it as continuing education done as it should be, starting with what really mattered.²³ Its practice was essentially that of a Zen monastery, organized primarily not by Henri Hartung but by his second wife, Sylvie, a practitioner of Za-Zen and a Tai Chi teacher who had spent time in Zen monasteries in Japan. Sylvie Hartung came from another of France's major Protestant families—her father had been governor of the Bank of France (president of the French reserve bank) and minister of finance under President de Gaulle. She had never been attracted by Islam or even especially by Traditionalism, but on marrying Henri Hartung she consented to adopt a "traditional" religious practice in place of Protestantism. She selected Catholicism but then found that as a Catholic she could not marry a divorcee, and so in 1966 she turned instead to the meditation techniques taught by Karlfried Graf Dürckheim, the follower of C. G. Jung who discovered Zen and Meister Eckhart while on a German mission in Japan in 1937.²⁴ From Dürckheim, Sylvie Hartung moved on to Za-Zen.

Traditionalism was evident in Henri Hartung's periodic lectures at his and his wife's center. Perennialism was also evident in Hartung's choice of regular guest lecturers. These included Adda Bentounès of the Algerian Alawiyya, who by then had a following of his own in Switzerland, and a Catholic priest, but the most important was a Zen *roshi* (abbot). Another periodic lecturer was Dürckheim, and a close friendship developed between the Dürckheims and the Hartungs. Because of Dürckheim's advanced age, he rarely traveled to Fleurier, but the Hartungs took members of the center on regular visits to Dürckheim's own center in Germany.

Henri Hartung died suddenly in 1988. Two years later Sylvie Hartung decided for personal reasons to withdraw from the center, which consequently ceased to operate in 1992, bringing this part of the history of Traditionalism to a close. Like Rose, Hartung cannot be described as a Traditionalist in the way that Schuon and Vâlsan can. Traditionalism was only one element in his public teaching, and for his followers was a stepping-stone of which they probably not even aware.

Small Is Beautiful

Another instance of Traditionalism's partial passage into the general culture of the West was one of the most successful books of the 1970s, *Small Is Beautiful: Economics as if People Mattered* (1973), by E. F. Schumacher. *Small Is Beautiful* sold several million copies—partly as a result of its inspired title, the suggestion of Schumacher's publisher (Schumacher wanted to call it *The Homecomers*).[25] As far as is known, Schumacher did not attend the Bilderberg Meeting at which Hartung spoke of the dangers of creating wretchedness, but he echoed Hartung's views. Schumacher, a British economist of German origin, attacked contemporary economics for its obsession with size and disregard of nonmaterial objectives, which meant that "innumerable qualitative distinctions are suppressed . . . [and] thus the reign of quantity celebrates its greatest triumph."[26] In his *Règne de la quantité* [The Reign of Quantity] 1945), Guénon argued that one of the central characteristics of the *kali yuga* was the replacement of quality by quantity.

Schumacher, like Hartung, identifies the wretchedness produced by inversion: "If human vices such as greed and envy are systematically cultivated, . . . if whole societies become infected by these vices, . . . actual people . . . find themselves oppressed by increasing frustration, alienation, insecurity and so forth."[27] The proper basis for economics was, Schumacher implied, spiritual— what he called "Buddhist economics," recognizing that "the teachings of Christianity, Islam or Judaism could have been used just as well as those of any other of the great Eastern traditions." "Buddhist economics must be very different from the economics of modern materialism, since the Buddhist sees the essence of civilization not in the multiplication of wants but in the purification of human character."[28]

Schumacher was an appreciative reader of Traditionalist works but was not himself a Traditionalist; he was a disciple less of Guénon than of Gurdjieff (like Pauwels), following a spiritual path within Buddhism and finally converting to Catholicism.[29] As it was for Rose, Traditionalism was one element in Schumacher's personal philosophy rather than a final answer itself—but it was an important element. In addition to being occasionally visible in *Small Is Beautiful*, Traditionalism was also one of the main sources of Schumacher's anti-modernism. This anti-modernism is implicit in much of *Small Is Beautiful*, and explicit in an unusual UN-funded report on the Burmese economy that Schumacher produced in 1955, in which he recommended that the Burmese government abandon all plans for economic development and concentrate instead on Buddhism.[30] "Modern materialistic scientism, . . ." he wrote elsewhere, "has destroyed even the last remnants of ancient wisdom, at least in the Western world."[31]

Traditionalist anti-modernism is not what made *Small Is Beautiful* a success, however, nor even Gurdjieffian spirituality. What was most appreciated were the elements of the book that argued for conservation of natural resources—arguments that helped launch the Green movement that was to characterize much of the late Western twentieth century. "Already," wrote Schumacher, "there is overwhelming evidence that the great self-balancing system of nature is becoming increasingly unbalanced." "Infinite growth in a finite environment is an obvious impossibility." "Non-renewable goods must be used only if they are indispensable, and then only with the greatest care and the most meticulous care for conservation."[32] These views derive not from Traditionalism, but from Anthroposophy, Rudolf Steiner's version of Theosophy. This had inspired the Soil Association, a British group that Schumacher joined in 1949 and that was one of the earliest bodies to press for what would later be called an ecological approach to agriculture.[33] Schumacher's views also derive from British industrial politics: he spent the latter part of his life working as an economic advisor for the British National Coal Board, the state-owned holding company for the British coal industry, and in the 1960s had been assigned the task of marshaling arguments against the British government's proposed closure of loss-making coal mines. His principal argument was that by the 1980s oil reserves would be starting to run out and coal mining would then return to its earlier importance.[34]

It is unclear whether Schumacher himself realized that his book was being read mainly for its arguments for ecology and that its anti-modernism and its plea for a spiritual basis for economics and for life in general were being ignored. The fame that attended his book's growing popularity may well have insulated him from this discovery, as he embarked in late 1973 on a worldwide series of lectures, the stresses of which led to his unexpected death in 1977 while he was traveling between speaking engagements.[35]

The Poet and the Prince

One of the most successful European attempts to introduce Traditionalism to the general public was sponsored by the English poet and literary critic Kathleen Raine. While Raine was an undergraduate student at Cambridge in the late 1920s, an interest in William Blake led her to Blake's sources, which she found included the original Perennialists of the Renaissance, including Marcilio Ficino.[36] She also identified similar sources behind Coomaraswamy's friend William Butler Yeats, whom she held to be "not a great poet 'in spite of' his studies in esoteric fields, but because of his great knowledge and learning in these fields of excluded knowledge."[37] These conclusions were received unenthusiastically by British academics, and Raine might have been dismissed as a crank were it not for the stature given her by her own poetry, the first collection of which—*Stone and Flower*—was published in 1943, with illustrations by Barbara Hepworth. Eighteen more volumes were published over the rest of the century, and in 1993 she was awarded the prestigious Queen's Gold Medal for Poetry.[38]

Raine's academic researches were accompanied by a spiritual search that led her through ritual magic (a group she identifies only as being descended from Crowley's Golden Dawn, to which Yeats had belonged) and finally to Hinduism.[39] Traditionalism seems to have played no major part in her search: Raine preferred the original Ficino to the later Guénon. She read the works of Guénon and other Traditionalists with interest, though, especially Coomaraswamy and *Le règne de la quantité*.[40] The combination of Ficino, Hinduism, and initiation led her to much the same conclusions as it had Guénon: that her age was the last age, the *kali yuga*.[41] She also reached the same conclusion about East and West as Guénon. "The materially poor East lacks what we in the West can provide," she told an Indian audience; "while our spiritually destitute materialist civilization looks to the Orient." "It is not in the streets of affluent London—or New York or Dallas—that faces of radiant beauty and the joy of life are to be seen. The rich . . . take their quiet desperation to the psychiatrists." Raine stressed that here she was referring to India as "a state of mind," not "political, economic and industrial India." On economics she echoed Schumacher, condemning technology in "the service of the profit motive, creating wants where none exist, in order to sell the products of the machines it has brought into being. Whereas every spiritually based civilization has placed the highest value not on multiplying wants but on reducing desire for material possessions."[42]

In 1980 Raine and three apparently Schuonian Traditionalists (Keith Critchlow, Phillip Sherrard, and Brian Keeble) together established *Temenos: A Review of the Arts of the Imagination*. "We did not use the word 'sacred,' since had we done so no-one would have taken us seriously," explained Raine later,[43] but the clue was there in the title: *temenos* in Classical Greek denoted the sacred center, usually of a place of worship. *Temenos* was from the first a somewhat Traditionalist journal, but never exclusively so.

Temenos attracted the attention of Sir Laurens van der Post, a South African friend and follower of Jung, and an early environmentalist. Van der Post was for many years a close friend of Prince Charles, the heir to the British throne, and has been seen as Prince Charles's spiritual mentor. In 1992 van der Post showed *Temenos* to the prince, who liked it enough to ask to meet Raine. Prince Charles then encouraged her to establish a Temenos Academy, which he housed within the Prince's Foundation, a body that acts as an umbrella for his cultural projects.[44]

Prince Charles is more of an anti-modernist than a Traditionalist, though he evidently reads Burckhardt with approval[45] and Traditionalist influences are increasingly visible in some of his speeches. In 2000, for example, in his capacity as lord high commissioner of the Church of Scotland, Prince Charles addressed the General Assembly of that Church as follows:

> We increasingly find ourselves in a secular age which is in danger of ignoring, or forgetting, all knowledge of the sacred and spiritual, and of those principles of order and harmony which lie at the very heart of the universe. . . . I have the greatest respect for the workings of the rational mind . . . but the inherent risk . . . is that we are in danger of unbalancing our lives. . . . Tradition, and the perennial wisdom which underlies so much of our deeper understanding of the visible and invisible worlds, have thereby become devalued or ignored.[46]

Traditionalism may also lie behind an approach to Islam that is significantly more sympathetic than is normal in British public life. In a 1993 speech given at the opening of the Oxford Center for Islamic Studies, of which Prince Charles is patron, he spoke powerfully against Western misunderstandings and fears of Islam, stressing the "common monotheistic vision" of Islam and Christianity and speaking of the need for "a metaphysical as well as a material dimension to our lives."[47] The reaction to this speech is evocative of the difficulties encountered by soft Traditionalism elsewhere: the mass circulation *Evening Standard* reported the speech under the headline, "Charles blasts lies of Saddam Hussein,"[48] concentrating on a passing topical reference and ignoring the substance of Prince Charles's speech almost entirely. Not all British newspapers took this line, of course, but in the end Prince Charles's speech probably did more for his own image in the Islamic world than for the image of Islam in Britain.

The most important organization within the Prince's Foundation that houses the Temenos Academy is the Prince of Wales's Institute of Architecture (established in 1992), which, like the prince himself, is more anti-modernist than Traditionalist. The other educational organization, however, is entirely Traditionalist. This is the Visual Islamic and Traditional Arts Programme (VITA), which was established in 1984 by Keith Critchlow and joined the Prince's Foundation in 1993.[49] VITA offered M.A., M.Phil., and Ph.D. courses, attracting about twenty students a year. These courses are primarily practical, teaching students to produce impressive work—miniatures following Mogul patterns, tiles following Ottoman patterns, and calligraphy and geometric mosaics of Islamic inspiration. To the extent that there is a theoretical element, it is purely Traditionalist—the works of Guénon, Schuon, Coomaraswamy, and other such authors. Visiting "tutors" include Nasr and Lings. The reactions of VITA's students to the Traditionalist component of their course vary: some feel that they have been tricked (this is not what they signed up for), some accept a Traditionalist approach to the arts to a greater or lesser degree, and some are sufficiently interested to go further, occasionally joining the Maryamiyya, which is well represented among the VITA faculty.[50]

More important than VITA, though, is the Temenos Academy, with its wider role. Traditionalists have been among the Temenos Academy's most frequent lecturers, but most lecturers have not been Traditionalists. Lectures have dealt with the arts (mostly poetry) and Islam (mostly Sufism) in about equal proportions, and then with Western esotericism (mostly Perennialism), and various other religions.[51] Seyyed Hossein Nasr spoke at the Temenos Academy, of which he is a fellow, on three occasions between 1992 and 2000.[52] Nasr and royal patronage are not the only connection between the Temenos Academy and the Imperial Iranian Academy of Philosophy. Like its Iranian predecessor, Temenos is a successful attempt to introduce Traditionalism into the intellectual mainstream, to include what Raine calls "excluded knowledge." There could be few better lobbyists for a neglected cause than Prince Charles. Lord Young (a prominent British businessman and friend of Prince Charles), talking of his work for a more fashionable issue—the environment—remarked of a conference in North Carolina attended by 100 leading businessmen: "Probably they just wanted to be photographed with him, but the results were good. . . . People going to private dinner parties at his London home or Highgrove (his country residence) end the evening by volunteering for all sorts of things they never intended. . . . He is living proof there is no such thing as a free lunch."[53]

There are limits, however, to what even Prince Charles can do for Traditionalism in the contemporary West. Much of the British popular press routinely greets his views and activities with a mixture of hostility and ridicule, and even a highly sympathetic article on him may end: "Of course, some of his subjects are convinced Prince Charles' theories are outlandish, if not barking mad. The spiritual and philosophical aspect of his crusade [against materialism] is considered either embarrassing, or half-baked in some parts of the realm."[54]

Aristasia

Aristasia is the post-1980s name of a group which, in slightly different form, was earlier known as The Romantics and The Olympians. It was started in the English university city of Oxford in the late 1960s by a female academic who used the name of "Hester StClare." StClare was born in the 1920s; other details of her career are unknown. A Traditionalist, in the late 1960s she began to gather a group of younger women, mostly Oxford students, who were dismayed by the "cultural collapse" of that decade.[55] They took Guénon one stage further: worse even than modernity was the "inverted society," the postmodern, contemporary era produced by the cultural collapse of the 1960s, an event often referred to by Aristasians as "the Eclipse." Inverted society—often referred to as "the Pit"—stands in much the same relation to modernity as modernity stood to tradition, argued "Alice Trent," StClare's most important follower. Not all that was produced before the Eclipse was worthless—Beethoven and Words-worth are clearly not "malignant aberrations," for example. Each phase in the cycle of decline may produce developments that, while "of a lower order than was possible to previous phases, . . . nonetheless are good and beautiful in their own right." Nothing produced after the Eclipse is of any worth at all, however (though theoretically something might be). In practice, all in the Pit is inver-sion—"the deliberate *aim* [is] an inverted parody of all that should be." The higher classes imitate the lowest, "family life and personal loyalty" are replaced by "a cult of 'personal independence,'" and even the earlier achievements of modernity are lost, as crime and illiteracy increase. Chaos is preferred to har-mony in art and dress, and masculinity replaces femininity.[56]

StClare, like Evola (though without any direct debt to him), added gender to Traditionalism. Evola was distinctly "masculinist," to the extent that his "ab-solute individual" was threatened with feminization as a result of modernity; Aristasia took the opposite line, that woman was threatened with masculini-zation. In Aristasian cosmology, the first age was not the age of the brahmin (as it had been for Guénon) but the age of the goddess. The rise of male deities and of a male-dominated society were the consequences of the earliest stages of decline. Modernity brought the triumph in the public sphere of "material and quantitative" male characteristics (aggression, warfare, and technical sci-ences) over "spiritual and qualitative" female characteristics—essentially "the principle of harmony or bonding." This was an early instance of inversion, since the female characteristics are inherently superior to the male ones, and the female is properly "the primary or fundamental sex." The final stage of decline—the Pit—brought "the ultimate triumph of patriarchy," normally de-scribed in the Pit as the general acceptance of feminist views. With the Eclipse, "the Masculine Principle has come to dominate the culture entirely, extirpating femininity even from the heart of women herself."[57]

The Aristasian elite, then, is entirely female, and not only female but "fem-inine." It also excludes men in order to avoid the risk of a return to the dom-ination of women by men, which was a product of decline, not a characteristic of primordial tradition. Further, it endorses a variety of Evola's *apoliteia* (though it does not use the term).[58] Since everything in the Pit is contaminated by inversion, "the entire tendency of every aspect of the culture is corrosive, and this corrosion is a ritual act that disrupts the soul, . . . that . . . furthers the pro-cess of psychic disintegration." It is thus necessary to control what enters our consciousness, just as we "will not normally pick up any interesting edible thing from the street and swallow it."

In addition to excluding the Pit from their lives as much as possible,

Aristasians attempt to recreate for themselves an environment corresponding to one preceding the Eclipse. Since "truly traditional . . . images . . . are too far from the everyday workings of our present consciousness," the era chosen for re-creation is the one immediately preceding the current one—the 1920s to 1950s. Aristasia, in addition to being the name of a Traditionalist group, is also a form of virtual reality (though Aristasians do not call it such, since they exclude neologisms as they exclude everything else characteristic of the Pit). Various aspects of pre-Eclipse life are painstakingly re-created in Aristasians' houses—1950s restaurants, 1940s clubs, 1930s homes. Aristasians dress in the clothes of their chosen decade, use the equipment and utensils of that decade, if possible drive the automobiles of that decade, and even watch the movies of that decade. This behavior is advanced as an alternative to the standard spiritual way of "sainthood" or "spiritual transcendence," for which only a few have the vocation.[59]

Aristasian Traditionalism is promoted through occasional magazine advertisements and on an elaborate website, which also includes Aristasian fiction. In Trent's "Strangers in Paradise" a non-Aristasian has just caused confusion by using the word "men" in conversation with two Aristasians:

> "Have you any idea what she's talking about?" asked the woman with the notebook.
> "Classical reference," said her colleague, Eileen. "Men—mythical creatures: like humans but very ferocious and cruel. Said to inhabit the Northern wastes in ancient times. Sabrina the Younger mentions them; so does Ulalua."[60]

Aristasian Traditionalism is presented more seriously in Trent's book The Feminine Universe. This book, aimed at the general reader, deals, for example, with Nietzsche before Guénon, and uses historical arguments with some skill. Aristasianism has also received some coverage in the British press and on television.[61]

At the end of the twentieth century Aristasia consisted of some 40 full-time, dedicated Aristasians, along with many part-time followers. Most Aristasians were in their 20s or 30s, with some older and a few younger; the most frequent occupation was "some connection to academia."[62] Almost all these Aristasians were in Britain—Aristasianism failed to find any significant following in America, perhaps because of cultural differences. Aristasia is permeated by the quirky humor characteristic of its Oxonian birthplace, where the expression of deeply held convictions is rarely free of an element of jest, and where no joke can be safely assumed not to conceal a very serious point.

British press coverage of Aristasia has emphasized less its Traditionalism than two aspects of its practice which, in the view of Trent, are more peripheral than central. One is the division of Aristasians into "blondes" and "brunettes," categories approximately corresponding to female and male in the outside world. This resulted in Aristasia's being described as "a lesbian enclave" by *The Pink Paper*, one of Britain's main gay and lesbian newspapers.[63] The other was the use of discipline—beating—seen by Aristasians as "a quest for purity . . . a means of spiritual submission,"[64] and by outsiders as sado-masochistic fetishism.

The role that lesbianism plays within Aristasia is unclear, if only because in the era before the Eclipse such things were not talked about and so Aristasians will not willingly talk about them either, but "intimate relations with men" are not encouraged.[65] The practice of submission, however, can (just about) be seen as being in line with more mainstream Traditionalist spirituality—the Sufi submits to his shaykh, and Trent is not wrong in her view that "submission to a higher power . . . is the very essence of spirituality," though one might wish to distinguish different varieties of submission.[66] Similarly, the separatism of the Aristasian community echoes the separatism of the Sufi order.

In a reminder of the ever-present potential political implications of Traditionalism, in 1995 Aristasia came under attack in *The Guardian* (a British liberal newspaper) for links with British National Party (BNP), a notorious extreme right group, when it was discovered that the BNP leader, John Tyndall, had written to "Marianne Martindale" (a prominent Aristasian): "I admire and respect what you are doing to the point of fascination." Martindale told *The Guardian*, "I personally have no interest in fascism," adding provocatively that she also had "no interest in democracy . . . [or in] any masculine political movement."[67]

12

Neo-Eurasianism in Russia

The collapse of the Soviet Union in 1991 brought a version of Western modernity to Russia and also brought to Russian politics an unusual variety of Traditionalism: Neo-Eurasianism. This ideology was developed by the centrally important Traditionalist Alexander Dugin and at first appealed principally to those sections of Russian society that rejected President Boris Yeltsin's policies and the idea of transforming Russia into some variety of liberal, democratic state on reasonable terms with the West. As the Russian political environment changed under President Vladimir Putin, Neo-Eurasianism moved from the margins into the political mainstream.

wrong!

Early Traditionalism in the USSR and Russia

Traditionalism Underground

Although Traditionalism was of necessity limited to dissident circles until the era of Perestroika, there were already Russian Traditionalists in the 1960s. Traditionalism first entered the Soviet Union through the Lenin Library in Moscow, which, for unknown reasons, was unusually well stocked with Traditionalist writers.[1] The attention of Yevgeny Golovin, a Russian poet known only to the circle of dissident or "independent" intellectuals he led, was drawn to these Traditionalist writers in 1962 or 1963 by references in Louis Pauwels's *Le matin des magiciens*—a distant echo of Pauwels's popularization of Traditionalism in Western Europe, discussed in the previous chapter.[2]

Golovin's interest in Traditionalism passed to his circle, one of many such small circles of intellectuals then to be found throughout the Soviet Union. Disenchanted with the increasingly stale orthodoxies of late Soviet Marxism-Leninism, these dissident or "independent" intellectuals inhabited the margins of Soviet life, boycotting institutions such as the Communist Party and Komsomols, membership of which was a requirement for access to jobs in areas such as academia and journalism where intellectuals normally work. Instead they worked as statisticians, librarians, or even street cleaners. Following an established Russian practice, they would meet in each others' flats or kitchens to talk and drink, but also to read and discuss philosophical, literary, and poetic works, sometimes circulated in *samizdat* (self-publishing, homemade copies) and sometimes of their own composition. Alternative music also flourished in this environment; Western genres such as rock and punk, frowned upon by the Soviet establishment, thus later acquired an intellectual respectability unknown in their countries of origin. Many of these intellectuals taught themselves foreign languages (often from parallel texts). Their self-education in the humanities frequently reached levels far beyond those commonly achieved by the self-taught in the West.[3]

Golovin's Soviet-era circle included Gaydar Jamal and Alexander Dugin, who became Russia's two most important Traditionalists. Jamal, who joined the circle in 1967, was a Muscovite of Azerbaijani origins whose education and upbringing were secular and Soviet rather than Islamic. As a young man, he had immersed himself in the library of philosophical works left by his maternal grandfather, an Ottoman Turk who migrated to Russia and participated in the October Revolution on the Bolshevik side and and who then taught at the prestigious State Institute for Theatrical Arts.[4] Dugin, who joined the circle in about 1980, was the son of a colonel in the Soviet army.

Golovin, Jamal, and (later) Dugin worked on reconstructing Traditionalism from the books they found in the Lenin Library, sometimes attempting to guess the contents of unavailable books from their titles alone. Although Guénon's *Symbolisme de la Croix* was unavailable (held in the "closed section" of the library), Evola's *Pagan Imperialism* (in the revised, more Traditionalist Leipzig edition of 1933) had been placed in the library's open collection when it was acquired in 1957—whoever was responsible for these decisions obviously looked no deeper than the books' titles. Russian Traditionalists, though taking their lead from Guénon's explanations of modernity, generally reacted to it (after 1991, at least) more on the model of Evola.

Traditionalism provided an intellectually satisfying explanation of the Soviet reality in which they lived and which they had rejected, but it did not move them to any variety of action. Dugin translated Evola's *Pagan Imperialism* into Russian in 1981, but his attempts to circulate it in *samizdat* met with little success. Neither the spiritual activity to which Guénon commonly led in the

West nor the political activity associated with Evola were possible in the Moscow of the 1960s and 1970s. Any possibility of political activity was excluded for obvious reasons, and spiritual activity was limited by the lack of the necessary infrastructure. Existing Traditionalist religious groups could not easily be contacted from the Soviet Union, though Vladimir Stepanov, a graduate of the Moscow Institute of Philosophy who belonged to Golovin's circle, did manage to contact a (non-Traditionalist) British neo-Sufi, the prominent novelist and poet Robert Graves.[5] Although Jamal joined the Naqshbandiyya Sufi order in Tajikistan in 1980, Sufism does not seem to have been important for him. When he took Golovin and Dugin for a month-long trip in the Zeravshan mountains in the northeast Pamirs later that year, they did not visit Jamal's shaykh, though they did visit the tombs of various Sufi saints.[6]

The closest Golovin's circle came to action was that occasionally they would become very drunk. What Dugin later called "excess in all forms" was seen as a form of revolt. This excess is visible in some of the novels of another member of Golovin's circle, novelist Yuri Mamleyev, described by one critic as the "master of the sexual and necrophilic grotesque."[7]

Traditionalism was found only in Moscow, though Graves's correspondent Stepanov was the agent for the introduction of Traditionalism into Estonia. He encouraged the interest in Traditionalism of Haljand Udam, an Estonian who between 1967 and 1971 was working on a Ph.D. thesis at the Moscow Institute of Oriental Studies.[8] Udam's original interest had been in Indology, and he found Guénon's *Introduction générale à l'étude des doctrines hindoues* while looking for works on Indian philosophy in a library catalog. Udam was impressed, and he located and read other Traditionalist works with the help of Stepanov, to whom he was introduced by his supervisor at the Institute of Oriental Studies. He then returned to Estonia and became Estonia's first Traditionalist. There was no significant contact between Udam and Golovin's circle in Moscow, however, and Udam later became a critic of the Russian Traditionalists.[9]

Golovin's circle seems to have attracted little official attention, although Jamal reportedly was committed to a mental institution more than once (then a standard way of controlling dissidents). The KGB evidently came to tolerate such informal circles, within certain limits—limits which Dugin evidently exceeded. In 1983 the authorities learned of a party in a painter's studio where Dugin had played the guitar and sung what he called "mystical anti-Communist songs," and Dugin was briefly detained. The KGB found forbidden literature in his room, principally books by Alexander Solzhenitsyn and Mamleyev (the novelist mentioned earlier, who had been in Golovin's circle but emigrated to America before Dugin joined).[10] Dugin was expelled from the Institute of Aviation, where he was then studying. He found employment as a street sweeper and continued reading in the Lenin Library with a forged reader's card.[11]

Traditionalism under Perestroika

The period of Perestroika[12] (1986–91) was in many ways a golden era for the "independent" intellectual. Quite unexpectedly, the previously unthinkable became possible and even popular. Restrictions were lifted; new areas became open to those without Communist Party membership; new ideas could be expressed. In 1988 the *Bulletin of the Estonian Oriental Society* even published a translation (by Udam) of Guénon's "Cycles cosmiques."[13]

It was during Perestroika that Russian Traditionalists first took active steps. In 1987 Dugin and Jamal together joined Pamyat' (Memory), later described by Dugin as "the most reactionary organization available." They hoped to influence it toward Traditionalism, rather as Eliade had hoped to use the Legion of the Archangel Michael in Romania, and Evola had hoped to use the Fascists, the Herrenclub, and the SS.

Pamyat' was the focus of popular opposition to Perestroika. Established in about 1974 by art restorers and historians and dedicated to the preservation of Russia's cultural heritage, it emerged in 1987 as a mass political organization,[14] possibly under KGB auspices as "a safety valve to let off the steam that dissidents were generating."[15] Pamyat' criticized Mikhail Gorbachev's reforms and claimed to be defending the true Russia; it attacked "Russophobia," Zionism, and the worldwide Masonic conspiracy.[16] "Russophobia" was understood as the threatened and actual weakening of the Soviet state,[17] the replacement of Soviet standards and values with liberal or even Western ones.

Dugin's and Jamal's attempts at infiltration of Pamyat' were no more successful than had been Eliade's or Evola's similar efforts earlier. Seminars they gave attracted respectable audiences (up to 100 people), and Dugin was appointed to Pamyat''s Central Council in late 1988,[18] but in 1989 they gave up and left Pamyat'; Dugin later described its members as "hysterics, KGB collaborators, and schizophrenics." Many others came to similar conclusions, and Pamyat' soon dwindled into insignificance. Its importance for Russian opposition politics was like that of Theosophy for Western esotericism: it was the forum that facilitated the emergence of figures who would later be important elsewhere.

After 1989 Jamal's and Dugin's activities ran on separate but parallel paths. In 1990, as Islamism began to emerge in the Soviet Union, Jamal was one of the founders of the Party of the Islamic Renaissance, discussed in the next chapter. After the collapse of the Soviet Union, Dugin helped found the not entirely serious National Bolshevik Party and became increasingly associated with two major figures in Russian political life. One was Gennady Zyuganov, the leader of the Communist Party of the Russian Federation (CPRF). The other, closer associate was Alexander Andreyevich Prokhanov, leader of a group known as the *Pochvenniki* (Patriots). Prokhanov was a prolific (and by some accounts not very good) novelist, whose most notable work was his 1982 *Derevo v tsentre Kabula* [A Tree in the Center of Kabul].[19] This novel of the Afghan war and other works on similar topics earned him the ironic sobriquet "the nightingale of the General Staff."[20]

Neo-Eurasianism

For Dugin, who was once arrested by the KGB as a dissident, to become an associate of Zyuganov, leader of the CPRF, was a surprising transformation. As we will see, there was later a second transformation of similar magnitude, when Dugin began to move from the sphere of the CPRF toward the political mainstream under President Putin. These transformations did not indicate inconsistency on Dugin's part. Like Evola, Dugin's primary loyalty was to his own ideology, not to other people's political movements.

Dugin's own explanation of his first transformation—from anti-Soviet dissident to associate of the Communist leadership—was twofold. First, in 1989 he made several trips to the West, addressing New Right audiences in France, Spain, and Belgium. These visits were important for bringing about a major change in Dugin's own orientation. Having for most of his life believed the "Soviet reality" to be "the worst imaginable," he found to his surprise that the Western reality was even worse—a reaction that was not uncommon among Soviet dissidents encountering Western realities. Second, the modification of his political position was completed by the events of August 1991, when a State Committee for the Extraordinary Situation [in the USSR], the GKChP, failed to establish control of the Soviet state during a poorly planned coup, and instead initiated the final dissolution of the Soviet Union. The document generally regarded as the manifesto of the GKChP was "Slovo k narodu" [A Word for the People], published on July 23, 1991, in *Sovietskaya Rossiya*, and written by Dugin's later associates Gennady Zyuganov and Alexander Prokhanov.[21] By his own account, Dugin was so disgusted by the crowds in Moscow calling for democracy, freedom, and the market that he finally found himself to be pro-Soviet, at the very point when the Soviet Union ceased to exist.

Beyond this explanation, we must look at the modifications Dugin made to the Traditionalist philosophy, and also at the special characteristics of Russian political life in the immediate post-Soviet period. Dugin's first modification was to "correct" Guénon's understanding of Orthodox Christianity, drawing a parallel with Coomaraswamy's earlier "correction" of Guénon's views on Buddhism. This correction is most clearly articulated in his *Metafisiki blagoivesti: pravoslavnyi esoterizm* [Metaphysics of the Gospel: Orthodox Esotericism] (1996). Here Dugin argues that the Christianity that Guénon rejected was Western Catholicism. Guénon was right in rejecting Catholicism but wrong in rejecting Eastern Orthodoxy, of which he knew little. According to Dugin, Orthodoxy, unlike Catholicism, had never lost its initiatic validity[22] and so remained a valid tradition to which a Traditionalist might turn. Dugin then proceeded to translate much of the Traditionalist philosophy into Orthodox terms.[23] Thus reoriented, Dugin's Traditionalism led not to Sufism as the esoteric practice of Islam, but to Russian Orthodoxy as both an esoteric and an exoteric practice.

Dugin's second modification of Traditionalism was to combine it with a doctrine known as Geopolitics or Eurasianism.[24] This doctrine has something in common with the views expressed in Samuel Huntington's *Clash of Civilizations*.[25] It sees conflict between blocs as inevitably produced by "objective" factors, not cultural ones as in Huntington's thesis but rather geographical ones. Geopolitical theory pits an Atlantic bloc, comprising maritime nations predisposed toward free trade and democratic liberalism, against a central and eastern continental Eurasian bloc, more inclined toward centralism and spirituality.

Russian Eurasianism has various origins, the earliest of which is the work of the nineteenth-century philosopher Konstantin Nikolayevich Leontyev,[26] who articulated ancient convictions of "Russian particularism." It was found also in Russian émigré writers of the 1920s,[27] who drew most importantly on the classic theorist of Geopolitics, the pioneering British geographer Sir Halford Mackinder.[28] Mackinder's thesis of a fundamental division between the "Eurasian heartland" and the Atlantic world was developed in his book, *Democratic Ideals and Reality*, published at the time of the Paris Peace Conference in 1919.[29] The intention of Mackinder, a Unionist [Conservative] member of Parliament and a staunch Imperialist, was to convince the Atlantic powers (Britain and America) of the need to intervene to ensure a balance between the two Eurasian powers, Russia and Germany. Ironically, his work attracted less attention in the Atlantic world than in the Eurasian world.[30]

Once Traditionalism is reoriented away from Hinduism and Sufi Islam toward Orthodoxy, it is an almost perfect complement to this Eurasianism. The Atlantic bloc can easily be identified with the *kali yuga*, modernity, absence of true spirituality, and the democracy of the most base which Evola so detested. Russia, on the other hand, is the repository of a vast and powerful initiatic tradition and has the finest possible spiritual and metaphysical justification for its inevitable struggle against the powers of darkness, incarnate in the Atlantic alliance. Whereas once the historic mission of the Soviet Union was to bring Communism to the world, it has now become the sacred mission of Russia to bring Orthodox Traditionalism to the world. In Dugin's own words, "the Eastern Church must accomplish her mission in the planetary context."[31] Dugin's "Traditionalized" version of Eurasianism will be referred to here as Neo-Eurasianism, Dugin's own term.[32]

Dugin's Political Activities

To complete the explanation of how a Traditionalist came to be aligned with Marxists, we must turn briefly to some special characteristics of Russian political life in the immediate post-Soviet period,[33] where the standard divide of Western politics into left, right, and center did not really apply. From the early days of Perestroika, Liberalism had been radical and Communism conservative. When organized political opposition to Perestroika surfaced within the Communist Party itself in 1990, crystalizing around the CPRF under Gennady Zyuganov, it was aligned ideologically with Prokhanov's Patriots. This alliance began the formation of a common front that is frequently described as "the Red-to-Browns," the CPRF being the Reds and the Patriots being the (fascist) Browns. Dugin himself preferred the label "Red-to-White."[34]

A more important divide than left and right was that between those, like Yeltsin, who accepted some vision of a liberal democratic Russia on reasonable terms with the West, who will be referred to as "Democrats," and those who rejected this vision, who will be referred to as "the Opposition." Different parts of the Opposition took various titles at various times (Communists, Patriots, nationalists, or even monarchists), but being in Opposition was generally far more important than the precise faction to which one belonged.[35]

In 1991 Dugin began to write in Prokhanov's newspaper *Den'* [Today]. He found Prokhanov "a statist patriot" but one unusually open to fresh ideas. The ideas that Prokhanov allowed Dugin to publicize in *Den'* were those of Evola and Guénon, and also of the Western European New Right: "anti-capitalists" (Dugin's phrase) such as Claudio Mutti, an Italian Muslim Evolian, and Alain de Benoist, the preeminent intellectual leader of the French New Right.

During this period, Dugin was decidedly of the Opposition, as were Zyuganov's Communists. For Dugin, Zyuganov's Opposition stance mattered more than his Marxism, which was anyhow not really very Marxist. In the words of Alexander Tsipko, once a political advisor to Gorbachev: "The very idea of putting the idea of the 'nation' and the 'state' above the idea of liberating the working class [as the CPRF clearly did] directly contradicts the spirit and theoretical doctrine of Marxism."[36]

Dugin and the Red-to-Browns

If it is understandable how a Traditionalist such as Dugin might want to ally himself with the CPRF, the question that remains is why the CPRF was interested in Neo-Eurasianism. The answer is that the various groups making up the Opposition shared interests and enemies but lacked a unifying ideology. Nationalism might at first sight have seemed a suitable ideology for Opposition purposes, but the ethnically based nationalism familiar in Western Europe since the French Revolution was hardly suitable in Russian conditions, since the Russian Federation is a multi-ethnic state. Ethnically based nationalism could play no part in the legitimization of either the Czarist or Soviet regimes,[37] and even Pamyat''s leader, Dmitry Vasilyev, was obliged to add a rider to his declaration that "our goal is to wake up the national consciousness of the Russian people," the addition being "and of all other peoples living in our motherland."[38] Taken to its logical extreme at the end of the twentieth century, ethnically based nationalism would have suggested that Russia's dominions be reduced even further than in 1991, to a small core of purely Russian territory. Although such an outcome was contemplated by a small number of radical Democratic intellectuals in Moscow, it would have been anathema to most ordinary Russians. It also suffered from the fatal practical drawback that it would have left unacceptable numbers of ethnic Russians stranded outside any purely ethnically Russian core.

Neo-Eurasianism, then, was a more inclusive form of nationalism better suited to Russian conditions. The Eurasian bloc, led by Russia, would include not only the whole of the Russian Federation but, in most interpretations, areas such as Ukraine and Belarus. In some views it would also include not just the territories of the former USSR, but also most of the Islamic world.

Relations between Russia and the Islamic world were a central paradox in Opposition and Neo-Eurasian thought. On the one hand, events in Afghanistan in the 1980s and in Chechnya and Moscow itself in the 1990s might have been expected to produce considerable hostility toward Islam and Islamism in the Russian army and general public, and anti-Islamic feeling was both encouraged and utilized by both President Yeltsin and President Putin. A certain amount of racist feeling against "black arses" from the Caucasus was general, and sometimes it resulted in racist attacks. Similar racist feeling has been routinely exploited by important sections of the extreme right in the West. On the other hand, the Soviet Union had long cultivated friendly relations with the Arab world, tending to see Middle Eastern states as actual or potential allies against America.[39]

Whatever the popular mood, the Russian Opposition generally spoke kindly of Islam. "I respect Islam and other religions," declared Pamyat''s Dmitry Vasilyev in 1989. "Khomeini is a great person who fights for Islam and the purity of the Islamic tradition. We are with those who have faith in God."[40] A similar line was taken later by most important figures in the Opposition (with the notable exception of Vladimir Zhirinovsky).[41] Dugin, Prokhanov, and Zyuganov all declared themselves in favor of an alliance with Islam. For Dugin, "The new phase of the Beast's world strategy consists in the subordination of the Russian people to global power, on the one hand, and in an attack against the most solid bastion of tradition, now represented by Islam, on the other."[42] For Zyuganov, "at the end of the twentieth century it is becoming more and more obvious that the Islamic way is becoming the real alternative to the hegemony of Western civilization. . . . Fundamentalism is . . . a return to the centuries-old national spiritual tradition . . . to moral norms and relationships between people."[43]

Zyuganov was an important figure in Russian political life, and Prokhanov was important to Zyuganov. Several commentators agree that Prokhanov was instrumental in Zyuganov's rapprochement with other Opposition groups, and so in his party's remarkable success in the December 1995 Duma elections, from which the CPRF emerged as the dominant party in the Duma,[44] a position it maintained in the 1999 elections, though its importance began to decline thereafter. There is also agreement that Prokhanov's newspaper *Den'* was crucial in popularizing Neo-Eurasianism and turning it into "the common focus of Russia's 'red-brown' coalition."[45] One commentator went so far as to declare that it was not the party organ, *Pravda 5*, but Prokhanov's newspaper "that represents the ideology of the communist mainstream."[46] "Zyuganov has used Eurasianism to reinvent the Communist Party," wrote another commentator, "and he has been fantastically successful in doing so."[47]

The role within the Opposition of Neo-Eurasianism, and so of Dugin himself, was central. This was the view of many Western observers, especially after Dugin's best-selling book, *Osnovi geopolitiki: geopoliticheskoye budushchee Rossii* [Geopolitical Foundations: The Geopolitical Future of Russia] (1997).[48] *Osnovi geopolitiki* was Dugin's most important and successful work. In 1997 it "was a topic of hot discussion among military and civilian analysts at a wide range of institutes . . . [though one observer's] impression was that there was more discussion than actual reading."[49] The interest of the Russian military in Dugin's book meant that much attention was also paid to it in specialized circles abroad. Dugin had already published "Geopolitics as Destiny" in the April 25, 1997, issue of *Krasnaya Zvezda* [Red Star], the army newspaper, and *Osnovi geopolitiki* also received the endorsement of the army, or at least of Lieutenant-General Nikolai Pavlovich Klotov, an instructor at the General Staff's Military Academy, a forum where Dugin had previously spoken at the invitation of Colonel-General Igor Nikolaevich Rodionov, later a minister of defense under President Yeltsin.[50]

Osnovi geopolitiki argued for an alliance with Islam. It also argued for the creation of a Berlin-Moscow-Tokyo axis to combat the American Atlantic threat, and for the return to Germany of Russia's Kalingrad enclave (the erstwhile Königsberg) and the return to Japan of the Kuril Islands, both taken by the Soviet Union in the aftermath of the Second World War. "The correlation between Dugin's ideas and those of the Russian establishment," wrote Charles Clover in the influential journal *Foreign Affairs*, "is too stark to be ignored." Clover cited as evidence the Russian suggestion in 1998 that the Kuril Islands might be returned to Japan, and Russia's rapprochement with Iran and Iraq.[51]

Both can be explained quite satisfactorily, of course, without reference to Dugin or Traditionalism,[52] but it is clear that Dugin's ideas seemed less eccentric to their Russian than to their Western audience.

The best analysis is perhaps that of the Democratic intellectual Igor Vinogradov, editor of the magazine *Kontinent*. Speaking of Eurasianism's origins in the 1920s, Vinogradov declared that it had "sufficiently revealed its gangrenous utopianism even then"—his objection to utopianism evidently being that it tends to lead to totalitarianism. Of the Neo-Eurasianists of the 1990s, Vinogradov said:

> They are undertaking a noisy galvanization of a reactionary utopia that failed long ago, an attempt to revive it through the injection of a new vaccine—a combination of "Orthodoxy" and "Islam" in the name of combating insidious "Zionism," putrid Western "Catholicism" and any kind of Jew-Masonry whatever . . . For all their [intellectual] ineptitude, they are very dangerous. After all, the temptation of religious fundamentalism in our century of unbelief and general spiritual corruption is attractive to many desperate people who have lost their way in this chaos.[53]

The credit for this revivification of a "failed" ideology must go to Dugin and Traditionalism, clearly the source of the "new vaccine" referred to.

Dugin's Neo-Eurasianism is not specifically or overtly Traditionalist. Although Traditionalist influences can easily be identified by the informed reader,[54] the word "tradition" does not appear in the glossary of his *Osnovi geopolitiki*, for example, and no Traditionalist or other philosophical authors are in the extracts from classic texts included in the book, which lead with Halford Mackinder.[55] The successful *Osnovi geopolitiki*, then, is another example of soft Traditionalism.

The National Bolshevik Party

Until Dugin's later alignment with the Kremlin, his most important political associations were with Prokhanov and the CPRF; after the success of *Osnovi geopolitiki*, directly with the CPRF: in early 1999 Dugin was appointed special advisor to Gennady Nikolayevich Seleznev, the CPRF speaker of the Duma.[56] He also maintained contacts with Western European rightists. Friendly relations were first established with Dugin's visits to the West in 1989 and continued with visits to Russia by de Benoist and his Belgian ally Robert Steuckers (the first of which took place in March 1992)[57] and with the publication of two collections of Dugin's articles in Italian by Mutti, in 1991 and 1992.[58] The political connection that first gave Dugin public prominence in Russia, however, and with which much of Dugin's writing was connected, was with a writer of a very different type from Prokhanov, Edvard Limonov.

Limonov had been a dissident poet like Golovin and, like Mamleyev, had emigrated to America, in 1974.[59] Like Dugin's, his reaction to Western realities had been one of disappointment and even disgust, documented in his most famous novel, *Eto ya, Edichka* [It's Me, Eddie] (New York, 1976).[60] He moved to France, taking French citizenship in 1987, and continued to write semi-autobiographical novels which were highly regarded both by those Russians who could read them, either abroad or in copies smuggled into the Soviet Union, and by many Westerners (most were translated into French as well as into other languages).

The collapse of the Soviet Union in 1991 meant that émigrés such as Limonov (and Mamleyev and Solzhenitsyn) could and did return to Russia.[61] For younger intellectuals, Limonov's return was even more significant than that of Solzhenitsyn. Limonov was widely interviewed, in the press and also on television, where for many liberal intellectuals he proved something of a disappointment. Though undeniably a fine poet and novelist, before the cameras he appeared less articulate and somewhat provincial. More disturbingly, he began to say "strange things." Liberals were finally forced to admit that Limonov's political views were those of the Opposition. In 1992, when the extreme nationalist Zhirinovsky presented his ironically named Liberal Democratic Party's future government of Russia, Limonov was one of his nine shadow ministers.[62]

Dugin met Limonov in the Opposition circles around Prokhanov and Zyuganov. Limonov was then ready to break with Zhirinovsky, who had become widely regarded as an unprincipled opportunist, and both he and Dugin were disappointed with the "archaism" of the existing Opposition. They accordingly determined on a joint *demarche*. Dugin wanted some sort of movement, but Limonov insisted on a formal political party, and so in 1993 they formed the National Bolshevik Party[63]—a striking title suggested by Dugin.[64] A third founding member of this party was the musician Yuri Letov, a drug-using anarchist punk music singer whose group, Grazhdanskaya Oborona (Civil Defense), had a significant following among the 12–20 age group.[65] After 1993 Limonov concentrated on political activities and stopped writing fiction.[66]

Limonov was the leader of the National Bolsheviks and the "man of action" behind its activities, but probably driven more by his reaction to the West in the 1970s than by Traditionalism or any particular ideology. The National Bolsheviks' first step was a Moscow-wide poster campaign calling for the boycott of imported goods, under the slogan "Yankees out of Russia!" This attracted some favorable attention to the party.[67] Subsequent slogans included "Drink kvass,[68] not Coca Cola," a creation of Dugin. Other activities were less successful. Party membership in Moscow never exceeded 500, and though it may have reached 7,000 in Russia as a whole, this is hardly a significant figure in a country of 150 million.[69] Limonov's alliances with two other Opposition parties were short-lived.[70]

In the 1995 Duma elections the National Bolsheviks campaigned as individuals rather than a party, having been repeatedly refused registration as a party by the ministry of justice.[71] Dugin ran in a St. Petersburg district while Limonov ran in Moscow. Dugin's campaign received wide publicity as a result of the support of Sergei Kuryokhin, a respected rock and jazz musician who also composed symphonies and whose band, Pop Mechanics, was "wildly popular." Kuryokhin's popularity derived partly from his "mystifications," as when he maintained on a major television channel that Lenin was in fact a mushroom. He organized a free pop concert under the title "Kuryokhin for Dugin"[72] and explained the National Bolshevik line in interviews such as one given to the St. Petersburg youth newspaper *Smena* [Change] in September 1995. Despite this support, Dugin polled only 2,493 votes, 0.85 percent of those cast. Limonov did slightly better in Moscow, with 1.84 percent (5,555 votes).[73]

Undaunted by this setback, Limonov stood again for office in May 1997 but failed to be elected governor of the Nizhni Novgorod region.[74] Dugin, on the other hand, concluded that Limonov's view of the National Bolsheviks' likely impact on the Russian electorate (as opposed to on Russian intellectuals) was unrealistic. He left the party in May 1998. The other founder of the party, the punk musician Yuri Letov, had paid little attention to it for some time (though in 1996 he wrote in the party journal, *Elementy*, of which more later).

There are undoubtedly elements of humor, reminiscent of Limonov's fiction, about the National Bolshevik Party. Its political program, for example, included the right of the party member not to listen while his girlfriend was talking to him, and the party's instructions on appropriate behavior in a cinema (visiting Western movies in groups of fifteen and vandalizing the auditorium) were surely not intended to be taken entirely seriously. What is one to make of the promise that "We shall crush the criminal world. Its best representatives will enter the service of nation and state. The rest will be annihilated by military means"? The party salute—the right arm raised for fascism with the fist clenched for Bolshevism, accompanied by a cry of "Da, smert'" (Death: yes!)— also had a hint of farce about it. These elements of the absurd clearly added to the National Bolshevik's countercultural appeal. Though it never admitted it, the National Bolshevik Party was more the embodiment of an attitude than it was a serious political organization. While the National Bolsheviks do take some action (individual National Bolsheviks have on occasion been arrested for minor acts of vandalism and breaches of the peace or, in Latvia, for drug offenses), the party's claim to aim at absolute power perhaps needs to be taken with a grain of salt. If the National Bolsheviks did by some unexpected means come to power, it is inconceivable that they could exercise that power in anything remotely approaching their current form.[75] The real importance of the National Bolshevik Party for Dugin was that for some years it was the base for his public appearances and his writing and publishing.

Between Parties

After Dugin left the National Bolshevik Party, the base for his activities became his own publishing house, Arktogeya (named after a Nordic version of Atlantis). Arktogeya published some translations of Western Traditionalists,[76] nine of Dugin's books (he usually wrote two books a year between 1993 and 1997),[77] and some novels of Gustav Meyrink, the "fantastic" early twentieth-century German writer from Prague, who was much interested in magic and the occult.[78]

Dugin also attempted, with mixed success, to spread his version of Traditionalism through a variety of journals and also through radio and the internet. Once again, the softest Traditionalism has been the most successful. A serious "theoretical" journal, *Elementy* [Elements], started in 1993 with an ambitious print run of 50,000 copies, but by 1996 this had been reduced to 2,000 copies.[79] A similar lack of public interest in hard Traditionalism was encountered by an independent esotericist publishing house, Byelovodiye, which published a number of translations of Guénon and Evola during the early 1990s[80] but stopped printing Traditionalist authors in about 1997.[81] In 1999 the only Traditionalist authors available in Moscow bookstores were Eliade and Burckhardt (one book, *Sacred Art in East and West*, 1999).[82]

More successful than *Elementy* was a weekly hour-long radio program, "Finis Mundi,"[83] hosted by Dugin and transmitted on Thursdays at midnight on a popular music station, FM 101. This "attracted a cult following of university students" (according to a Moscow newspaper)[84] with an eclectic selection of music (from Wagner to Edith Piaf) mixed with Dugin's Traditionalist message and a discussion of a single philosopher for each show: Guénon for the first, Nietzsche for the eighth. The program was cancelled in 1997, however, after only sixteen weeks, according to Dugin, for political rather than journalistic reasons.

The impact of Dugin's massive website, www.arctogaia.ru, is hard to judge. In 1999 it contained sections on metaphysics, politics, literature, and erotics[85] and discussion forums on Traditionalism, Hermeticism, literature, and Old Belief. These discussion forums seemed to be used by a small number of people, but the audience of www.arctogaia.ru may expand as Internet connectivity grows in Russia. It is possible that the impact of Dugin's website in America and Europe was greater than in Russia.[86]

By the late 1990s Dugin's most important means of access to the Russian public (apart from the occasional appearance on national television)[87] was a page in Prokhanov's newspaper *Zavtra* [Tomorrow], the successor to *Den'* [Today], which had been banned in the aftermath of Yeltsin's use of armed force against a recalcitrant Duma in October 1993. Dugin's page—a supplement entitled "Yevraziyskoye Vtorzheniye" [Eurasian Invasion]—can hardly have appealed to the same audience as *Zavtra* itself. *Zavtra* was distinctly populist, with lead stories such as "Yeltsin—thief. Dyachenko—thief?" (Dyachenko is Yeltsin's daughter), features on military aviation, and exposés of Democratic political figures as American spies or Jewish agents. Dugin's "Yevraziyskoye Vtorzheniye," in contrast, was much more intellectual. A distinctly post-modern layout quite different from the rest of *Zavtra* might be complemented by a thought for the day from Emerson (for example, "The hero is he who possesses an unmoving center"), and the complement to *Zavtra*'s lead story on "Yeltsin—thief. Dyachenko—thief?" was "National Existentialism: The Body as Performance."[88]

The Eurasia Movement and Party

By 2000 as the firmer hand of President Vladimir Putin gave Russian political life a measure of certainty that contrasted favorably with the drift and very visible corruption of the late Yeltsin years, it was clear that the Opposition was becoming increasingly marginal. The National Bolshevik Party received a ter-minal blow when Limonov was imprisoned for illegal possession of firearms and other similar groups began to break up. Even the CPRF seemed doomed, too dependent on elderly voters and too mired in its Soviet past.[89]

Dugin concluded that the Opposition in general and the CPRF in partic-ular were getting nowhere and would get nowhere.[90] The CPRF seemed to him to have been absorbed into the system it was meant to be opposing, and despite its flirtation with Neo-Eurasianism, its nationalism remained too much based on Russian ethnicity.[91] Although Dugin continued to publish his "Yevraziys-koye Vtorzheniye" supplement in Prokhanov's *Zavtra*, his main focus shifted to what he called "radical centrism." This new position, publicly adopted in 2001 with the foundation of a Eurasia Movement, was centrist in that it en-dorsed President Putin as a patriot who appeared committed to the restoration of Russian power and receptive to the idea of Russia as a Eurasian power. It was radical in that Dugin's Neo-Eurasianism was central to the Eurasia Move-ment, and in that the liberal elements in Putin's political program were tol-erated rather than endorsed.[92]

The timing of Dugin's announcement of the Eurasia Movement seems to have been determined by the registration, some months before, of a Eurasian Party of Russia by a Duma deputy, Abd al-Wahid Niyazov (born Vadim Med-vedev). Niyazov, though a Russian convert to Islam who endorsed much or all of Dugin's Neo-Eurasianism and had associated with Jamal, was not a Tradi-tionalist.[93] That he chose the title "Eurasian" for his party was rather a measure of the success of Dugin's ideology—or, in Dugin's eyes, an "attempt to usurp Eurasian ideology."[94] Niyazov's objective was to establish a party that would represent Muslims within the Democratic system but would not be purely Islamic. Neo-Eurasian nationalism gave him both a justification for a multiconfessional party and a way to stress his and his party's loyalty to the Russian state.[95]

Dugin established his Eurasia Movement with three varieties of support, two of which made it a far more serious organization than the National Bolshevik Party. First were a number of fellow Traditionalists, including two members of the original Soviet-era dissident circle of Yevgeny Golovin: Golovin himself and Yuri Mamleyev, the novelist whose books had gotten Dugin into trouble with the KGB when he was a student at the Institute of Aviation.[96] The second variety of support came from respected individuals such as Dr Alexander Panarin, a prominent political scientist who held the chair of political science at Moscow State University.[97] The third came from figures close to the Kremlin and from intelligence officers. There were many rumors that Putin's close aide Gleb Pavlovsky sponsored the Eurasia Movement in one way or another, but Pavlovsky was not officially a member of the movement.[98] Formal members did, however, include the well-known television personality Mikhail Leontyev, said to be "the president's favorite journalist," and Mufti Talgat Taj al-Din, the shaykh al-Islam of Russia.[99]

Taj al-Din had in 1980 been appointed mufti of the European USSR and Siberia (a position established by Catherine the Great in 1789), according to some under KGB sponsorship, and had followed the Soviet line. In 1985, for example, he joined three other Soviet Muftis in condemning the "undeclared war . . . waged on [the Afghan people] by American imperialists and their henchmen"—the *mujahidin*.[100] Despite periodic challenges, he retained his post and much of his influence through Perestroika and under Yeltsin and Putin.[101] His previous career strongly suggests that Kremlin approval of the Eurasia Movement would have had much more weight with him than his assessment of the movement's aims, and his participation, like that of Leontyev, strongly suggests Kremlin support.

There were many reports that the Eurasia Movement received generous financial support from branches of associations of retired officers of the SVR and FSB, the foreign intelligence and domestic security agencies into which the Soviet KGB had been divided in 1991.[102] Dugin's second-in-command in the Eurasia Movement, Peter Yevgen'evich Suslov, was also a former intelligence officer. After service in the KGB's First Main Directorate, Suslov retired from the SVR as a colonel in 1995.[103] According to one controversial and unconfirmed report, he had specialized in assassinations and was linked with Maxim Lazovsky, a former KGB and FSB officer implicated in allegedly fabricating "Chechen terrorist" bombings in Moscow in 1994.[104] Support from retired FSB and SVR officers does not definitely indicate the active support of serving officers or of the FSB itself, but it does imply at least a cooperative relationship with the FSB and the Kremlin. Given that President Putin himself had once served in the KGB's First Main Directorate (later the SVR), there was a tendency for intelligence officers to be entrusted with certain delicate tasks—

not because those tasks were necessarily related to intelligence work, but because intelligence officers were seen as being trustworthy, reliable, and effective. There is thus a possibility that, in one way or another, Suslov was a Kremlin representative in the Eurasia Movement's leadership.

As a result of these types of support, the Eurasia Movement quickly acquired over 50 provincial branches and a membership of 2,000, a respectable figure for a movement, if not for a political party. What was perhaps more important, the cooperative relationship with the Kremlin meant that the Eurasia Movement began to take on some of the characteristics of a respected foreign policy think tank, similar in function (if not in ideological orientation) to RAND or the Council on Foreign Relations. Many believed that the Kremlin on occasion took advice from the Eurasian Movement and that it sometimes used the movement to float its own policy proposals.[105]

Dugin's movement followed Neo-Eurasian theory in being multiconfessional. In addition to Mufti Taj al-Din there were representatives of Russia's three other established religions—Orthodoxy, Judaism, and Buddhism. Given the close relations between the Orthodox hierarchy and the Kremlin, Orthodox participation reflected the centrist more than the radical element in Dugin's approach. Radicalism rather than centrism was visible in the movement's representative of Judaism, Rabbi Avraam Shmulevich, but the religions that really mattered were Orthodoxy and Islam.

Islamic participation might have been either centrist or radical. As we will see in the next chapter, Dugin's former associate Jamal was by this time firmly embedded in radical Islamism, generally if inaccurately described in Russian as "Wahhabism." Dugin, however, here preferred centrism to radicalism. He distinguished carefully between "Wahhabism" and "traditional Islam," condemning the former and praising the latter. Mufti Taj al-Din welcomed the Eurasia Movement as "our answer to supporters of Satanic Wahhabism,"[106] and opposition to radical Islamism is also visible in the activities of Peter Suslov, the ex-SVR officer who was Dugin's second-in-command. In early 1999 Suslov established a foundation called *Yedineniye* (Unity).[107] It was formally independent of the Eurasia Movement, but in the context of a conference organized by the Eurasia Movement (on "Islamic Threat or Threat to Islam?") it proposed a settlement of the conflict in Chechnya jointly with a Chechen separatist leader, Kozh-Ahmad Nukhaev, also a former intelligence operative. The basis of this settlement was a proposed division of Chechnya into Russian and autonomous zones as well as the replacement of radical "Wahhabi" Islam by traditional, Sufi Islam.[108] It is not clear to what extent this plan was backed by the Kremlin (it was one of a number of plans being proposed at the time).

Dugin's "radical centrism" and Kremlin connections did not in any way turn him or his movement into a Kremlin puppet, as could be seen in the wake of the September 11, 2001, attacks on America. Mufti Taj al-Din (as would have been expected) immediately followed the Kremlin line in condemning the attacks. Dugin, too, immediately expressed his condolences and made clear his condemnation of "the acts of the assassins against innocent people."[109] However, he also wrote that the planes that destroyed the Twin Towers were "the swallows of the apocalypse," parallels to the bullets from the gun of Gavrilo Princip in Sarajevo in 1914 that ignited the First World War. The "swallows" of September 11, he declared on September 12, would force America to respond in a way that would ignite a possibly apocalyptic "war between [American] unipolar globalism . . . and all the rest of the world."[110] He believed that in this war Russia should (presumably only at first, though he did not say this) remain neutral while improving its relations with the Eurasian bloc,[111] and accordingly he saw the pro-Atlantic stance adopted by Putin as "the first major geopolitical mistake made by the president." In Dugin's view, America's action in Afghanistan "deal[t] a crushing blow to the Eurasianist strategy in Central Asia." He argued, however, that Putin should nevertheless be supported, because the alternatives were worse.[112] This incident clearly demonstrates that the radical element of Dugin's "radical centrism" proved stronger than the centrist element. In other words, Dugin was faithful to his promise that "we are only led by the interests of Russia in a long-term perspective. If defending the long-term interests are not politically convenient, or if they contradict the present situation, we defend them just the same."[113]

In 2002 the second congress of the Eurasia Movement resolved to transform the movement into a political party, the Eurasia Party (a title differing slightly from that of Niyazov's party, the Eurasian Party).[114] The implication was that Dugin intended to register his party and take part in the 2003 Duma elections, but at the present time, the significance of this transformation remains to be seen.

Similarly, the significance of Traditionalism and of Neo-Eurasianism for Russian politics still remains to be seen. Since 1991, Neo-Eurasianism has been growing in importance in the evolving discourse on Russia's future, a discourse in which alternatives to Western-style liberal democracy have significant support. Dugin may be going too far in seeing Guénon as an unrealized Marx (a parallel that might cast Dugin as a new Lenin, though Dugin himself does not draw this second parallel). He has, however, clearly demonstrated that "soft" Traditionalism can exercise significant influence in Russian political life.

Israeli Neo-Eurasianism

Dugin's Neo-Eurasianism was watched with interest by political radicals around the world. I will consider here, however, only one instance of the export of Neo-Eurasianism—to Israel, where it is represented by two organizations,

Be'ad Artzeinu (To our homeland) and the MAOF Analytic Group. In concentrating thus on Israel, I am following Dugin's own assessment of the importance of Israeli Neo-Eurasianism.[115]

The MAOF Analytic Group of Vladimir Bukarsky is the less important of the two organizations. This group, which is loosely aligned with a number of other ultranationalist groups to the right of the Likud Party, was established in 1997 to promote nationalism among Russian immigrants by means of pamphlets, seminars, and guided tours of Jewish settlements in Judea, Samaria, and Gaza (the Occupied Territories).[116] It has a large website, entirely in Russian, and one of the 24 categories there is devoted to Neo-Eurasianism, with articles by Dugin and other writers on familiar Neo-Eurasian themes.[117] Neo-Eurasian views are also to be found in the more recent writings of Bukarsky elsewhere. This group appears to be interested only in propagating its views, not in any direct action.

The more important group is Be'ad Artzeinu, which in 2002 claimed several hundred members, all of Russian origin. Two of its leaders were in Moscow for the founding congress of the Eurasia Movement, Rabbi Avraam Shmulevich and Avigdor Eskin, both Israeli citizens of Russian origin.[118] At present, Be'ad Artzeinu has launched only one action—a protest outside the Latvian embassy in Tel Aviv in April 2001—but the previous activities of Eskin suggest that other actions may be expected.

The Be'ad Artzeinu protest was in defense of Vassily Kononov, who had been sentenced to prison in Latvia in 2000 for war crimes committed in 1944 (ordering the execution of six civilians, including a pregnant woman). From the Latvian perspective, Kononov was guilty of a war crime, since the civilians were Latvians and Kononov had been a member of a militia accompanying the invading Soviet army.[119] From Be'ad Artzeinu's point of view, Kononov was innocent, because the Latvians he ordered killed were probable Nazi sympathizers, and the trial and conviction of Kononov was a clear sign of resurgent Nazism in Latvia.[120] From a Russian perspective, Kononov was innocent, since he had been a resistance fighter acting under Soviet authority, and his trial was a clear sign of anti-Russian feeling. Russian reaction was so strong that President Putin granted Kononov honorary Russian citizenship.[121] Two separate groups of National Bolsheviks entered Latvia in Kononov's defense, and one of them even attempted to blow up the tower of St. Peter's Church in central Riga, the Latvian capital.[122] Although Dugin was no longer associated with the National Bolsheviks at the time of the Be'ad Artzeinu protests, the alignment between Israeli and Russian nationalists visible in the Kononov case is striking.

The biography of Shmulevich illustrates how an Israeli can become a Neo-Traditionalist, on the face of it a surprising development, given both Traditionalism's and Neo-Eurasianism's emphases on Islam and Dugin's previous connection with groups widely seen as fascist and anti-Semitic. Shmulevich was brought up in Murmansk by secular Soviet parents, vaguely aware that he was

"Jewish" but in no way religious. After rediscovering the religion of his grandmother, he emigrated to Israel and became a Hasidic (pietist) rabbi (it is not
clear in what order these two events took place).[123] The Hasidim, who are in
some ways the Judaic equivalent of the Sufis, are fiercely Orthodox, and the
fiercely Orthodox generally take one of two extreme positions regarding the
State of Israel. At one extreme, they may reject it as an irreligious, blasphemous
attempt to hasten the redemption. At the other extreme, they may see Israel
as an element in the redemption. In this case, Israel's unexpected conquest of
Judea and Samaria in 1967 is seen as a divine gift, and any attempt to relin-
quish these "occupied" territories is blasphemous.[124] This is the position that
Shmulevich took. He joined some 250 others in a controversial, symbolically
important, and heavily defended "settlement" in the center of Hebron, a city
of some 40,000 Arab inhabitants, known by them as al-Khalil.[125]

In Israeli terms, Shmulevich and his companions are indisputably radical,
generally described in the press as "right-wing extremists" (in Israeli use, the
terms "right" and "left" are applied in a very different sense to that in America
and Europe, principally denoting approaches to the Palestinian question: the
left favors land for peace, and the right does not). The Neo-Eurasianist approach
to the Palestinian question is well illustrated by the activities of Avigdor Eskin,
another Hebron settler of Russian origin, an associate of Shmulevich, and a
member of Dugin's Eurasia Movement.

Eskin became famous in 1995 when he responded to the Oslo accords by
pronouncing on Prime Minister Yitzak Rabin a *pulsa d'nura* (lashes of fire in
Aramaic), an ancient Kabballistic death curse, believed generally to work within
a period of 30 days. Eskin called on "the angels of destruction that they take a
sword to this wicked man . . . for handing over the Land of Israel to our enemies." Thirty-two days later, Rabin was shot by Yigal Amir (not a settler, but
rather a student from Herzliya), and as a result, in 1997 Eskin was sentenced
to four months in prison for incitement.[126] On his release, he began to prepare
two projects designed to ignite a Palestinian reaction that would destroy the
Oslo accords: catapulting a pig's head into the grounds of the Dome of the
Rock on the Temple Mount during Ramadan, and placing another pig's head
on the grave of a Izz al-Din al-Qassm (a Palestinian national hero killed by the
British Mandatory authorities in 1935). The Israeli security services discovered
these plans, as well as a plan to burn down a building belonging to an Israeli
leftist group, Dor Shalom, and Eskin and an accomplice were arrested. In 1999
Eskin was sentenced to two and a half years in prison.[127] Ironically, a year later
Ariel Sharon's visit to the Temple Mount led to much the same result that
Eskin's projects had aimed at, igniting the second *intifada*.

Eskin and Shmulevich's participation in a Eurasia Movement that aims to
embrace much of the Islamic world is clearly paradoxical. The alliance with
Islam was clearly not the element of Neo-Eurasianism that appealed to them.
What did appeal was the anti-American elements in Neo-Eurasianism, which

fit well with many settlers' view of their own government as betraying them, the Jewish people, and Zionism, under American pressure. Even the government of Prime Minister Sharon seemed to many settlers only a slight improvement on that of Prime Minister Rabin, in that it did not entirely reject the possibility of compromise with the Palestinians and it appeared amenable to American pressure. Shmulevich's explanation of this betrayal was the "process of subordination of the political elite to Western influence,"[128] against which Neo-Eurasianism struggles.

Shmulevich and Eskin are Neo-Eurasianists rather than Traditionalists, and there is no evidence that either of them has ever read Guénon. Even their Neo-Eurasianism is a consequence rather than a cause of their other activities—Eskin's stance preceded the development of Neo-Eurasianism, and his first known political activity was in 1979, when, at age 19, he and three other young settlers were arrested for breaking into Palestinian houses in Hebron, where they "overturned furniture and assaulted inhabitants."[129] Three years later, in 1981, Eskin was again arrested, this time during a protest in front of the Soviet Airline Aeroflot's offices in New York, and charged with "rioting, unlawful assembly, disorderly conduct and attempted criminal mischief."[130] The Israeli Neo-Eurasianists represent a development of Dugin's activities that can not even be described as "soft" Traditionalism. To the extent that they make use of an ideology partly derived from Traditionalism, however, they too are descended—albeit indirectly—from Guénon's work.

13

The Islamic World

The first country in the Islamic World to encounter Traditionalism was Iran. Though the Islamic Revolution ended Nasr's activities there, Traditionalism survived the revolution and by the end of the twentieth century had come to play a role in the public debate on the future direction of the Islamic Republic. Traditionalism had by that time also appeared in the general discourse of other Islamic countries, notably Turkey and Malaysia, and in the Russian Federation, which has a significant and long-established Muslim population.[1] In the Arab world, however, Traditionalism remained in general absent from public discourse. In Algeria it was dismissed as irrelevant, and in Morocco it played a role closer to that in the West, providing answers to the individual spiritual searches of some Westernized Moroccans but having no discernible impact on the wider society.

Guénon in North Africa

The renewed popularity of Traditionalist writings in Europe after the 1960s had an impact on Francophone North Africa, especially Algeria and Morocco, rather as it did in Moscow at about the same time. A small group of Algerian dissident intellectuals began to read Guénon in about 1967. They were opposed to the socialist and materialist ethos of the Algerian regime, the Front de libération nationale (National liberation front, FLN), which had led Algeria to independence through the bloody war with France that helped establish the concept of "revolutionary war" in Italy[2] and which had then established a socialist one-party state.

One of these dissident intellectuals, Rachid ben Eissa, launched a series of workshops for university students that aimed to wean young Algerians away from socialist materialism and thereby to start an Islamic renaissance within Algeria.[3] Their main speaker was Algeria's leading Islamist intellectual, Malek Bennabi, and a guest speaker was Roger Garaudy, then a member of the Central Committee of the French Communist Party and later France's most famous convert to Islam—and, incidentally, an enthusiast of Guénon.[4] Traditionalist analyses were the center of Ben Eissa's attack on modernity. Given the FLN's hold over Algeria's cultural and intellectual life, it would have been hard if not impossible to hold such workshops independently, so Ben Eissa created an Office for Islamic Sociological Studies in the Ministry of Education which allowed him to arrange the workshops in the ministry's name (they were usually held in public schools during school vacations). These workshops operated every summer from 1969, lasting for three or four days and attracting some 120 to 140 students each. Most of the students had a technical or natural sciences background—humanities students were abandoned as a lost cause.

There were, however, no translations of Guénon's work into Arabic, though Rachid ben Eissa considered one. He concluded that although such ideas in French might help turn Algerians who were educated in essentially a French system toward Islam, in Arabic they would only scandalize Algeria's less educated readers, who would likely "misunderstand" them and see them as un-Islamic or even anti-Islamic.

Traditionalism did not take root in Algeria. After expressing some initial interest, Bennabi concluded that Guénon and other Traditionalists spoke to the problems of the West, not to the problems of Algeria, which in his view were political and economic more than spiritual. Interest in an Islamic solution to these problems—that is, in Islamism, or radical political Islam—grew, and interest in Traditionalism declined. Ben Eissa's workshops were discontinued, and Ben Eissa left Algeria for a career abroad, finally ending up at UNESCO headquarters in Paris. Ben Eissa's cousin Hamza ben Eissa had written, in French, two books on modernity which were Traditionalist in every respect— Hamza ben Eissa even attempted, with some success, to reproduce Guénon's own style. These books failed to find a publisher. Support for Algeria's main Islamist group, the Front Islamique du Salut (Islamic Salvation Front, FIS) produced an FIS victory in independent Algeria's first free elections in 1991, and civil war the following year.

In Morocco, where political conditions were more relaxed and economic conditions less severe than in Algeria, Traditionalism was more successful. It played an important part in a Sufi renaissance among the elite that started in the 1970s, led by a Sufi order, the Budshishiyya. Even so, Guénon has never been translated into Arabic there, for much the same reasons that Ben Eissa abandoned the idea of a translation in Algeria.

The Budshishiyya is not a Traditionalist order—its shaykh, Hamza ibn Abi'l-Abbas, has never read Guénon, though he has certainly heard of him.[5] However, in the view of Ahmad Qustas, a one-time *muqaddam* of the Budshishiyya for the important Fez region, the works of Guénon played some part in bringing to the order almost all those of its members who come from what Qustas calls the "Francophone milieu"—that is, Moroccans educated in French, the elite who may speak the Moroccan dialect of Arabic at home but are more at ease reading in French than in Arabic.

The Budshishiyya has been spectacularly successful in recruiting from this milieu, as well as from the social classes immediately below it, a considerable achievement given the ignorance of and hostility to Sufism that is prevalent in this milieu, and the distance between the lifestyles of the elite and Islam.[6] Traditionalism can reach this milieu as other approaches cannot. When Zakia Zouanat, a Francophone Budshishi and a Traditionalist, was interviewed on Sufism by the large circulation French-language magazine *Demain*, she used the interview not to talk about her own shaykh but to praise Guénon's "incommensurable work" which had "bestowed greater nobility on Sufism."[7] This emphasis may have resulted purely from her enthusiasm for Guénon but may also have been calculated. In articles of her own, Zouanat goes to great pains to address her Francophone readers' misconceptions about Sufism, such as presenting it as a repository of "that universal dimension that puts it in touch with what is most profound in man's inspiration towards freedom, in the search for the absolute," and hastening to reassure her readers that it is not un-Islamic or fanatical.[8] That Zouanat herself is not just unveiled but even glamorous must also reassure her readers. It is likely, then, that Zouanat emphasizes Guénon because she regards his work as the best point of access to Sufism for her readers. For her as for Abd al-Halim Mahmud in Egypt, the endorsement of Sufism by a "civilized" Frenchman is welcome and useful.

Guénon became known in Morocco's Francophone milieu in the 1960s as he did in Algeria, and he was read along with Sartre and Camus.[9] It was generally known by Guénon's Moroccan readers (unlike most of his Western readers) that he himself had become Muslim and a Sufi, and he was commonly (if not entirely accurately; see chapter 4) associated with Abd al-Halim Mahmud, whose writings were also popular in Morocco. Guénon's Traditionalism thus pointed his Moroccan readers toward Sufism more directly than it did his European and American readers, and no Moroccan Traditionalists are known to have proceeded from Guénon to non-Islamic destinations. This is so partly because Sufism, though in eclipse, remained "present beneath the surface" for even the most modern Moroccan, and partly because of the almost total absence of New Age "spiritualist" groups in Morocco. Although the French-language section of a major Casablanca bookstore might follow the standard Western classification of "Spirituality" in arranging its books, all the books on sale in this section will typically deal with Islam (save perhaps for one or two on Christianity).[10] Of such books on Islam, many more will deal with Sufism than would be the case in the Arabic section of such a bookshop, reflecting the tastes of the French reading public.

Guénon's own books were not generally on sale at the end of the twentieth century, partly because Guénon's main French publisher (Gallimard) was too expensive for the Moroccan market, but they could be ordered fairly easily if required. Plenty of works by other Traditionalists that would lead the interested reader to Guénon were available, however.[11] These included books by Fawzy Sqali, a Moroccan of the Francophone milieu who, like Qustas, became a Budshishi *muqaddam*.

Fawzy Sqali

In addition to being the most important Moroccan Traditionalist, Sqali is also a good example of how Traditionalism can bring modern Moroccans back to their origins, which according to Qustas is one of the major tasks of the Budshishiyya. Both Sqali's grandfathers had been *ulama* (religious scholars) at the Qarawayyin in Fez (the leading institution of learning in the Islamic West), and Sufis as well, followers of a Moroccan branch of the Khalwatiyya Order. Sqali's father, on the other hand, was a senior hospital administrator, bilingual in French and Arabic, a busy man who had no interest in Sufism (though he prayed the ritual prayers). Sqali's schooling was entirely in French, at the Mission culturelle française in Fez, and his university education (from 1973) was at the University of Paris, where he studied sociology and from where he obtained a *doctorat d'État* (Ph.D.) in anthropology.[12]

Sqali, then, was a thoroughly modern Moroccan. During his first four years in Paris, his interests were much like those of any student in the 1970s, though he remained on the fringes of political activity and never joined any political group or movement. Dissatisfaction with this mode of life, however, led him on a spiritual search for "the essential." His first interest was in Taoism, as might easily have been the case for any Parisian student of purely French origins in the 1970s, rather as Nasr's first interests were in Hinduism. Though Taoism seemed to offer a beautifully stripped-down "essential," Sqali found that it did not indicate any feasible course of action. His resultant disappointment reflected the general Islamic emphasis on practice noted in chapter 4.

Sqali therefore began to turn to the Islam of his Moroccan childhood, reading the Koran and even beginning to pray the ritual prayers again, "all on my own, in the middle of Paris!" as he later recalled—Paris and prayer occupy opposite ends of a spectrum for a Moroccan Francophone. In addition, Sqali began to buy books on Islam and Sufism—a French translation of Rumi, a

book on Ibn Arabi by Nasr's associate Henry Corbin, and books by Traditionalists: Guénon's *Aperçus sur l'ésotérisme islamique et le taoïsme* (a posthumous
collection of articles), which combined Sqali's first and second interests; a book
by the Maryami Jean-Louis Michon; and two books by Martin Lings, the French
translations of *What Is Sufism?* and *Sufi Saint*.[13]

While such books might have led a Frenchman to Schuon and the Maryamiyya, and had indeed led even the Iranian Nasr to this destination, for Sqali
they were more of a stepping-stone. They led him to "decode" (his word) what
he already knew, and to return to Morocco in search of a spiritual master. Sqali's
original plan was to go to the South, the remote, desert region of Morocco which
has been least touched by modernity, an adventurous trip on which an uncle
proposed to accompany him. Before the trip could start, however, Sqali heard
much of the lamented fate of a relation by marriage, a businessman named
Tahir Rais, who was at the time thought by the family to have been lost to a
variety of cult. Rais had in fact become a follower of one of the most important
Moroccan shaykhs of the late twentieth century, Hamza al-Budshishi.

Although the Budshishiyya was in fact an entirely normal Islamic Sufi
order, Tahir Rais's entry into it alarmed and dismayed his family. Because of
their inaccurate conceptions of what a Sufi was, Shaykh Hamza sounded to
them like an impostor and a charlatan, or at the least deluded. The fact that
his order was known to have attracted young men who were previously irreligious—open drinkers of alcohol, for example—only made things stranger. One
exception was an elderly man who, after listening to the discussions in Casablanca, remarked that those assembled should be careful of what they said
about Hamza al-Budshishi, who might well be a living saint. Sqali was of a
similar view: what he heard reminded him of Lings's description of Ahmad al-
Alawi, of the spiritual master that his Traditionalist readings had described. He
obtained an invitation to a Budshishi *dhikr* ceremony, entered the order, and
traveled to the *zawiya* at Madagh, near Oujda on the Moroccan-Algerian border,
where he spent one week.

The function of Traditionalism for Sqali had been important but essentially
ancillary. It was the religion into which he had been born, not Traditionalism,
that directed his search to Sufism and to the shaykhs of Morocco, but it was
his readings of Traditionalist authors that gave him "very exact references" and
made easy the identification of Shaykh Hamza as the master he was seeking.
These readings also helped to validate the choice that Rais had made independent of such readings: during the week that Sqali spent with him after meeting
him at the first Budshishi *dhikr* he attended, Rais's wife was fascinated and
relieved to hear of the historical respectability of this variety of Sufism from
Sqali, who based his explanations on his readings in Paris.

Other forms of validation were also at work. On meeting Shaykh Hamza,
Sqali immediately recognized him as the master who had appeared to him in
his dreams around the time of his departure from Paris, and the question

Shaykh Hamza asked him—"So you want to return the soul [ruh] to its origin [asliha]?"—seemed to have a double meaning, since the word asl (in Sufi parlance, an implied reference to God) can be taken to mean "tradition" as well as "origin." Another validation came on Sqali's return to Fez. His family's reaction to his joining the Budshishiyya was "general panic," and his dismayed mother took him to lunch with her father, Idris, the retired Qarawayyin teacher, so that he could explain to Sqali that what he was doing was not Islam and not required by Islam. During this lunch, conversation ran on unusual lines, with everyone talking about religion and spirituality, and Idris himself telling stories of Sufis from Fez's past which none present had heard before. Sqali's mother, rather surprised, reminded her father that this was not what he was meant to be doing, and Idris said he would come to that later. However, instead he took his grandson aside and asked him if it was a "severe" way he had taken. Sqali replied that he had seen no severity in the Budshishiyya, to which his grandfather replied, "Hold to it, then, for dear life." Sqali felt he had come home in more ways than one. Since then Sqali has followed the Budshishiyya and eventually became a Budshishi muqaddam.

Moroccan Traditionalism

Both Sqali and Qustas, then, are Budshishi muqaddams familiar with Traditionalism. Qustas, though, cannot be considered a Traditionalist. He heard of Guénon from some English converts to Islam only after entering the Budshishiyya in 1975.[14] He is not himself from the Francophone milieu but rather is the son of a Darqawi Sufi Imam, and for some time he taught in the Islamic Studies program at the Qarawayyin, now a university. He appreciates Guénon's work and makes use of it in his current role as muqaddam for North America (his function, though the title does not exist), but it has no consequences for his own spiritual or intellectual life. On the contrary, he is extremely critical of those Traditionalists who become "stuck" in Perennialism and is dismissive of the utilitarian approach to the Sharia of many Traditionalists, stressing that the Sharia is the vessel that must hold the haqiqa (truth, God). A number of former Maryamis are among those Americans who have come to him and the Budshishiyya, and Qustas is therefore exceptionally well informed about the more scandalous aspects of the Maryamiyya's later years; at one point he tried to convince some leading Maryamis that they should warn other Maryamis away from Schuon. In one sense, then, Traditionalism as a practice has no harsher critic than Qustas.

In contrast, there is still much of the Traditionalist about Sqali. On the one hand, he stresses that Traditionalism is one expression of spiritual truth but is not in any way a spiritual path. In his view it is confused with a spiritual path only by those who have insufficient spiritual experience, who have not properly encountered a real spiritual path. Sqali argues that it is not only the works of

Guénon that present the risk of being taken for the definitive spiritual doctrine, that even Ibn al-Arabi can (but should not) be taken in this way. In his view, to take any single corpus as a definitive doctrine is incompatible with Sunni Islam; the definitive guide is the shaykh, in his own case shaykh Hamza.

On the other hand, Traditionalism was something more than a stepping-stone for Sqali. He continued to read Guénon and found that as he progressed in the Budshishiyya and as his own spiritual understanding deepened, so the works of Guénon meant more and more on each rereading. His Budshishi activities in France keep him in touch with the French Traditionalist milieu. He also has a private project for what might be called the retraditionalization of society—though he himself calls this project "Sufism's contribution to society . . . from a traditional point of view." This project is expressed in his participation in a number of associations with semi-Traditionalist objectives;[15] he is also the founder and director of the annual Fez Festival of the Sacred Musics of the World. This festival has since 1994 grown in importance and size, in 2000 attracting not only Nasr but also Jacques Attali, a prominent French public figure with an interest in Islam;[16] in 2001 it expanded to include a parallel conference, the first being on the theme of "A soul for globalization," to which a wide range of international intellectual figures were invited. Sqali emphasizes the connection between the objectives of this festival and the past of the city of Fez, not only the spiritual and scholarly capital of the western Islamic world, but also a city where the three Abrahamic religions have flourished side by side. There is something of the Perennialist in this view.

From the point of view of those who encounter the Budshishiyya, however, there is little difference between Sqali and Qustas. Both understand Traditionalism well enough to explain, in effect, that the Budshishiyya is the best available traditional initiation. Sqali's first and most important book, La voie soufie (1985),[17] also serves these ends. According to Sqali, it resulted partly from his own attempt to form a "synthesis" of Traditionalism and Sufism, to link Traditionalism with the classical Sufi texts he was reading and with his own experience of the Budshishiyya, to "develop doctrinal coherence." La voie soufie is not an overtly Traditionalist book, however. It includes Guénon, Schuon, and a few other Traditionalist authors in its bibliography and makes use of a few Traditionalist concepts such as the division between vertical and horizontal,[18] but in appearance and structure it is more a scholarly work than anything else, though it makes clear that its author is both a Muslim and a committed Sufi. The first part of the book is a survey of Islamic cosmology and metaphysics, drawing partly on more modern sources such as the Amir Abd al-Qadir and partly on classical sources such as Ibn al-Arabi. This part might equally serve to Islamize a Traditionalist's understanding of these questions, or to impress a non-Traditionalist with the range and subtlety of Islamic thought. Sqali stresses, however, that Sufi "doctrine is essentially the expression of a lived experience"[19]—the first sentence in the book, and a point emphasized numerous times—and the second part of the book is an introduction to that lived experience. One section is devoted to the order and the shaykh, and another is a guide to the Sufi path as someone entering an order such as the Budshishiyya might experience it.

According to its author, *La voie soufie* led many French Traditionalists to him and thus to the Budshishiyya. This effect may be explained by the book's quality: the second part is excellent, both from a Sufi and a scholarly point of view, though many readers no doubt find the first part somewhat hard going. The book also guards against the disappointment which a French Traditionalist or intellectual might feel on encountering the realities of Sufism in the Islamic world; it explains, for example, that not all Sufi orders retain the spirituality that attended their foundation.[20] For the theoretically minded, it explains the relative dearth of recent first-quality intellectual works by Sufis in terms of a shift in perspective, from the expression of spiritual knowledge in writing to its interior realization, specifically rebutting any possible charge of "what has been called Muslim decadence."[21] This is a response to the idealization of the East that was visible in the younger Guénon[22] and is still present among many Western Traditionalists.

Sqali became the Budshishi *muqaddam* for France while still a student. After joining the Budshishiyya and with the permission of his new shaykh, he returned to France to continue his education.[23] He was given an *ijaza* by Shaykh Hamza almost immediately afterwards, and by 2000 the Budshishiyya had *zawiyas* in Paris, Strasbourg, Nantes, Montpelier, Aix-en-Provence, Nice, and Marseilles, some large and some small.[24] The Marseilles *zawiya* included Le Derviche, an "oriental café" open to the general public, incorporating a bookshop, library, and sales of oriental handicrafts.[25] The Budshishiyya is one of France's more important Sufi orders and is also beginning to expand into Spain, England, and the United States.[26]

The Budshishiyya's success in attracting members in France, as in Morocco, may be due to its highly effective publications and outreach events, and its success in retaining members may be due to its relaxed approach to the application of the Sharia. It may also be due to networks: once one or two members of a social group have joined an order, others are likely to follow them, and likely to feel at home when they arrive.

The Budshishiyya's French publications and outreach events are designed to appeal to that segment of the French public that is interested in alternative spirituality, but Traditionalists are also kept in mind. Thus the semi-annual magazine that Sqali established in 1998, *Soufisme, d'orient et d'occident* [Sufism: In East and West] covers selected Sufi persons, events, and books. It contains translations of classic Sufi texts (Rumi, Abd al-Qadir al-Jilani) and articles on topics such as *dhikr* and the Qarawayyin mosque. Rather as Zakia Zouanat presented Sufism to Francophone Moroccans in terms of "man's inspiration towards freedom," an editorial in *Soufisme* speaks of Sufism's objective in terms of "the transformation of being" rather than mentioning God or Islam.[27] The first issue of *Soufisme* planned for 2001 addressed Traditionalists specifically, advertising in advance its cover story, "Concerning an unpublished correspondence of René Guénon."

The French Budshishiyya has organized outreach events such as an annual "Rencontres Méditerranéenne sur le soufisme" [Encounters on Sufism], a series of meetings, films, exhibitions, and concerts in Marseilles and a number of other French cities, which in 2000 attracted about a thousand people to a total of 30 events.[28] Sqali himself makes regular public speeches, sponsored by organizations such as the Association Espaces/Expressions at the Sorbonne, and since the late 1990s also sponsored by a Budshishi organization, the Association l'isthme. Meetings at the Rencontres of 2000 were addressed not only by Sqali, but also by Khaled Bentounès, an Alawi shaykh known to many Traditionalists, and Guéndé Jeusset, a Franciscan monk who had spent 20 years in the Ivory Coast and had evidently become somewhat universalist in the process—he spoke of a Tijani shaykh there being as much his own spiritual master as St. Francis of Assisi.[29]

Sqali has the permission of Shaykh Hamza to "base himself on European structures,"[30] even to the extent (according to one source) of sometimes hedging his answers to the question of whether it is necessary to be Muslim to be Sufi.[31] The application of the Sharia on matters such as dress is relaxed: Sqali stresses that he has no desire "to dress Frenchmen in turbans" and that when cultural conflicts occur between Budshishis of French and Moroccan origin, his concern is not to integrate Frenchmen into the cultural milieu of North African immigrants but rather to integrate immigrants into the mainstream cultural milieu of France. Sufism, he says, is like water and will take the form of the vase into which it is poured.

The Budshishiyya is not a Traditionalist order in the way that the Maryamiyya or Ahmadiyya or even Válsan's Alawiyya are. The emphasis is not on Guénon and Traditionalism but on Shaykh Hamza and Sufism. That the Budshishiyya was one of the very few Sufi orders to break through into modernity in the Arab world owed more to its shaykh's charisma and to organizational talents than to Traditionalism—but the role that Traditionalism plays in its continued expansion is one measure of the success of the breakthrough. No other order can receive Traditionalist intellectuals so smoothly. Shaykh Hamza is happy to accept and lead those whose intellectual worlds derive from Guénon and Sartre, as well as those whose worlds are more purely Islamic.

The Islamic Republic of Iran

Traditionalism played no public part in the early years of the Islamic Republic, as the turmoil of the war with Iraq and of the consolidation of the revolution shifted the focus from intellectual to practical matters. Nasr's academy survived,[32] without its imperial title—students went through the academy's library whiting out the hated word "imperial" from the rubber stamps on the library books, and even from the title pages of past issues of the academy's journal.[33] It has been of little importance since, however, except in the academic study of philosophy, and today it is poorly funded in comparison with its glorious beginnings. It no longer has a journal or any publications, and the blue tiles are chipped in places.

Reactions to the Revolution

Some former members of the academy moved away from Tehran and politics. Ayatollah Ashtiyani, for example, went to the holy city of Mashhad, where he continued to teach Mulla Sadra; he had been an admirer of Khomeini as a philosopher, describing him as "the seal of the philosophers and gnostics of our time," but had no interest in the revolution.[34] The Imperial Academy's former deputy director, Hadi Sharifi, moved to London, where he established and for many years ran the Furqan Foundation, a body that continued the academy's interest in original texts by undertaking the monumental task of locating, preserving, and cataloging manuscripts of Islamic scholarship worldwide.[35]

Traditionalism, however, remained alive in Iran. Nasr and Corbin and Chittick were replaced by other former members of the academy, notably Gholam-Reza A'avani, who in about 1984 became director in Nasr's place, and by other traditional (but not Traditionalist) scholars.[36] A university professor in a city outside Tehran replaced Nasr as *muqaddam* of the Maryamiyya but, as before, the order itself remained relatively small.[37]

Some Traditionalists played an active part in postrevolutionary politics. Nasrullah Purjavadi, who was previously disappointed by the Imperial Academy's failure to change anything of importance, was appointed to the Shura-ye ali-ye Enqalab-e Farhangi (Council for the Cultural Revolution),[38] the main task of which was the purging of Iran's universities. Reza Davari Ardakani, who had encountered Traditionalism while studying at Tehran University, and Abd al-Karim Soroush, the young intellectual who had turned from Nasr to Shariati before the revolution, were also appointed to this council. It is not known whether the other members of this council had read Guénon or not (there were seven in all), but these three appointments indicate the penetration of Traditionalism into significant areas of Iranian life. They also illustrate the three varieties of Traditionalist found in Iran. At one extreme are hard Traditionalists like Purjavadi, who may be Maryamis or may belong to some other Sufi order (Purjavadi was a Ni'matollahi). At the other extreme are people like Soroush, who are familiar with Traditionalist ideas and writers but for whom Traditionalism was never of much interest, or ceased to be of interest. In between are people like Davari: Traditionalism has contributed to their views, but their lives have not been deeply affected by it and they do not belong to Traditionalist organizations. Such people are the Iranian equivalents of Schumacher, soft Traditionalists.

Traditionalists adopted a variety of stances over the subsequent decades as the Islamic Republic matured. In 2001 many university professors, especially in the field of philosophy, were either Traditionalists or well acquainted with Traditionalism: most of these made no public declarations of their positions. Some continued to support the postrevolutionary regime. Haddad Adil, one of Nasr's closest former associates, who had been rejected as a minister of culture soon after the revolution because of his association with Nasr and so with the court,[39] became a conservative member of parliament. He was said to be very close to the Supreme Leader, Ayatollah Khameini, whose son was married to Adil's daughter.[40] Davari also remained close to the regime and became president of the Academy of Science and a leading conservative intellectual. Others took opposing positions: Laleh Bakhtiar, a half-American Traditionalist who had earlier edited a revolutionary Islamic women's magazine, *Mahjuba*, and established an organization to translate Shariati's works into English,[41] left Iran for a career as a psychologist in America, where she ended up working for Kazi Publications, America's premier Islamic publisher.[42] Purjavadi remained in Iran (and became director of the Iran Universities Press) but finally found himself aligned with the liberals; he expressed regret that "tradition" and "Islam" had become masks behind which "certain people" worked for their own interests, reducing them to insistence on details of female dress, campaigns against alcohol, and the strengthening of xenophobia. Though he remained a Traditionalist (publishing a Persian translation of Lings's *Sufi Saint* in 1999), he also decided that Islam needs to change in order to survive. Schuon and Nasr, he believed, had often propagated ideas of a variety which, when incorporated into an ideology, proved dangerous and destructive—even to the future of Islam.[43]

Another former member of Nasr's academy, Daryush Shayegan, left for France after the revolution and also found himself aligned with the liberals on his return to Iran. In 1977 he published *Asia dar barabir gharb* [Asia versus the West], a book that attacked the West as the home of modernity.[44] While studying Sanskrit and traveling in India in the late 1960s, however, Shayegan was already wondering whether there still existed any traditional society, or only "civilizations in transition" toward modernity. By the 1990s he had concluded that there was no such a thing as a traditional society, and that it hardly mattered. Modernity was "inevitable and epidemic" but also multicultural. Starting in America, "cultures are forming a mosaic . . . and it is no longer possible to chain them together in a linear formation." Religion *can* coexist within modernity, he concluded, since human spiritual needs exist independent of context—as can be seen from the popularity in the West of Eastern spiritual teachings, from Yoga to Tibetan Buddhism. The implication is that the fight against Western modernity is not only pointless but unnecessary.[45]

Enough Traditionalists remained in Iran, then—on both sides of the political divide—to respond to the revival of interest in Traditionalism that began in the 1990s. This renewal was first visible among teachers and students of architecture: "the style of Dr. Nasr" became much discussed as an architectural style that was not of the West. A 1973 book by Laleh Bakhtiar and Nader Ardalan, published by Chicago University Press with an introduction by Nasr, has been much read (*The Sense of Unity: The Sufi Tradition in Persian Architecture*).[46] After the mid-1990s a number of new translations of Traditionalist books were published—translations of Guénon and Schuon and also of Nasr and two other Maryamis, Burckhardt and Lings.[47] Lings's work on Shakespeare was widely discussed and was admired by popular preachers such as Husayn Ilahi Qumsha'i.[48] Growing interest in Traditionalism among students was also reported in the late 1990s, both in Qom and in the main university system.[49]

The Religious Pluralism Debate

In 1998 Traditionalism became more generally prominent as a side effect of a public debate on religious pluralism. This debate arose not because of any practical question concerning the status of religious minorities in the Islamic Republic, but because of the status of the man who started it, Soroush, and because of its implications for Iran's reception of reformist ideas, ideas often associated with non-Muslim America. The religious pluralism debate was important as an intellectual reflection of the political struggle going on between the conservative forces represented by the Supreme Leader, Ayatollah Khameini, and the reformists, represented by President Khatemi.[50]

The religious pluralism debate was started by Soroush in 1998 with an article which he later developed into a book. The article was provocatively entitled "Siratha-ye mustaqim" [Straight Paths (plural)], a reference to the Fatiha, in which believers ask God to guide them on the Straight Path (singular). In his article and book Soroush argued that truth is one. As he explained to an interviewer, "Truths everywhere are compatible; no truth clashes with any other truth. . . . One truth in one corner of the world has to be compatible with all truths elsewhere, or else it is not a truth."[51] This view, disarmingly simple though it may sound, has an implication made explicit in Soroush's title: that more than one Path may be Straight, that Islam does not have a monopoly on truth.

Soroush's article and book caused a stir. They also revived an interest in the Traditionalist theory of Transcendent Unity, which was aired during 1998–99 in a number of periodicals issued in Qom, starting in 1998 with *Ma'rifat* [Gnosis], the journal of the Imam Khomeini Research Institute. Also in 1998 *Naqd ve Nazar* [Commentary and Views], issued by the Office of Islamic Propaganda of the Qom Hawze, devoted a special issue to Transcendent Unity and to the Traditionalists.[52] When the newly established Qom Center for Studies on Religion started a journal—*Haft Aman* [Seven Heavens]—in 1999, the first article in its first issue dealt with Traditionalist views on Transcendent Unity.[53] All these articles were broadly supportive of Soroush's overall conclusions about religious pluralism, though on their own, different bases.

One Traditionalist, Davari, had been on the other side during an earlier high-profile debate launched by Soroush. This was a debate on modernism, again started by an article of Soroush which later became a book, in this case "Qabz va bast-e Te'orik-e Shari'at" [Expansion and Contraction in the Theory of the Sharia]. The Sharia, argued Soroush, is transcendent and eternal, but the interpretation of the Sharia is a profane science, which should make use of the discoveries of the natural and social sciences. This argument aroused considerable controversy, being seen—correctly—as an attack on the religious establishment and as a call for a general revision of the Sharia, that is, a modernization of the Sharia.[54]

Davari responded not so much to Soroush's basic argument as to his implied conclusion, arguing that in reality Westerners had not so much modernized their religion as lost it altogether. This was not the first time that Soroush and Davari had clashed: in the 1980s it had been Soroush who had replied to Davari. In a 1982 book Davari had argued that the West was not so much a political organism as a "totality," that this totality had resulted from the replacement of tradition by modernity, and that therefore one could not think of safely adopting elements from the West. Davari's views are commonly traced to Heidegger,[55] but his view of the West's loss of its religion through the replacement of tradition by modernity is characteristically Traditionalist.[56]

The Future of Traditionalism in Iran

Davari is not the only conservative to hold Traditionalist views. Some of the more intellectual circles in the politically important Basij militia, for example, are reported to favor Nasr's return to Iran as a matter of urgency. There is a feeling that Nasr can speak to the new generation that is reading Freud, and that visibly has little commitment to the revolution, in a way that others cannot.[57]

Ironically, it was as Traditionalism was beginning to assume new postrevolutionary relevance that the academy suffered the fate it had avoided at the revolution itself; it was abolished.[58] Despite its formal abolition, the academy had become an established feature on the Iranian intellectual landscape and continued to be referred to as "the Academy" even when it no longer legally existed. A'avani and the others made the best of a new task of teaching Western philosophy,[59] though A'avani explained the interest of working on Western philosophy in terms of the interest a physician might find in studying disease.[60]

Finally, Aʿavani arranged for the statute for a new academy ("Academy II") to be approved by the minister of culture, and for the new academy to be housed in the same building as the original academy, so that "the Academy" formally returned to life, even though it had no budget.

Perhaps surprisingly, Traditionalism never seems to have come under significant attack in Iran for its Western and non-Islamic origins and content—origins about which contemporary Traditionalists are quite frank, as in the special issue of *Naqd ve Nazar* referred to earlier. The views expressed in that journal would cause general outrage if published in Arabic in Guénon's adopted Cairo or elsewhere in the Arab Sunni world, as both Algerian and Moroccan Traditionalists recognized. That they have not caused outrage in Iran is partly because Traditionalists have been somewhat careful about what has been translated into Persian, and partly because of the relative openness of Iranian intellectual life. Hujjat al-Islam Sadiq Larijani, a mullah teaching at the Madrasa-yi Vali-yi Asr in Qom, for example, said that his only real criticism of Guénon was that his works were insufficiently analytic. As to their content, he remarked that Soroush expresses ideas that are considerably more shocking.[61]

There have been only two known exceptions to the general toleration of Traditionalism in the Islamic Republic. One was the reaction of Husayn Ghaffari, a philosopher at Tehran University who at one point announced an intention to write against the Traditionalist conception of the Transcendent Unity of religions—but is not known actually to have written anything on this subject.[62] The other was an article published in Maʿrifat in reply to the earlier article on Transcendent Unity in that journal. It attacked Traditionalism on two grounds: the origins of its ideas (which were traced back to Encausse and nineteenth-century French occultism, though not to Ficino) and the contradiction of the theory of Transcendent Unity by strict and classical interpretations of the Koran and *hadith*.[63] Perhaps significantly, the author of this article was not a product of the Qom system but rather an American philosopher, Dr. Muhammad Legenhausen, who had taken a job at the Imam Khomeini Research Institute after teaching at Rice University.[64]

Turkey

Traditionalism in Turkey has not yet produced any of the features we have seen elsewhere. There is no equivalent of the Budshishiyya or of the Iranian Academy of Philosophy. Instead there is a definite and growing interest in Traditionalist works, fed by numerous translations, among intellectuals—the Turkish equivalent of the Moroccan Francophone milieu, though in Turkey this elite is not associated with proficiency in any foreign language. Its main marker is instead what in French is called *laïcisme*, the variety of secularism developed in France which implies not state neutrality to religion, but rather the active exclusion of religion from the public sphere.

It is the philosophy of which *laïcisme* is a part that makes Turkish interest in Traditionalist so remarkable. Since the 1920s the Turkish Republic has been committed to a philosophy sometimes called Kemalism, after Kemal Atatürk, the widely revered father of modern Turkey. Kemalism is a philosophy not only of *laïcisme* but of uncompromising modernization and Westernization, directly opposed to tradition—and therefore opposed by Traditionalism. In the view of one Turkish Traditionalist, the works of Guénon are in a Turkish context more subversive than those of Khomeini.

Although occasional references indicate that a few Turkish intellectuals and writers had read some of Guénon's books in French by the 1940s, and there were occasional mentions of Guénon during the 1970s (usually as a commentator on modernity),[65] it was not until 1979 that the first Traditionalist writing appeared in Turkey. This was a translation of Guénon's, "Le *tawhid*," which appeared in *Kubbealti Akademi Mecmuasi*,[66] a small-circulation journal covering mostly literary and historical topics, read primarily by academics and intellectuals. The translator was Mustafa Tahrali, who, like Sqali, had encountered Guénon while studying in Paris (though earlier, during the 1960s) and had been in touch with Traditionalists there, notably Ahmad Vâlsan, the eldest son of Michel Vâlsan. On returning to Turkey after completing a Ph.D. thesis on the Rifa'iyya Sufi order at the Sorbonne in 1973, Tahrali taught in the theology department of Marmora University, finally becoming a professor and head of the section for the study of Sufism.[67]

Tahrali's 1979 translation was the first of many. By the end of the twentieth century, Turks could read most of Guénon's books as well as many of Evola's and Eliade's. Surprisingly, Evola was generally seen as a writer on spiritual rather than political topics, and his connections with the right were little known.[68] Traditionalism has not had any political impact in Turkey.[69]

Various Maryamis had also been translated, notably Schuon and Lings and, most important, Nasr.[70] Nasr became Turkey's most popular Traditionalist writer. Almost all of his works had been translated by 2000, and two volumes of his articles (some originally appearing in Persian and never translated into any Western language) were republished only in Turkish. The reason was mostly (in the view of one of his translators) that he speaks directly to the Turkish concern with Islam in a way that other Traditionalists did not. With Guénon one was obliged to make connections; Nasr made them himself.

None of these translations had large print runs, each selling a maximum of 1,000 copies a year, but all were published by more or less mainstream publishers and were sold in most major bookshops that stocked books on Islam.[71] There is, then, a definite if limited interest in Traditionalism, parallel to the interest that developed in the 1980s in the works of Seraphim Rose's early teacher, Alan Watts, in books on religion and science such as Fritjof

Capra's *The Tao of Physics* (1975) and Paul C. W. Davies's *God and the New Physics* (1983), and in new translations of Rumi and Ibn Arabi.[72] In Morocco Guénon was read alongside Camus; in Turkey Nasr is read alongside Watts. A short article of mine on the history of Traditionalism was translated into Turkish by a general literary magazine, *Hece*, where it appeared along with poetry, reviews, and short stories.

The popularity of Nasr is one indicator that Turkish Traditionalism is decidedly Islamic—more so than Iranian Traditionalism, where the emphasis is more philosophical. Another indicator is that some Traditionalist works were specially edited for the Turkish market: for example, only the first chapter of Guénon's *Introduction générale à l'étude des doctrines hindoues*, was brought out (this chapter is an introduction to Eastern doctrines in general), since the Turkish public was felt to have little interest in Hinduism. Even in the absence of editing such as this, translation into Turkish has sometimes involved Islamization, as when the word *din* (religion, by implication Islam) is used to translate "tradition."[73]

There has also been more opposition to Traditionalism as being un-Islamic in Turkey than in North Africa or Iran. A journalist associated with the Islamist movement, Zübeyir Yetik, in 1992 published *İnsanin Yüceliği ve Guenoniyen Batinilik* [Human Greatness and Guénonian Esotericism],[74] as well as several articles in the magazine *Haksöz* arguing, according to one Traditionalist, against a return to the bronze age—hardly what Guénon was suggesting. Traditionalism is also said to have attracted little enthusiasm from the Turkish religious establishment.[75] This relatively greater opposition may be due to the fact that in Turkey anyone can read Traditionalists whereas in Morocco and Algeria only those with a French education can. Iran's Islamic intellectuals are, in general, more tolerant of unusual views of Islam than are Turkish or Arab Islamic intellectuals.

Despite all these publications, there are no Traditionalist organizations in Turkey. That there is no important Traditionalist Sufi order (there are only half a dozen Maryamis, all in the city of Konya) follows the pattern of Iran and Morocco—a Traditionalist order is not needed where there are already plenty of indigenous orders. The reason there is no equivalent of the Budshishiyya is perhaps that there is no Turkish order specializing in "modern" Turks in the way that the Budshishiyya specializes in "modern" Moroccans—though a magazine published by the Naqshbandiyya Order, *İlim ve Sanat* [Science and Art], did in 1987 publish one Traditionalist article on Guénon,[76] and an unidentified professor of physics who became a Khalwati shaykh in the late 1990s read Guénon's books with interest.

Similarly, Turkey's leading Traditionalists all operate individually. A colleague of Turkey's earliest Traditionalist, Tahrali, is Mahmud Kiliç, the most prominent of the younger Traditionalists, who arranged the publication of much of Nasr's work (sometimes under an alias). Kiliç comes from a Sufi family—his grandfather was a Sufi shaykh in Kosovo. He seems himself to be a more active Sufi than Tahrali, who is a "follower" of the Turkish Rifa'i shaykh Ken'an Rifa'i[77]—but only in the sense of following his written works, since Rifa'i's order was disbanded in the 1920s, as required by early Kemalist legislation, and Rifa'i died in 1950. Both Kiliç and Tahrali have written Traditionalist articles of their own, usually in somewhat specialist journals such as *Kubbealti Akademi Mecmuasi* (which published the first translation of Guénon in 1979). In addition, there are two other academics, one a popular Islamic philosopher and the other a well-known psychiatrist, Kemal Sayar, who writes on Sufi psychology.[78]

Given this absence of identifiable Traditionalist organizations, it is hard to estimate the size of the Traditionalist movement in Turkey. Kiliç and Tahrali receive a number of letters from readers[79] and know of a small number of Turks they have introduced to a variety of orders. These include one famous Turk, Ayşe Şasi, a popular female movie director who became a Khalwati. Kiliç may also refer people to the Lausanne *zawiya* of the Algerian Alawi shaykh Banda bin Murad[80] if he feels that cultural differences between them and Turkish Sufis would be likely to create difficulties—he anyhow recommends those who go to Turkish shaykhs not to discuss Guénon in the *zawiya*. In addition, an unknown number of people have presumably found shaykhs on their own without reference to Tahrali or Kiliç. Though it may be harder for an inhabitant of Istanbul in 1999 to find a shaykh on his or her own than for an inhabitant of Cairo or Fez, it is still a lot easier than for an inhabitant of Rome or Los Angeles.

The impact of Traditionalism in Turkey, then, has been twofold: to guide an unknown number of individuals to Sufism, and to introduce Traditionalist ideas into the discourse of the new generation of disenchanted Westernized intellectuals—much the same people to whom Traditionalism appeals in the West. This is a class of growing importance in Turkey. As in Russia, the final significance of Traditionalism in Turkey remains to be seen.

Islamism in Russia

Islamic Traditionalism in Russia, like Dugin's Eurasianism, derives from Golovin's 1960s circle of dissidents. Like Dugin's Eurasianism, Russian Islamic Traditionalism is primarily political—in fact, Islamist rather than Islamic.

As was seen in the last chapter, Gaydar Jamal joined and left Pamyat' along with Dugin. He then became one of the founding members of the Party of the Islamic Renaissance (PIR), established in 1990 by Ahmad Qadi Aktaev in Astrakhan (a city on the Volga estuary in the Russian Federation). While far from being the largest or most important political organization of Muslims in the whole of the ex-USSR, the PIR is the only significant party to cover the whole of the Russian Federation; all other groups are regionally based. The PIR is thus of key importance in Russia proper, that is, outside the Muslim republics.[81]

Jamal was initially the PIR's ideologist, editor of its organ *Tavhid* [Unity], and director of its research center in Moscow. Early issues of *Tavhid* are distinctly Traditionalist in tone.[82] In the first issue Jamal analyzed the state of Islam in Traditionalist terms, adding a historical angle rarely found elsewhere, derived in this case from Islamist writings. Islam, he pointed out, existed in time and was subject to decline just as everything else was. Further, there had been no *real* Islamic government since the death of the Prophet, and certainly not since the Mongols. Matters had grown much worse since then, since the "post-colonial elites" in the Islamic world were either nationalists (and hence enemies of universal Islam) or "atheist cosmopolitan[s]," equally enemies of true Islam.[83]

An article published in 1991 reveals Jamal's debt to Evola. After comparing the existential significance of death in Evolian Traditionalism to the metaphysical significance of death (the final return to God) in Islam, he argues that "authentic Islam and the authentic right are non-conformist; their vital character consists of opposition, disagreement, non-identification." René Daumal, the surrealist painter discussed in chapter 4, would have approved. For a Christian, "God is almost synonymous with hyper-conformism," whereas Islam is a "protest . . . against the reduction of God to 'consensus.'" The political right and Islam both fight the snares of the world, including self-deification and "profane elitarianism."[84]

This Traditionalist Islamism proved too extreme for many. The PIR split in 1992 over the issue of relations with Yeltsin and his project of Russian democracy: most of the PIR aligned with this project, while Jamal led a more radical minority away from the party toward alliances with radical Islamists in the Middle East and with the domestic opposition to Yeltsin, in the form of the Communist Party of the Russian Federation (CPRF) under Gennady Zyuganov and the rightist "Patriots" under Alexander Prokhanov.[85] Both men were associates of Jamal from his time in Pamyat', and both also associated with the other major Traditionalist in Russia, Dugin. This "red-brown-green alliance" will be discussed further.

Jamal's relations in the Middle East were with men such as Hasan al-Turabi, the leader of the Sudanese Islamic Front and for many years the *éminence grise* behind the Islamist military regime in the Sudan. The PIR was thus replaced as Jamal's institutional framework by the Islamic Committee of Russia—a network of such Islamic Committees was established under al-Turabi's guidance at a conference in Khartoum in 1993 in order to unite the leaders of various radical Islamist movements such as Turabi's own National Islamic Front, Hamas in Palestine, and the Hezbollah in Lebanon. Jamal became leader of the Moscow branch of this Islamic Committee.[86] In a 1999 interview he spoke of contacts with the Hezbollah, Hamas, the Wolves of Islam (a Chechen group), and the Afghan Taliban.[87] At this time, Jamal was one of the major two or three voices of radical Islamism in the Russian Federation.

Jamal's own political associations within Russia have been with the Opposition. In mid-1999, Prokhanov's *Zavtra* carried an interview with Jamal, announcing the formation of a united front of "green and red" between Jamal's Islamic Committee of Russia and the Movement in Support of the Army, Defense Industry and Military Science, an independent opposition group aligned with the CPRF and run by the chairman of the Duma State Security Committee with the aid of a retired army colonel-general of Cossack origin, Albert Makashov.[88]

The unlikely alliance between a radical Islamist and a Movement in Support of the [Russian] Army when the Russian army was entering its second round of conflict with Islamists in the Caucasus[89] was made possible by neo-Eurasianism. As a retired army officer and local official of the Movement in Support of the Army said at the time: "We all are children of one mother regardless of ethnicity and religion. The name of our mother is Russia."[90] For the Movement in Support of the Army, those killing Russian soldiers in the Caucasus were rebels, not Chechens or Muslims; appropriate measures should be taken against rebels, whether Chechen or Russian or Cossack, Muslim or Orthodox. The war that the army was fighting in 1999 was emphatically not one against Muslims as such.

For Jamal and for the Movement in Support of the Army, the real enemy was Yeltsin, whose administration was accused by Makashov of having taken no adequate steps after the first Chechen war to resolve the situation there, and also the Israelis: "A card is being played in order to provoke a quarrel between Orthodoxy and Islam," declared Makashov at a press conference, going on to blame "those in the Middle East who are unhappy about being neighbors with the Arab world."[91] Similarly, for Jamal the conflict in the Caucasus served the interests of Yeltsin and of the Israelis. Foreign conflicts drew attention away from Yeltsin's domestic failures and led to increased Russian-Israeli cooperation, which assisted Israeli attempts to extradite certain Arab Islamists living in Russia, thus serving the interests of the "Atlantist lobby."[92] Such explanations echo the views of much of the Opposition as well as of many ordinary Russians—Russians are often fond of conspiracy theories.[93]

Radical Islamism and Traditionalism are in general incompatible; they take fundamentally different views of tradition, of the future of humanity, and of course of religions other than Islam.[94] Possibly for this reason, Jamal has modified his own position to the extent that he can hardly be described any longer as purely Traditionalist—Dugin in fact described him privately as "post-Traditionalist."[95] He is critical of the apparent contradiction between Guénon's practice of Islam and the concentration in his writing on Hinduism,[96] and at least by implication he has criticized Evola for confusing the political with the spiritual.[97] To some extent, then, Jamal should be regarded as one for whom Traditionalism became a stepping-stone rather than a destination.

Jamal is, however, not the only Traditionalist Muslim who is a radical Islamist. Another is the Italian Claudio Mutti, a one-time follower of Evola's follower Franco Freda, the proponent of armed spontaneity. Mutti, who lost his job at the University of Bologna and served a prison term for his terrorist activities, turned his attention to more spiritual matters in the early 1980s and converted to Islam. Two factors influenced this conversion: the writings of Guénon, to which he had been led by the writings of Evola, and Colonel Qaddafi. Guénon had convinced him of the need for a "path of realization," something Evola had not accomplished. Qaddafi is a more unusual source. Freda had had an interest in Qaddafi and Islam; he wrote in *Quex* about Evola's requirement for a spiritual basis for action in terms of the relationship between the "lesser jihad" (armed conflict) and the "greater jihad" (the struggle to subdue the lower self), and he published a translation of some of Qaddafi's speeches.[98] This translation had been done by Mutti, presumably from French—Mutti, who had taught Hungarian and Romanian at the University of Bologna before his dismissal, does not know Arabic. Mutti had originally seen Qaddafi as the leader of a spiritually based jihad against the modern West and saw Islam as "the spiritual force that might animate and direct the 'revolt against the modern world.'" Although he later changed his mind about Qaddafi, he did not change his mind about Islam.[99]

Mutti's Islam is militant and political. He has published Italian translations of Jamal's work, and also of the Ayatollah Khomeini. That Islam is installed on top of his early Evolianism is symbolized by the decor of his office, which is predominantly Islamic but includes a Nazi standard propped behind the filing cabinet. Mutti has also made unusual attempts to "Europeanize" the history of Islam. The Ottoman Empire, he points out, was European as well as Arab and Asian, with a variety of grand viziers, admirals, and generals being of European origin. Alexander the Great is as much an Islamic figure (as Dhu'l-Qarnayn) as a European one, and Plato was incorporated into Islamic thought as well as European thought. Mutti even identifies one of the Companions of the Prophet Muhammad, Suhayb al-Rumi, as a European.[100]

Mutti is not known to have any significant personal following or to have engaged in any political or armed action after the 1980s. He is important, however, as one of the focal points in the late twentieth-century international network of Traditionalists, linking smaller Traditionalist groups in Romania, Hungary, Italy, France, and Russia.

Assessment

The role played by Traditionalism in the Islamic World and Russia and the role commonly played by Traditionalism in the West differ fundamentally. In the West most Traditionalist groups are small and isolated, and Traditionalism remains marginal, even though many individual Traditionalists have addressed Western audiences effectively. With rare exceptions, the most successful books of Western Traditionalists have been "soft" and have not dealt with Traditionalism per se. Pure Traditionalism has only ever interested a tiny minority of the Western public, and the concerns of Western Traditionalists are generally marginal to the general discourse of the West. In Iran and Turkey and Russia, however, Traditionalists are much more integrated into their societies and take part in the mainstream discourse—or, in Russia, in the less prominent of two mainstream political discourses. This is less true in Morocco, where the pattern is closer to that in the West—because the element in Moroccan society that is interested in Traditionalism is itself close to the West.

It seems paradoxical that a philosophy that derives from the Italian Renaissance and was developed in early twentieth-century France and Switzerland should be more at home in contemporary Iran, Turkey, and Russia than in the West. A Traditionalist might argue that this apparent paradox reflects the difference between Western modernity and Islamic tradition. This explanation is not entirely satisfactory, however. Much of Iran was very modern at the time of the revolution, and Turkey is the Islamic world's most self-consciously modern country. Russia, though differing from the West in many important ways, is also a modern rather than a "traditional" country. The most traditional countries of the Islamic world have shown the least interest in Traditionalism. Guénon is unknown in Egypt today, and Arabic is one of the few major languages in which almost no Traditionalist works are available. And neither Algerian nor Moroccan Traditionalists, in the end, considered that there was any point in making them available in that language.

Iran and Turkey, in contrast to Egypt and non-Francophone Morocco, have an equivalent of Guénon's Western audience—small but important. Russia has a larger one. It is not the presence of tradition in Iran and Turkey that allows Traditionalism into the intellectual mainstream, but the presence of modernity. Similarly, it is not the presence of modernity that excludes Traditionalism from mainstream Western discourse, but rather the absence of any real Western interest in some of the central questions that interested Guénon. One such question is the one now beginning to be asked in Turkey for the first time since the nineteenth century and is of pressing concern in Russia: East or West? Another is a central question for Iran today—modernization, or isolation for the sake of traditional religion? These are the very questions that Guénon's original writings addressed.

misunderstanding is that there is one modernism.
what is rejected is this particular modernism—too
materialistic, too predatory, too deadly to all.

14

Against the Stream

In the years before the 1927 publication of his *Crise du monde moderne*, René Guénon constructed an anti-modernist philosophy, Traditionalism, which flowered chiefly after the 1960s. Before the Second World War, Traditionalism was a small intellectual movement (Guénon in Cairo and his various correspondents) with one single active organization, the Sufi order led by Frithjof Schuon in Basel. By the start of the 1960s the intellectual movement had lost its center and was becoming increasingly diverse. There were soon a handful of active organizations, mostly Sufi but some Masonic. Then over the next four decades Schuon's order flourished before in part failing, Eliade transformed the academic study of religion, terrorists inspired by Baron Julius Evola caused havoc in Italy, and Traditionalism entered the general culture of the West. Finally it appeared in Iran, Turkey, and Russia. At the end of the twentieth century there were so many Traditionalist or partly Traditionalist organizations that it was no longer possible to count them.

It might seem strange that Traditionalism should benefit thus from the 1960s, a decade in which modernity visibly advanced. This is in fact not so extraordinary. On the one hand, alienation from modernity appears to increase as modernity advances. On the other hand, the advance of modernity requires the rejection of the status quo, and the past can be appealed to as much as the future by those who reject the present. The Renaissance produced something new by looking back to the classical age, and the Reformation also produced something new by looking back to early Christianity. Modernity may be produced by anti-modernism, and anti-modernism by

Islanism same

modernity. As Douglas Allen has shown, Eliade's work has much in common with postmodernism; what Allen says of Eliade is also true of the movement from which he came. Both Traditionalism and postmodernism reject "the tyranny and domination of the modernist idols of science, rationalism, and 'objectivity.'" Both see the Enlightenment as "narrow, oppressive, hierarchical, reductionist." For both, "rational scientific discourse is only one of the ways that human beings construct their 'stories' about reality."[1]

The number of those who rejected Western modernity and were alienated from contemporary society increased during the 1960s, just as the attractiveness of such previously established alternatives as Moscow-aligned Communist parties began to decline. It was from among dissenters such as these that Traditionalists were always drawn. There were even more dissenters from Western modernity outside the West, of course, and during the final quarter of the twentieth century some of them began to receive Traditionalist ideas with enthusiasm. The most interesting future developments in the history of Traditionalism may lie in these areas. Though it is too early to say, Traditionalism in the West may have run its course and may be in the process of being reabsorbed into the common stock of Western ideas from which it first emerged.

One of France's most eminent scholars of religion, Antoine Faivre, a professor at the same Sorbonne that refused Guénon a Ph.D., recently confessed himself at a loss to explain the success of what he called "one of the most curious cultural phenomena of our age."[2] I would suggest that the success of Traditionalism derives not only from the symbiotic relationship between modernity and anti-modernism, but also from the particular synthesis made by Guénon.

Guénon's philosophy was not especially original. It was composed of a number of elements, most of which had been part of Western thought for centuries. His achievement was to form an entirely new synthesis out of these ideas, and then to promote his synthesis to the point where it could be taken further by others—by Schuon into religious organizations, by Evola into politics, by Eliade into scholarship, and finally by Nasr and Dugin into the non-Western world.

Guénon's synthesis combined an emphasis on inversion, an idea older than the Book of Revelation (the source from which it is most familiar to Westerners), with a number of other ideas that had already been synthesized for him during the previous century. The oldest of these was the idea that Wisdom might be found in the East, an idea visible in the Sicily of Frederick II in the thirteenth century (at which point it was indisputably and objectively true).[3] The second oldest idea was Perennialism, which I have traced back to Marsilio Ficino in the fifteenth century. Neither of these ideas was rare at the start of the twentieth century, and by the end of that century they were both commonplace. Travel in India had become as standard a part of the education of the European university student as the Grand Tour had once been in part of the education of the European aristocrat, while yoga and Zen had become commonplace features of American life. The Perennial Philosophy remained little known by that name, but some sort of universalism had become the norm in the West—not even the Catholic Church dared to continue to claim an absolute monopoly of religious truth, and many Westerners tended to take it for granted that any given religion was, in one way or another, little different in its essentials from any other. *[not what is meant]*

The idea that Wisdom resided in the East was part of the original Perennialism, the East at that point consisting of classical Greece and biblical Israel and Egypt, represented by Hermes. Hinduism's replacing Hermes first appears with Reuben Burrow at the close of the eighteenth century and became more widespread during the nineteenth century, finally and most influentially through the Theosophical Society. It is the Theosophical Society that is the start of the visible development of Traditionalism, as of so many other movements, but one more synthesis was required to provide Guénon with his starting point. This was with the concept of initiation, again a very old concept, that becomes visible in its characteristic modern form with the emergence of modern Masonry in the seventeenth century. Perennialism, Hindu Wisdom, and initiation were all part of the Martinist Order of Guénon's first master, Dr. Gérard Encausse, who made the distinction between exoteric and esoteric religion that was to become a central aspect of Traditionalism. Guénon's second master, Count Albert de Pouvourville, promoted a similar synthesis, replacing Hinduism with Taoism. Much the same synthesis is found in the painter Ivan Aguéli, except that here—for the first time—Islam and Sufism take the place of Hermeticism, Hinduism, and Taoism. This synthesis continued independently of Traditionalism and was visible at the end of the twentieth century in the poet Katherine Raine, an initiate and enthusiast of Ficino who found her home in Hinduism.

It is clear that Guénon received this last synthesis from Encausse and de Pouvourville. The origins of his emphasis on inversion are less certain. De Pouvourville's stress on the danger to the West of the spiritual superiority of the East is one source, since it was implicit in this view that in at least one important respect the West had regressed rather than progressed. Regression is also implicit in Perennialism, which looks for truth in the past rather than the future, though no Perennialist before de Pouvourville seems to have followed this implication to its logical conclusion. Catholic polemics against Masons and Satanists are another source, since it was under Catholic auspices that Guénon's first writings on counterinitiation appeared. Perhaps the most important source of all, however, was Guénon's own youthful experiences among Martinists and neo-Gnostics, and of course his own venture of the Renewed Order of the Temple. These enterprises no doubt have seemed laughable to most readers of this book, and it is understandable that they appeared to the more mature Guénon as the opposite of what they claimed to be, as paths to error rather than to truth. Guénon's <u>occasional paranoia</u> may also have contributed to his identifying the forces of counterinitiation.

Inversion comprehends regression and counterinitiation. When a look at possibilities for initiation in the modern West makes clear the death of esotericism there, inversion can easily be synthesized with the search for Wisdom in the East. Perennialism does not follow automatically, but, when combined with these other two elements, it produces Traditionalism.

Inversion and the search for Wisdom in the East both have something in common with Orientalism, as analyzed by Edward Said.[4] Said showed how much Western understanding of the Middle East derived more from the self-understanding of the West than from anything that actually existed in the Middle East. Being rational was part of the Western self-image: the Middle East was unlike the West, so it was irrational. In the nineteenth century, when Western women were seen primarily as moral and virtuous, the Western understanding of the Muslim woman focused on the libidinous occupant of the harem. When the image of Western woman changed to emphasize emancipation, the Muslim woman was seen in terms of subordination and the veil. This model can be profitably applied even today: the Western press tends to ignore the possibility that public opinion might exist in the Middle East, except in references to the (dark, frightening, and irrational) "Arab street," because public opinion is what exists and matters in the West.

The general Traditionalist view of the Orient is in many ways an inverse form of Orientalism. Both Traditionalism and Orientalism are dualistic systems, both derive from the nineteenth century, and both share the important methodological failing of overreliance on texts and underreliance on observation. Like Orientalism, Traditionalism tends to portray the world outside the West as the mirror of the West. The difference is that the comparison is complimentary toward the non-West. Instead of contrasting a Middle East peopled by childlike irrational beings incapable of organization and self-discipline to a mature, disciplined, scientific and rational West, Traditionalism contrasts a West characterized by modernity, materialism, and mere technical skill to a Middle East of tradition, spirituality, and wisdom. This understanding of the Middle East is arguably no more accurate than that of the classic Orientalist.

One further element was still required for the Traditionalist philosophy to reach its final form. This was the development of Guénon's conception of initiation to include practice, a development that occurred only in the 1930s once Guénon had encountered the practice of Islam in Egypt. Traditionalism until that point had concentrated on texts and ideas. Though Aguéli and de Pouvourville had both traveled beyond Europe, neither seems to have placed much emphasis on practice. Religious practice, visible in 1920s France principally on Sundays, was everywhere in 1930s Egypt—visible in the ritual prayers shopkeepers performed in their shops, audible in the call to prayer five times every day, unavoidable in the disruption of most aspects of life every Ramadan. There is no direct evidence that it was these experiences that led Guénon to conclude that initiation must imply actual practice, but that seems very likely.

Guénon's own modification of Traditionalism during the 1930s to include practice was not the only modification. Most other important Traditionalists added modifications of their own. Dr Ananda Coomaraswamy, as a distinguished art historian, introduced a lasting emphasis on aesthetics found in many parts of the Traditionalist movement, notably in Schuonian Traditionalism. He also made the first, largely unsuccessful, attempt to integrate Traditionalism into formal scholarship—Guénon had turned his back on academia after his thesis was refused by the Sorbonne. It was Dr. Mircea Eliade who later most successfully integrated Traditionalism into scholarship, translating "tradition" into "archaic religion" and Wisdom into "universally valid myth and symbol," and adding a fair measure of academic rigor to his writings.

Evola made the most dramatic modifications to Guénonian Traditionalism, to the extent that some contemporary Traditionalists, partly motivated by embarrassment at Evola's politics, would prefer to exclude him from Traditionalism altogether. Evola's earlier readings of Nietzsche and Bachofen led to an emphasis on realization not through religious practice but through action, through the revolt that the painter René Daumal had seen as lacking from Guénon's own writings. For Guénon the priestly caste was superior to the warrior caste, but Evola disagreed. In the circumstances of the 1920s, 1930s, and 1940s Evolian Traditionalism pointed toward the political right, separating it definitively from Guénonian Traditionalism, which was essentially apolitical. These two branches of Traditionalism remained linked, however, as can be seen from the "leftist" Henri Hartung's repeated visits to Evola during the 1960s. Evolian Traditionalism underwent further modifications after the Second World War with the insertion of Existentialism, which led—with Franco Freda's help—to an understanding of *apoliteia* that brought bloody mayhem.

Coomaraswamy, Eliade, and Evola all proceeded from the earlier version of Traditionalism, which did not emphasize practice. Frithjof Schuon proceeded from the final version and modified Traditionalism in quite another direction, adding the characteristic organizational form of the Sufi order. It is from this point onward that we can really speak of a Traditionalist movement rather than just a philosophy. Schuon also developed Perennialism into a universal mission of his own that led ultimately to disaster. In reaction, Michel Vâlsan modified Schuonian Traditionalism in the direction of extreme orthodoxy, leading back to non-Traditionalist Islam, a destination his followers shared with Dr. Fawzy Sqali. Within Schuon's Traditionalism, Dr. Hossein Nasr then modified Traditionalism for consumption in the more modern segments of the Islamic world, adding an emphasis on "Islamic Philosophy" and for the first time connecting Traditionalism directly with non-Western scholarship. Nasr shares with Eliade the distinction of being a leading Traditionalist scholar.

It is unclear whether one of the latest modifications of Traditionalism, the replacement of both priest and warrior by woman at the hands of the Aristasians, should be regarded seriously as the equipping of Traditionalism for another new group (women), or as amusing evidence of the passing of Traditionalism into the general culture of the West. Deep seriousness has been characteristic of all other Traditionalists; perhaps the element of humor in Aristasia will prevent its spreading beyond very limited circles.

Alexander Dugin was responsible for the last major modification of the twentieth century, equipping Traditionalism for the European East by adding Orthodox Christianity and the Eurasian geopolitical theories of Sir Halford Mackinder. More indebted to Evola than to Guénon, Dugin's Neo-Eurasianism seemed to some to threaten consequences as lamentable as Evola's.

The politics of Dugin and Evola and the disaster of Schuon's later Maryamiyya in Bloomington have led some to argue that Traditionalism, as both a movement and a philosophy, is irredeemably evil. Numerous Traditionalists have, however, recognized and successfully avoided evil while remaining Traditionalists. Eliade distanced himself from the Legion of the Archangel Michael as it began to turn itself into a Nazi clone, and Vâlsan distanced himself not only from events in Romania but also from the disaster looming over the Maryamiyya. Nasr may have accidentally contributed to the Iranian Revolution, but he did his best to prevent this revolution, and two less important Iranian Traditionalists (Daryush Shayegan and Nasrullah Purjavadi) were prominent among those Iranians who condemned the evils that the revolution ushered in.[5] Schuon and Paul de Séligny are more difficult cases, but it seems clear that evil or good depend more on the individual Traditionalist than on Traditionalism itself.

The Traditionalist movement has undeniably failed in certain areas, but in others it has succeeded. At least on a grand scale, it has failed in its original objective, as defined in 1924 by Guénon in Orient et Occident. Western civilization at the start of the twenty-first century is not observably any more based in spiritual tradition than it was in the 1920s. If there are more non-Western spiritualities in the West now than in the 1920s, their presence cannot be traced only to the efforts of a Traditionalist elite. On a less grand scale, however, Traditionalists have been among the most effective of those writers, lecturers, and educators who have introduced Western audiences to Islam, to Sufism, and to a more sympathetic approach to non-Western religion generally, both within academia and beyond. Traditionalists have also played an important part in guiding parts of Masonry toward something that might be described as spirituality, and they have succeeded to their own satisfaction in the earliest objective, that of reassembling the debris of the primordial tradition. Traditionalism is complete and internally coherent.

It is the least ambitious projects of Traditionalists that have proven most successful. "Soft" Traditionalism, books that are informed by a Traditionalist analysis but do not stress it, has reached far wider audiences than "hard" Traditionalism. It is this soft form of Traditionalism that has touched the lives of many who did not know it—though few readers of this book have likely heard of Traditionalism per se, many have encountered soft Traditionalist authors and interpretations. This relationship is not, of course, restricted to Traditionalism—the works of George Orwell were more widely read in the West than were those of Karl Marx.

Frontal attacks on modernity have, in contrast, usually achieved the opposite of their intention. E. F. Schumacher's anti-modernism fed into further modernization, and rather than destroying the bourgeois state, the activities of Italian terrorists in the 1970s produced a revulsion against extremism which markedly strengthened the status quo. Vâlsan's unambitious Sufi order, which aimed merely to lead those who came to it along the standard paths of Sufism, achieved its objectives; Schuon's universal mission transformed his order into a religious movement that was distinctively modern (as the germ of a new religion), and that Guénon would surely have identified as counterinitiation.

It is only outside the West that frontal attacks on Western modernity by Traditionalists have met with any success, in Iran and then in Russia. The favorable reception given to Traditionalists in these countries derives from their alignment with established anti-Westernism. Traditionalists in Iran and Russia were going with the stream. In the West, "hard" Traditionalism was going against the stream. Soft Traditionalism generally avoided the mainstream. In general, initiatives that go with historical streams may modify the direction of those streams somewhat, whereas initiatives that go against streams are normally either sunk or (like Schumacher, Freda, or Schuon) turned around by the stream and proceed in the opposite direction. In these terms, Vâlsan led his followers from one stream to another; they are now far closer to the mainstream of Islam than to anything Western.

Individuals who have become Traditionalists were almost without exception already out of the stream. Schuon and Burckhardt, like Aguéli and Eberhardt before them, came from artistic, nonconformist backgrounds, as did the Traditionalist sympathizer Thomas Merton. Von Meyenburg and Pallavicini came from aristocratic backgrounds, out of tune with the times, as did Count de Pouvourville and Baron Evola,[6] and of course also two Traditionalist sympathizers, the claimant to the throne of France and the heir to the throne of the United Kingdom. Coomaraswamy and Nasr were the products of cultural mixing and had no stream of their own in the first place. In fact, the only important Traditionalist *not* to come from a background or community out of tune with the times was Guénon himself, the only child of a solidly bourgeois insurance loss assessor.

The mainstream of the twentieth century was progressive, in the sense of hoping for progress, if not in the pre-First World War sense of believing in the inevitability of progress. No progressive has ever become a Traditionalist, not even a non-Western progressive. The highly progressive Egyptian intellectual Taha Husayn rejected Traditionalism and Guénon himself with scorn, the progressive Algerian Islamist Malek Bennabi rejected Traditionalism as irrelevant, and the progressive Iranian Islamist Ali Shariati made no use whatsoever of Traditionalism in his work.

NO ?

An awareness of the importance of following a stream is implicit in a strategy known in French as *entrisme* (entry-ism), a term usually used in a political context to indicate the opportunistic infiltration of an organization with a view to influencing it from within. *Entrisme* was used by numerous Traditionalists, usually with more success on subsequent than on first attempts. Traditionalists have sometimes attempted *entrisme* with little to show for their effort. Eliade, Evola, Dugin, Jamal, and Pallavicini failed to achieve their objectives with the Legion of the Archangel Michael in Romania, the Italian Fascist Party, the SS, Pamyat' and the Party of the Islamic Renaissance in Russia, and the Catholic Church—it was the Catholic Church that dominated the Islamo-Christian dialogue which Pallavicini attempted to Traditionalize, without success. In all cases, these are or were centrally controlled and rigidly structured organizations which it would be hard for anyone to infiltrate.

In contrast, Traditionalists have enjoyed success with political alliances and loose-knit communities, usually on their second or third attempt at *entrisme*— Eliade and to some extent Nasr in American academia, Dugin with the Red-Brown Alliance and Jamal with the network of "Islamic Committees," and Evola with the ultra-Conservative circles around the Berlin Herrenclub (these circles themselves then failed, or rather were dismantled by the Nazis, but that is another matter). Evola also successfully infiltrated the issue of racialism, though his initiatives were ended from outside by the Fascist regime. Pallavicini has done better with the loosely knit community of official and semi-official international Islamic organizations than with the Catholic Church.

racism is not Islamic

One of three exceptions is von Sebottendorf, not anyhow a Traditionalist, who failed ludicrously in his attempt to infiltrate the Germanen-Orden and succeeded only in helping the Nazi Party to part of its name. There was no successful second attempt by von Sebottendorf. In the United Kingdom, Critchlow has successfully Traditionalized much of the Temenos Academy and the Prince's Foundation without (so far as is known) having suffered any earlier failures. In France, Hartung was successful in infiltrating executive education but later judged this infiltration to have been turned by the stream.

"Hard" Traditionalism has been rejected not only by progressives and by the mainstream of twentieth-century Western history, but by two other distinct groups: fully traditional people, and most scholars. Almost the entire population of the Arab world has ignored Traditionalism, evidently because the Arab world is not modern enough to receive it. Religious figures solidly embedded in their own traditions have also often rejected Traditionalism in whole or in part—Jacques Maritain for the Catholic Church, Seraphim Rose for the Orthodox Church, and Ahmad Qustas for Islam.

Except in Dugin's version, Traditionalism has not usually claimed to be compatible with Christianity (though Schuon's universalism claimed to encompass Christianity, as it did all religions). Many Traditionalists, however, have regarded themselves as Muslim. Though any Muslim who subscribes to any form of universalism is departing from what is generally accepted to be the consensus of Islam, many Traditionalists might be judged Muslim by Muslims on the basis of their practice: Nasr, Vâlsan, Pallavicini, and Guénon himself. Others, notably Schuon, would be and have been rejected. The relationship between Traditionalism and scholarship is a curious one. On the one hand, the entire field of contemporary religious studies bears the imprint of Eliade's soft Traditionalism, and many leading Traditionalists have been scholars. On the other hand, every non-Traditionalist scholar who has looked at Traditionalism since Professor Sylvain Lévi rejected Guénon's Ph.D. thesis in 1921 has come to much the same conclusion: these people are not serious. They ignore history, and they ignore anything that does not fit their theories. In the words of Antoine Faivre, Traditionalism "de-historicizes and de-spatializes its ontological predicates. . . . Its propensity to search everywhere for similarities in the hope of finally finding a hypothetical Unity is evidently prejudicial to historico-critical research, that is to say empirical research, which is more interested in revealing the genesis, the course, the changes, and the migrations of the phenomena that it studies." As Faivre recognizes, anyone who sets out knowing the "truth" is unlikely to recognize anything unexpected that they meet on the way.[7]

It is not the function of this book to defend Traditionalism, but it seems clear that those who condemn Traditionalism as not serious are missing the point. Traditionalism makes a claim to represent the ultimate truth, just as religion or some types of philosophy do. As Douglas Allen said, "rational scientific discourse is only one of the ways that human beings construct their 'stories' about reality." To judge Traditionalism as one would a university thesis makes no more sense than to dismiss Christianity for having insufficient evidence of Christ's divinity, or to dismiss Islam for ignoring crucial elements of the doctrine of the Trinity. On the other hand, Guénon did submit his work to Lévi as a thesis, and so Lévi was right to recommend its refusal.

Notes

A list of my main interviewees appears before the bibliography; places and dates of interviews are given there rather than in individual notes.

Material unlikely to interest most readers has been made available as "additional notes" available on the Web. Such material is indicated by "See AN" and a number. Thus "See AN 2" refers the interested reader to additional note 2 for the chapter in question, at http://www.traditionalists.org/anotes.

1. TRADITIONALISM

1. *Shorter Oxford English Dictionary*, third ed.

2. René Guénon, *La crise du monde moderne* (Paris: Bossard, 1927) and *La métaphysique orientale* (Paris: Chacornac, 1939); Julius Evola, *Rivolta contro il mondo moderno* (Milan: Hoepli, 1934). The title of this book draws on Guénon's *Crise du monde moderne* and Evola's *Rivolta contro il mondo moderno*.

3. The summary of the Traditionalist philosophy given in this chapter is of necessity a brief one and emphasizes especially those elements which were of most importance for the subsequent history of the Traditionalist movement. Readers interested in the Traditionalist philosophy as a philosophy should start with Guénon's *Crise du monde moderne*, or read any of the other books written by the Traditionalists themselves. A good overview is given in William W. Quinn, *The Only Tradition* (Albany, N.Y.: SUNY Press, 1996).

4. René Guénon, *L'introduction générale à l'étude des doctrines hindoues* (Paris: M. Rivière, 1921).

5. Lévi, report to Dean Ferdinand Brunot, quoted in Marie-France James, *Ésotérisme et Christianisme: autour de René Guénon* (Paris: Nouvelles éditions latines, 1981), p. 194.

6. Lévi, report to Dean Brunot.

7. Victor Cousin, *Cours de philosophie* (Paris: Pichon et Didier, 1828).

8. Jean Filliozat, "Rien sans l'orient?" *Planète+*, April 1970, p. 124.

9. Lévi, report to Dean Brunot.

10. At least he did not include it among the two criticisms he added to Noële Maurice-Denis's review of the *Introduction générale* (in *La Revue universelle*, July 1921, discussed later).

11. Agostino Steuco, a Vatican librarian and Christian Platonist, author of *De perenni philosophia* [Concerning the Perennial Philosophy], 1540, dedicated to Pope Paul III.

12. Ficino's most important work was *Theologica Platonica de animarum immortalitate* [The Platonic Theology of the Immortality of the Soul] (1482), in which he examined the question of immortality in the light of the writings of Plato as well as of Catholic theology.

13. Paul Oskar Kristeller, Introduction, *The Letters of Marsilio Ficino* (London: Shepheard-Walwyn, 1975). Available online at http://easyweb.easynet.co.uk/orpheus/ficino.htm [June 14, 2001].

14. Kristeller, Introduction.

15. The reasons for this are considered in chapter 2.

16. James, *Ésotérisme et Christianisme*, p. 194.

17. *Le Théosophisme, histoire d'une pseudo-religion* (Paris: Nouvelle Librairie Nationale, 1921); *L'erreur spirite* (Paris: M. Rivière, 1923).

18. The unusual photograph of an immersed crucifix in Serrano's "Fluid Mysteries" series caused much controversy in the 1980s and 1990s.

19. Discussion with anonymous Traditionalist, 1994.

20. René Guénon, *Orient et Occident* (Paris: Payot, 1924; reprint, Paris: Guy Trédaniel, 1993), p. 19. I have edited the quote as follows: "Modern Western civilization appears in history as a veritable anomaly . . . among all those that we know . . . , this civilization // accompanied by a corresponding intellectual regression . . . [which] has reached a point where today's Occidentals no longer know what pure intellectuality might be . . . hence their disdain."

21. Guénon, *Orient et Occident*, p. 187.

22. Guénon, *Orient et Occident*, p. 115.

23. Oswald Spengler, *Der Untergang des Abendlandes; Umrisse einer Morphologie der Weltgeschichte* (2 vols., Munich: Beck, 1919–22).

24. Guénon, *Orient et Occident*, pp. 169–87.

25. Guénon, *Orient et Occident*, p. 186. I have again edited the passage for directness as follows: "If the elite . . . does not have the time // mentality as a whole . . . this elite would be . . . the symbolic 'ark' // it would however receive . . . the bases of a new development // But . . . there would still be . . . difficult problems: the ethnic revolutions . . . would certainly be most serious . . . It would be much preferable for the West . . . to acquire a civilization . . . appropriate to its own conditions, sparing it . . . from being more or less unpleasantly assimilated."

26. Guénon, *Orient et Occident*, pp. 174, 177, 184–85, and 188.

27. Guénon, *Orient et Occident*, p. 177.

28. *L'homme et son devenir selon le Védânta* (Paris: Bossard, 1925); *La crise du monde moderne* (Paris: Bossard, 1927). See AN 1 for the other four.

29. René Guénon, *La crise du monde moderne* (Paris: Folio, 1999), p. 187.

30. Quoted in Paul Chacornac, *La vie simple de René Guénon* (1958; reprint, Paris: Editions traditionnelles, 1986), p. 79.

31. See http://www.d.edu/Departments/Maritain.

32. Nöele Maurice-Denis Boulet, "L'ésotériste René Guénon: Souvenirs et jugements," *La pensée catholique: Cahiers de synthèse* 77 (1962), 24–25.

33. Boulet, "L'ésotériste René Guénon," pp. 18 and 26–27, and Jean Borella, "René Guénon and the Traditionalist School," in *Modern Esoteric Spirituality*, ed. Antoine Faivre and Jakob Needleman (New York: Crossroads, 1992), p. 373.

34. Boulet, "L'ésotériste René Guénon," 77, pp. 35–36.

35. That Maritain and others recommended Guénon to the Frères des Ecoles chrétiennes (who ran the école des Francs-Bourgeois) is supposition, but under the circumstances reasonable supposition.

36. Quoted in James, *Ésotérisme et Christianisme*, p. 198.

37. Amèlée d'Yvignac, in *Revue de philosophie* November–December 1924, quoted in James, *Ésotérisme et Christianisme*, p. 225.

38. Bernard Allo, OP, review in *Revue des sciences philosophiques et théologiques*, quoted in James, *Ésotérisme et Christianisme*, p. 227.

39. In 1946–47, according to James, *Ésotérisme et Christianisme*, p. 389.

40. James, *Ésotérisme et Christianisme*, pp. 233–34, and James, *Ésotérisme, Occultisme, Franc-Maçonnerie et Christianisme aux XIX et XX siècles. Explorations bio-bibliographiques* (Paris: Nouvelles éditions latines, 1981), p. 145.

41. Olivier de Frémond.

42. James, *Ésotérisme et Christianisme*, pp. 243–44, 255–56, and 262–63.

43. For the others, see AN 2. Zoccatelli, *Le lièvre qui rumine: Autour de René Guénon, Louis Charbonneau-Lassay et la Fraternité du Paraclet* (Milan: Archè, 1999), p. 16.

44. Guénon, *Crise du monde moderne*, pp. 195–201.

45. Reconstructed from the draft of a letter from Charbonneau-Lassay to Guénon, April 1928, printed in Zoccatelli, *Lièvre qui rumine*, pp. 61–62.

46. Maurice Clavelle [Jean Reyor], "Document confidentiel inédit," unpublished typescript.

47. A number of books on Martinism, etc., were found in his private library after his death. See Igor Volkoff, "Voyage à travers la bibliothèque de René Guénon," *Egypte nouvelle*, October 9, 1953, reprinted in Xavier Accart, ed., *L'Ermite de Duqqi: René Guénon en marge des milieux francophones égyptiens* (Milan: Archè, 2001). See pp. 220–21.

48. Chacornac, *Vie simple*, p. 63. There has been a certain amount of speculation about the identity of the Indian lady, who has sometimes been identified wrongly as Guénon's wife and sometimes as the wife of an unknown guru of Guénon. It seems likely to me that the portrait was purely decorative.

49. Chacornac, *Vie simple*, p. 84, and for the lack of enthusiasm Jean Reyor, "De quelques énigmes dans l'oeuvre de René Guénon," in *René Guénon* [Cahiers de l'Herne], ed. Jean-Pierre Laurant and Paul Barbanegra (Paris: Ed. de l'Herne, 1985), pp. 137–38.

50. André Braire, interview.

51. James, *Ésotérisme et Christianisme*, p. 298.

52. James, *Ésotérisme et Christianisme*, p. 298. Jourd'Heuil was in Rome some ten years before Maritain is said to have tried to get Guénon's books put on the Index, but she might have found Guénon some lasting sympathizers at the Vatican. Another reason that Guénon was never put on the index may have been the influence of Cardinal Daniélou (see chapter 6).

53. Chacornac, *Vie simple*, p. 84.

54. Jean-Pierre Laurant, e-mail, October 11, 2001.

55. In the introduction of his translation of part of *La crise du monde moderne*, published in 1935. Quoted in Roger Lipsey, *Coomaraswamy*, vol. 3: *His Life and Work* (Princeton, N.J.: Princeton University Press, 1977), p. 169.

56. *Catalogue of the Indian Collections in the Museum of Fine Arts* (Boston: Museum of Fine Arts, 1923–30); *History of Indian and Indonesian Art* (New York: E Weyhe, 1927).

57. His encyclopedic knowledge resulted partly from the ten years he spent cataloguing the Boston museum's vast collection (Lipsey, *Coomaraswamy*, p. 135).

58. For the details, Lipsey, *Coomaraswamy*, pp. 145–48. The speculation is mine alone.

59. That Guénon provided the big ideas while Coomaraswamy provided the scholarship is the view of Lipsey, *Coomaraswamy*, p. 172, with which I entirely agree. Most important, Coomaraswamy persuaded Guénon to drop his characterization of Buddhism as a Hindu heresy of little interest. Marco Pallis, "A Fateful Meeting of Minds: A. K. Coomaraswamy and R. Guénon," *Studies in Comparative Religion* 12 (1978), 180–81.

60. *A New Approach to the Vedas: An Essay in Translation and Exegesis* (London: Luzac, 1933).

61. Quoted in Lipsey, *Coomaraswamy*, p. 177. See also pp. 163–64.

62. Eric Schroeder, "Memories of the Person," in *Coomaraswamy*, ed. Lipsey, vol. 3, p. 285.

63. *The Transformation of Nature in Art* (Cambridge, Mass.: Harvard University Press, 1934); *Hinduism and Buddhism* (New York: Philosophical Library, 1941). For more on Coomaraswamy's Traditionalism, see Giovanni Monastra, "Ananda K. Coomaraswamy: de l'idéalisme à la tradition," *Nouvelle Ecole* 47 (1995).

64. Lipsey, *Coomaraswamy*, vol. 3, p. 186.

65. Coomaraswamy to Marco Pallis, 1944, reprinted in Lipsey, *Coomaraswamy*, vol. 3, p. 184.

66. Eric Schroeder, quoted in Lipsey, *Coomaraswamy*, vol. 3, p. 206.

67. Walter E. Clark, Review of Ananda K. Coomaraswamy, *Hinduism and Buddhism* (New York: Philosophical Library, 1943), *Harvard Journal of Asiatic Studies* 8, no. 1 (March 1944), 63–70. The reviewer, clearly an Indologist in the classic tradition, devotes five whole pages to listing dubious interpretations, mostly etymological ones.

68. Lipsey, *Coomaraswamy*, vol. 3, p. 162.

69. Lipsey, *Coomaraswamy*, vol. 3, pp. 254–57.

70. *Histoire d'un enfant du pays d'Egypte* (reprint, Paris: F. Rieder, 1924).

71. Jean-Pierre Luccioni, "Bonjean, Bosco et la 'doctrine,'" in *Henri Bosco, mystère et spiritualité: Actes du IIIe colloque international Henri Bosco (Nice, 22–24 mai 1986)*, no editor (NP: Librairie Jose Corti, 1987), p. 168.

72. Bonjean, "Souvenirs et réflexions sur René Guénon," *Revue de la Méditerranée*, March–April 1951, pp. 214–20, quoted in Chacornac, *Vie simple*, p. 83.

73. Pierre Alibert, *Gleizes: biographie* (Paris: Editions Gallérie Michèle Heyraud, 1970), pp. 207–9.

74. See Alibert, *Gleizes*.

75. See Eddy Batache, *Surréalisme et tradition: la pensée d'André Breton jugée selon l'oeuvre de René Guénon* (Paris: Editions traditionnelles, 1978).

76. Christian Allègre, Review of Phil Powrie, *René Daumal, étude d'une obsession* (Geneva: Droz: 1990), *Erofile: Electronic reviews of French & Italian Literary Essays* 18 (December 1991) [online]. Available http://www2.wheatoncollege.edu/Academic . . . cDept/French/Erofile/archive/ero18.html [May 24, 2000].

77. "Michel Camus, Daumal, profil perdu," *Poésie d'hier et d'aujourd'hui* [online]. Available http://www.mygale.org/mirra/metaphys.html [2000].

78. Diary 1928, in Daumal, *L'évidence absurde, essais et notes I (1926–1934)* (Paris: Gallimard, 1972). Reproduced in *Cybrairie ambulante*, October 10, 1997 [online]. Available http://www.chez.com/freecyb/cybrairie/grandjeu.htm [May 5, 2000].

79. Jean-Paul Enthoven, "Dumont l'intouchable" [interview with Louis Dumont], *Le nouvel observateur*, January 6, 1984, reprinted in Roland Lardinois, "Louis Dumont et la science indigène," *Actes de la recherche en sciences sociales*, 106–107 (March 1995), 11 and 18. My thanks to Marc Gaborieau for bringing Dumont's connection with Guénon to my attention.

80. Henri Bosco, *Hyacinthe* (Paris: Gallimard, 1940).

81. Quoted in Xavier Accart, "Du *Jardin enchanté* à l'ermitage Saint-Jean: La réception de l'oeuvre de René Guénon par Henri Bosco," in *Henri Bosco, Actes de colloque international de Narbonne 13–14 juin 1997*, no editor (Narbonne: Les cahiers du CERMEIL, 1997).

82. Accart, "Du *Jardin enchanté*."

83. Henri Bosco, "Trois rencontres," *Nouvelle Revue Française*, November 1951, p. 276.

84. Stefano Salzani and PierLuigi Zoccatelli, *Hermétisme et emblématique du Christ dans la vie et dans l'oeuvre de Louis Charbonneau-Lassay (1871–1946)* (Milan: Archè, 1996), pp. 16–17.

85. *Bestiaire du Christ: la mystérieuse emblématique de Jésus-Christ* (Paris: Desclée, De Brouwer, 1940). The *Bestiaire*, 1,000 pages with 1,157 woodcuts, was published when enough subscriptions for it had been raised, but most copies were then destroyed in a warehouse by German action during the Second World War. See Salzani and Zoccatelli, *Hermétisme et emblématique*, pp. 11–13 and 55–56, and E. Mila, "Charbonneau-Lassay y el esoterismo católico en el siglo XX," online at *Disidencias: OnLine Press*. Available http://members.es.tripod.de/disidentes/arti44.htm [June 1, 2000].

2. PERENNIALISM

1. Paul Chacornac, *La vie simple de René Guénon* (1958; reprint, Paris: Editions traditionnelles, 1986), pp.16–27.

2. Gérard Encausse defended his doctoral thesis in 1894, on "L'anatomie philo-

sophique et ses divisions, augmentée d'une essai de clarification méthodologique des sciences anatomiques." Marie-Sophie André and Christophe Beaufils, *Papus, biographie: la Belle Epoque de l'occultisme* (Paris: Berg International, 1995), p. 115.

3. André and Beaufils, *Papus*, pp. 8–14.

4. As a young man Olcott had dropped out of New York University for financial reasons and moved to Ohio, where he farmed and wrote a standard work on sorghum cultivation. After a spell as agricultural correspondent for the *New York Tribune* in the 1850s, action as a signals officer during the Civil War, and a successful assignment as a commissioner at the War Department, Olcott was called to the New York Bar in 1868.

5. Quoted in Bruce F. Campbell, *Ancient Wisdom Revived: A History of the Theosophical Movement* (Berkeley: University of California Press, 1980), p. 29. See also pp. 2–7 and 21–22.

6. In his *De rebus sacris et ecclesiasticis exercitationes*. For Ficino and for Hermes and Casaubon, see Wouter J. Hanegraaff, *New Age Religion and Western Culture: Esotericism in the Mirror of Secular Thought* (Leiden: Brill, 1996), pp. 388–91, and Paul Oskar Kristeller, Introduction to *The Letters of Marsilio Ficino* (London: Shepheard-Walwyn, 1975). See also David Stevenson, *The Origins of Freemasonry: Scotland's Century, 1590–1710* (Cambridge: Cambridge University Press, 1988), pp. 82–82, and Antoine Faivre, "Histoire de la notion moderne de Tradition dans ses rapports avec les courants ésotériques (Xve–XXe siècles)," *Aries*, unnumbered volume, *Symboles et Mythes* (c. 2000), pp. 9–12.

7. Arthur Edward Waite, "The French Mystic and the Story of Modern Martinism," online at *Martinist Information Page*. Available http://www.icbl.hw.ac.uk/bill/ TFMSOMM.html [May 8, 1996]. Encausse in fact claimed de Saint-Martin as the order's founder, probably with little justification.

8. Saint-Martin, *De l'esprit des choses* (Paris: 1800), quoted in Umberto Eco, *Foucault's Pendulum* (San Diego: Harcourt Brace Jovanovich, 1989), p. 173.

9. Emile Dermenghem, *Joseph de Maistre mystique* (1923; reprint, Paris: La Colombe, 1946), pp. 48–51.

10. De Maistre, *Mémoire au Duc de Brunswick* (1781), quoted in Faivre, "Histoire de la notion moderne de Tradition," p. 18.

11. For the Asiatick Society, see J. M. Steadman, "The Asiatick Society of Bengal," *Eighteenth Century Studies* 10 (1977).

12. Reuben Burrow, "A Proof that the Hindoos Had the Binomial Theorem," *Asiatick Researches: Transactions of the Society Instituted in Bengal for Inquiring into the History and Antiquities, the Arts, Sciences and Literature, of Asia* 2 (1799), 488–89. Steadman, "Asiatick Society," drew my attention to this important article.

13. Notably Thomas Maurice in his "A Dissertation on the Indian Origin of the Druids and on the Striking Affinity which the Religious Rites and Ceremonies, Anciently Practised in the British Islands, Bore to Those of the Brahmins" (*Indian Antiquities* 6, 1812), and Godfrey Higgins in his *The Celtic Druids* (London: Rowland Hunter, 1829). See Catherine Robinson, "Druids and Brahmins: A Case of Mistaken Identity?" *DISKUS* 6 (2000) [online]. Available http://www.uni-marburg.de/ religionswissenschaft/journal/diskus [February 1, 2002].

14. Quotations from Emerson taken from Russell B. Goodman, "East-West Phi-

losophy in Nineteenth-Century America: Emerson and Hinduism," *Journal of the History of Ideas* 51 (1990), 627, and Stephen E. Whicher, ed., *Selections from Ralph Waldo Emerson: An Organic Anthology* (Cambridge, Mass.: Riverside Press, 1960), p. 104.

15. *The Dial* carried work by Emerson, and *The Western Messenger* work by James Freeman Clarke, author of the popular *Ten Great Religions: An Essay in Comparative Theology* (Boston, 1871). Not only Hinduism, but also the Romantic-Perennialist idea of "the identity of the religious *sentiment* [my emphasis] under all its great historic forms" and the need for a "mutual interchange of experience between the East and the West" were promoted by a non-Transcendentalist ex-Unitarian minister, Samuel Johnson, also a reader of Victor Cousin. See Carl T. Jackson, "The Orient in Post-Bellum American Critical Thought: Three Pioneer Popularizers," *American Quarterly* 1 (1970), 69–75. These are all variations on the theme of transmission through Cousin and Transcendentalism.

16. In Whicher, ed., *Selections*, pp. 139–40.

17. Aldous Huxley, *The Perennial Philosophy* (1944; New York: Harper and Brothers, 1945).

18. The Baltic states came under German control before being absorbed into the Russian Empire, and most Baltic landowners were thus of distant German origin, normally with the rank of baron and German surnames. By the nineteenth century, however, the Baltic barons were culturally indistinguishable from the rest of the imperial aristocracy.

19. Campbell, *Ancient Wisdom*, pp. 2–7 and 21–22.

20. "Bey" was the Ottoman, and so also the nineteenth-century Egyptian, equivalent of the British title "Sir." "Tuitit" bears no resemblance to any Egyptian name of the time.

21. Campbell, *Ancient Wisdom*, pp. 23–24 and 25–26.

22. Estimate of size from Poul Pedersen, "Tibet, Theosophy, and the Psychologization of Buddhism," unpublished paper delivered at a conference on "Mythos Tibet" held at the University of Bonn, May 10–12, 1996. This relocation of the Theosophical Society to India coincided with the beginning of its expansion, much of which was in India (and also Burma and Ceylon)—in 1885, 106 of 121 lodges were in these three countries—but also in Europe and America.

23. Peter Washington, *Madame Blavatsky's Baboon: A History of the Mystics, Mediums and Misfits Who Brought Spiritualism to America* (New York: Schocken Books, 1995), pp. 66–67.

24. *Isis Unveiled: A Master-key to the Mysteries of Ancient and Modern Science and Theology* (New York: J. W. Bouton, 1877); *The Secret Doctrine: The Synthesis of Science, Religion and Philosophy* (London: Theosophical Pub. Co., 1888).

25. Campbell, *Ancient Wisdom*, pp. 34 and 40.

26. Samuel Dunlap, *Sôd, the Son of Man* (London: Williams and Norgate, 1861); Joseph Ennemoser, *The History of Magic* (London: H. G. Bohn, 1854); John Dowson, *A Classical Dictionary of Hindu Mythology and Religion, Geography, History, and Literature* (London, Trübner, 1879); Horace Wilson, trans., *Vishnu Purana: A System of Hindu Mythology and Tradition* (London, J. Murray, 1840). This at least was the conclusion of William Coleman, an American scholar of Pali texts with an interest in spiritism (Campbell, *Ancient Wisdom*, pp. 34 and 41). See Coleman, "The Source of Madame

Blavatsky's Writings," in *A Modern Priestess of Isis*, ed. Vsevolod Soloviev (London, 1895: 353–66). There are other theories, but it is generally agreed that the works were extensively plagiarized.

27. See Washington, *Madame Blavatsky*, esp. pp. 37 and 81. This raises an alternative possibility for the transmission of what may be called Vedic Perennialism to Guénon, since Bulwer Lytton was in contact with Eliphas Lévi (pseudonym of Alphonse-Louis Constant), a defrocked French priest who combined occultism with an interest in the Vedas and a belief in a single universal religious tradition (Washington, *Madame Blavatsky*, p. 37). A similar conviction of "the existence of a great Unity" in "the basis [*fond*]" of all religions can be found in Antoine Fabre d'Olivet, *L'Histoire philosophique du genre humaine* (1822) (I, 1, quoted in Faivre, "Histoire de la notion moderne de Tradition"). The line from Fabre d'Olivet through Lévi is also a plausible one but is not emphasized here for reasons of clarity.

28. Campbell, *Ancient Wisdom*, pp. 87–93, and Washington, *Madame Blavatsky*, pp. 80–81.

29. The Theosophical Society continues to exist and has given rise to numerous other movements, of which the most important is Rudolf Steiner's Anthroposophy. See Washington, *Madame Blavatsky*, for the history of later Theosophy.

30. *Lotus*, July–August 1887, quoted in André and Beaufils, *Papus*, p. 37.

31. Sufi initiation may be divided likewise: the exoteric significance of "taking" an order is that a new Sufi joins a community and can benefit from the spiritual instruction of the shaykh, while the esoteric significance is that the new Sufi receives *baraka* [approximately, grace] by joining him or herself to the chain of shaykhs that goes all the way back to the Prophet and through the Prophet to God himself.

32. Stevenson, *Origins of Freemasonry*, pp. 5–19.

33. Stevenson, *Origins of Freemasonry*, pp. 20, 26–31, 44–50, and 87–96.

34. Stevenson, *Origins of Freemasonry*, pp. 196–99 and 230–31.

35. Antonio Coen and Michel Dumesnil de Grammont, *La Franc-Maçonnerie Ecossaise* (Nice: SNEP, 1946), p. 15.

36. Stevenson, *Origins of Freemasonry*, pp. 6–7.

37. G. Rocca, ed., *'Abdul-Hadi: Ecrits pour La Gnose* (Milan: Archè, 1988), pp. 33–48.

38. André and Beaufils, *Papus*, pp. 54–57.

39. The words are those of Georges Descormiers, a follower of Encausse, quoted in Philippe Encausse, *Papus, le "Balzac de l'occultisme": vingt-cinq années d'occultisme occidental* (Paris: Pierre Belfond, 1979), p. 31.

40. See K. Paul Johnson, *Initiates of Theosophical Masters* (Albany, N.Y.: SUNY Press, 1995), pp. 1–10, for a discussion of Blavatsky's understanding of initiation.

41. André and Beaufils, *Papus*, p. 11, and André Braire, interview.

42. André and Beaufils, *Papus*, pp. 84–86.

43. André and Beaufils, *Papus*, p. 86.

44. André and Beaufils, *Papus*, pp. 93–94, and Chacornac, *Vie simple*, pp. 31–33.

45. Encausse, *Papus*, p. 34.

46. Waite, "French Mystic."

47. Quoted in Encausse, *Papus*, p. 52.

48. André and Beaufils, *Papus*, pp. 65–70 and 116–17.

49. Bryan R. Wilson, *The Social Dimensions of Sectarianism: Sects and New Religious Movements in Contemporary Society* (Oxford: Clarendon Press, 1990).

50. "Vurgey" (pseud.), "L'Age de Sphinx," *Le Voile d'Isis* May 6, 1891, p. 3.

51. This is the conclusion of Professor Jean Filliozat, a distinguished French Indologist, according to whom Guénon's "expositions [of Hindu doctrine] are in general in conformity with Indianist scholarship of his time, the published works of which he followed." Filliozat, "Rien sans l'orient?" *Planète+*, April 1970, p. 124.

52. For example, Guénon not only used Léon Wieger's poor translation of the *Tao Te Ching*, but as a consequence ended up quoting as part of the original text an inadequately labeled gloss of Wieger. See Pierre Grison, "L'Extrême-Asie dans l'oeuvre de René Guénon," in *René Guénon* [Cahiers de l'Herne], ed. Jean-Pierre Laurant and Paul Barbanegra (Paris: Ed. de l'Herne, 1985), p. 145. Alain Daniélou also mentions Guénon's reliance on B. G. Tilak's very dubious *The Arctic Home of the Vedas*. Daniélou, "René Guénon et la tradition hindoue," in *René Guénon* [Dossiers H], ed. Pierre-Marie Sigaud (Lausanne: L'Age d'Homme, 1984), p. 137.

53. Maurice Clavelle [Jean Reyor], "Document confidentiel inédit," unpublished typescript.

54. Clavelle [Reyor], "Document confidentiel."

55. André and Beaufils, *Papus*, pp. 268–70; Clavelle [Reyor], "Document confidentiel."

56. André and Beaufils, *Papus*, pp. 270–73, and Clavelle [Reyor], "Document confidentiel."

57. *The Secret Doctrine*, quoted in Campbell, *Ancient Wisdom*, p. 49.

58. Emerson, "Nature," in *Selections*, ed. Whicher, pp. 21 and 24.

59. Roger Lipsey, *Coomaraswamy*, vol. 3: *His Life and Work* (Princeton, N.J.: Princeton University Press, 1977), pp. 9–10.

60. Lipsey, *Coomaraswamy*, vol. 3, pp. 10, 14, and 42. The speculation about events at Wycliffe is my own; the environment of the British boarding school is a tough one.

61. Lipsey, *Coomaraswamy*, vol. 3, pp. 17–18.

62. For the cousins, Lipsey, *Coomaraswamy*, vol. 3, p. 41.

63. Lipsey, *Coomaraswamy*, vol. 3, pp. 22–25.

64. *Mediæval Sinhalese Art, Being a Monograph on Mediææval Sinhalese Arts and Crafts, Mainly as Surviving in the Eighteenth Century, with an Account of the Structure of Society and the Status of the Craftsmen* (Broad Campden: Essex House Press, 1908).

65. Lipsey, *Coomaraswamy*, vol. 3, pp. 26, 33, 40, 53, and 69–72.

66. Lipsey, *Coomaraswamy*, vol. 3, pp. 122–26. The trustee was Dr. Deman W. Ross.

67. Giovanni Monastra, "Ananda K. Coomaraswamy: de l'idéalisme à la tradition," *Nouvelle Ecole* 47 (1995).

68. Lipsey, *Coomaraswamy*, vol. 3, pp. 42–45.

69. See Kathleen Raine, *Blake and Tradition* (Princeton, N.J.: Princeton UP, 1968).

70. Quoted in Lipsey, *Coomaraswamy*, vol. 3, p. 108.

71. Quoted in Lipsey, *Coomaraswamy*, vol. 3, p. 109.

72. Monastra, "Ananda K. Coomaraswamy."

73. My thanks for this information to Dr. Marco Pasi, a Crowley expert.

3. GNOSTICS, TAOISTS, AND SUFIS

1. Lance S. Owens, "An Introduction to Gnosticism," *The Gnostic Society Library* [online]. Available http://home.online.no/noetic/nagham/nhlintro.html [July 12, 2001].

2. René Le Forestier, *L'Occultisme en France aux XIXe et XXe siècles: L'église gnostique*, ed. Antoine Faivre (Milan: Archè, 1990), pp. 9–37.

3. It is not clear who Valentine I was. Marie-France James, *Ésotérisme et Christianisme: autour de René Guénon* (Paris: Nouvelles éditions latines, 1981), pp. 81–82.

4. The group also included an individual named Faugeron (who later helped Guénon found his Order of the Temple) and Yvon Le Loup (a bank clerk and Encausse's librarian). Maurice Clavelle [Jean Reyor], "Document confidentiel inédit," unpublished typescript; Marie-Sophie André and Christophe Beaufils, *Papus, biographie: la Belle Epoque de l'occultisme* (Paris: Berg International, 1995), pp. 128–29; and Philippe Encausse, *Papus, le "Balzac de l'occultisme": vingt-cinq années d'occultisme occidental* (Paris: Pierre Belfond, 1979), p. 37.

5. Le Forestier, *Occultisme en France*, p. 69, and Jean-Pierre Laurant, *L'ésotérisme chrétien en France au XIX siècle* (Lausanne: L'Age d'Homme, 1992), p. 141.

6. Jean Kostka [pseud. of Jules-Benoît Doinel], *Lucifer démasqué* (Paris: Delhomme et Briguet, 1895). See Le Forestier, *Occultisme en France*, pp. 71–74, and André and Beaufils, *Papus*, pp. 127–28.

7. Another ex-occultist, Paul Rosen (originally a Pole), published *Satan et compagnie, association universelle pour la destruction de l'ordre sociale* [Satan & Co: A universal corporation for the destruction of social order] (Paris, 1888), followed by *L'ennemie sociale, historie documentée de la Franc-Maçonnerie de 1717 à 1890* [The enemy of society: A documented history of Freemasonry from 1717 to 1890] (Paris, 1890), dedicated to Pope Leo XIII.

8. Faugeron led the Catholic Gnostic Church. André and Beaufils, *Papus*, pp. 128–29, 275, and 278.

9. James, *Ésotérisme et Christianisme*, p. 82; André and Beaufils, *Papus*, pp. 275–76; and Clavelle [Reyor], "Document confidentiel."

10. Nöele Maurice-Denis Boulet, "L'ésotériste René Guénon: Souvenirs et jugements," *La pensée catholique: Cahiers de synthèse* [Paris] 77 (1962), 23.

11. According to de Pouvourville himself, "le Thien dianhien" and "le Bachlieu." Marie-France James, *Esotérisme, Occultisme, Franc-Maçonnerie et Christianisme aux XIX et XX siècles. Explorations bio-bibliographiques* (Paris: Nouvelles éditions latines, 1981), p. 221. I take "Thien dianhien" as Thien dia hoi, the Vietnamese form of T'ien-ti hui, and "Bachlieu" as Bac Lieu. Hue-Tam Ho Tai, *Millenarianism and Peasant Politics in Vietnam* (Cambridge, Mass.: Harvard University Press, 1983), pp. 55 and 62.

12. Hue-Tam Ho Tai, *Millenarianism*, pp. 20 and 35–37; Julian F. Pas and Man Kam Leung, *Historical Dictionary of Taoism* (Lanham, Md.: Scarecrow Press, 1998), pp. 1–3, 212–16; and Barend J. Ter Haar, *Ritual and Mythology of the Chinese Triads: Creating an Identity* (Leiden: Brill, 1998), pp. 7 and 344. For his career, James, *Esotérisme, Occultisme*, pp. 219–20. My thanks to Jean-Pierre Laurant for further information, derived from his interviews with de Pouvourville's nephew, Guy de Pouvourville.

13. *Le Tonkin actuel* (Paris: A. Savine, 1891).

14. Jean-Pierre Laurant, *Matgioi, un aventurier taoïste* (Paris: Dervy livres, 1982), pp. 30 and 41–42.

15. *L'art indo-chinois* (Paris: Librairies-imprimeries réunies, 1894); then *Les sept éléments de l'homme de la pathogénie chinoise* (Paris: Chamuel, 1895) and *Le Taoïsme et les sociétés secrètes chinoises* (Paris: Chamuel, 1897).

16. Published under de Pouvourville's pseudonym Mat-Gioi as *De l'autre côté du mur: récits chinois des guerres de 1883* (Haiphong [Vietnam]: F.-H. Schneider, 1897) and reissued as *L'Annam sanglant* [Bleeding Annam] in 1911.

17. James, *Esotérisme, Occultisme*, p. 221.

18. The translations were *Le Tao de Lao-Tseu* and *Le Te de Lao-Tseu* (Paris: Librairie de l'art indépendant, 1894). He also published a translation of the *Traité des influences errantes de Quangdzu* (Paris: Bibliothèque de la Haute Science, 1896).

19. See also James, *Esotérisme, Occultisme*, p. 221.

20. De Pouvourville and Louis Champrenaud, *Les enseignements secrets de la Gnose* [The Secret Teachings of Gnosis] (Paris, 1904). This book was followed by *La voie métaphysique* (Paris, 1905) and *La voie rationnelle* (Paris: L Bodin, 1907).

21. Jean-Pierre Laurant, *Le sens caché selon René Guénon* (Lausanne: L'Age d'homme, 1975), p. 53.

22. Boulet, "L'ésotériste René Guénon," p. 22. Noële Boulet, the most useful source on Guénon at this time (because soon afterward she became a close friend of Guénon, and she never herself was a Traditionalist) was convinced that it was from de Pouvourville that Guénon derived his dismissal of Catholicism as a "sentimental form" of religion.

23. De Pouvourville, editorial, *Le Continent* 1, no. 1 (1906), 11–16.

24. It ceased publication in 1907 after only ten issues. There is no reason to suppose that this Hans Richter was the painter Hans Richter.

25. *L'opium, sa pratique* (Paris: Editions de l'Initiation, 1903).

26. De Pouvourville, "La question de l'opium," *Le Continent* 4 (1906–7), 289–310, and Laurant, *L'ésotérisme chrétien en France*, p. 178. Guénon admitted the use of opium (as an "aid to meditation") before 1912 (Boulet, "L'ésotériste René Guénon," p. 22); that he acquired this habit from de Pouvourville is a reasonable speculation.

27. In "Pages dédiées à Mercure," *La Gnose* 1911 (reprinted in *'Abdul-Hadi: Ecrits pour La Gnose*, ed. G. Rocca [Milan: Archè, 1988]), for example, Aguéli argued that "esoteric Islam" (Ibn al-Arabi's Sufism) was very close to Taoism as explained by de Pouvourville, and he identified both with "primordial tradition" (using much the same phrase as Guénon had) and with the Islamic concept of *din ul-fitra* [original religion]. He also showed some interest in de Pouvourville's racial concerns, though he did not follow his theories, ascribing the "decadence" of Orientals to "ethnic heterogeneity" but adding that away from the towns and cities of the Orient one can find "as much collective morality and individual virtue as in the best countries of Europe." Aguéli, "Pages," p. 24.

28. Rocca, ed., *'Abdul-Hadi: Ecrits*, p. xv.

29. André and Beaufils, *Papus*, pp. 124–25 and 136; James, *Ésotérisme et Christianisme*, p. 105; and Le Forestier, *Occultisme en France*, pp. 88–89. See AN 1.

30. James, *Ésotérisme et Christianisme*, pp. 105–14 and 127, and André and Beaufils, *Papus*, p. 276

31. Paul Chacornac, *La vie simple de René Guénon* (1958; Paris: Editions tradition-nelles, 1986), p. 47, and Laurant, *Matgioi*, p. 62. There is some doubt that de Pou-vourville was actually in a position to initiate anyone into a Triad, since the path from Tao-chung [assistant] to Tao-shih [gentleman of the Tao] is a long and complex one involving various stages, which de Pouvourville would hardly have had time to com-plete. Only a Tao-shih can perform rituals on his own. See Pas and Man Kam Leung, *Historical Dictionary of Taoism*, pp. 258–60. The date of 1912 usually given for these events is wrong—see Rocca, Introduction, p. xix, p. xix.

32. Viveca Lindqvist, *Ivan Aguéli 1869–1917: centre culturel suédois, Paris 11 mars– 24 avril 1983* (Paris: Centre culturel suédois, 1983), p. 6.

33. For Bernard and Theosophy, Jean-Pierre Laurant, "La 'non-conversion' de René Guénon (1886–1951)," in *De la conversion*, ed. Jean-Christophe Attias (Paris: Cerf, 1998), p. 135. In 1907 Aguéli wrote an enthusiastic obituary of Olcott. He also retained a somewhat Theosophical version of Perennialism, in 1907 ascribing Theos-ophy's lack of success among Muslims to the fact that "no Theosophist really knew the secret doctrines of Islam and thus could not find Theosophy in Muslim formu-las." Aguéli, obituary of Colonel Olcott, *Il Convito* 2 (1907), 62–64, reprinted in Rocca, ed., *'Abdul-Hadi: Ecrits*, p. xiii.

34. Marie Huot, *Les courses de taureaux à Paris, 1887, 1889, 1890: Conférence faite le mercredi 11 juin 1890, à la salle des Capucines* (Paris: Ligue populaire contre la vivi-section, 1890); Alphonse Séché, *Les muses françaises: anthologie des femmes poètes (XXe siècle)* (Paris: Louis Michaud, 1908), p. 162; and Lindqvist, *Ivan Aguéli*, p. 8.

35. Séché, *Les muses françaises*, p. 162. See AN 2 for a poem of Huot.

36. Hilary Hocking and Ingrid Holmgren, *Ivan Aguéli* (Sala: Sala Art Society, n.d.), p. 2.

37. Aguéli's teacher Bernard spent 1894–1904 in Egypt, but this fact does not seem to have been Aguéli's reason for going there, since Aguéli did little or no paint-ing during these years.

38. Rocca, ed., *'Abdul-Hadi: Ecrits*, p. xvi, and Chacornac, *Vie simple*, p. 45.

39. Lindqvist, *Ivan Aguéli*, p. 8. For Aguéli's career, also see Chacornac, *Vie sim-ple*, pp. 42–48.

40. Salvatore Bono, *Orientalismo e Colonialismo: La ricerca di consenso in Egitto per l'impresa di Libia* (Rome: Istituto per l'Oriente C. A. Nallino, 1997), pp. 33–37 and 58–61.

41. Bono, *Orientalismo*, pp. 42–44 and 47–50.

42. A *mufti* is primarily a scholar but is often forced into a political role. Mu-hammad Illaysh in 1881 joined the anti-European uprising led by Colonel Ahmad Ur-abi. After Urabi's army was defeated in 1882 by the British army. which was to re-main in Egypt until 1956, Muhammad Illaysh was imprisoned, and it was in prison that he died. Knut S. Vikør, *Sufi and Scholar on the Desert Edge: Muhammad b. 'Ali al-Sanusi and his Brotherhood* (London: Hurst, 1995), pp. 250–51.

43. The report of Abd al-Rahman's close relations with Abd al-Qadir in Damas-cus (Michel Vâlsan, *L'islam et la fonction de René Guénon: recueil posthume* [Paris: Ed. de l'Oeuvre, 1984], p. 35) is a dubious one, because it is not clear where Vâlsan got his information from, and also because Vâlsan reports that Abd al-Rahman was able to return to Cairo after being amnestied by Queen Victoria, which cannot possibly be the case.

44. See K. Paul Johnson, *The Masters Revealed: Madame Blavatsky and the Myth of the Great White Lodge* (Albany, N.Y.: SUNY Press, 1994), pp. 68–69.

45. Bono, *Orientalismo*, p. 57, and Rocca, ed., *'Abdul-Hadi: Ecrits*, pp. xiii–xiv. Ethiopia, of course, has only a minority Muslim population.

46. Vâlsan, *L'islam et la fonction de René Guénon*, p. 37.

47. Fred De Jong, *Turuq and Turuq-linked Institutions in Nineteenth Century Egypt: A Historical Study in Organizational Dimensions of Islamic Mysticism* (Leiden: Brill, 1978), pp. 27–28, 113, and 173–74.

48. Laurant, "Non-conversion," p. 135, and Rocca, ed., *'Abdul-Hadi: Ecrits*, pp. viii and ix–x.

49. Roger Shattuck, *The Banquet Years: The Origins of the Avant Garde in Paris, 1885 to World War I* (1958; New York: Vintage Books, 1968), pp. 24, 211, and 215.

50. Lesley Blanch, *The Wilder Shores of Love* (London: John Murray, 1955), pp. 275–76.

51. See Isabelle Eberhardt, *Departures: Selected Writings Translated from the French* (San Francisco: City Lights, 1994).

52. Blanch, *Wilder Shores of Love*, pp. 275–78.

53. Sanua was a politically radical journalist and language teacher, who in his youth had supported the Italian nationalist Carbonari and in later life supported the anti-colonialist Islamic nationalism of Jamal al-Din al-Afghani. He belonged to the same Masonic lodge in Cairo as did al-Afghani, and when al-Afghani went to Paris it was Sanua who taught him French. Johnson, *Masters Revealed*, pp. 52–55; K. Paul Johnson, *Initiates of Theosophical Masters* (Albany, N.Y.: SUNY Press, 1995), p. 77.

54. Johnson, *Initiates*, pp. 168 and 171–72.

55. This account of Eberhardt in Algeria is pieced together from various sources and is something of a reconstruction. See especially Blanch, *Wilder Shores of Love*, and Karim Hamdy, "The Intoxicated Mystic: Eberhardt's Sufi Experience," in *Departures*, pp. 225–42; I have also used Tanya Monier, "Isabelle Eberhardt, Colonial Heretic," unpublished paper delivered at the annual meeting of the Middle East Studies Association held in San Francisco, November 22–24, 1997.

56. Johnson, *Initiates*, p. 171.

57. The phrase "Sufi order"—*tariqa* in Arabic—may be used in two senses: to describe a distinct group of Sufis who follow one particular shaykh, or to describe a spiritual lineage. For a fuller introduction to Sufism, see my short work, *Sufism: The Essentials* (Cairo: American University in Cairo Press, 2000). See also AN 3. For the Rahmaniyya and Eberhardt's contacts, see Julia A. Clancy-Smith, *Rebel and Saint: Muslim Notables, Populist Protest, Colonial Encounters (Algeria and Tunisia, 1800–1904)* (Berkeley: University of California Press, 1994), pp. 217–22 and 233–48.

58. Eberhardt was not the first French visitor to Bu Sada. In 1884 the soon-to-be-celebrated orientalist painter Etienne Dinet had visited there with an entomological expedition and had subsequently become Muslim. See Denise Brahimi, *Les terrasses de Bou-Saada* (Algiers: Entreprise Nationale du Livre, 1986).

59. Blanch, *Wilder Shores of Love*, pp. 298–99.

60. The many followers of teachers such as Inayat Khan and writers such as Idries Shah would disagree with this statement. However, from a factual and historical point of view, non-Islamic Sufism is not found in the Islamic world (though there

are, of course, occasional sectarian movements that become non-Islamic, sometimes of Sufi origin, as there are new religious movements anywhere and everywhere).

61. Von Sebottendorf's alter ego, Erwin Torre (see later), concludes after reading Rumi's *Mesnawi* that Christianity is basically the same as Islam, and he reaches an understanding of "the unity of spiritual nature with God." Rudolf von Sebottendorf, *Der Talisman des Rosenkreuzers* (Pfullinger in Württemberg: Johannes Baum Verlag, 1925), p. 37. He also maintains that Europe needs "Oriental culture" more than Turkey needs Westernization (pp. 74–75), and at the start of the book there are numerous set-piece denunciations of Western materialism, contrasted with "Oriental spirituality." In reality, the various Turkish and Egyptian characters at the start of von Sebottendorf's book who explain "Oriental spirituality" would have been far more likely to preach mainstream Islam to him. "Oriental spirituality" is, of course, a Western rather than an Oriental concept.

62. Von Sebottendorf claimed to have been adopted as an adult by an elderly Freiherr von Sebottendorf, an event that seems unlikely, and for which there is no other evidence. Nicholas Goodrick-Clarke, *The Occult Roots of Nazism: The Ariosophists of Austria and Germany, 1890–1935* (Wellingborough: Aquarian Press, 1985), pp. 140–41.

63. Much of von Sebottendorf's biography is cautiously reconstructed here on the basis of an autobiographical novel, von Sebottendorf, *Talisman*, which is more of a novel in the first part and more clearly autobiographical after about 1908. See also Goodrick-Clarke, *Occult Roots of Nazism*, pp. 135–52.

64. Von Sebottendorf, *Talisman*, pp. 53–55. The approximate date is deduced from pp. 72–73.

65. There were close relations between many Bektashis and Turkish Masons after the prohibition of the order in 1826, mostly from 1839, with many Ottoman liberals being both Bektashi and Masons. See Irène Mélikoff, *Hadji Bektach: un mythe et ses avatars* (Leiden: Brill, 1998), pp. 241–44, and Thierry Zarcone, *Mystiques, philosophes et francs-maçons en Islam: Riza Tevfiq, penseur ottoman (1868–1948), du soufisme a la confrérie* (Paris: Institut français d'études anatoliennes d'Istanbul, 1993).

66. The variety of numerology described by von Sebottendorf is based around the interpretation of the letters *alaf, lam,* and *mim* in the Koran, the key to which is said to be an ancient tablet of Indian origin given to the Prophet and passed by him to his successor Abu Bakr, and then by Abu Bakr to Ali. From Ali, its secrets passed to certain Sufi orders. Von Sebottendorf, *Talisman*, p. 71, and von Sebottendorf, *Die Praxis der alter türkischen Freimaurerei: Der Schlüssel zum Verständnis der Alchimie* (1924; reprint, Freiburg im Breisgau: Hermann Bauer, 1954), pp. 12–13. This story is certainly not widespread among Sufis, and I know of no other mention of it, though it may have been circulating among Bektashis at the time.

67. Erwin Torre received the Bektashi order's "cord" (which from the context may mean *wird*, daily practice, normally the consequence of entering a Sufi order) from a Bektashi shaykh, with whom was been studying Arabic and the Koran after the dawn ritual prayer. In answer to the question "Do you believe in God?" Erwin replied" "Yes, I believe that God is One"—which might be an affirmation of the Muslim understanding of God, or equally the Perennialist understanding. Von Sebottendorf, *Talisman*, pp. 50–51. The *wird* which Erwin received, however, bears little resem-

blance to any Sufi *wird* I know, and the whole event bears no resemblance whatsoever to any of the Bektashi ceremonies described in Mélikoff, *Hadji Bektach*. Elsewhere (*Talisman*, p. 34) von Sebottendorf displays familiarity with the practice of non-Bektashi Sufis, and he has presumably transferred non-Bektashi Sufi practice to a fictional Bektashi context. The familiarity is more that of an informed outsider than of an insider.

68. Von Sebottendorf, *Talisman*, pp. 73–78. Paradoxically, von Sebottendorf may have started his own pseudo-Masonic lodge in 1910 in Istanbul, but this failed to prosper.

69. Von Sebottendorf, *Praxis der alter türkischen Freimaurerei*, pp. 9–10.

70. Boulet, "L'ésotériste René Guénon," pp. 18 and 26–27.

71. Michel Chodkiewicz, the contemporary French scholar of Ibn al-Arabi, has criticized some of Aguéli's translations from Arabic—see Chodkiewicz, "L''Offrande au Prophète' de Muhammad al-Burhanpuri," *Connaissance des religions*, June–Sept. 1988, pp. 30–40, esp. p. 30—and he is no doubt right. My contention is not, however, that Aguéli was a first-rate scholar like Chodkiewicz, but that he was far more than an amateur.

72. Laurant, "Non-conversion," p. 136.

73. Notably Stanislas de Guaita, reviver in 1888 of the Cabalistic Order of the Rose-Cross. James Webb, *The Occult Underground* (La Salle, Ill.: Open Court, 1974), p. 174.

74. André and Beaufils, *Papus*, pp. 160 and 168.

75. Catalogue of Bibliothèque nationale de France.

76. Boulet, "L'ésotériste René Guénon," p. 22.

77. Chacornac, *Vie simple*, p. 46.

78. Clavelle [Reyor], "Document confidentiel"; André and Beaufils, *Papus*, p. 338.

79. Lindqvist, *Ivan Aguéli*, pp. 10 and 30. Subversive in the eyes of the British, then at war with the Ottoman Empire, itself in alliance with the Central Powers.

80. Chacornac, *Vie simple*, pp. 47–48.

81. Lindqvist, *Ivan Aguéli*, pp. 5, 8, and 10–11.

82. The museum, the Aguéli Museum in Sala, was established in 1962 (Hocking and Holmgren, *Ivan Aguéli*, pp. 3–4). The novel was Torbjörn Säfve's *Ivan Aguéli: en roman om frihet* (Stockholm: Prisma, 1981). According to Laurant, "Non-conversion," Axel Gauffin, in his *Ivan Aguéli: människan, mystikern, målaren* (Stockholm: Sveriges allmänna konstförenings publikation, 1940–41), reports that Aguéli converted from Islam to the new Bahai religion. I have been unable to confirm this report, and it is not repeated anywhere else.

83. He is said to have written one more religious work, *Sainte Thérèse de Lisieux*, signifying a return to Catholicism (Laurant, *Matgioi*, p. 93). This book is not to be found in the French National Library, however, and de Pouvourville's nephew Guy de Pouvourville expressed severe doubts, in an interview with Jean-Pierre Laurant, about any return to the Church by his uncle (my thanks to Jean-Pierre Laurant for this information).

84. See also *L'homme qui a mis les Boches dedans* (Paris: Editions Figuière, 1919), *La greffe* (Paris: Editions Figuière, 1922), and *Chasseur de pirates* (Editions du Monde Moderne, 1928).

85. André and Beaufils, *Papus*, pp. 324–34.

86. James, *Esotérisme, Occultisme*, pp. 96–97.

87. André and Beaufils, *Papus*, pp. 338 and 340–42.

4. CAIRO, MOSTAGANEM, AND BASEL

1. Nöele Maurice-Denis Boulet, "L'ésotériste René Guénon: Souvenirs et jugements," *La pensée catholique: Cahiers de synthèse*, 77 (1962), 41.

2. Boulet, "Ésotériste René Guénon," 78–79 (1962), 140.

3. Guénon to Charbonneau-Lassay, March 18, 1929, and April 11, 1929, reprinted in PierLuigi Zoccatelli, *Le lièvre qui rumine: Autour de René Guénon, Louis Charbonneau-Lassay et la Fraternité du Paraclet* (Milan: Archè, 1999), pp. 53 and 58–59.

4. From Guénon's reply (April 11, 1929) to a missing letter from Charbonneau-Lassay, it appears that Charbonneau-Lassay attempted to excuse Françoise on the grounds that she was feeling isolated.

5. Boulet, "Ésotériste René Guénon," 77, 41.

6. This is the deduction of Robin Waterfield, *René Guénon and the Future of the West: The Life and Writings of a 20th-Century Metaphysician* ([UK]: Crucible Press, 1987). Shillito's husband had died at about the same time as Guénon's wife.

7. Paul Chacornac, *La vie simple de René Guénon* (1958; Paris: Editions traditionnelles, 1986), pp. 91–92. Chacornac calls Shillito "Madame Dina" and her husband "Hassan Farid Dina" but is evidently confused by Egyptian names. In Egyptian usage, "Madame" is prefixed not to the family name but to the first name, and Dina is anyhow a female first name, not a family name. Wives retain their own family name on marriage. Shillito's husband would thus have been Hassan Farid, identified as an engineer. If Shillito had taken the Egyptian Muslim first name of Dina, she must have converted to Islam—she would otherwise have kept her original name of Mary, which can easily be turned into Arabic as "Maryam." She would not have had to convert to marry Hassan Farid, since Muslim men are allowed to marry Christian or Jewish women and in Egypt sometimes do. Her conversion must have been the consequence of conviction.

8. Maurice Clavelle [Jean Reyor], "Document confidentiel inédit," unpublished typescript.

9. Waterfield, *René Guénon*, p. 56.

10. Faruq al-Hitami, interview.

11. Chacornac, *Vie simple*, p. 111. Under Egyptian law, nationality passed through the father. The nationality of the mother and the place of birth were irrelevant. Guénon's children would thus have required residence permits from birth, and it was evidently to relieve them of this requirement that Guénon took Egyptian citizenship— not out of any form of Egyptian patriotism. See also pp. 93–94.

12. In this discovery he was neither the first nor the last Westerner. Significant numbers of Westerners find themselves unexpectedly entranced by Cairo despite its many problems, sometimes visiting for days and staying for decades. Only a few of these become Muslim. For most it is what a Traditionalist would identify as "the traditional way of life" that appeals, even if they do not entirely follow it themselves.

13. Jean-Louis Michon, "Dans l'intimité de Cheikh Abd al-Wahid—René Guénon— au Caire, 1947–49," *Sophia* 3,2 (1997), reprinted in Xavier Accart, ed., *L'Ermite de Du-*

qqi: René Guénon en marge des milieux francophones égyptiens (Milan: Archè, 2001), p. 258.

14. See especially René Alleau and Marianne Scriabine, *Actes du colloque international René Guénon et l'actualité de la pensée traditionnelle (Cérisy-la-Salle: 13–20 juillet 1973)* (Braine-le-Comte [Belgium]: Editions du Baucens, 1979).

15. Michon, "Dans l'intimité de Cheikh Abd al-Wahid," p. 256.

16. A further peculiarity is probably more apparent than real. A photograph of a special corner in Guénon's house used for the ritual prayer appears in Accart, *Ermite de Duqqi* (plate 25). The floor and walls are covered with straw matting, as is common in North Africa (but not Egypt), and there is a candle, as in a Turkish (but not usually an Egyptian) mosque. Given that an anonymous informant reports that Guénon followed normal Muslim practice (in spreading a prayer mat where convenient, praying, and then folding the mat up again afterwards), and given the non-Egyptian elements in this photograph, which was anyhow taken in 1953 (after Guénon's death), it is possible that the corner was created by the photographer rather than Guénon, as visual proof of Guénon's piety.

17. Muhammad Guénon, interview. He also took the Qadiriyya, according to Seyyed Hossein Nasr, "Frithjof Schuon et la tradition islamique," *Frithjof Schuon, 1907–1998: Etudes et témoignages,* ed. Bernard Chevilliat (Avon: Connaissance des Religions, 1999), p. 126.

18. This judgment is based on Michael Gilsenan, *Saint and Sufi in Modern Egypt: An Essay in the Sociology of Religion* (Oxford: Oxford University Press, 1973).

19. Guénon to F. Schuon, November 28, 1932. My thanks to Jean-Baptiste Aymard for this reference.

20. Sufi involvement in politics is, in fact, probably almost as old as Sufism itself.

21. Guénon, in *Etudes traditionnelles,* 1948, quoted in Jean-Pierre Laurant, "La 'non-conversion' de René Guénon (1886–1951)" in *De la conversion,* ed. Jean-Christophe Attias (Paris: Cerf, 1998), p. 139. Guénon wrote almost exactly the same thing in a letter to Alain Daniélou, August 27, 1947, quoted in Thierry Zarcone, "Relectures et transformations de Soufisme en Occident," *Diogène* 187 (January 2000), 145–60. The phrase "move in" [*s'installer*] is used by Guénon elsewhere; Zarcone draws attention to its significance in "Relectures et transformations."

22. Guénon, letter to Pierre Colard, 1938, quoted in Laurant, "Non-conversion," p. 139.

23. Igor Volkoff, "Voyage à travers la bibliothèque de René Guénon," *Egypte nouvelle* October 9, 1953. Reprinted in Accart, *Ermite de Duqqi.* See pp. 220–21. No Arabic books are mentioned here, and none were in Guénon's library in the 1980s, according to two informants. It is of course possible that some had existed, were not noticed by Volkoff, and had been sold by the 1980s.

24. This was Michel Vâlsan, for whom see chapters 5 and 6 (Michel Chodkiewicz, interview).

25. This point is also suggested by the awkward and unformed handwriting (according to Accart, *Ermite de Duqqi,* p. 169) of his only known writing in Arabic, his signature to his application for Egyptian citizenship. I have not seen this signature; in his correspondence Guénon used the Arabic script for ritual phrases such as the *bismillah,* and in this case the writing is well formed but perhaps not very fluent.

26. Alleau and Scriabine, *Actes*, pp. 47 and 91.

27. India: Alain Daniélou (see chapter 6). Guénon's main correspondent in Brazil was Fernando Guedes Galvão, who in 1948 published the first Portuguese translation of *Crise du monde moderne*. A Traditionalist presence in Brazil survived until the end of the century, latterly under Luiz Pontual (Luiz Pontual, e-mail, August 11, 2000).

28. Chacornac, *Vie simple*, p. 99, for the attack, and Michon, "Dans l'intimité de Cheikh Abd al-Wahid," p. 257, for the explanation.

29. Martin Lings, interview.

30. Michon, "Dans l'intimité de Cheikh Abd al-Wahid," p. 258.

31. Marie-France James, *Esotérisme, Occultisme, Franc-Maçonnerie et Christianisme aux XIX et XX siècles. Explorations bio-bibliographiques* (Paris: Nouvelles éditions latines, 1981), pp. 231–33 ; Jean-Baptiste Aymard, "Frithjof Schuon (1907–1998). Connaissance et voie d'intériorité. Approche biographique," in *Frithjof Schuon*, ed. Chevilliat, p. 39; and also Accart, *Ermite de Duqqi*, pp. 51–52. See also Valentine de Saint-Point, "René Guénon," *L'Egypte nouvelle*, January 25, 1952, reprinted in *Ermite de Duqqi*, p. 157, and Jean Moscatelli, letter to the editor of *France-Asie*, April 28, 1953, reprinted in *Ermite de Duqqi*, p. 213.

32. Sadek Sellam, "Un frère des hommes," in *L'Islam et l'Occident: Dialogues*, ed. Najm-oud-Dine Bammate (Paris: UNESCO, 2000), pp. 13–15.

33. Faruq al-Hitami, interview.

34. Thierry Zarcone, "Le cheikh al-Azhar Abd al-Halim Mahmud et René Guénon: entre soufisme populaire et soufisme d'élite," in *Ermite de Duqqi*, ed. Accart, pp. 274–76.

35. It is advanced principally in Ibrahim M Abu-Rabiʿ, "Al-Azhar Sufism in Modern Egypt: The Sufi Thought," *Islamic Quarterly* 32 (1988), 207–35. Many of the allegedly Traditionalist attitudes of Mahmud could have come from anywhere, and every time Abu-Rabiʿ alleges a precise Traditionalist view of Mahmud, the footnote cites a work of Guénon, not of Mahmud—except on one occasion when the work of Mahmud cited seems not to exist (the reference in the citation is incomplete).

36. Martin Lings, interview.

37. Abd al-Halim Mahmud, "Al-ʿarif bi'Llah shaykh Abd al-Wahid Yahya," in Mahmud, *Al-madrasa al-Shadhiliyya al-haditha wa imamha Abu'l-Hasan al-Shadhili* (Cairo, n.d.), pp. 229–54. My conclusions are supported by discussions in 2001 with Hatsuki Aishima, then a graduate student working on a thesis on Mahmud at the University of Kyoto. Aishima had not found any development of any of the characteristic Traditionalist themes in Mahmud's work.

38. *Al-Marifa* was edited by Mustafa Abd al-Raziq, Shaykh al-Azhar 1945–47. See Accart, *Ermite de Duqqi*, p. 47. Al-Raziq's tenure at Al Azhar was a period more of reform than of tradition.

39. Ahmad Badawi, interview.

40. Quoted in Albert Hourani, *Arabic Thought in the Liberal Age, 1798–1939* (Cambridge: Cambridge UP, 1983), pp. 328–29. My thanks to Mona Abaza for this quotation.

41. Accart, *Ermite de Duqqi*, p. 45.

42. This is hypothesis, based on the change in Guénon's writings.

43. *Aperçus sur l'initiation* (Paris: Chacornac, 1946).

44. Clavelle, "Document confidentiel."

45. Clavelle, untitled document reprinted in Zoccatelli, *Lièvre*, pp. 121–22. Barbot's name and some other details from Stefano Salzani and PierLuigi Zoccatelli, *Hermétisme et emblématique du Christ dans la vie et dans l'oeuvre de Louis Charbonneau-Lassay (1871–1946)* (Milan: Archè, 1996), pp. 64 and 66–69. Reyor's document gives the name as Estoile internelle, but this must be a misprint—E. Mila has "éternelle"— see Mila, "Charbonneau-Lassay y el esoterismo católico en el siglo XX," online at *Disidencias: OnLine Press.* Available http://members.es.tripod.de/disidentes/arti44.htm [June 1, 2000].

46. Reyor in C. Tacou, ed., *Mircea Eliade* [Cahier de l'Herne] (Paris: Editions de l'Herne, 1978), pp. 122–23. Charbonneau-Lassay's diary suggests that his motivation for reviving the Fraternité des Chevaliers du divin Paraclet was to stop people from leaving Christianity, according to PierLuigi Zoccatelli, e-mails, July 2 and 4, 2001.

47. Reyor in Zoccatelli, *Lièvre*, p. 123, and Mila, "Charbonneau-Lassay."

48. Reyor in Zoccatelli, *Lièvre*, pp. 123–24; for Reyor's suggestion, Salzani and Zoccatelli, *Hermétisme et emblématique*, p. 79.

49. Letter of Thomas to Abbé André Gircourt, June 24, 1947, reprinted in Zoccatelli, *Lièvre*, pp. 137–38. The description of the practices themselves is reprinted in *Lièvre*, pp. 127–33.

50. They were often referred to as "la Thomasine." Zoccatelli, e-mails.

51. Charbonneau-Lassay, letter to Abbé André Gircourt, January 16, 1946. Reprinted in Zoccatelli, *Lièvre*, pp. 65–66.

52. Mila, "Charbonneau-Lassay."

53. Where not otherwise indicated, information on French Masonry and the Traditionalist role in it derives from interviews with Claude Gagne and Pierre Mollier as well as discussions with other French and foreign Masons. I am not myself a Mason, and therefore my informants were all obliged to be circumspect when dealing with me. I would like to thank my Masonic informants for their unfailing courtesy when dealing with a "profane" interviewer, and to warn my readers that in this section I have been unusually dependant on unconfirmed evidence and on speculative reconstruction.

54. Clavelle, "Document confidentiel."

55. My thanks to Jean-Pierre Laurent for this information.

56. Napoleon's brother Joseph, various generals, and Chief of Police Fouché were all Masons. Antonio Coën and Michel Dumesnil de Grammont, *La Franc-Maçonnerie Ecossaise* (Nice: SNEP, 1946), pp. 23 and 27–28.

57. Oswald Wirth, *La Franc-Maçonnerie rendue intelligible à ses adeptes*, 3 vol.s, vol. 2: *Le compagnon* (1931?; Paris: Dervy livres, 2000), pp. 22–23.

58. "Freemasonry . . . teaches men to build themselves collective happiness on earth, without forbidding them to believe in a future life if they so wish" (Wirth, *Franc-Maçonnerie rendue intelligible*, vol. 2, p. 51).

59. Wirth, *Franc-Maçonnerie rendue intelligible*, vol. 2, passim.

60. Pierre Chevallier, *Histoire de la franc-maçonnerie française*, vol. 3, *La Maçonnerie: Eglise de la République (1877–1944)* (Paris: Fayard, 1975), gives credit almost equally to Guénon (p. 405).

61. Wirth's views on many subjects are hardly compatible with Guénon's or indeed with those of any believing Muslim, Jew, or Christian. He maintains, for exam-

ple, that the human soul is not an absolute—it can be modified by "anger, drunkenness or madness"—and that "the individual is an ephemeral and particularized manifestation of the species, which alone possesses a wider life, joined to the great universal life." Only participation in the totality of humanity can give us immortality, since it is only humanity as a whole that is immortal. See Wirth, *Franc-Maçonnerie rendue intelligible*, vol. 2, pp. 83–84.

62. Jean-Pierre Laurent, "René Guénon (1886–1951) et la Franc-Maçonnerie" *Travaux de Villard d'Honnencourt* 9 (1984, 2): 15–20, p. 17.

63. J. Corneloup, *Je ne sais qu'épeler* (Paris: Vitiano, 1971), pp. 99–100, and Denys Roman, *René Guénon et les destins de la Franc-Maçonnerie* (Paris: Les éditions de l'oeuvre, 1982), p. 159.

64. William Stoddart, "Titus Burckhardt: An Outline of his Life and Works," in *Mirror of the Intellect: Essays on Traditional Science and Sacred Art*, ed. Titus Burckhardt (Cambridge: Quinta Essentia, 1987), pp. 3 and 5.

65. Frithjof Schuon, *Erinnerungen und Betrachtungen* ([Switzerland]: privately printed, 1974), p. 12.

66. Where no other source is given in what follows, information derives from Schuon, *Erinnerungen und Betrachtungen*, and Harald von Meyenburg, interview.

67. Aymard, "Frithjof Schuon," p. 7, supplemented by Aymard, e-mail, February 3, 2003. There are various suggestions in Schuon, *Erinnerungen und Betrachtungen*, that Schuon's father was interested in spirituality and the Vedas.

68. Schuon, *Erinnerungen und Betrachtungen*, p. 7.

69. Schuon, *Erinnerungen und Betrachtungen*, p. 7.

70. Schuon to Albert Oesch, 1932, quoted in Aymard, "Frithjof Schuon," p. 12.

71. Aymard, "Frithjof Schuon," p. 12, and Nasr, "Frithjof Schuon," pp. 124–25.

72. Schuon, *Erinnerungen und Betrachtungen*, pp. 13–14. See AN 1.

73. Aymard, "Frithjof Schuon," p. 6.

74. Schuon, *Erinnerungen und Betrachtungen*, pp. 41 and 57, and Aymard, "Frithjof Schuon," p. 7.

75. This conversion had evidently been agreed upon before Schuon's father's death, since Schuon's father had expressed a wish that his children become Catholic before his death. Aymard, e-mail.

76. Schuon, *Erinnerungen und Betrachtungen*, pp. 6–7, and 12.

77. Aymard, "Frithjof Schuon," p. 7.

78. Schuon, *Erinnerungen und Betrachtungen*, pp. 48–49.

79. Schuon, *Erinnerungen und Betrachtungen*, p. 7.

80. Schuon, *Erinnerungen und Betrachtungen*, p. 40.

81. The recurrence of this unusual term in the name of Charbonneau-Lassay's Fraternity and Schuon's diary is striking. I have not, however, been able to find any link between the two and so must assume that it is coincidence. The term is not totally obscure, especially in a Catholic context. It is used several times in the Gospel of St. John.

82. Schuon, *Erinnerungen und Betrachtungen*, p. 66.

83. Von Meyenburg, fax, July 2002, for the meetings and Schuon's visits to them. Von Meyenburg does not specify who was in the group; Aymard (e-mail) supposes that it was the group established by Hans and Ernst Küry, two brothers with

whom Schuon corresponded but who did not play an important part in the later history of the Alawiyya.

84. Schuon, *Erinnerungen und Betrachtungen*, p. 100. Aymard (e-mail) places these events in 1934, but Schuon describes the event in the context of having just written the poem "Du bist der Traum." This was written before he went from Basel to Lausanne. *Erinnerungen und Betrachtungen*, pp. 97, 99.

85. Martin Lings, *A Sufi Saint of the Twentieth Century: Shaikh Ahmad al-'Alawi, His Spiritual Heritage and Legacy* (London: George Allen & Unwin, 1971), esp. pp. 63–66.

86. This Yemeni sailor was Muhammad Qasim. On his death in 1999, the Yemeni president sent his brother to England for Muhammad Qasim's funeral. See Muhammad al-Maysali, obituary of Muhammad Qasim al-Alawi, *The British-Yemeni Society Website* [online]. Available http://www.al-bab.com/bys/obits/alawi.htm [July 4, 2001].

87. The reason for the suspicion was not that Sufi orders are military organizations dedicated to jihad, but more because once the French had destroyed or taken control of North African state institutions and structures, the Sufi orders were all that was left to act as an organizational basis for resistance.

88. Robert Caspar, in "Mystique musulmane. Bilan d'une décennie (1963–1973)," *Institut de Belles Lettres Arabes* [Tunis] 135 (1975), pp. 81–82, reports the popularity but finds it difficult to explain. For Probst Biraben, Jean-Pierre Laurant, e-mail, October 11, 2001.

89. Lings, interview, reports that the sailors bought the ticket. Von Dechend, however, remembers that she bought the ticket (Aymard, e-mail, citing his interview with von Dechend).

90. Aymard, "Frithjof Schuon," p. 14.

91. For a beautiful description of the *zawiya*, see Schuon, letter of early January 1933, reprinted in Schuon, *Erinnerungen und Betrachtungen*, p. 73.

92. Schuon, *Erinnerungen und Betrachtungen*, pp. 71–72.

93. Schuon, *Erinnerungen und Betrachtungen*, pp. 71–74 and 77.

94. Schuon, *Erinnerungen und Betrachtungen*, pp. 8, 71, and 74.

95. Schuon, *Erinnerungen und Betrachtungen*, p. 8.

96. Von Meyenburg, interview.

97. Burckhardt, unnamed text, quoted in Schuon, *Erinnerungen und Betrachtungen*, pp. 87–88.

98. Schuon, *Erinnerungen und Betrachtungen*, p. 84, and Aymard, "Frithjof Schuon," p. 17.

99. Al-Alawi is generally reported as holding universalist views, but it is not clear to what extent or at what level.

100. Schuon, *Erinnerungen und Betrachtungen*, p. 84.

101. Burckhardt in Schuon, *Erinnerungen und Betrachtungen*, pp. 86 and 88.

102. Burckhardt in Schuon, *Erinnerungen und Betrachtungen*, p. 89.

103. Schuon, *Erinnerungen und Betrachtungen*, p. 94.

104. Schuon, *Erinnerungen und Betrachtungen*, p. 95.

105. Schuon, *Erinnerungen und Betrachtungen*, p. 94.

106. Schuon, *Erinnerungen und Betrachtungen*, p. 16.

107. Schuon, *Erinnerungen und Betrachtungen*, p. 122. From the text it is conceivable that this appointment was also part of the visions of the Prophets and the Buddha, but this is not the case, since the same episode is described quite factually in a letter from Schuon to Hans Küry, February 20, 1935 (my thanks to M. Aymard for quoting the relevant passage, e-mail).

108. For example, "Sidi Alawi" to Cyril Glasse (undated; private collection), Aymard, "Frithjof Schuon," p. 16, and Roland Goffin, interview with Khaled Bentounès, "Entrevista con Khaled Bentounes," *Symbolos* 19 [online]. Available http://www.geocoties.com/symbolos/s19rgoff.htm [July 4, 2001].

109. Khaled Bentounès, interview.

110. Von Meyenburg suggests that it was Schuon's view that while "as a convention, an *ijaza* is necessary for giving initiation, in emergency cases any initiate can give initiation, as any baptized can baptize if no priest is available" (fax, July 2002). Other past or present followers of Schuon make similar suggestions, though without the reference to baptism. If this was Schuon's logic, it depends heavily on the Christian parallel. In the Islamic world there is no concept of "emergency cases" requiring admission into a Sufi order.

111. Von Meyenburg, interview and fax, July 2002.

112. Von Meyenburg, fax, July 2002. Aymard cites Hans Küry as reporting the same incident with Schuon continuing the *dhikr* (e-mail), and in general as having Schuon rather than Burckhardt lead the group from the beginning. Since I never interviewed Küry, I am unable to resolve this discrepancy and simply follow von Meyenburg's version.

113. Von Meyenburg, interview.

114. Schuon to Burckhardt, May 1939. I have used a later typed transcript of this letter.

115. William Stoddart, for example, cited Koran 29:45 in an e-mail (February 2003). This verse starts "Recite what is inspired in you of the Book [Koran] and establish ritual prayer, for ritual prayer preserves you from wrong and iniquity," and continues, depending on one's interpretation, either "and remembrance of God is without doubt most important" or "but remembrance of God is more important." Difficulty arises because in Arabic "most important" and "more important" are the same. Schuonians prefer "more important," and (of more importance) emphasize the Arabic word translated as "remembrance"—*dhikr*. At least some Schuonians take *dhikr* in this context to refer to the Sufi practice of repetitive prayer, called *dhikr*. The use of the word in that sense is generally considered to postdate the Koran, and so "remembrance" is the meaning generally understood. That these Schuonians interpret a verse generally taken to underline the importance of the ritual prayer to mean almost the exact opposite is an indication of their distance from the Islamic mainstream, but also, in a sense, of their sincerity.

116. Schuon, *Erinnerungen und Betrachtungen*, p. 100.

117. Schuon, *Erinnerungen und Betrachtungen*, pp. 104–18.

118. To judge by the reference in Schuon's letter [to Burckhardt?] of May 5, 1944, reprinted in Schuon, *Erinnerungen und Betrachtungen*, p. 125.

119. Schuon, *Erinnerungen und Betrachtungen*, p. 122. Aymard disputes my chronology (e-mail); the passage, written in 1944, describes events in Mostaganem and permission to use the All-Highest Name, and comments that he "later" stopped using

it, associating this cessation with his worldly love. It is not entirely clear when "later" was, but I think my interpretation of this passage is the most likely one.

120. Von Meyenburg, interview. Aymard disputes this phrase (e-mail), but there is some collateral evidence to support von Meyenburg's recollection.

121. Schuon, *Erinnerungen und Betrachtungen,* p. 132.

122. For example, Schuon, *Erinnerungen und Betrachtungen,* p. 95.

123. Clavelle, "Document confidentiel."

124. Clavelle, "Document confidentiel."

125. Von Meyenburg, interview. Clavelle, "Document confidentiel," has one hundred, but von Meyenburg is the more reliable source.

126. The spiritual status of an individual saint may be private, but anything that could be described as an order in an organizational sense is almost invariably public.

127. Schuon, *Erinnerungen und Betrachtungen,* pp. 95 and 138. Aymard questions this chronology (e-mail), but the first event is clearly dated to early 1937, whereas the second event happened about two years after the death of al-Alawi.

128. Schuon, *Erinnerungen und Betrachtungen,* p. 95.

129. Von Meyenburg, interview.

130. Schuon, *Erinnerungen und Betrachtungen,* pp. 8, 136, and Aymard, "Frithjof Schuon," pp. 25–26.

131. Chodkiewicz, interview.

132. Guénon, letter to Vasile Lovinescu, March 1938, quoted in Julius Evola, *Le chemin du cinabre* (Milan: Archè and Arktos, 1983), pp. 199–200.

133. Schuon, *Erinnerungen und Betrachtungen,* p. 139.

134. Aymard, "Frithjof Schuon," p. 27.

135. James, *Esotérisme, Occultisme,* pp. 84–85, and von Meyenburg, interview.

136. Von Meyenburg, interview.

137. Schuon, *Erinnerungen und Betrachtungen,* pp. 9 and 37.

138. Schuon, letter of August 18, 1943, reprinted in Schuon, *Erinnerungen und Betrachtungen,* p. 120

139. Schuon, *Erinnerungen und Betrachtungen,* pp. 262–63.

140. Schuon's interest in the Virgin Mary in fact existed even before this: in about 1934 he composed a poem to the Virgin. Schuon, *Erinnerungen und Betrachtungen,* p. 154.

5. FASCISM

1. Defined here pragmatically, as authoritarian regimes that ultimately fought the Western Allies on the Axis side during the Second World War.

2. These are the words of Rudolf von Sebottendorf's alter ego Erwin Torre in his autobiographical novel *Der Talisman des Rosenkreuzers* (Pfullinger in Württemberg: Johannes Baum Verlag, 1925), pp. 81–97.

3. Nicholas Goodrick-Clarke, *The Occult Roots of Nazism: The Ariosophists of Austria and Germany, 1890–1935* (Wellingborough: Aquarian Press, 1985), pp. 41–64 and 128–29.

4. Von Sebottendorf, through his *alter ego* Erwin, *Talisman,* p. 101.

5. Goodrick-Clarke, *Occult Roots of Nazism,* pp. 142–46 and 150, and von Sebottendorf, *Talisman,* pp. 99–102.

6. Albrecht Götz von Olenhusen, "Zeittafel zur Biographie Rudolf von Sebotten-dorfs (1875–1945)," printed after 1969 in an unidentified journal, pp. 81–86; Götz von Olenhusen, "Bürgerrat, Einwohnerwehr und Gegenrevolution: Freiburg 1918–1920. Zugleich ein Beitrag zur Biographie des Rudolf Freiherr von Sebottendorff," in *Beiträge zur europäischen Geistesgeschichte der Neuzeit. Festschrift für Ellie Howe zum 20. September 1990*, ed. Götz von Olenhusen and others (Freiburg: Hochschule Verlag, 1990), pp. 122–26; and Goodrick-Clarke, *Occult Roots of Nazism*, pp. 147–49 and 151–52.

7. This is the entirely convincing conclusion of Goodrick-Clarke, *Occult Roots of Nazism*, pp. 193–98 and 201–2. Myth, however, later became reality, with the growth of occultist Neo-Nazi groups during the 1970s and 1980s. See Nicholas Goodrick-Clarke, *Blak Sun: Aryan Cults, Esoteric Nazism, and the Politics of Identity* (New York: New York University Press, 2002), especially pp. 108–9 and 14–17.

8. *Bevor Hitler kam: Urkundlichen aus der Frühzeit der nationalsozialistischen Bewegung* (Munich: Deukula-Grassinger, 1933).

9. Götz von Olenhusen, "Zeittafel zur Biographie," p. 88, and Herbert Rittlinger, *Geheimdienst mit beschränkter Haftung: Bericht vom Bosporus* (Stuttgart: Deutsche Verlags–Anstalt, 1973), p. 184.

10. Rittlinger, *Geheimdienst*, pp. 184–85 and 326. Rittlinger supposes von Sebottendorf received help from important friends, since his return to Turkey from a concentration camp would otherwise be inexplicable.

11. Goodrick-Clarke, *Occult Roots of Nazism*, p. 146.

12. For an alternative account of Evola's intellectual development, see Goodrick-Clarke, *Black Sun*, pp. 53–66.

13. Julius Evola, *Le chemin du cinabre* (Milan: Archè and Arktos, 1983), p. 69. On p. 85 he says that he even criticized Guénon in his *Saggi sull'idealismo magico* (1925).

14. *Rivolta contro il mondo moderno* (Milan: Hoepli, 1934; reprint, Rome: Edizioni Mediterranee, 1993).

15. H. T. Hansen, "Julius Evola und der Sexus" in Julius Evola, *Die Grosse Lust–Metaphysik des Sexus* (n.p.: Fischer Media Verlag, 1998).

16. *Arte astratta, posizione teorica* (Zurich: Magliano e Strini, 1920); *La parole obscure du paysage intérieur* (Zurich: Collection Dada, 1920). Evola, *Chemin du cinabre*, pp. 17–22, and Alain de Benoist, "Bibliographie de Julius Evola." My thanks to M. de Benoist for letting me use this unpublished and exhaustive bibliography. Richard Drake, "Julius Evola and the Ideological Origins of the Radical Right in Contemporary Italy," in *Political Violence and Terror: Motifs and Motivations*, ed. Peter H. Merkl (Berkeley: University of California Press, 1986), for the *Revue bleu*, and Hansen, "Julius Evola und der Sexus," for the fingernails.

17. This interest was reflected in Evola's early works, *Saggi sull'idealismo magico* [Essays on magic idealism] (1925) and *L'uomo come potenza. I Tantra nella loro metafisica e nei loro metodi di autorealizzazione magica* [Man as power: Tantra as metaphysics and as method of magical self-realization] (1926). Evola, *Chemin du cinabre*, pp. 30–31.

18. H. T. Hansen, "Die 'magische' Gruppe von Ur in ihrem Historischen und esoterischen Umfeld," in Julius Evola, *Schritte zur Initiation* (Bern: Scherz-Ansata, 1997), and Evola, *Chemin du cinabre*, p. 69. For Reghini, Dana Lloyd Thomas, "Arturo Reghini: A Modern Pythagorean," *Gnosis Magazine* 59 (Summer 1997), available http://www.geocities.com/integral_tradition/reghini.html [December 26, 2002].

19. Evola, *Chemin du cinabre*, p. 79.

20. Sibilla Aleramo, *Amo, dunque sono* (1927; reprint, Milan: A. Mondadori, 1940).

21. Hansen, "Julius Evola und der Sexus."

22. Evola, *Chemin du cinabre*, pp. 85–89. Evola also acknowledges the influence of Hermann Wirth, but this was less important.

23. Evola, *Chemin du cinabre*, pp. 8–10 and 28–29.

24. *Teoria dell'individuo assoluto* (Turin: Fratelli Bocca, 1927).

25. Joseph Campbell, Introduction, *Myth, Religion and Mother Right: Selected Writings of J. J. Bachofen*, ed. Ralph Manheim (Princeton, N.J.: Princeton University Press, 1967), pp. xxxiv–xliv.

26. Jakob Burckhardt not only valued Bachofen's work but was related to him by marriage—Bachofen's wife, Louise, was a Burckhardt. Campbell, Introduction, pp. xxxiv, and li–liv, and George Boas, Preface, *Myth, Religion and Mother Right*, ed. Manheim, pp. xi–xx. According to Campbell, Nietzsche was a frequent visitor to Bachofen's house in the 1870s (p. xlvi).

27. *Autorité spirituelle et pouvoir temporel* (Paris: J. Vrin, 1929).

28. Evola, *Rivolta contro il mondo moderno*, passim and Evola, *Chemin du cinabre*, pp. 90–92, 106—7, and 125–26.

29. Evola, *Chemin du cinabre*, p. 92.

30. Lloyd Thomas, "Arturo Reghini."

31. Evola, *Chemin du cinabre*, pp. 70–71.

32. Evola, *Chemin du cinabre*, p. 97.

33. *Imperialismo pagano. Il fascismo dinnanzi al pericolo euro-cristiano* (Rome: Atanor, 1928).

34. Hansen, "Die 'magische' Gruppe von Ur." Reghini was committed to Masonry and shared the views expressed in *Imperialismo pagano*, seeing Roman paganism as infinitely superior to Christianity, which he dismissed not only as sentimentality (following Guénon) but also as the religion of a "spiritual proletariat." See Evola, *Chemin du cinabre*, p. 69.

35. Evola, *Chemin du cinabre*, pp. 87 and 93, and Hansen, "Die 'magische' Gruppe von Ur."

36. Evola, *Chemin du cinabre*, pp. 94–95.

37. Evola, *Chemin du cinabre*, pp. 70–75.

38. Evola, *Chemin du cinabre*, pp. 93–96.

39. *La tradizione ermetica. Nei suoi simboli, nella sua dottrina e nella sua "Arte Regia"* (Bari: Laterza, 1931). Evola, *Chemin du cinabre*, p. 103.

40. *La tradizione romana* (Milan: Flamen, 1973). Evola, *Chemin du cinabre*, pp. 87–88; Hansen, "Die 'magische' Gruppe von Ur"; and Renato del Ponte, "Le correnti della tradizione pagana romana in Italia," *Agiza* 7 (c. 1996). Available http://utenti .tripod.it/centrostudilaluna/delponte.htm [May 17, 2000].

41. *Maschera e volto dello spiritualismo contemporaneo. Analisi critica delle principali correnti moderne verso il "sovrannaturale"* (Turin: Bocca, 1932).

42. Evola, *Chemin du cinabre*, p. 107–13.

43. Evola, *Chemin du cinabre*, pp. 112–13.

44. Evola, *Chemin du cinabre*, p. 104.

45. Rio de Janeiro: Rocco, 1991. This interpretation is the only sign of Tradition-

alist influence in the book, which is otherwise determinedly modern. Coelho's interpretation of alchemy probably came through Mircea Eliade (discussed later).

46. Hansen, "Die 'magische' Gruppe von Ur."

47. This is Hansen's view, on the basis also of other research (personal communication).

48. Evola, *Chemin du cinabre*, p. 69.

49. Hartung in fact asked about the "individuated individual" ("Rencontres Romaines au milieu des ruines," unpublished manuscript, March 1984), but the question is essentially the same.

50. This statement was made in 1974. See Claudio Mutti, "Evola e l'Islam," *Heliodromos: Contributi per il fronte della Tradizione* [Siracusa] 6 (Spring 1995), 52–53.

51. Hartung, "Rencontres."

52. Evola, *Chemin du cinabre*, pp. 96–99.

53. Evola, *Chemin du cinabre*, p. 101.

54. *Heidnische Imperialismus* (Leipzig: Armanen, 1933).

55. De Benoist, "Bibliographie."

56. H. T. Hansen, "Julius Evola und die deutsche konservative Revolution," *Criticon* [Munich] 158 (April/June 1998), 16–33.

57. Evola, *Chemin du cinabre*, p. 75.

58. Hansen, "Julius Evola und die deutsche konservative Revolution."

59. Evola, *Chemin du cinabre*, p. 134.

60. It appears in the modern form *ting* in the names of contemporary Scandinavian parliaments.

61. Evola, *Chemin du cinabre*, pp. 134–35, and Hansen, "Julius Evola und die deutsche konservative Revolution."

62. Evola, *Chemin du cinabre*, pp. 136–37, and Hansen, "Julius Evola und die deutsche konservative Revolution."

63. Hansen, "Julius Evola und die deutsche konservative Revolution."

64. Evola, *Chemin du cinabre*, p. 137.

65. *Il mistero del Graal e la tradizione ghibellina dell'Impero* (Bari: Laterza, 1937).

66. Hansen, "Julius Evola und der Sexus."

67. This summary sees events in a somewhat Evolian light.

68. Evola, *Chemin du cinabre*, pp. 129–30. This is an extreme oversimplification of complex events.

69. Hansen, "Julius Evola und die deutsche konservative Revolution."

70. The details that are known are taken from the minutes of the meeting that rejected these proposals, and the visit to Wewelsburg is reported in a 1939 Italian police report (though since another such report of 1930 has Evola as a follower of Rudolf Steiner engaged in spreading German imperialism in close relations with the German crown prince and Mrs. Krupp, such reports on Evola must be treated with caution). See Hansen, "Julius Evola und die deutsche konservative Revolution." Evola himself is silent on any contacts with the SS in *Chemin du cinabre*, reporting only his contacts with the ultra-Conservatives, but then even Evola would by then have had cause to regret contacts with the SS.

71. Wiligut was instructed to review four lectures of Evola, one stated to have been given in Berlin in 1937, and three in 1938, as well as *Heidnische Imperialismus—*

Goodrick-Clarke, *Occult Roots of Nazism*, pp. 188–83 and 189–190. Wiligut's occultist connection was in the late 1920s, with the Ordo Novi Templi, a neo-Templar group, established in 1907 by Jörg Lanz von Liebenfels, a former Cistercian. Von Liebenfels was (predictably) connected with the Theosophical Society, but some of his ideas were far from those of the Theosophists. Interpreting the biblical Fall as the miscegenation of divine early Aryans with pygmies, in 1905 he proposed returning the Aryans to their earlier divine state; his proposals included the sterilization of inferior races, or possibly their deportation to Madagascar, or, alternatively, their ritual incineration. See Goodrick-Clarke, *Occult Roots of Nazism*, pp. 90–97, 100, and 180.

72. Goodrick-Clarke, *Occult Roots of Nazism*, p. 190.

73. Hansen, "Julius Evola und die deutsche konservative Revolution," for the minutes of the meeting of August 11, 1938. Hansen puts an entirely different interpretation on these minutes, emphasizing the unreliability of the report of Evola's 1938 visit and merely quoting its reference to Evola's plans as not to be supported because they were utopian. Hansen has probably seen the original minutes, and I have not, a fact that makes my own reinterpretation somewhat less certain, but it seems to me that the meeting could not have decided to cut off *further* access to *führenden Dienststellen* unless Evola had previously had access, and that a meeting at a high enough level to be attended by Himmler would not have bothered to consider Evola's plans unless they had been in some fashion addressed to the SS. This suggests that the *führenden Dienststellen* referred to were within the SS. Goodrick-Clarke, *Occult Roots of Nazism* (to which Hansen does not refer; he may not know of the Wiligut report) gives no details of the speeches that Wiligut was asked to report on, and only one (that of 1937) is specifically stated to have been given in Germany; it is thus possible that the three June 1938 speeches were given elsewhere, possibly even in Italy, and had come to the attention of Himmler for some other reason. It seems unlikely, however, that there is no connection when three speeches given in June 1938 are reviewed by the SS and the giver of those speeches is on the agenda of a high-level SS meeting in August 1938. It must be stressed, though, that further research in this area is needed.

74. Goodrick-Clarke, *Occult Roots of Nazism*, pp. 179 and 190.

75. *Sintesi di dottrina della razza* (Milan: Hoepli, 1941).

76. Evola, *Chemin du cinabre*, pp. 151–52 and 157.

77. Evola, *Chemin du cinabre*, pp. 153 and 156, and de Benoist, "Bibliographie."

78. Evola, *Chemin du cinabre*, p. 154.

79. Evola, *Chemin du cinabre*, p. 154, and Hansen, "Julius Evola und die deutsche konservative Revolution." Evola himself, of course, puts it rather differently.

80. De Benoist, "Bibliographie."

81. Evola, *Chemin du cinabre*. pp. 159–62. Goodrick-Clarke, *Black Sun*, pp. 66–67.

82. For Reghini, H. T. Hansen, "Mircea Eliade, Julius Evola und die Integrale Tradition," in Julius Evola, *Über das Initiatische* (Sinzheim: AAGW, 1998). For *Ur*, Evola, *Chemin du cinabre*, p. 137. "Distant" in the geographical sense but also in the metaphorical. In the late 1930s Evola sent some books to Eliade with a covering note beginning, "I remember you perfectly"—Claudio Mutti, *Julius Evola sul fronte dell'est* (Parma: All'insegna del Veltro, 1998), p. 94—which implies that Eliade had requested the books in a letter containing a phrase such as "you may remember that Reghini [or

someone] mentioned me to you in. . . ." The date 1927 is the latest possible, given the Evolian content of Eliade's "Ocultismul în cultura europeanā," published in *Cuvântul* in December 1927. It is also the earliest, since *Ur* did not exist before 1927.

83. For Theosophy, Natale Spineto, "Mircea Eliade and Traditionalism," *Aries* NS 1, no. 1 (2001), 68. Saint Martin is less well established.

84. Spineto, "Mircea Eliade," p. 68.

85. Mircea Eliade, *Journal III, 1970–1978* (Chicago: University of Chicago Press, 1989), p. 161.

86. Robert Ellwood, *The Politics of Myth: A Study of C. G. Jung, Mircea Eliade, and Joseph Campbell* (Albany, N.Y.: SUNY Press, 1999), p. 81.

87. The encounter seems to have taken place in about 1933. In 1934 Lovinescu published an article on the Holy Grail in *Etudes traditionnelles*—Claudio Mutti, Introduction, *La Dacia iperborea*, Vasile Lovinescu (Parma: All'insegna del Veltro, 1984), p. 11. There is also a passing reference to Evola in an article published by Lovinescu in that year in *Vremea* [Bucharest] (Mutti, *Julius Evola sul fronte dell'est*, p. 23).

88. Mutti, *Julius Evola sul fronte dell'est*, p. 22.

89. Mutti, Introduction, *Dacia iperborea*, p. 11. The articles on Dacia are collected and translated as *Dacia iperborea*.

90. Adriana Berger, "Mircea Eliade: Romanian Fascism and the History of Religions in the United States" in *Tainted Greatness: Antisemitism and Cultural Heroes*, ed. Nancy A. Harrowitz (Philadelphia: Temple University Press, 1994), pp. 55–56.

91. Mutti, "La vita e i libri di Vasile Lovinescu" in *La colonna traiana* [sic], Vasile Lovinescu (Parma: All'insegna del Veltro, 1995), p. 20.

92. Mutti, "Vita e libri," p. 20.

93. Eliade's earliest Traditionalist article was published in December 1927, while he was a 20-year-old undergraduate student. This is "Ocultismul în cultura europeanā" [Occultism in European culture], which appeared in the magazine *Cuvântul* [Youth] December 1, 1927, pp. 1–2, and drew on an article of Evola published in Italy the previous month, "Il valore dell'occultismo nella cultura contemporanea" [The Value of Occultism in Contemporary Culture], *Bilychnis*, November 11, 1927, pp. 250–69. In 1932 Eliade described Guénon as "a remarkable occultist, with a solid understanding, who always knows what he is talking about" ("Spritualitate şi mister feminin" [Spirituality and Feminine Mystery], *Azi* [Today], April 1932). In his 1935 review of Evola's *Rivolta contro il mondo moderno* (1933) in *Vremea* (March 31, 1935, p. 6), Eliade is more cautious, calling Evola "one of the most interesting personalities of the war generation." From 1935 onward, though, there are only occasional references to Traditionalist authors. See Mutti, *Julius Evola sul fronte dell'est*, pp. 22, 97–98, and Hansen, "Mircea Eliade."

94. Spineto, "Mircea Eliade," p. 67.

95. Quoted in Hansen, "Mircea Eliade."

96. Eliade, *Journal III*, pp. 162–63.

97. Since Eliade did not deny Evola's charge of missing acknowledgments, he could only be seeking to explain why those acknowledgments (the presence of which would constitute "overt Traditionalism") were absent. In this context, mention of his non-Traditionalist audience seems to imply that he did not want to put that audience off. Of course he could simply mean that he saw no point in referring to (Traditionalist) authors whom his own readers would never read, but this interpretation is un-

likely, given that Eliade must have understood the dual purpose of source citation. Elsewhere, Eliade more or less admitted to Traditionalism. In 1940, while writing a novel (*Viaţa Nouă* [New Life]), he wrote in his diary of one of his characters, Tulin: "Tulin will say things which . . . I have never had the courage to express in public. I have only, at times, confessed to a few friends my 'traditionalist' views (to use René Guénon's term)." Quoted in Spineto, "Mircea Eliade," p. 68.

98. In a letter of 1949, Guénon wrote of Eliade: "He is more or less entirely in agreement, essentially, with traditional ideas, but dare not show it too much in what he writes, since he is afraid of colliding with officially accepted conceptions." Steven M. Wasserstrom, *Religion after Religion: Gershom Scholem, Mircea Eliade, and Henry Corbin at Eranos*, (Princeton, N.J.: Princeton University Press, 1999), p. 272.

99. In *Comentarii la legenda Meşterului Manole* [Commentary on the Legend of Master Manole] (Bucharest: 1943), quoted in Spineto, "Mircea Eliade," p. 73.

100. Mircea Eliade, "Some Notes on *Theosophia perennis*: Ananda K. Coomaraswamy and Henry Corbin" [Review of Roger Lipsey, *Coomaraswamy*, 3 vols., Princeton, N.J.: Princeton University Press, 1977], *History of Religions* 19 (1979), 169–71.

101. Spineto, "Mircea Eliade," mentions: "the concepts of anthropo-cosmic correspondence, of the symbol, of the sacred center, of the 'cyclical' quality of traditional time, of human construction as a repetition of cosmogony, of sacrifice as a reintegration, and of the archetype" (p. 68). Many of these are either not central to either Traditionalism or Eliade's work, or else they are found in both but also elsewhere. Eliade does indeed view traditional time as cyclical, but in a very different way from Guénon.

102. This objective is deduced from his earlier association with Traditionalism, a deduction that seems to be supported by the arguments I will show later. Of course Eliade—like everyone—must have had multiple objectives.

103. Douglas Allen, "Mircea Eliade's View of the Study of Religion as the Basis for Cultural and Spiritual Renewal," in *Changing Religious Worlds: The Meaning and End of Mircea Eliade*, ed. Bryan S. Rennie (Albany, N.Y.: SUNY Press, 2000), pp. 211 and 214–25. See also Bryan S. Rennie, Introduction, *Changing Religious Worlds*, ed. Rennie, pp. ix–xxiv

104. "Folclorul ca instrument de cunoştere" [Folklore as an Instrument of Knowledge], 1937, reprinted in *Insula lui* [The Island], *Euthanasius* (Bucharest: Fundaţia regalā pentru literaturā şi arte, 1943). Quoted in Mutti, *Julius Evola sul fronte dell'est*, p. 22.

105. He also on occasion substituted "soteriological" for "initiatic"—see example in Spineto, "Mircea Eliade," p. 69. For Eliade, "archaic" religion included even contemporary Hinduism (see Rennie, "The Religious Creativity of Modern Humanity: Some Observations on Eliade's Unfinished Thought," *Religious Studies* 31 [June 1995], 221–35), just as Hinduism was "traditional" for the Traditionalists.

106. Spineto, "Mircea Eliade," p. 75.

107. In *L'épreuve du Labyrinthe, entretien avec C H Rocquet* (Paris: 1978), quoted in Enrico Montanari, "Eliade e Guénon," *Studi e Materiali di Storia della Religioni* 61 (1995), 133.

108. N. J. Girardot, "Smiles and Whispers," in *Changing Religious Worlds*, ed. Rennie, p. 157.

109. Lovinescu's support is deduced from his 1934 article "Mistica fascismului"

[The Mysticism of Fascism], *Vremea* January 14, 1934 (Mutti, *Julius Evola sul fronte dell'est*, p. 23). He also knew Codrianu personally (Mutti, *Julius Evola sul fronte dell'est*. p. 21). Eliade's support is discussed later.

110. Larry L. Watts, *Romanian Cassandra: Ion Antonescu and the Struggle for Reform, 1916–1941* (Boulder, Col.: East European Monographs, 1993), pp. 132–33, and Berger, "Mircea Eliade," p. 56. The judgment on Legionary anti-Semitism is from Watts, p. 183.

111. Radu Ioanid, *The Sword of the Archangel: Fascist Ideology in Romania* (Boulder, Col.: East European Monographs, 1990), pp. 54–55, and Watts, *Romanian Cassandra*, pp. 158–60.

112. Z. Ornea, *The Romanian Extreme Right: The Nineteen Thirties* (Boulder: East European Monographs, 1999), pp. 204 and 206.

113. *Vremea* 10: 476 (1937), quoted in Berger, "Mircea Eliade," pp. 63–64.

114. "Why I Believe in the Victory of the Legionary Movement," *Buna Vestire* [Good Tidings], December 17, 1937. German translation in *Deutsche Stimme* 11 (1998), available online at http://members.tripod.com/centenar/ccd4.html [May 2000].

115. "Bucuresti Centru Viril," *Vremea* 8: 835 (1935), and "Pilotii Orbi" [Blind pilots], *Vremea* 10: 505 (1937), quoted in Berger, "Mircea Eliade," pp. 56 and 63.

116. Or 1936 or 1938—see discussion in Mutti, *Julius Evola sul fronte dell'est*, pp. 13–15.

117. Evola, *Chemin du cinabre*, p. 137.

118. Mutti, *Julius Evola sul fronte dell'est*, pp. 25–26.

119. Florin Mihaescu, "René Guénon, Frithjof Schuon, Vasile Lovinescu et l'initiation," in *Frithjof Schuon, 1907–1998: Etudes et temoignages*, ed. Bernard Chevilliat (Avon: Connaissance des Religions, 1999), pp. 195–97.

120. Ioanid, *Sword of the Archangel*, p. 141 for Lupu.

121. Maurice Clavelle [Jean Reyor], "Document confidentiel inédit," unpublished typescript, and Muhammad Vâlsan, interview.

122. In Eliade, "Initiation et monde moderne," *Travaux de Villard de Honnecourt* 1 (1980). Quoted in Wasserstrom, *Religion after Religion*, pp. 41–42.

123. Watts, *Romanian Cassandra*, pp. 173–76; Ellwood, *Politics of Myth*, p. 82; and Ornea, *Romanian Extreme Right*, p. 216.

124. Marie-France James, *Esotérisme, Occultisme, Franc-Maçonnerie et Christianisme aux XIX et XX siècles. Explorations bio-bibliographiques* (Paris: Nouvelles éditions latines, 1981), p. 336, and Bryan Rennie, "Mircea Eliade," *Routledge Encyclopedia of Philosophy* (1998).

125. Watts, *Romanian Cassandra*, pp. 228–29, and Ornea, *Romanian Extreme Right*, p. 219.

126. Mutti, "Vita e libri," p. 22.

127. The formulation, though not the charge itself, is from Kelley Ross, "Mircea Eliade (1907–1986)," *The Proceedings of the Friesian School*, Fourth Series, 1996– [online]. Available http://www.friesian.com/eliade.htm.

128. Ross, "Mircea Eliade."

129. *A patrulea hagialîc: exegeza nocturna a Crailor de Curtea-Veche* (Bucharest: Cartea Româneasca, 1981); Mutti, "Vita e libri," p. 22; and e-mail from Mihai Marinescu, September 1, 2001.

130. For events after Lovinescu's death, see AN 1.

131. For details, see AN 2.

6. FRAGMENTATION

1. There was obviously an unidentified Traditionalist in the Brazilian diplomatic service. Brazil declared war on the Axis in August 1942.

2. French Masonry was officially dissolved in 1940 and its assets and records seized. Lists of former Masons, who were prohibited from public employment and subject to various other disabilities, were published in the *Journal officiel* [Official Gazette]. Numerous anti-Masonic exhibitions and publications were arranged. Antonio Coen and Michel Dumesnil de Grammont, *La Franc-Maçonnerie Ecossaise* (Nice: SNEP, 1946), pp. 6 and 57–60.

3. Martin Lings, interview.

4. Alain Daniélou, "René Guénon et la tradition hindoue," in *René Guénon* [Dossier H], ed. Pierre-Marie Sigaud (Lausanne: L'Age d'Homme, 1984), pp. 138–39, and Marie-France James, *Esotérisme, Occultisme, Franc-Maçonnerie et Christianisme aux XIX et XX siècles. Explorations bio-bibliographiques* (Paris: Nouvelles éditions latines, 1981), pp. 88–89.

5. André Gide, *Journal 1939–1949: Souvenirs* (1954; Paris: Gallimard, 1979), p. 254. The Traditionalist in question was Abdallah Haddou, identified either as Georges or as Guy Delon. Nothing more is known of him.

6. Henri Bosco, "Trois rencontres," *Nouvelle Revue Française*, November 1951, p. 279.

7. *La grande Triade* (Nancy: Revue de la Table Ronde, 1946). Denys Roman, *René Guénon et les destins de la Franc-Maçonnerie* (Paris: Les éditions de l'oeuvre, 1982), p. 160.

8. This is the estimate of Claude Gagne, who as well as being a later Venerable of the Grande Triade was also archivist of the French Grand Lodge.

9. The future grand master was Antonio Coën. Taken from Register of Lodge Membership of the Grande Triade, of which I was allowed to see the first pages.

10. Roman, *René Guénon*, p. 166.

11. Roman, *René Guénon*, pp. 165–66.

12. Henri Hartung, *Spiritualité et autogestion* (Lausanne: L'Age d'Homme, 1978), pp. 28–35, and Sylvie Hartung, interview. Hartung's report, "La Chine communiste et le problème communiste chinois," was presented in September. Henri Hartung, "Articles et conférences," unpublished manuscript, July 1, 1983.

13. Henri Hartung, *Présence de Ramana Maharshi* (1979; Paris: Dervy livres, 1987), p. 36.

14. In 1947 he defended a thesis on "L'hévéaculture et le problème de caoutchouc en Indochine Française." Hartung, "Articles et conférences."

15. Hartung to Guénon, May 2 and July 13, 1949, and Guénon to Hartung, May 19, 1949. Collection of Sylvie Hartung.

16. Vâlsan to Schuon, November 1950, private collection.

17. Catherine Schuon, "Frithjof Schuon: Memories and Anecdotes," *Sacred Web* 8 (1992), 37–38.

18. Personal observation on several occasions.

19. Frithjof Schuon, *Erinnerungen und Betrachtungen* ([Switzerland]: privately printed, 1974), p. 12.

20. *Black Elk Speaks* (New York, William Morrow, 1932).

21. Michael Fitzgerald, "Le rôle de Frithjof Schuon dans la préservation de l'esprit de l'indien peau-rouge" in *Frithjof Schuon, 1907–1998: Etudes et témoignages*, ed. Bernard Chevilliat (Avon: Connaissance des Religions, 1999), p. 186, and Bernadette Rigal-Cellard, "La religion des sioux oglalas" in *Le facteur religieux an Amérique du Nord: Religion et groupes ethniques au Canada et aux Etats-Unis*, ed. J. Beranger and P. Guillaume (Bordeaux: CNRS, 1984), pp. 245–48.

22. Catherine Schuon, "Frithjof Schuon," p. 41.

23. Fitzgerald, "Rôle de Frithjof Schuon," p. 187, and Jean-Baptiste Aymard, "Frithjof Schuon (1907–1998). Connaissance et voie d'intériorité. Approche biographique," in Chevilliat, ed., *Frithjof Schuon, 1907–1998*, p. 32.

24. *The Sacred Pipe: Black Elk's Account of the Seven Rites of the Oglala Sioux* (Norman: University of Oklahoma Press, 1953). Aymard, "Frithjof Schuon," p. 32.

25. Rigal-Cellard, "Religion des sioux oglalas," p. 245.

26. Fitzgerald, "Rôle de Frithjof Schuon," p. 187.

27. Maurice Clavelle [Jean Reyor], "Document confidentiel inédit," unpublished typescript. Relations between Guénon and Schuon seem to have continued much as before until then, since in 1947 Schuon even sent Guénon for correction the proofs of his most important book, *De l'unité transcendante des religions* [The Transcendent Unity of Religions], which was published in 1948 (Claude Gagne, interview).

28. Clavelle, "Document confidentiel."

29. "Orthodox Islam" is here defined as Guénon would have defined it: mainstream Islam as practiced by pious Sufis in countries such as Egypt.

30. Clavelle, "Document confidentiel."

31. Hartung, notes of conversation with Cuttat, July 23, 1950, and open letter from Vâlsan to Schuon, November 1950. I was not allowed to read the letter myself but only to take notes as it was read aloud to me; some parts may have been omitted, but I am confident that none were added and that the general tone of the letter was not significantly changed.

32. The same point was made by a later Schuonian in 2002: "Such dispensations were never made into a principle that was broadly applied." Michael Fitzgerald, "Frithjof Schuon: Providence without Paradox," *Sacred Web* 8, 2002.

33. Harald von Meyenburg, interview.

34. Vâlsan to Schuon, November 1950.

35. Schuon, "Taçawwuf," undated typed text.

36. Fitzgerald, "Frithjof Schuon."

37. Vâlsan to Schuon, November 1950.

38. What to do about fasting under such circumstances has engaged Muslims for centuries. The question did not arise during the early years of Islam and so received no definitive answer at that time. After Islam spread north, it was realized that fasting from dawn to dusk in July in certain latitudes would amount to committing suicide. One pragmatic answer to this problem has been to fast according to the times of dawn and dusk at some other place, such as Mecca.

39. The only purpose of *tayammum* is to pray, and it is usually harder for a Mus-

lim in the West to find somewhere to pray than it is to find somewhere to do ablutions. Such permission might conceivably have been useful for someone working where he or she could lock the door of an office but not the door of a public bathroom.

40. There are no other grounds on which such relaxations can be based. The Sharia permits the limited delaying of ritual prayer and fasting for those who are traveling or fighting, and exempts certain categories of person (pregnant women, for example) from fasting altogether—but that is all.

41. For example, I once heard a Sufi shaykh give such permission to a Norwegian soldier serving with his country's army in the peacekeeping forces in Lebanon. The reaction of the Norwegian army to a soldier who converted to Islam in Lebanon and starting praying in public can only be imagined.

42. The phrase "essentialization" is used to describe Schuon's "dispensations" much later, in Fitzgerald, "Frithjof Schuon," but it is likely that the underlying concept was to be found also in the 1940s.

43. Vâlsan to Schuon, November 1950. Vâlsan refers to drinking wine or port but, according to von Meyenburg, the permitted drink was beer, not wine—on the grounds that beer contains less alcohol than wine. Von Meyenburg, fax, July 2002.

44. There were reports that some of the hijackers of September 11, 2001, had been seen drinking vodka, but these reports must be treated with extreme caution.

45. Von Meyenburg, fax, July 2002.

46. Schuon to Burckhardt, May 1939, addressing on this point not Burckhardt personally but rather "all the *zawiyas*." I have used a later typed version of the letter.

47. Clavelle, "Document confidentiel," supplemented by interview with A1 (see list before bibliography). I have not seen this *ijaza*, the existence of which has sometimes been questioned. There is, however, far less controversy surrounding Maridort's *ijaza* than Schuon's.

48. Vâlsan to Schuon, November 1950. Contemporary Maryami informants did not dispute this point.

49. PierLuigi Zoccatelli, e-mails, July 2 and 4, 2001, and Zoccatelli, *Le lièvre qui rumine: Autour de René Guénon, Louis Charbonneau-Lassay et la Fraternité du Paraclet* (Milan: Archè, 1999), p. 31.

50. Zoccatelli, *Lièvre qui rumine*, p. 33. See AN 1.

51. Jean-Pierre Laurant, *Les sens caché selon René Guénon* (Lausanne: L'Age d'homme, 1975), pp. 241–42.

52. See Clavelle, "Document confidentiel inédit," and Roman, *René Guénon*, p. 167. A somewhat neutral observer, Corneloup, echoes these interpretations in J. Corneloup, *Je ne sais qu'épeler* (Paris: Vitiano, 1971), pp. 114 and 117.

53. Or possibly a third attempt. Another lodge was established in France during the 1950s by Romanian Traditionalist refugees; no further details of this are known, however.

54. My thanks to PierLuigi Zoccatelli for this information.

55. This contention of Reyor has been contested but, given Guénon's conviction that he was being spied on, seems plausible.

56. Clavelle, "Document confidentiel inédit," and Lings, interview.

57. Lings was even called in by the police on one occasion for questioning about

these strange symbols (Lings, interview). An unrelated informant, an American teaching in Cairo at that time, confirmed that it was quite normal in the late 1940s for foreign mail to arrive showing clear signs of having been read by the censor.

58. Hartung, note of conversation with Cuttat, August 27, 1950.

59. Clavelle, "Document confidentiel."

60. James, *Esotérisme, Occultisme*, pp. 85–86.

61. Sylvie Hartung, interview.

62. Sylvie Hartung, interview. The non-Schuonian Alawis were followers of Khaled Bentounès.

63. Vâlsan to Schuon, September 17, 1950. For Guénon's approval, Michel Chodkiewicz, interview.

64. Guénon, letter of October 9, 1950, reproduced in Dominique Devie, "The File on the Schuon Case: The History of a Pseudo-Guénonian Cult" [online]. Available http:/www.mygale.org/oo/cret/ltguenon.htm [December 13, 1996].

65. Vâlsan to Schuon, November 1950.

66. Hartung, notes of conversation with Cuttat, July 23, 1950.

67. Clavelle, "Document confidentiel."

68. Valentine de Saint-Point, "René Guénon," *L'Egypte nouvelle*, January 25, 1952, reprinted in *L'Ermite de Duqqi: René Guénon en marge des milieux francophones égyptiens*, ed. Xavier Accart (Milan: Archè, 2001), pp. 158–59.

69. Gabriel Boctor, "Une visite à l'ermite de Dokki," *La Bourse égyptienne*, January 22, 1951, reprinted in Accart, ed., *Ermite de Duqqi*, p. 103.

70. Paul Chacornac, *La vie simple de René Guénon* (1958; Paris: Editions traditionnelles, 1986), pp. 112–24; Lings, letter to Schuon, January 11, 1951 (private collection; French translation in Accart, ed., *Ermite de Duqqi*, pp. 239–41); and S Katz, letter to Swami Siddheswarananda, February 6, 1951, printed in Accart, ed., *Ermite de Duqqi*, pp. 241–42. Whithall N. Perry, "Aperçus," in *Frithjof Schuon, 1907–1998: Etudes et témoignages*, ed. Bernard Chevilliat (Avon: Connaissance des Religions, 1999), pp. 90–91. See AN 2.

71. Accart, ed., *Ermite de Duqqi*, pp. 53–54.

72. Various informants.

73. The origin of this belief has not been established. For the last wish, Katz to Siddheswarananda, February 6, 1951.

74. For the attempt to sell the library, Igor Volkoff, "Voyage à travers la bibliothèque de René Guénon," *L'Egypte nouvelle*, October 9, 1953, reprinted in Accart, ed., *Ermite de Duqqi*, pp. 218–23. My thanks to Jean-Pierre Laurant for news of the television.

75. Lings, interview.

76. Perry, "Aperçus," pp. 100–101.

77. Martin Lings and Faruq al-Hitami, interviews. For Levy, see also Andrew Rawlinson, *The Book of Enlightened Masters: Western Teachers in Eastern Traditions* (Chicago: Open Court Press, 1997). I have used the somewhat longer manuscript of this book, for which I would like to thank Dr. Rawlinson.

78. Accart, ed., *Ermite de Duqqi*, pp. 57–60.

79. Accart, ed., *Ermite de Duqqi*, p. 61.

80. Gamal Abdul Nasr was a nationalist, not an Islamist. After French troops joined British and Israeli troops in invading Egyptian territory in 1956 during the

Suez Crisis—known in Egypt as the Tripartite Aggression—the memory of a single French convert to Islam was not going to make much difference to anything.

81. Clavelle, "Document confidentiel," supplemented by Gagne, interview.

82. Gagne, interview, and other informants.

83. Pietro Nutrizio, ed., *René Guénon e l'Occidente* (Milan: Luni Editrice, 1999), passim. The quotations are from Ugo Darbesio, review of the *Etudes traditionnelles* review of Jean Reyor, *Pour un aboutissement de l'oeuvre de René Guénon* (Milan: Archè, 1988), *Rivista di Studi Tradizionali* 68–69 (1989), 245–48.

84. Muhammad Guénon and A1 (see list before bibliography), interviews.

85. Muhammad Vâlsan, interview. Where no other source on this order is given, information comes from Muhammad Vâlsan or Michel Chodkiewicz.

86. By Chodkiewicz, who was in a position to judge and seemed not to be exaggerating.

87. Muhammad Vâlsan, interview.

88. At least two books, and 25 shorter translations in *Etudes traditionnelles* between 1951 and 1971. See bibliography in Michel Vâlsan, *L'islam et la fonction de René Guénon: recueil posthume* (Paris: Editions de l'Oeuvre, 1984).

89. This *dhikr* was followed, in the normal way, by a homily, drawing mostly on the Koran or Ibn al-Arabi; Guénon was referred to only occasionally.

90. Estimates vary between 65 (Chodkiewicz) and 200 (Muhammad Vâlsan).

91. Only rarely exceeded in the case of new orders, that is. A long-established order may have thousands of not very dedicated followers.

92. See J. Storch and R. Françon, "La difficile naissance de la semeuse," *Documents Philatéliques* 110, no. 4 (1986) [online]. Available http://www.chez.com/koechlin/semeuse/semeuse-doc1.htm. There is also a Musée Oscar Roty with a website at http://www.coeur-de-france.com/roty.html. After 2002 a modernized version of the *Semeuse* appeared on certain Euro coins minted in France

93. The surname is, of course, Polish, but the Chodkiewicz family had been established in France since 1832, brought there by an army officer who fled Russia after an unsuccessful insurrection in 1831. All information on Chodkiewicz comes from an interview with him, confirmed where possible from other sources.

94. In fact, at the Ecole des Hautes Etudes en Sciences Sociales, a prestigious institute.

95. In 1998 the *Revue de l'histoire des religions*—a venerable academic journal established in 1880—published six articles in a special issue dealing with Christian and Muslim orders (vol. 215, no. 1). One was by Chodkiewicz, one by Gril, and one by Eric Geoffroy, not a Traditionalist but a reader of Guénon, a Muslim, and the son-in-law of Vâlsan's closest follower, René Roty. The three articles on Christian orders were written by scholars with no connection to Vâlsan.

96. See, for example, Yacoub Roty, *L'attestation de foi: première base de l'Islam* (Paris: Maison d'Ennour, 1994). The approach in this book is typical of Vâlsan's order—it is based purely on classic Islamic sources until the last chapter, which deals with the "providential work" of Guénon, talks of the dangers of contemporary rationalism, and recommends the reading of six of Guénon's most important works.

97. He was known to members of the Grand Triad, occasionally wrote on Masonry (for example, a three-part article on "Les derniers hauts grades de l'Ecossisme et la réalisation descendante" in *Etudes traditionnelles* in 1953), and suspected approv-

ingly that Illaysh was a Mason (Vâlsan, *L'islam et la fonction de René Guénon*, pp. 30–31), which may well have been the case. Chodkiewicz, however, is clear that Vâlsan was not a Mason (interview).

98. Muhammad Vâlsan, interview.

99. Vâlsan, *L'islam et la fonction de René Guénon*, p. 13.

100. Various informants. None of these successor orders wished to have further details made public.

101. Pallavicini, interview. Where no other source is given, information on Pallavicini and the Ahmadiyya derives from Pallavicini, or from observation during a visit to the Ahmadiyya in Milan in 1996, including informal interviews with other Ahmadis.

102. Various informants.

103. For further information on this order, see my *Saints and Sons: The Making and Remaking of the Rashidi Ahmadi Sufi Order, 1799–2000* (Leiden: Brill, forthcoming).

104. Ali Salim, interview.

105. Ali Salim and Muhammad Zabid, interviews.

106. Pallavicini, interview.

107. "Centro Studi Metafisici 'René Guénon,'" undated leaflet.

108. "Centro Studi Metafisici 'René Guénon,'" and Pallavicini, interview.

109. Examples taken from notes to Abd-al-Wahid Pallavicini, *Islam interiore: La spiritualità universale nella religione islamica* (Milan: Arnoldo Mondadori, 1991), which reprints many of Pallavicini's lectures.

110. Davide Gorni, "La moschea divide già via Meda," *Corriere della Sera* October 26, 2000.

111. I observed the *dhikr* in Milan and later in Singapore.

112. Avoidance of syncretism is stressed repeatedly by Pallavicini in both his writings and his speeches. My assessment of following the Sharia is based on observation and discussion and on the absence of any accusations of departures from it among the many accusations made against Pallavicini by his opponents (other than occasionally giving the Islamic *salamat* greeting to non-Muslims). Though the Ahmadiyya is not known to have departed from Islam, Pallavicini has made occasional minor errors in his exposition of it—confusing Koran and *hadith* (sayings of the Prophet) as the source of something, for example. These are accidental errors, not departures.

113. Pallavicini, interview.

114. Conclusion on analysis of lectures reprinted in Pallavicini, *Islam interiore*.

115. Various informants.

116. Various informants.

117. Various Reuters reports.

118. Franco Cardini, "Religioni di guerra e di pace," *Il Giornale* [Milan], October 29, 1985.

119. Stefania Trabucchi, "Un centro per capire l'Islam: Lo 'shaikh' Pallavicini e l'incontro tra Allah e Roma," *Corriere della Sera*, July 30, 1990, p. 18.

120. This is the view of Dr. Stefano Allievi (personal communication).

121. "Abdu-l-Hadi" [pseud.], letter to the editor, *Messaggero dell'Islam*, December 15, 1986, p. 15.

122. Stefano Allievi (personal communication).

123. "*In memoriam* René Guénon," reprinted in Abd-al-Wahid Pallavicini, *L'islam intérieur: La spiritualité universelle dans la religion islamique* (1991; Paris: Christian de Bartillat, 1995), pp. 103–13.

124. *Communita Islamica* 1992, pp. 11 and 13–14. This was the single issue of *Communita Islamica* produced during 1992 and was devoted entirely to attacking Pallavicini.

125. Muhammad Zabid (interview) has no knowledge of his father's writing any such letter, which was in Italian, a language that his father did not know. Though the letter might have been translated into Italian by someone else, its contents are simply incorrect. Muhammad Zabid and Ali Salim (interviews) both confirm that Pallavicini did enter the Ahmadiyya and receive an *ijaza;* Shaykh Abd al-Rashid would not have denied giving an *ijaza* if he had in fact done so (he could have canceled it if he wished). The deciding factor is that the letter contains the statement that Pallavicini's acts are "null and void of any *traditional* foundation" [my emphasis]. Only someone familiar with Traditionalism could have written that; it is not a phrase that could occur to any Arabic or Malay speaker unless he had read deeply in Traditionalist works, which Shaykh Abd al-Rashid had not.

126. Pallavicini, *L'islam intérieur*, pp. 163–64.

127. Various informants.

128. Pallavicini, interview, supported by a variety of corroborative evidence.

129. Various Ahmadi informants.

130. Francesco Battistini, "Moschea: AN diserterà la fiaccolata di protesta," *Corriere della Sera*, October 31, 2000.

131. Elisabetta Rosaspina, "Milano: Un quartiere contro la moschea," *Corriere della Sera*, October 30, 2000.

132. Various reports in *Corriere della Sera*, October 2000.

133. Jean Tourniac [Jean Granger], *Johannes Eques A Rosa Mystica. La Francmaçonnerie chrétienne-templière des Prieures Ecossais Rectifies: Réflexion sur l'organisation prieurale et l'esprit du rite* (Paris: SEPP, 1997), pp. 11–13 and 78.

134. Tourniac published fifteen books between 1965 and 1993 on Masonry, symbolism, Eastern Christianity, and Judaism as well as on pure Traditionalism. Two volumes on Judaism were also brought out posthumously.

135. The name chosen this time was S. F., though informants varied on whether these letters stood for Sainte Fraternité or Sein de Famille.

136. Its ritual was distinguished by a new Masonic grade invented by Guénon, that of Chevalier (or perhaps Maître) d'Orient et d'Occident.

137. Tourniac, *Johannes Eques*, passim, and Roman, *René Guénon*, pp. 153–54.

138. Tourniac's first book, in 1965, was *Symbolisme maçonnique et tradition chrétienne* (Paris: Dervy, 1965). Baylot and Riquet together published *Les Francs-Maçons: dialogue entre Michel Riquet et Jean Baylot* (Paris: Beauchesne, 1968).

139. Tourniac, *Johannes Eques*, p. 81.

140. My thanks to Father Jérôme Lacordaire for these details.

141. These comments are based on a reviews of the *Travaux de la loge nationale de recherches Villard de Honnecourt* and the *Cahiers Villard de Honnecourt*.

142. Patrick Géay, Editorial, *La Règle d'Abraham* 1 (April 1996), 3–6.

7. THE MARYAMIYYA

1. Frithjof Schuon, *Erinnerungen und Betrachtungen* ([Switzerland]: privately printed, 1974), pp. 137–38.

2. Jean-Baptiste Aymard, "Frithjof Schuon (1907–1998). Connaissance et voie d'intériorité. Approche biographique," in *Frithjof Schuon, 1907–1998: Etudes et témoignages*, ed. Bernard Chevilliat (Avon: Connaissance des Religions, 1999), p. 43.

3. Schuon, *Erinnerungen und Betrachtungen*, p. 9.

4. A3, interview. See list before bibliography.

5. Whithall N. Perry, "Aperçus," in *Frithjof Schuon*, ed. Chevilliat, pp. 100–102.

6. Schuon, *Erinnerungen und Betrachtungen*, pp. 152 and 267.

7. Schuon, *Erinnerungen und Betrachtungen*, p. 159, and Aymard, "Frithjof Schuon," p. 50. Yellowtail was the husband of the first Native American to become a certified nurse, and the brother of the first Native American to become superintendent of a reserve. Michael Fitzgerald, "Le rôle de Frithjof Schuon dans la préservation de l'esprit de l'indien peau-rouge," in *Frithjof Schuon*, ed. Bernard Chevilliat, p. 190. The White Buffalo Woman is central to the Lakota foundation myth, bringing to the Native Americans their first sacred pipe.

8. Schuon, *Erinnerungen und Betrachtungen*, p. 166.

9. Schuon, *Erinnerungen und Betrachtungen*, p. 169.

10. Schuon, *Erinnerungen und Betrachtungen*, pp. 141–42.

11. Schuon, *Erinnerungen und Betrachtungen*, pp. 167 and 169.

12. Schuon, *Erinnerungen und Betrachtungen*, pp. 173–83, supplemented by Bernadette Rigal-Cellard, "La religion des sioux oglalas" in *Le facteur religieux an Amérique du Nord: Religion et groupes ethniques au Canada et aux Etats-Unis*, ed. J. Beranger and P. Guillaume (Bordeaux: CNRS, 1984), pp. 248–51, and J. Vahid Brown, e-mail, December 2002.

13. Schuon, *Erinnerungen und Betrachtungen*, p. 180.

14. Schuon, *Erinnerungen und Betrachtungen*, p. 200.

15. Schuon, *Erinnerungen und Betrachtungen*, pp. 9,190–91, and 212–59.

16. Schuon, *Erinnerungen und Betrachtungen*, p. 9.

17. Schuon, *Erinnerungen und Betrachtungen*, p. 264.

18. Schuon, *Erinnerungen und Betrachtungen*, p. 265.

19. Schuon, *Erinnerungen und Betrachtungen*, p. 263.

20. Schuon, *Erinnerungen und Betrachtungen*, p. 266.

21. Schuon, *Erinnerungen und Betrachtungen*, p. 295.

22. Schuon, *Erinnerungen und Betrachtungen*, pp. 272 and 266.

23. Schuon, *Erinnerungen und Betrachtungen*, p. 268.

24. Henri Hartung, *Présence de Ramana Maharshi* (1979; Paris: Dervy livres, 1987), p. 44.

25. In 1967 Schuon and his party missed the boat they had been intending to take to Tangier and so decided to go through Spain and take the boat from there. On the way they visited the renowned "Macarena" Virgin in Seville, to whom Schuon ascribed the untroubled remainder of the journey. *Erinnerungen und Betrachtungen*, p. 274.

26. Aymard, "Frithjof Schuon," pp. 53–54.

27. Schuon, *Erinnerungen und Betrachtungen*, p. 153.

28. The words are those not of Schuon but of Aymard, "Frithjof Schuon," p. 50.

29. Jean-Baptiste Aymard, e-mail, February 2003.

30. Aymard says that the paintings were never used for meditation (e-mail), but various Maryami sources strongly suggest that they were at least an informal focus for meditation.

31. Lings, reporting Schuon. Lings, "Frithjof Schuon. Un regard autobiographique," in *Frithjof Schuon*, ed. Chevilliat, p. 85.

32. Aymard, "Frithjof Schuon," pp. 53 and 58.

33. In fact, it is Abraham who is commonly used as the figure who unites all three monotheistic religions, since Abraham has an approximately equal status in all three. The Virgin Mary has no place in Judaism, even though the house of David does. There is no established "hierarchy of women" in Islam, and if there were, the more obvious candidates for occupying its summit would be Hagar (Abraham's wife, in Islam), or in more recent times Fatima, the daughter of the Prophet Muhammad, or perhaps his wife Aysha. That some Turkish Muslims venerate Mary at Ephesus says nothing much about Muslim attitudes toward the Virgin Mary as a whole: Turkish popular Islam is much influenced by Alevism, which incorporated the Christian cult of the Virgin and differs in so many ways from Sunni and Shi'i Islam that it would be considered an entirely separate religion were it not that such a classification would have very difficult implications for relations between Turkey's sizable Alevi minority and the Sunni majority.

34. "Concerning the Paintings," typed text, undated. Its author might also be Patricia Estelle (pseud., discussed later).

35. By the time of Schuon's death there were some 1,200 such texts in circulation. For dates and collection, Aymard, e-mail. Aymard describes the texts not as "canonical" (my phrase) but as "méthodiques."

36. Description from my own review of a selection of these texts.

37. For the justification, "Points of Reference," c. 1985, unsigned and undated document in the hand of Catherine Schuon. For the facts, various informants. For the date, A5, interview (see list before bibliography).

38. Names were provided by various informants and are consistent. Since the women thus linked to Schuon are in most cases still alive, and in some cases have children, no good purpose would be served by the publication of these details, however.

39. Burckhardt to "Abd al-Hayy," August 4, 1957.

40. Seyyed Hossein Nasr, "Intellectual Autobiography." *The Philosophy of Seyyed Hossein Nasr*, ed. Lewis E. Hahn (Chicago: Open Court, 2001), p. 4, and various informants in Iran. Where no other source is given, information such as this is common knowledge in Iran and derives from various informants who have confirmed each other.

41. Nasr himself writes that he was sent to America to get away from a household dominated by the weakening health of his father, who had been seriously injured in an accident and died shortly after Nasr left for America (Nasr, "Intellectual Autobiography," pp. 10–11). These circumstances explain why Nasr's parents might have thought that he would be better off away from home, but they do not explain why he was sent on what in 1945 was a long and difficult trip to America.

42. Nasr, "Intellectual Autobiography," pp. 16–19, and Nasr, interview.

43. Adnan Aslan, *Religious Pluralism in Christian and Islamic Philosophy: The Thought of John Hick and Seyyed Hossein Nasr* (Richmond, Surrey [U.K.]: Curzon, 1998), p. 15.

44. "In Quest of the Eternal Sophia," in *Philosophes critiques d'eux-mêmes / Philosophische Selbstbetrachtungen*, ed. André Mercier and Suilar Maja (Bern: Peter Lang, 1980), p. 115. Quoted in Aslan, *Religious Pluralism*, p. 16.

45. Nasr, "Intellectual Autobiography," p. 27.

46. "Islamic philosophy" as thus used is essentially *hikma dhawqiyya*, "sapiential philosophy," a term taken from Suhrawardi, who distinguished "sapiential philosophy" from "discursive philosophy." The essence of Suhrawardi's distinction is that sapiential philosophy approaches the divine, whereas discursive or Aristotelian philosophy does not. For Suhrawardi, a true *arif* (knower of God) needed both varieties. For the distinction, A'avani interview.

47. "Conceptions of Nature and Methods Used for its Study by the Ikhwan al-Safa, al-Biruni, and Ibn Sina," 1958.

48. For Nasr's teachers, see AN 1. Ali Tabandeh, *Hurshid tabande* (Tehran: Haqiqat, 1998), pp. 46, 48, 51–53, 65–75, 80–82, and 87.

49. New York: Praeger, 1966; London: Allen & Unwin, 1968; New York: Schroder Books, 1972.

50. Between 1964 and 1968 Harvard University Press published Nasr's doctoral thesis, as *An Introduction to Islamic Cosmological Doctrines: Conceptions of Nature and Methods Used for Its Study by the Ikhwan al-Safa, al-Biruni, and Ibn Sina* (1964), and two other important books, *Three Muslim Sages: Avicenna, Suhrawardi, Ibn Arabi* (1964) and *Science and Civilization in Islam* (1968). All three of these books were significant works of scholarship and have subsequently been reprinted and republished a number of times in English; *Science and Civilization in Islam* has also been translated into French and Italian. They were preceded by some minor works in Persian: *Ahamiyat-i tahqiq dar falsafah-'i Islam dar 'asr-i hazir* [Importance of Studying Islamic Philosophy Today] Tehran: S.N., 196–?, *Vujud va takassur-i an* [Being and its Polarization] Tehran: Daniskkadah-i Adabiyat, 196–? The Persian translations of the three books were published as follows: *An Introduction to Islamic Cosmological Doctrines* immediately, *Three Muslim Sages* in 1967, and *Science and Civilization in Islam* in 1972.

51. Some interviewees report that Nasr's wife was a personal friend of the empress.

52. A2, interview (see list before bibliography). Where no other source is given, information on the academy derives from this source.

53. Nasr, Preface, *Sophia Perennis* 1, no. 1 (1975), 7.

54. In 1975 the shah even replaced Iran's long-established Islamic *hijri* calendar, which counted years from the Prophet Muhammad's establishment of the first Islamic polity in Medina, with one that counted years from the accession of Cyrus the Great in 559 B.C. The use of *falsafah* (philosophy) rather than *hikma* in the academy's title was probably due to the same reason.

55. Nasrullah Purjavadi, for example, was a Ni'matollahi (interview).

56. The leading authority after his own teacher, Tabataba'i, with whom Nasr had himself studied. Ali Tabandeh, *Hurshid tabande*, p. 97, and A'avani, interview.

57. Yahya Alawi, interview.

58. Corbin was the successor to Massignon at the Ecole Pratique des Hautes Etudes of the Sorbonne. He had been working on Suhrawardi since 1939, in Istanbul initially and after the Second World War, then in Paris and Iran, and later on Mulla Sadra. Steven M Wasserstrom, *Religion after Religion: Gershom Scholem, Mircea Eliade, and Henry Corbin at Eranos* (Princeton, N.J.: Princeton University Press, 1999), pp. 146–47. He published a translation of Mulla Sadra's *Kitab al-mashazir* in 1964.

59. Wasserstrom, *Religion after Religion*, p. 42, for Eliade's participation. Mircea Eliade, "Some Notes on *Theosophia perennis*: Ananda K. Coomaraswamy and Henry Corbin" [Review of Roger Lipsey, *Coomaraswamy*, 3 vols., Princeton, N.J.: Princeton University Press, 1977], *History of Religions* 19 (1979), 173–76, esp. 173.

60. Antoine Faivre, interview. This view was supported by other informants. For the parallels, see especially Henry Corbin, "The Force of Traditional Philosophy in Iran Today," *Studies in Comparative Religion* 2 (1968), 12–26.

61. Nasr, "Intellectual Autobiography," p. 50.

62. A'avani, interview.

63. Pierre Lory, interview.

64. The opening address, delivered by the Empress Farah, was printed in *Sophia Perennis* 1, no. 2 (Autumn 1975). Many participants in conferences of this sort, of course, completely ignore the set theme.

65. While the size of the Iranian Maryamiyya is not certain, it may not have exceeded 12 persons, though one estimate puts its membership after the Revolution as high as 70.

66. With the possible exception of an early work in Persian, *Ahamiyat-i tahqiq dar falsafah-'i Islami dar 'asr-i hazir* [The Importance of Studying Islamic Philosophy Today], published in the 1960s, which I have not located or read.

67. List in *Sophia Perennis* 1, no. 2 (Autumn 1975), 133–38.

68. These comments are based on a review of the first six issues.

69. Muhammad Legenhausen, interview.

70. He on occasion recommended Guénon (whom he compared to Max Planck) to his followers. Shariati, "A Glance at Tomorrow's History" [online]. Available http://www.shariati.com/tomorrow/tomorrow1.html and http://www.shariati.com/tomorrow/tomorrow2.html [April 2001], and Ali Rahnema, *An Islamic Utopian: A Political Biography of Ali Shariati* (London: I. B. Tauris, 1998), p. 161.

71. He never attacked Shariati in writing but frequently spoke critically of him (Soroush, interview).

72. Soroush, interview.

73. Julian Baldick, review of Tabatabazi, *Shi'ite Islam* (London: Allen & Unwin, 1976), *Times Literary Supplement*, April 30, 1976, p. 526.

74. Actually, "head of the Empress's Private Bureau." Nasr became involved in high politics almost by accident—see his "Intellectual Autobiography," p. 72. For one of Nasr's diplomatic missions, see Parviz C. Radji, *In the Service of the Peacock Throne: The Diaries of the Shah's Last Ambassador to London* (London: Hamish Hamilton, 1983), p. 270.

75. Nasr, "Intellectual Autobiography," p. 72.

8. AMERICA

1. In Switzerland: Lausanne, Basel, and Geneva. In France: Reims and Nancy. In England: London. In Argentina: Buenos Aires. In America: Bloomington, Berkeley, and Washington D.C.

2. For Borella, various sources. For Rama Coomaraswamy, A5, interview (see list before bibliography); e-mails.

3. A5 and A7, interviews (see list before bibliography).

4. Since many of these are still teaching, it would not be helpful to specify their names or institutions.

5. James H. Forest, *Living with Wisdom: A Life of Thomas Merton* (Maryknoll, N.Y.: Orbis, 1991), pp. 6–16.

6. Aldous Huxley's *Ends and Means* turned his attention to mysticism, Jacques Maritain's *Art and Scholasticism* and the example of Gerard Manley Hopkins confirmed a predilection for Catholicism. Blake was the first subject of Merton's Ph.D. thesis, later replaced by Hopkins. See Forest, *Living with Wisdom*, pp. 47–55, 73, 79 and 90.

7. My thanks to Jean-Baptiste Aymard (e-mail, February 2003) for this suggestion.

8. Forest, *Living with Wisdom*, pp. 125 and 128.

9. Quoted in Forest, *Living with Wisdom*, p. 118.

10. Sidney H. Griffith, "Merton, Massignon, and the Challenge of Islam" in *Merton & Sufism: The Untold Story*, ed. Rob Baker and Gray Henry (Louisville, Ky.: Fons Vitae, 1999), pp. 59 and 68.

11. Rob Baker, "Merton, Marco Pallis, and the Traditionalists" in *Merton & Sufism*, ed. Baker and Henry, pp. 203–5.

12. Quoted in Baker, "Merton, Marco Pallis," p. 204.

13. Blake, who had been very important to Merton (see n. 6) and was also a perennialist.

14. Baker, "Merton, Marco Pallis," p. 195, and Forest, *Living with Wisdom*, pp. 126 and 173.

15. Baker, "Merton, Marco Pallis," pp. 217–19.

16. Merton, journal entry for June 16, 1966, *The Journals of Thomas Merton*, vol. 6: *Learning to Love*, ed. Christine M. Bochen (San Francisco: Harper San Francisco, 1997), quoted in Baker, "Merton, Marco Pallis," pp. 220–21.

17. Baker, "Merton, Marco Pallis," p. 223. According to William Stoddart (e-mail, February 2003), there was no Merton-Schuon correspondence.

18. Seyyed Hossein Nasr, "What Attracted Merton to Sufism," in *Merton & Sufism*, ed. Baker and Henry, p. 9.

19. The quotations and itinerary are from Forest, *Living with Wisdom*, pp. 201–7. The speculations are entirely mine. Forest was aware neither of Merton's interest in Traditionalism nor of the existence of the Traditionalist movement.

20. Forest, *Living with Wisdom*, pp. 208–25. Of course, had there been anything unusual about the circumstances of Merton's death, many of his colleagues at the conference might have felt obliged to conceal that fact.

21. Harper Collins estimate on the 1991 paperback cover. *The Religions of Man* grew out of a successful 17-part television series of the same name, broadcast on Na-

tional Educational Television in 1955. Diane Hue Balay, "Can a 76-Year-Old Retired Minister Become a Media Star?" (March 21, 1996), online at *UMR Communications*. Available http://www.umr.org/HThust.htm. [May 18, 2000].

22. G. McLeod Bryan, *Voices in the Wilderness: Twentieth-Century Prophets Speak to the New Millennium* (Macon, Ga.: Mercer University Press, 1999), p. 101.

23. Huston Smith, "Bubble Blown and Lived In: A Theological Autobiography," *Dialog* 33, No. 4 (Fall 1994), 276–77.

24. Bryan, *Voices*, p. 101.

25. Smith, "Bubble Blown," p. 275.

26. Smith, introduction to *The Transcendent Unity of Being* by Schuon (New York: Harper & Row, 1975), pp. ix–xi; Smith, "Bubble Blown," p. 276, and fax, July 29, 2001.

27. Smith, "Bubble Blown," p. 277.

28. Smith, "Bubble Blown," p. 278.

29. Smith, "Bubble Blown," p. 279.

30. Mary Rourke, "Our Culture, Our Beliefs, Our Responsibilities: Explorer of the World's Spirituality," *Los Angeles Times*, July 21, 1999, p. E 1+, and Marilyn Snell, "The World of Religions according to Huston Smith," *Mother Jones* 22, No. 5 (November–December 1997), 40–43.

31. Bryan, *Voices*, and Snell, "World of Religions."

32. This is the view of Gene R. Thursby (e-mail, May 19, 2000); I did not myself hear the address.

33. Smith, "Bubble Blown," p. 278.

34. Transcripts available online at http://www.intuition.org/fxv/smith.htm, smith2.htm, and smith3.htm [May 2001].

35. See my "Decade analysis" at http://www.traditionalists.org/bibliog/anal1 .htm#Decade.

36. Why this should be the case is a mystery. The number of Jews becoming Traditionalists seems roughly in proportion with the composition of the populations of the countries concerned. See, however, discussion of Rabbi Léon Askénazi in chapter 10.

37. See my "Traditionalist Writings" at http://www.traditionalists.org/bibliog/ gwrite.html.

38. Marcia Z. Nelson, "Islamic Publishing Is Poised for Growth,"*Publishers Weekly*, November 13, 2000, supplemented from catalogs, interviews, and various other sources.

39. "Moslems: East Comes West," *The Economist*, April 3, 1976, p. 30. For Mahmud, contemporary photographs. For Queen Elizabeth opening the festival, Stoddart, e-mail; the *Economist* report says only that she opened one of the exhibitions.

40. For finances, Alistair Duncan (once secretary of the trust), fax, January 31, 2000. The UAE government gave £1,250,000 (about $15 million at 2000 prices), and the governments of six other Muslim countries together contributed a further £600,000. For the trustees, Duncan, *World of Islam Festival Trust 1973–1983* (London: privately printed, n.d.). For Beeley, Obituary of Sir Harold Beeley, *Daily Telegraph* [London], July 31, 2001.

41. "If there could be said to be a single man who stands for, and indeed to a large extent inspired, the *batin* of the Festival, it is Frithjof Schuon." Peter Lamborn

Wilson, "The World of Islam," *Sophia Perennis* [Tehran] 2, no. 2 (Autumn 1976), 108. Of all the commentators on the festival in London, only the novelist Doris Lessing seems to have spotted that many offerings came "from a similar stable." Doris Lessing, "The Ones Who Know" [Review article], *Times Literary Supplement*, April 30, 1976, p. 515.

42. Wilson, "The World of Islam," p. 109. See also Michael Levey, "The Twin Pillars of Islam," *Times Literary Supplement*, April 30, 1976, p. 518.

43. *Times Literary Supplement*, April 30, 1976.

44. For these, see Christian Bonaud, *L'Imam Khomeyni, un gnostique méconnu de XXe siècle* (Beirut: Al-Bouraq, 1997).

45. See my "Schuonian Writers: Biographic analysis" at http://www.traditionalists.org/bibliog/bibindx.htm.

46. Islam is commonly presented to the Western public either by self-consciously "modern" Muslims or by political activists. The "modern" Muslims often adopt a somewhat apologetic tone, frequently trying to justify Islamic practices in terms of contemporary social science or—in severe cases—in terms of natural science. These spokespeople are generally not found to be very impressive—the apologetic tone is noted, and the rationalizations are dismissed as self-serving. They do not, however, commonly evoke actual hostility, which is the usual effect of radical Islamists, who seem to be angry with everybody—so everybody gets angry with them in return.

47. This approach is somewhat ironic, given the general Traditionalist emphasis on the esoteric/exoteric distinction, but it was the consequence of the emphasis on the esoteric.

48. These comments are based on my own experience of the consequences of assigning some of these articles to undergraduate classes.

49. Anonymous correspondent, e-mail, May 2001.

50. James W. Morris, "Ibn ʿArabî in the 'Far West': Visible and Invisible Influences," *Journal of the Muhyiddin Ibn ʿArabi Society*, 29 (2001), 87–122. The quotations are taken from a prepublication lecture version of this article.

51. Frithjof Schuon, *Erinnerungen und Betrachtungen* ([Switzerland]: privately printed, 1974), p. 295.

52. These interpretations are strongly resisted by Aymard (e-mail), but are suggested by the last few pages of Schuon's *Erinnerungen und Betrachtungen*. Schuon has written repeatedly of the various stages of his life, and he ends his memoirs by speculating that in 1973 (when he was writing that book) a new stage might be beginning. In this connection he mentions two events. One was a conference in Houston, Texas, where Léo Schaya presented a paper drawing attention to a relationship between the activities of the Maryamiyya and the eschatological function of Elijah—here Schuon is at the least quoting with approval an implicit comparison between him and Elijah. The other event was the visit of a German *sadhu* from Sri Lanka, which he interprets in connection with a dream he had in the 1940s in which he was fused with Kali; he clearly sees much significance in this dream. Schuon, *Erinnerungen und Betrachtungen*, pp. 302–4.

53. Schuon, letter of December 19, 1980, to Léo Schaya, in which Schuon comments that "the human instrument for the manifestation of the *Religio Perennis* at the

end of time had to be a Westerner." He can hardly have been referring to any Westerner but himself.

54. Published in *Studies in Comparative Religion* 12 (1978), 131–75.

55. Schuon to Hans Küry, May 15, 1981, and Schuon to unidentified follower,
April 29, 1989, quoted in Jean-Baptiste Aymard, "Frithjof Schuon (1907–1998). Connaissance et voie d'intériorité. Approche biographique," in *Frithjof Schuon, 1907–1998:
Etudes et témoignages,* ed. Bernard Chevilliat (Avon: Connaissance des Religions,
1999), p. 59.

56. Three contemporary Schuonians, e-mails, February 2003.

57. Frithjof Schuon, "Quelques critiques," in *René Guénon* [Dossier H], ed. Pierre-
Marie Sigaud (Lausanne: L'Age d'Homme, 1984), pp. 57 and 80.

58. Schuon, "Quelques critiques," p. 57.

59. The last issue describes itself as "93rd year," but Philippe Encausse gives
1890 as the date of the first issue. Encausse, *Papus, le "Balzac de l'occultisme": vingt-
cinq années d'occultisme occidental* (Paris: Pierre Belfond, 1979), p. 31. Perhaps the discrepancy is due to the years during which publication was suspended, such as during
the Second World War.

60. André Braire, interview.

61. Richard B. Forsaith, interview, and other informants.

62. Forsaith, interview.

63. For the fact of the sign, Catherine Schuon, "Frithjof Schuon: Memories and
Anecdotes," *Sacred Web* 8 (1992), 59.

64. In a letter of October 19, 1980, Schuon explained to Léo Schaya that the
move was "a question of moving away from the *Religio formalis* [presumably Islam] by
virtue of moving towards the *Religio perennis.*" The alternative explanation was given,
for example, by Nasr (interview).

65. Forsaith, interview.

66. Harald von Meyenburg, interview.

67. A7, interview (see list before bibliography).

68. Forsaith and A5 (see list before bibliography), interviews.

69. Forsaith, interview.

70. Forsaith, interview; Mark Koslow, "Black Elk, Joseph Epes Brown and the
Schuon Cult" (unpublished typescript, private collection); A7, interview (see list before
bibliography); and Jean-Paul Schneuwly, interview. Schuon "married" Estelle in about
1989, having "married" his second "vertical" wife in 1974 (A5, interview, see list before bibliography).

71. Michael Fitzgerald, "Frithjof Schuon: Providence without Paradox," *Sacred
Web* 8, 2002.

72. Forsaith, A7 (see list before bibliography), and Schneuwly, interviews.

73. For the use of *pneumatikos,* four undated short texts of Schuon: 1034, 1035,
1082, and "Au sujet d'une personnalité pneumatique." For the use of *avatar* and for
one interpretation of *pneumatikos,* von Meyenburg, interview, and von Meyenburg,
fax, July 2002. For the less dramatic interpretation of *pneumatikos,* Aymard, e-mail,
and Stoddart, e-mail.

74. Catherine Schuon, "Frithjof Schuon: Memories and Anecdotes," *Sacred Web*
8 (1992), 43–46.

75. Schuon, numbered paper dated 1981, quoted in Fitzgerald, "Frithjof Schuon."

76. Forsaith, interview. According to Stoddart, "he sang chiefly Arabic *qasidas.* For a time he added an Indian chant" (e-mail).

77. Some informants specify the Rite of the Sacred Pipe and the Sun Dance, while others deny that these were performed but are not explicit about what actually took place during the "Indian Days." Yellowtail had a close relationship with Inverness Farms—he regarded all followers of Schuon as automatically members of the Crow tribe—but he was still an outsider, according to some informants.

78. Forsaith, interview; Mark Koslow, "Schuon and Thomas Yellowtail" (unpublished typescript, private collection); and photographs of Indian Days in a private collection.

79. A8 (see list before bibliography), letter to Koslow, undated, probably from 1995. The description of S. E. Lambert (untitled sworn declaration, October 9, 1992) coincides with A8's. The description of Mark Koslow ("Schuon and Thomas Yellowtail," "Evidence of the Involvement of Children," unpublished typescripts, private collection) suggests a somewhat larger and more ritualized gathering. Other Schuonians suggest that these accounts were all orchestrated by critics of the group.

80. Schuon, "Beauty," text no. 1018.

81. Schuon, "Beauty's Requirement," text no. 316.

82. Forsaith, interview confirmed by A7 (interview, see list before bibliography).

83. Schuon, "Au sujet du Gouvernement de la Tarîqah," handwritten text, undated.

84. Forsaith, interview. As was said in chapter 4, other Alawis have disagreed, supporting Schuon's *ijaza.*

85. A7, interview (see list before bibliography).

86. Connor (another letter), Lambert (declaration), and A5 (interview, see list before bibliography).

87. *State of Indiana v. Frithjof Schuon,* Indictment, Monroe Circuit Court, filed October 11, 1991. Also Mark Koslow, interview, confirmed by Sergeant (retired) Jim Richardson, interview.

88. Kurt Van der Dussen, "Schuon Indictments Dropped," *The Herald-Times* [Bloomington], November 21, 1991, p. 1.

89. Kurt Van der Dussen, "Prosecutor Explains Reasons for Dropping Case," *The Herald-Times* [Bloomington], November 21, 1991, p. A9.

90. Richardson, interview; Koslow, "Schuon and Thomas Yellowtail."

91. "Information on Indictments of Frithjof Schuon," press release, November 21, 1999.

92. Indiana Code 35–42–4–3 and 35–42–4–8.

93. Koslow, interview.

94. Robert Miller, the country prosecutor, quoted in Robert Niles, "Charges Dropped against Schuon," *Indiana Daily Student,* November 21, 1991, p. 1.

95. The marine contract of conditional sale had been given as part security for a $12,000 loan to Vidali (Judgment, *Stanley Jones v. Aldo Vidali,* Case B118448, California Municipal Court, County of San Diego, El Cajon Judicial District, October 22, 1993). Vidali's son Ari acquired a one-third interest in the *Arcadaldo* in 1982; Vidali then sold the boat in about 1992 (Order, *Ari Vidali v. Aldo Vidali,* Case 654460, Cali-

fornia Superior Court, County of San Diego, San Diego Judicial District, December 1992).

96. Ziauddin Sardar, "A Man for All Seasons," *Impact International*, December 1993, pp. 33–36.

97. Contempt Order, *Michael Pollack and Sharlyn Romaine v. Aldo Vidali*, Case 92–1060 S, US District Court for the Southern District of California, October 26, 1992.

98. Von Meyenburg, interview.

99. Catherine Schuon, "Frithjof Schuon," p. 60.

100. The leadership passed on Schuon's instructions to two senior Maryamis; Estelle's influence waned after she remarried. A6 (see list before bibliography), e-mails, 2002.

101. I have not seen the fence myself, but it was reported by a colleague who drove to Inverness Farms in 2002. For the open discussion of the Maryamiyya, see many of the more recent articles used for this book, or visit www.worldwisdom.com.

102. Catherine Schuon, "Frithjof Schuon," p. 45.

103. "Lettre de S. Ibrâhîm à un accusateur marocain," c. 1978.

104. Little would be gained by retelling here the often moving stories of such people.

105. Forsaith, interview.

106. Danner to Forsaith, October 20, 1988.

107. Patrick Ringgenberg, "Frithjof Schuon: Paradoxes et Providence," *Sacred Web* 7, 2001. The quotation is taken from the French manuscript rather than the published English translation.

108. Forsaith, interview.

109. Smith, "Bubble Blown," p. 277.

9. TERROR IN ITALY

1. Gianfranco De Turris, *Elogio e difesa di Julius Evola: Il Barone e i terroristi* (Rome: Edizioni Méditerranée, 1997), pp. 50, 52, 59, 61.

2. EM [pseud.], "Sobre los 'años de plomo': las estrategias políticas en Italia," address to "Las Jornadas sobre el MSI," online at *Disidencias OnLine/Press*. Available http://members.es.tripod.de/disidentes/arti33.htm [October 23, 2001].

3. De Turris, *Elogio e difesa*, pp. 51–52.

4. EM, "Años de plomo."

5. Franco Ferraresi, *Minacce alla democrazia: La Destra radicale e la strategia della tensione in Italia nel dopoguerra* (Milan: Feltrinelli, 1995), p. 109. I have relied extensively on this work for information. My interpretations, however, often differ significantly from those of Dr. Ferraresi.

6. Ferraresi, *Minacce alla democrazia*, pp. 112–13.

7. Human sacrifice is thought by scholars to have been practiced by the Etruscans but not the Romans.

8. H. T. Hansen, "Die 'magische' Gruppe von Ur in ihrem Historischen und esoterischen Umfeld," in Julius Evola, *Schritte zur Initiation* (Bern: Scherz-Ansata, 1997); Renato Del Ponte, "Le correnti della tradizione pagana romana in Italia," *Agiza*

7 [c. 1996], online at http://utenti.tripod.it/centrostudilaluna/delponte.htm [May 17 2000]; and Claudio Mutti, interview.

9. Ferraresi, *Minacce alla democrazia*, pp. 137, 140–41.

10. Most notably Clemente Graziani, "La Guerra rivoluzionaria," *Ordine Nuovo* 2 (April 1963); 11–27. See Ferraresi, *Minacce alla democrazia*, p. 136.

11. Ferraresi, *Minacce alla democrazia*, pp. 129–31.

12. Ferraresi, *Minacce alla democrazia*, pp. 133–34.

13. Ferraresi, *Minacce alla democrazia*, pp. 127–29.

14. Ferraresi, *Minacce alla democrazia*, pp. 232–34.

15. Ferraresi, *Minacce alla democrazia*, pp. 175–87. Freda's responsibility for the attacks of December 12, 1969, is probable rather than proven beyond doubt, but his group's responsibility for other attacks with similar objectives is more or less clear.

16. Ferraresi, *Minacce alla democrazia*, pp. 175–81. The cause of this fall has never been established, but he presumably jumped or was pushed.

17. Dario Fo, "Morte accidentale di un anarchico" (Turin: Einaudi, 1974).

18. Ferraresi, *Minacce alla democrazia*, p. 173.

19. Ferraresi, *Minacce alla democrazia*, pp. 220–24, 229.

20. Ferraresi, *Minacce alla democrazia*, p. 242.

21. H. T. Hansen, "Der Ritt auf dem Tiger: Anmerkungen zum Buch," in Julius Evola, *Cavalcare la Tigre / Den Tiger reiten* (Engerda: Arun, 1997).

22. Julius Evola, *Cavalcare la Tigre: Orientamenti esistenziali per un'epoca della dissoluzione* (1961; Rome: Edizioni Méditerranée, 1995), pp. 149, 151.

23. Evola, *Cavalcare la Tigre*, pp. 151–52.

24. For example, in Hansen, "Ritt auf dem Tiger." An interesting parallel, which may or may not have occurred to Evola, is the Islamic concept of *hijra* (emigration), fundamental to the more extreme varieties of late twentieth-century political Islam.

25. Ferraresi, *Minacce alla democrazia*, pp. 101, 296, and De Turris, *Elogio e difesa*, p. 99.

26. Ferraresi, *Minacce alla democrazia*, p. 302.

27. There were echoes of Freda in both the organizational method and the apparent objectives of the terrorists who carried out the attacks on America on September 11, 2001.

28. Ferraresi, *Minacce alla democrazia*, pp. 243, 277.

29. Ferraresi, *Minacce alla democrazia*, pp. 287–88, 317–19.

30. Ferraresi, *Minacce alla democrazia*, p. 300. The view is now that it was the right, though the exact group has still not been identified.

31. Ferraresi, *Minacce alla democrazia*, pp. 103, 303–4.

32. Ferraresi, *Minacce alla democrazia*, pp. 277–79, 316–17, 320–24, 338–40.

33. Hansen, "Ritt auf dem Tiger." Hansen's conclusions, however, are the opposite of mine.

34. Henri Hartung, "Rencontres Romaines au milieu des ruines," unpublished manuscript, March 1984, entry for June 25, 1971. Hartung was probably not aware of these groups' involvement in terrorism.

35. Ferraresi, *Minacce alla democrazia*, p. 103. For the significance of Qaddafi, see Nicholas Goodrick-Clarke, *Black Sun: Aryan Cults, Esoteric Nazism, and the Politics of Identity* (New York: New York University Press, 2002), p. 69.

36. Roger Griffin, "Revolts Against the Modern World: The Blend of Literary

and Historical Fantasy in the Italian New Right," *Literature and History* 11 (Spring 1985), 111.

37. See my http://www.traditionalists.org/web/political01.html#Evolians.

38. For the link with Freda, Ferraresi, *Minacce alla democrazia*, p. 195.

39. See http://www.fondazione-evola.it [June 24, 2001].

40. The Alleanza Nazionale groups were the Circolo Azione Giovani in Verona and the Circolo Azione Giovani "René Guénon" Talenti in Rome.

41. Ruotolo Guido, "Il PM di Verona Papalia: 'C'e' un vero pericolo" [interview with Procurator Guido Papalia], *La Stampa*, December 30, 2000, p. 7, and Margret Chatwin, "Fronte Nazionale," July 29, 2001, *Informationsdienst gegen Rechtsextremismus* [online]. Available http://www.idgr.de/lexikon/stich/f/fronte-nazionale/fronte-n .html [October 23, 2001].

42. Chatwin, "Fronte," on the basis of reports in *Il Secolo XIX* (July 25, 2001), ascribed to sources in the Italian security services.

43. Claudio Mutti, *Julius Evola sul fronte dell'est* (Parma: All'insegna del Veltro, 1998), pp. 43–55.

44. The groups were Kard-Kerezst-Korona Szövetség, the School of Tradition and Transcendence of Árpád Szigeti, and Apokalipszis Iskolája (School of Apocalypse). Mutti, *Julius Evola sul fronte dell'est*, pp. 48, 53–55, and http://www.euroasta.com/apoka [June 21, 2001]. Mutti does not mention Apokalipszis Iskolája.

45. Mutti, *Julius Evola sul fronte dell'est*, pp. 57–59, and http://www.extra.hu/ tradicio [June 24, 2001]. Hungarian Traditionalism clearly deserves further study, which I myself am not linguistically equipped to perform.

46. Del Ponte, "Correnti della tradizione pagana romana."

47. De Benoist, interview, and reading of some New Right works. For the purely political influence of Evola in England, see Goodrick-Clarke, *Black Sun*, pp. 49–50, 52 and 68–71.

10. EDUCATION

1. Adriana Berger, "Mircea Eliade: Romanian Fascism and the History of Religions in the United States" in *Tainted Greatness: Antisemitism and Cultural Heroes*, ed. Nancy A. Harrowitz (Philadelphia: Temple University Press, 1994), pp. 64–65, and H. T. Hansen, "Mircea Eliade, Julius Evola und die Integrale Tradition," in Julius Evola, *Über das Initiatische* (Sinzheim: AAGW, 1998).

2. Evola wanted Eliade to help get his [Evola's] books published in France, and although Eliade either could or would not help him, Evola translated Eliade's *Shamanism and Archaic Ecstacy Techniques* into Italian, under the pseudonym of Carlo d'Altavilla (Hansen, "Mircea Eliade, Julius Evola").

3. Steven M. Wasserstrom, *Religion after Religion: Gershom Scholem, Mircea Eliade, and Henry Corbin at Eranos* (Princeton, N.J.: Princeton University Press, 1999), pp. 3, 24, and 317–18; Edmund Leach, "Sermons by a Man on a Ladder," *New York Review of Books* 7 (October 20, 1966), 28.

4. Wasserstrom, *Religion after Religion*, p. 153.

5. The student who remembers him as a Traditionalist is William Quinn, whose Traditionalist Ph.D. dissertation Eliade strongly supported. Natale Spineto, "Mircea Eliade and Traditionalism," *Aries* NS 1, no.1 (2001). This dissertation was later pub-

lished as William W. Quinn, *The Only Tradition* (Albany, N.Y.: SUNY Press, 1996). The low profile is reported by another research student, N. J. Girardot, "Smiles and Whispers," in *Changing Religious Worlds: The Meaning and End of Mircea Eliade*, ed. Bryan S. Rennie (Albany, N.Y.: SUNY Press, 2000), pp. 152–53. It seems more in line with other reports. Eliade continued writing novels in Romanian while at Chicago, even though they had no readers other than his wife and a few close friends (Rachela Permenter, "Romantic Postmodernism and the Literary Eliade," *Changing Religious Worlds*, ed. Rennie, pp. 95–116).

6. Karlfried Graf Dürckheim and Alphonse Göttmann, *Dialogue sur le chemin initiatique* (Paris: Cerf, 1979), p. 149. In Berger, "Mircea Eliade," for example, Eliade is described as "deeply interested by the spiritualist theories of anti-Semites such as the Italian Julius Evola and the Frenchman René Guénon." This is a drastic oversimplification.

7. A Chair in his name was also endowed at the University of Chicago in 1985. Berger, "Mircea Eliade," p. 66.

8. See Carl Olson, "Eliade, the Comparative Method, Historical Context, and Difference," in *Changing Religious Worlds*, ed. Rennie, esp. pp. 60–93 and 70–71.

9. This distinction between autonomous and "heteronomous" approaches was made by Eliade's pupil Ioan Petru Culianu, and in the view of Roger Corless, Eliade "was the leader and, in the event, the capstone" of the autonomous approach. See Corless, "Building on Eliade's Magnificent Failure," in *Changing Religious Worlds*, ed. Rennie, pp. 3–9.

10. A judgment as broad as this is, of course, open to dispute, but it is shared by others. Thus: Eliade "more than anyone else at this time in the United States rescued the study of religion not only from a jealous Abrahamic God and a narrow provincial theology . . . but also from the reductive scientistic rationalization of the secular academy" (Girardot, "Smiles and Whispers," p. 149).

11. Rudolf Otto, *Das Heilige* (1917; reprint, Munich: Biederstein, 1947). See Kelley Ross, "Mircea Eliade (1907–1986)," *The Proceedings of the Friesian School*, Fourth Series, 1996– [online] (available http://www.friesian.com/eliade.htm); Ross, "Rudolf Otto (1869–1937)" (available http://www.friesian.com/otto.htm); and Ross, "Jakob Friedrich Fries (1773–1843)" (available http://www.friesian.com/fries.htm).

12. See Bryan S. Rennie, Introduction to *Changing Religious Worlds*, ed. Rennie, pp. ix–xxiv.

13. Douglas Allen, "Mircea Eliade's View of the Study of Religion as the Basis for Cultural and Spiritual Renewal," in *Changing Religious Worlds*, ed. Rennie, p. 208.

14. See Rennie, Introduction.

15. Leach, "Sermons," p. 28.

16. Wasserstrom, *Religion after Religion*, p. 45. Wasserstrom sometimes goes too far, however: to describe the popular writer Louis Pauwels as "another significant influence on Eliade" (p. 77) is putting the cart before the horse. If anything, Eliade influenced Pauwels.

17. To judge, at least, from the general tone of Mircea Eliade, "Some Notes on *Theosophia perennis*: Ananda K. Coomaraswamy and Henry Corbin," *History of Religions* 19 (1979), 167–76.

18. Today there are sections for Islam and for Ethics, groups for Lesbian-Feminist Issues and for Ritual Studies, and seminars for Buddhist Relic Veneration and Swedenborg Issues and Influences.

19. Antoine Faivre, "Presentation du Dossier ['Pérennialisme']," *Aries* 11 (1990), 5–6; Leonard J. Bowman, "Unity that Honors Diversity: Perennialism and Metaphor," *Aries* 12–13 (1990–91), 45; and interviews and e-mails with other scholars involved in the group.

20. Thursby, e-mails, May 2000.

21. Sheldon R. Isenberg and Gene R. Thursby, "Esoteric Anthropology: 'Devolutionary' and 'Evolutionary' Orientations in Perennial Philosophy," *Religious Traditions* 7–9 (1984–86), pp. 177–226.

22. "Esoteric Anthropology: 'Devolutionary' and 'Evolutionary' Orientations in Perennial Philosophy" was published in *Religious Traditions* 7–9 (1984–86), 177–226, and "A Perennial Philosophy Perspective on Richard Rorty's Neo-Pragmatism" in the *International Journal for Philosophy of Religion* 17 (1985), 41–65. Both are available online through http://web.clas.ufl.edu/users/gthursby/pub/.

23. Wouter J. Hanegraaff, "Some Remarks on the Study of Western Esotericism," *Esoterica* 1 (c. 1998), 6, and Bernd Radtke, "Between Projection and Suppression: Some Considerations Concerning the Study of Sufism," in *Shi'a Islam, Sects and Sufism: Historical Dimensions, Religious Practice and Methodological Considerations*, ed. Fred De Jong (Utrecht: M.TH. Houtsma Stichting, 1992), p. 71. Radtke identified the scholars but not the movement from which they came.

24. In fact, initially at the sixth section of the Ecole Pratique des Hautes Etudes, which in 1975 became the Ecole des Hautes Etudes en Sciences Sociales. Marc Gaborieau, "Louis Dumont (1911–1998)," *Journal Asiatique* 287 (1999), 1–2.

25. Louis Dumont, *Homo hierarchicus. Essai sur le système des castes* (Paris: Gallimard, 1966).

26. Louis Dumont, *Essais sur l'individualisme. Une perspective anthropologique sur l'idéologie moderne* (Paris: Du Seuil, 1983). See Roland Lardinois, "Louis Dumont et la science indigène," *Actes de la recherche en sciences sociales* 106–7 (March 1995).

27. Gaborieau, "Louis Dumont," p. 3.

28. Lardinois, "Louis Dumont," pp. 23–34.

29. Marc Gaborieau, personal communication, April 2003.

30. Lardinois, "Louis Dumont," p. 12, n. 5.

31. Lardinois, "Louis Dumont," pp. 25–26. The commentator was writing in *Libération*, November 17, 1983, and is cited by Lardinois.

32. Paul Fenton, "Qabbalah and Academia: The Critical Study of Jewish Mysticism in France," *Shofar: An Interdisciplinary Journal of Jewish Studies* 18, no. 2 (Winter 2000). Fenton identifies the influence of Guénon on Ashkénazi and Gordin but does not examine it in any depth. My thanks to Vahid Brown for drawing Professor Fenton's article to my attention.

33. Léon Askénazi, "L'histoire de ma vie," available online at http://www.manitou .org.il/la_vie.html [June 26, 2003]. Where no other source is given, information comes from this brief autobiography, supplemented from "Portrait: Rav Léon Yehouda Askénazi," available online at http://www.col.fr/fsju/education/manitou.htm [February 18, 1999], and "Biographie," available online at http://www.manitou.org.il/ biographie.htm [June 26, 2003].

34. He was initially recruited as a student, but quickly became a teacher.

35. Askénazi, "L'histoire de ma vie."

36. Elyakim Simsovic, e-mail exchange, June 2003. Simsovic was a close follower of Askénazi who sometimes taught his lessons for him when Askénazi was ill

toward the end of his life. He and Askénazi discussed Guénon on a number of occasions.

37. Paul Fenton, e-mails, June 2003.

38. Charles Mopsik, "Quelques échos de la cabale dans la pensée française du vingtième siècle," *Journal des Études de la Cabale* 1 (1997), online at http://www.chez .com/jec2/artmop.htm [June 26, 2003].

39. After his emigration to Israel, Askénazi remained in close contact with France, and he also established a Mayanot Institute in Jerusalem, somewhat on the model of the Gilbert Bloch School. This was replaced in 1983 with a network of Jewish Study Centers (Yaïr) for the teaching of orthodox Judaic culture to Jews of modern Western background.

40. Fenton, e-mails, June 2003.

41. Comments based on Simsovic, e-mails, and on review of websites connected with Askénazi.

42. Fenton, e-mails.

43. Mopsik, "Quelques échos de la cabale." See Benamozegh, *Israël et l'humanité* (Paris, 1885). Simsovic disagrees somewhat with Mopsik's reading of Benamozegh (e-mails).

44. Simsovic, e-mails.

45. Askénazi, "L'histoire de ma vie."

46. Simsovic, e-mails.

47. Sylvie Hartung, interview, and G. Engelhard, "Sciences humaines, une formule nouvelle de l'enseignement supérieure," *Réforme*, September 1953, p. 3.

48. IBM France newsletters for 1957, "Préparer les jeunes cadres à accéder à de plus hauts emplois," *Figaro*, January 17, 1956, and "L'institut des sciences humaines ouvre une nouvelle section," *Le Monde*, January 24, 1956, p. 7.

49. Jean Sénard, "Pour se cultiver : d'abord savoir couper le téléphone," *Figaro Littéraire*, February 24, 1962; Jean Papillon, "1953–1963: L'Institut des sciences et techniques humaines à dix ans" (n.p., n.d.), and other contemporary press reports.

50. To judge from one videotape of him speaking (collection of Sylvie Hartung).

51. The Loi sur la formation professionnelle continue. Henri Hartung, *Le temps de la rupture: éducation permanente et autogestion* (Neuchatel [Switzerland]: A la Braconnière, 1975), p. 23.

52. Including *Le Monde, Le Figaro, France-Soir,* and *L'Express.*

53. Hartung, *Pour une éducation permanente* (Paris: Fayard, 1966), p. 12.

54. Sénard, "Pour se cultiver."

55. Henri Hartung, "Rencontres Romaines au milieu des ruines," unpublished manuscript, March 1984.

56. Hartung, "Rencontres Romaines," May 14, 1965.

57. Numbers from Jean Papillon, "Rencontre université-entreprises pour l'anniversaire de l'Association des sciences et techniques humaines," *Le Figaro*, January 13–14, 1968.

58. Henri Hartung, *Ces princes du management: le patronat français face a ses responsabilités* (Paris: Fayard, 1970), p. 11.

59. Sylvie Hartung, interview. Where no other source is given, information on Henri or Sylvie Hartung comes from Sylvie Hartung.

60. Hartung, *Princes du management,* p. 12.

61. Hartung, *Princes du management,* p. 116.

62. He continued to believe that May 1968 had been an appropriate response to the alienation of the individual produced by the forces of the modern world, a response that was for once collective rather than merely individual, but he regretted that it had quickly been taken over by established structures that used it to their own ends—politicians, trades unions, politicized students, and the like. Sylvie Hartung, interview.

63. Hartung, "Rencontres Romaines."

64. Hartung, "Rencontres Romaines."

65. Hartung, *Princes du management,* p. 12.

66. Henri Hartung, *Spiritualité et autogestion* (Lausanne: L'Age d'Homme, 1978), p. 144.

67. The distinction is made later, in Henri Hartung, *Ici et maintenant* (Laval: Siloe, 1989), p. 30.

68. Various contemporary press reports.

69. Official English translation of Hartung's address. Typescript.

70. Comments based on review of Hartung's own file of reviews.

71. Hartung, *Princes du management,* p. 92.

72. *L'Humanité* June 22, 1970.

73. Jean Vuilleumier, *Tribune de Genève,* April 22, 1970.

74. *Entreprise,* April 11, 1970.

75. Comte de Paris to Hartung, March 25, 1970.

76. He took the order from a "Sidi Abdallah al-Alawi," who is otherwise unknown. Yves Camicas and Claude Camicas, *Les gens du blâme: une secte au quotidien* (Milan: Archè, 1995), p. 37.

77. Camicas and Camicas, *Gens du blâme,* p. 11 and passim. Where no other source is given, information derives from *Gens du blâme.* This is a problematic source, since it is a revised version of an account that was originally written as a novel and is an attack on de Séligny by two former followers. It is a work of definite literary merit and a revealing insight into what is popularly called the "cult mentality." Accounts of "cults" by hostile ex-followers are notoriously unreliable as evidence, however, and the paucity of corroborating evidence means that the account that follows must be regarded as provisional. Especially provisional is the identification I have made of Hocquard with "Joseph" in *Gens du blâme,* since certain details do not match. In other respects, however, such external evidence as I have confirms *Gens du blâme,* which is internally consistent.

78. Camicas and Camicas, *Gens du blâme,* pp. 17–39.

79. Camicas and Camicas, *Gens du blâme,* p. 77.

80. These comments are based on a review of the entire series of *Je suis.*

81. Camicas and Camicas, *Gens du blâme,* pp. 260–73.

82. Henri Le Mire, *Le voleur d'âme: réponse a Beatrice Le Mire* (Paris: Société de production littéraire, 1978), pp. 69–71.

83. Le Mire, *Voleur d'âme,* p. 58.

84. Béatrice Le Mire, *Sauvez-moi, sauvez-moi!* (Paris: Albin Michel, 1977), p. 62.

85. Masthead of *Je Suis,* May 15, 1962.

86. Le Mire, *Sauvez-moi,* passim.

87. Hocquard, *Mozart* (Paris: Du Seuil, 1970), p. 2.

88. Camicas and Camicas, *Gens du blâme*, p. 144.

89. Camicas and Camicas, *Gens du blâme*, pp. 133–34.

90. Le Mire, *Voleur d'âme*, pp. 71, 89.

91. Camicas and Camicas, *Gens du blâme*, p. 400.

92. Le Mire, *Voleur d'âme*, pp. 123–29.

93. Le Mire, *Voleur d'âme*, pp. 131–40; Jean de Rebervilliers, afterward to Camicas and Camicas, *Gens du blâme*, pp. 299–302.

94. De Rebervilliers, afterward, pp. 299–302.

11. EUROPE AFTER 1968

1. Abellio, unlike Pauwels, was taken seriously by the French elite as a novelist, philosopher, and public intellectual. Guénon and Evola were two sources among many for Abellio, along with Foucault and Jung and Steiner, and so Abellio is both a means and a measure of Traditionalism's penetration into general French culture. Antoine Faivre, "Histoire de la notion moderne de Tradition dans ses rapports avec les courants ésotériques (XVe–XXe siècles)," *Aries* vol. hors série, "Symboles et Mythes" (c. 2000), pp. 43–44, and Jean-Pierre Lombard, Avant propos, in *Raymond Abellio* [Cahier de l'Herne], ed. Jean-Pierre Lombard (Paris: Ed. de l'Herne, 1979), pp. 9–10.

2. Louis Pauwels and Jacques Bergier, *Le Matin des magiciens, introduction au réalisme fantastique* (Paris: Gallimard, 1960).

3. Dominique Dhombres, "Louis Pauwels, alchimiste d'une étrange mixture idéologique," *Le Monde*, January 30, 1997.

4. Editorial announcement, *Planète*, January–February 1970, p. 4.

5. Review of *Planète* editions for 1970.

6. Dhombres, "Louis Pauwels."

7. The evidence for this increase is anecdotal, but convincing.

8. Damascene Christensen, *Not of This World: The Life and Teachings of Fr. Seraphim Rose, Pathfinder to the Heart of Ancient Christianity* (Forestville, Cal.: Fr. Seraphim Rose Foundation, 1993), pp. 21, 35–36, 52, 54, and 68.

9. Christensen, *Not of This World*, pp. 70, 79, 81, 98, and 190.

10. Rose, unpublished draft, probably of his incomplete book *The Kingdom of Man and the Kingdom of God*, quoted in Christensen, *Not of This World*, pp. 125–26.

11. Quoted in Christensen, *Not of This World*, p. 651.

12. Christensen, *Not of This World*, pp. 637–44.

13. *Orthodoxy and the Religion of the Future: Can the Orthodox Church Enter a "Dialogue" with Non-Christian Religions?* (Platina, Cal.: Saint Herman of Alaska Brotherhood, 1976); *The Soul after Death: Contemporary After-death Experiences in the Light of the Orthodox Teaching on the Afterlife* (Platina, Cal.: Saint Herman of Alaska Brotherhood, 1980).

14. Christensen, *Not of This World*, passim. For the Russian reception of Rose's books and publications, my thanks to Boris Falikov.

15. Jean-François Mayer, *Confessions d'un chasseur de sectes* (Paris: Cerf, 1990), pp. 27–46.

16. Pierre Assouline, *Les nouveaux convertis: enquête sur des chrétiens, des juifs et des musulmans pas comme les autres* (Paris: Gallimard, 1992), p. 250.

17. Ali Schutz, interview.

18. Abbot Silvano, e-mails, November 1998.

19. In *Foucault's Pendulum* (San Diego: Harcourt Brace Jovanovich, 1989), quotations from a variety of Traditionalist writers are used as chapter epigraphs, and there are numerous other references to Traditionalism. There is even a character who is "interested in joining together again the fragments of a lost Tradition" (p. 433) called Agliè—a name that might easily be inspired by Aguéli. But despite all these references, there is nothing Traditionalist in either the plot or characters of the book. Eco has plundered Western esotericism for stones for his own mosaic.

20. See my http://www.traditionalists.org/web/guenonian.html.

21. Sylvie Hartung, interview.

22. Sylvie Hartung, interview.

23. Martha Biberstein and Bruno Biberstein, "Henri Hartung : pour deux fois formateur d'adultes," unpublished typescript, May 21, 1982.

24. Karlfried Graf Dürckheim and Alphonse Göttmann, *Dialogue sur le chemin initiatique* (Paris: Cerf, 1979), pp. 19–27.

25. Barbara Wood, *E. F. Schumacher: His Life and Thought* (New York: Harper & Row, 1984), pp. 348 and 352. This is a semi-autobiographical account by Schumacher's daughter.

26. E. F. Schumacher, *Small Is Beautiful: Economics as if People Mattered* (1973; New York: Harper & Row, 1989), p. 32.

27. Schumacher, *Small Is Beautiful*, p. 37.

28. Schumacher, *Small Is Beautiful*, pp. 55, 59, and 64.

29. Wood, in *E. F. Schumacher,* is explicit about Gurdjieff, Buddhism, and Catholicism but largely silent on Traditionalism. Schumacher's debt to Traditionalism is very visible, however, in his less well-known *A Guide for the Perplexed* (1977; London: Vintage, 1995), where he describes Guénon as "one of the few significant metaphysicians of our time," p. 135. His library was well stocked with Traditionalist works. See online catalog, available http://www.schumachersociety.org/fritzlib.html [May 24, 2000].

30. Wood, *E. F. Schumacher*, p. 249.

31. Schumacher, *Guide for the Perplexed*, p. 14.

32. Schumacher, *Small Is Beautiful*, pp. 31 and 51.

33. Wood, *E. F. Schumacher*, pp. 221–22.

34. Wood, *E. F. Schumacher*, pp. 300–303.

35. Wood, *E. F. Schumacher*, pp. 352–67.

36. *Blake and Tradition*, Princeton, N.J.: Princeton University Press (Bollingen Series), 1968.

37. Kapila Vatsyayan, "Kathleen Raine Speaks" [interview with Kathleen Raine], *IGNCA [Indira Gandhi National Center for the Arts] Newsletter* 3, no. 3 (October–December 1995), online at IGNCA website, http://ignca.nic.in/nl_00902.htm [June 14, 2001]. See Raine's *Yeats, the Tarot, and the Golden Dawn* (Dublin: Dolmen Press, 1972), and her *Yeats the Initiate: Essays on Certain Themes in the Work of W. B. Yeats* (Savage, Md.: Barnes & Noble Books, 1990).

38. This medal has been awarded annually since 1935, on the recommendation of the poet laureate ("Gilt-edged poets," *Sunday Telegraph*, January 3, 1993, p. 20).

39. Vatsyayan, "Kathleen Raine Speaks."

40. Kathleen Raine, letter to Stephen Overy replying to e-mail from the author, June 15, 2001.

41. Raine herself does not use the phrase in her writing (or at least not frequently enough for me to have encountered it), but this was evidently the conclusion of Margaret Williams, an American graduate student who visited Raine in the mid-1980s, as expressed in Williams's fine poem entitled "Kali Yuga: June 1995," online at *William Butler Yeats Seminar Homepage* (California State University, Northbridge). Available http://www.csun.edu/hceng029/yeats/rainepoem.html [June 2001].

42. Kathleen Raine, "India and the Modern World," speech reprinted in *Lapis* (n.p., n.d.), formerly online at http://www.opencenter.org/lapis/raine.html (taken from Google.com cache).

43. Vatsyayan, "Kathleen Raine Speaks."

44. Vatsyayan, "Kathleen Raine Speaks"; Maggie Parham, "She Will Not Cease from Mental Fight," *The Times* [London], April 18, 1992.

45. He quoted him twice in speeches in 1996. See http://www.princeofwales.gov .uk/speeches [June 2001]. Prince Charles's own position might be described as anti-modernist Jungian-Emersonian universalism. At the opening of his Institute of Architecture he defined "spirit" as "that overwhelming experience of awareness of a oneness with the Natural World, and beyond that, with the creative force that we call God which lies at the central point of all. . . . It is both 'pagan' and Christian, and in this sense is surely the fundamental expression of what we call religion." In the same speech Prince Charles spoke against "scientific rationalism" as "destroying the traditional foundations on which so many of our human values had been based for thousands of years." "The Inauguration of the Prince of Wales's Institute of Architecture," January 1992, available http://www.princeofwales.gov.uk/speeches/architecture _30011992.html [online] (June 24, 2001). Jungianism is confirmed in other sources, e.g., by Commander Richard Aylford, Prince Charles's private secretary, reported in Kate Muir, "The Selling of the Prince of Wales," *The Times* [London] March 30, 1992. The most important difference between Traditionalism and a position such as this is the absence of the element of initiation. It is not known whether or not Prince Charles is a Mason. Family tradition makes it likely that he is, but there is no evidence as to how seriously he takes Masonry or to what variety of lodge (if any) he belongs.

46. Charles, Prince of Wales, Address to the General Assembly of the Church of Scotland, Edinburgh, May 20, 2000. Available http://193.36.68.132/speeches/scotland _20052000.html [June 24, 2001].

47. "Islam and the West," speech given in the Sheldonian Theatre, Oxford, October 27, 1993. Available http://www.princeofwales.gov.uk/speeches/religion_27101993 .html [October 30, 2001].

48. Gervase Webb, "Charles Blasts Lies of Saddam Hussein," *Evening Standard* [London], October 27, 1993, p. 2.

49. VITA was originally established in 1984 as a program within the Royal College of Arts, a prominent London art school—the "Royal" indicates earlier patronage rather than any connection with the present prince of Wales. Critchlow was also involved in the Institute of Architecture as director of studies, and he is also a fellow of the Temenos Academy. He is the key Traditionalist in the Prince's Foundation.

50. VITA website (http://www.princes-foundation.org/foundation/edu-vita.html). Prince of Wales, "Inauguration,"and Eric Broug (VITA MA student), e-mails, September 2001.

51. Comments based a review of back issues, catalogs of recorded lectures for sale, etc.

52. Catalog of recorded lectures for sale.

53. Quoted in Muir, "Selling."

54. Muir, "Selling."

55. "Alice Trent," e-mails, June 27–30, 2001. Where no other source is given, information on Aristasia derives from this correspondence.

56. "Alice Lucy Trent," *The Feminine Universe: A Complete Outline of the Primordial Feminine Essentialist Philosophy* (London: Golden Order Press, n.d.), pp. 8, 30–32, 34–35, 38, 40, and 44.

57. Trent, *Feminine Universe*, pp. 9, 11–14, 27, 44, and 49–50. For early civilizations, Trent cites the work of James Mellaart. For the biological rather than social origins of " 'conventional femininity' " she cites Anne Moir.

58. Trent has never read Evola (e-mail), and bases herself on Guénon, but she has come to some similar conclusions independently.

59. Trent, *Feminine Universe*, pp. 103–11 and 115–25.

60. Trent, "Strangers in Paradise," *Femmeworld Modular Femmefiction* [online]. Available http://www.aristasia.org/femmeworld/Modula.html [June 26, 2001].

61. In 1996, Channel 4 broadcast a documentary on Aristasia.

62. Trent, e-mails.

63. Quoted in Francis Wheen, "A Firm Hand behind Sweethearts," *The Guardian* [London], March 18, 1998, p. 10.

64. Trent, *Feminine Universe*, p. 126.

65. Trent, e-mails.

66. Trent, *Feminine Universe*, p. 122. The "higher power" is defined cautiously by Trent in the "absence of a living feminine tradition" and given "awareness of the dangers of attempting to create or 'revive' one" (Trent, e-mails).

67. Francis Wheen, "The Tortured Past of Miss Martindale," *The Guardian* March, 1, 1995, p. T5.

12. NEO-EURASIANISM IN RUSSIA

Parts of this chapter were originally presented at CESNUR's 14th International Conference, Riga, Latvia, August 29–31, 2000, under the title "Russian Traditionalism."

1. For further comments, see AN 1.

2. Alexander Dugin, interview. Where no other source is given, information derives from Dugin, confirmed from other sources when possible.

3. See AN 2.

4. Gaydar Jamal, interview. According to other sources, he may have attended the Oriental Institute in Moscow and been expelled from it in 1969.

5. Haljand Udam (e-mails, March–June 2000). See AN 3.

6. Jamal joined the branch of the Naqshbandiyya led by Eshon-e Khalifat. Dugin and Jamal, interviews.

7. Caryl Emerson, "The Russians Reclaim Bakhtin," *Comparative Literature* 44 (1992), 415–24.

8. The thesis was on Suhrawardi, one of Nasr's "Islamic philosophers."

9. Udam, e-mails. See AN 4.

10. See AN 5.

11. Dugin found a card in the street and substituted his own photograph for that of the original reader.

12. See AN 6.

13. Udam, e-mails.

14. See AN 7.

15. "Yakovlev Blames KGB for Rise of Fascist Groups" [Interview with Alexander Yakovlev], *Izvestia*, June 17, 1998, p. 5. Translation from *Current Digest of the Post-Soviet Press*. Some sources in the Russian press are taken from this digest. See AN 8.

16. See AN 9.

17. See AN 10.

18. Stephen D. Shenfield, *Russian Fascism: Traditions, Tendencies, and Movements* (New York: ME Sharpe, 2000). My thanks for permission to use a draft chapter from this book

19. Alexander Prokhanov, *Derevo v tsentre Kabula* (Moscow: Sov. pisatel', 1982).

20. For more on Prokhanov, see AN 11.

21. See AN 12.

22. The various Western Traditionalists who sought their valid initiatic tradition in Orthodoxy tacitly support Dugin's view.

23. See Dugin's summary of his book, "La Métaphysique de la Bonne Nouvelle" [online]. Available http://web.redline.ru/arctogai/bies.htm [May 31, 1997]. See AN 13.

24. "Eurasianism" is also used. In fact geopolitics is more of a field of study than a single theory, and it is possible to study geopolitics without subscribing to any of the theories discussed in this chapter. For the sake of simplicity, however, I will use "Geopolitics" to denote what might be called the Mackinder-Haushofer school, "Eurasianism" to denote its earlier Russian forms, and "Neo-Eurasianism" to denote the Dugin-Traditionalist school.

25. Samuel P. Huntington, *The Clash of Civilizations and the Remaking of World Order* (New York: Simon & Schuster, 1996).

26. See AN 14.

27. See AN 15. For a good discussion of earlier Eurasianism, see Ryszard Paradowski, "The Eurasian Idea and Leo Gumilëv's Scientific Ideology," *Canadian Slavonic Papers* 41 (1999), 19–32.

28. Mackinder was a key figure in the establishment of geography as a respectable academic discipline in Britain, the first reader in geography at the University of Oxford (in 1887), and later the first director of the London School of Economics and Political Science (in 1904).

29. The basic thesis of *Democratic Ideals and Reality: A Study in the Politics of Reconstruction* (London: Constable, 1919) was first expressed in "The Geographical Pivot of History," a paper given to the Royal Geographical Society in 1904.

30. See AN 16.

31. Dugin, "Métaphysique de la Bonne Nouvelle."

32. Alexander Dugin, "Landmarks of Eurasianism," available online at http://www.eurasia.com.ru/vehi4.html [June 19, 2002].

33. See also the excellent paper of Mikhail Epstein, "Main Trends of Contemporary Russian Thought," delivered to the Twentieth World Congress of Philosophy, Boston, August 10–15, 1998. Available online at http://www.bu.edu/wcp/Papers/Cont/ContEpst.htm.

34. Alexander Tsipko, "Russia's Difficult Path Toward Democracy: Moral and Ideological Preconditions for Overcoming the Legacies of the Communist System in Russia," *International Review of Sociology* 7 (1997), 267–318; Dugin, "Landmarks of Eurasianism." See AN 17.

35. In their *Politicheskiy extremizm v Rossii* [Political Extremism in Russia] (Moscow: Panorama, 1996), Alexander Verkhovsky, Anatoly Papp, and Vladimir Pribylovsky "meticulously show how [Opposition groups] have over the years become interpenetrated through shared personnel and organizational interminglings . . . [to] constitute, despite their ideological differences, a relatively uniform core" (Andreas Umland, "The Post-Soviet Extreme Right," *Problems of Post-Communism* 44, no. 4 [July–August 1997], 53–61).

36. Tsipko, "Russia's Difficult Path."

37. David G. Rowley, " 'Redeemer Empire': Russian Millenarianism," *American Historical Review* 104 (1999), 1582–1602, esp. 1597–99.

38. Walter Ruby, "Of Russia, 'Memory,' and the Jews" [interview with Vasilyev], *Jerusalem Post*, March 7, 1989.

39. See AN 18.

40. Ruby, "Of Russia."

41. See AN 19.

42. Interview with Claudio Mutti, translated in *Alternative terceriste* 27 (December 1990), 5. Quoted in Deborah Cook, "Origins and Metamorphoses of the New Right: An Interview with Pierre-Andre Taguieff," *Telos* 98–99 (Winter 1993 / Spring 1994), 159–72.

43. Gennady Zyuganov, *The Geography of Victory*, quoted in. Charles Clover, "Dreams of the Eurasian Heartland," *Foreign Affairs* 78, no.2 (March–April 1999).

44. With 21.7 percent of votes and 58 seats in single-mandate districts (Tsipko, "Russia's Difficult Path"). Most explicit is Specter: "Perhaps more than any man in Russia, [Prokhanov] helped forge . . . the powerful alliance of Communists and nationalist groups that [made] Gennady A. Zyuganov . . . the main challenger for the presidency" in 1996. Michael Specter, "Muse of Anti-Yeltsin Forces: He Is Feared, Never Ignored," *New York Times*, May 2, 1996, p. A1. For the importance of this alliance in the 1995 election results, see Tsipko, "Russia's Difficult Path."

45. Andrei P. Tsygankov, "Hard-Line Eurasianism and Russia's Contending Geopolitical Perspectives," *East European Quarterly* 32 (1998), 315–34.

46. Dmitry Shlapentokh, " 'Red-to-Brown' Jews and Russian Liberal Reform," *Washington Quarterly* 21, no. 4 (Autumn 1998), 107–26.

47. Clover, "Dreams," pp. 91–93.

48. A paperback abridgement of this work was published in 1999 under the title *Nash Put'* [Our Way].

49. Jakob Kipp, quoted in Shenfield, *Russian Fascism*.

50. "Ostritt," *Antifaschistische Nachrichten*, April 1998 [online]. Available http://

www.infolinks.de/an/1998/04/012.htm [July 28, 1999]. Also Jacob W. Kipp, "Forecasting Future War: Andrei Kokoshin and the Military-Political Debate in Contemporary Russia" (January 1999), *US Army, Foreign Military Studies Office* [online]. Available http://call.army.mil/call/fmso/issues/kokoshin.htm [June 14, 2000].

51. Clover, "Dreams."

52. Japan for decades has been demanding the return of the Kuril Islands as the price for normalization of relations with first the Soviet Union and then Russia. Foreign Minister Yevgeny Primakov, an Arabist who was director of the Institute of Oriental Studies in Moscow from 1977 to 1985, and who had devoted most of his adult life to fostering Soviet relations with the Arab world, might be expected to incline toward the Soviet Union's traditional allies in the Middle East; as Clover himself remarks, Primakov emphasized the Soviet Union's role as "guardian of the East" before Eurasianism, Traditionalism, or even Perestroika were even heard of, in his *The East after the Collapse of the Colonial System* (Moscow, 1983).

53. Vinogradov, in Yelena Yakovich, "*Kontinent* in Moscow: Voice of Russian Culture" [interview with Igor Vinogradov], *Literaturnaya Gazeta,* July 22, 1992, p. 5

54. See AN 20.

55. He also includes Pyotr Savitsky, John Turner, Cara Schmidt, Karl Haushofer, and John Pavulesko.

56. Seleznev announced this appointment in an interview on Radio Russia in February 1999 (Ivan Kurilla, "Geopolitika i kommunizm" [Geopolitics and Communism], *Russki Zhurnal* 23, February 1999). Seleznev was a member of the Central Committee of the Communist Party and editor of *Pravda* since 1991 (Russian National News Service, online at http://www.nns.ru/persons/selez.htm).

57. Cook, "Origins."

58. Under the title *Continente Rusia* in Italian by Claudio Mutti's publishing house in 1991, and as *Rusia: misterio del Eurasia* (Madrid: Grup Libro, 1992).

59. Biographical data here from Russian National News Service, online at http://www.nns.ru/persons/limonov.html [August 1, 1999]. According to Shenfield, *Russian Fascism,* Limonov knew, but was not close to, Golovin and Mamleyev in the 1970s.

60. See AN 21. Limonov's regret at his emigration resulted in an attempt to return to the Soviet Union, but although the Soviet press made the most of the recantation of a dissident both well known and well regarded in certain circles, Limonov (who had lost his Soviet citizenship on leaving the Soviet Union) remained abroad.

61. By some accounts, Mamleyev divided his time between Paris and Moscow after 1991. This information and the liberal reaction to Limonov's return (discussed later) from Boris Falikov (interview).

62. Federal Information Systems Corporation, press conference given by Vladimir Zhirinovsky and others, June 22, 1992. See AN 22.

63. Dugin, interview. Where no other source is given, information is derived from Dugin.

64. Dugin derives it from Nikolai Vasilievich Ustralov's *Rossiya u okna vagona* [Russia from a Train Window], published in Harbin (China) in 1926. See introduction to an extract of Ustralov, "Pust' pravit imya ego" [Let His Name Rule], reprinted in *Yevraziyskoye Vtorzheniye,* August–September 1999.

65. Dugin, interview.

66. *Limonov protiv Zhirinovskogo* [Limonov against Zhirinovsky], 1994, is his

only post-1993 work in the Lenin Library. According to Shenfield, *Russian Fascism*, however, a book entitled *Anatomy of Love* was at one point to be published in 1998.

67. Sander Thoens, "Neo-Fascists Launch Boycott," *Moscow Times*, July 23, 1994.

68. A popular Russian drink, less sweet and more solid than its American rival.

69. Figures from Shenfield, *Russian Fascism;* the assessment is my own. Shenfield sees the National Bolsheviks as a significant party, "the largest middle-range fascist organization in Russia," with "considerable potential for further growth."

70. See AN 23.

71. Shenfield, *Russian Fascism*.

72. He was not alone in using this tactic. Chernomyrdin also organized free pop concerts, importing Western stars.

73. Reports in the *St. Petersburg Times* by Sergei Chernov (September 26, 1995, March 19, 1996, and July 14, 1996) and Sarah Hurst (December 12, 1995), and by Alexander Kan in the *Moscow Times* (September 28, 1995). Appreciation of Kuryokhin by Boris Falikov (interview). See AN 24.

74. Christian Lowe, "Campaign Heats Up in Nizhni Novgorod," *Moscow Times*, May 20, 1997.

75. Details from Shenfield, *Russian Fascism;* the assessment, however, is purely my own.

76. A translation of Guénon's *Crise du monde moderne* was published in 1993, and Dugin's own translation of Evola's *Heidnischer Imperialismus* in 1994.

77. See AN 25.

78. The translations were *Golem. Valipurgieva noch* [The Golem (1915) and Walpurgisnacht, (1917)] (1990) and *Belyi Dominikanetz* [The White Dominican] (1993). For Meyrink's interests, see Antoine Faivre, *The Eternal Hermes: From Greek God to Alchemical Magus* (Grand Rapids, Mich.: Phanes, 1995).

79. *Elementy* was the official journal of the National-Bolshevik Party; it carried articles on the Western European right and various "alternative-mystical" questions as well as on Traditionalism. Its title deliberately echoed the title of a successful French journal, *Éléments*, edited by de Benoist. *Elementy*'s connection with the Western European New Right was further underlined by the inclusion of de Benoist, Mutti, and Steuckers on its editorial committee, which also included Prokhanov. Dugin's enthusiasm for this connection was not shared by de Benoist himself, however; he originally advised Dugin against the use of the name *Elementy*, and as soon as became aware that he was on the editorial committee, he wrote requesting that he be removed from it. De Benoist later explained that although he liked Dugin personally and was sympathetic toward his views, he felt that he and Dugin were following very different intellectual lines in very different circumstances and he did not want any responsibility for a publication in a language he could not read (de Benoist, interview). By 1996 Prokhanov had also left the editorial committee. When he left the National Bolshevik Party and so lost control of *Elementy*, Dugin replaced it with a new journal of his own, *Miliy Angel* [Dear Angel].

80. For example, a translation of the *Reign of Quantity* in 1994. A full survey of translations is not possible because the Lenin Library's collection in its role as a library of deposit is incomplete after 1991. The name Byelovodiye refers to a promised land of the Old Believers, comparable to Atlantis in the Western esoteric tradition.

81. Telephone conversation with the publisher's office, August 1999.

82. Moscow, Aleteia, 1999, acknowledging the 1967 edition by Perennial Books, London.

83. Finis Mundi: The end of the world. For the relationship between millenarianism, "secular millenarianism," and Russian imperialism, see Rowley, "Redeemer Empire."

84. Alexander Bratersky, "Radio from the End of the World," *Moscow Times*, February 13, 1997. Details of program themes from http://www.arctogaia.com/public/fm .htm [online], where recordings of the programs may be played.

85. See AN 26.

86. This section derives from exploration of www.arctogaia.ru in July 1999, of www.geocities.com/CapitolHill/6824/ in January 1997, and of a growing number of linked sites in 2001–2.

87. See AN 27.

88. *Zavtra*, August–September 1999. For the publication history of "Yevraziyskoye Vtorzheniye," see AN 28.

89. A good analysis of this trend is contained in Andreas Umland, "Towards an Uncivil Society? Contextualizing the Decline of Post-Soviet Russian Extremely Right-Wing Parties," paper presented to the Post-Communist Politics and Economics Workshop, Harvard University, May 15, 2002.

90. These events took place after research for this book was complete. Given the significance of these developments, however, this section (on the Eurasia Movement and Party) was added to the manuscript at the last moment. It is, therefore, somewhat tentative in nature.

91. Dmitry Shlapentokh, "Russian Nationalism Today: The Views of Alexander Dugin," *Contemporary Review*, July 2001, p. 32.

92. Dugin, "The Eurasia Movement at a Difficult Stage," address to the Political Council of the Eurasia Movement, Moscow, October 11, 2001, online at http://utenti .lycos.it/ArchivEurasia/dugin_mps011011.html (June 17, 2002); Grigory Nekhoroshev, "Eurasians Decide to Rely on Vladimir Putin," *Nezavisimiya Gaezeta*, April 24, 2001, p. 2; Yelena Dorofeyeva, "Eurasia Movement Created in Russia," ITAR-TASS News Agency wire report, April 21, 2001.

93. Dmitri Glinski-Vassiliev, "Islam in Russian Society and Politics: Survival and Expansion," Program on New Approaches to Russian Security, Harvard University, policy memo no. 198, May 2001, p. 5. Niyazov apparently converted shortly after his arrival in Moscow from Siberia in about 1990 (Glinski-Vassiliev, e-mail, June 2002), so it is unlikely that he encountered Traditionalism before his conversion.

94. Dugin, "Landmarks of Eurasianism."

95. See AN 29.

96. Nekhoroshev, "Eurasians Decide to Rely on Vladimir Putin."

97. Umland, "Towards an Uncivil Society?"

98. These rumors are widely reported.

99. For membership of the movement, see "communiqué" of April 21, 2001, available online at http://www.arctogaia.com/public/eng/congress.html June 17, 2002].

100. The *mujahidin* were then described as "sabotage gangs raised and trained by foreign instructors . . . [which], prodded by American dollars . . . shed the blood of

their own brothers, while still calling themselves Muslims." Dispatch of the Telegraph Agency of the Soviet Union, October 24, 1985.

101. Galina M. Yemelianova, "New Muftis, New Russians?" online at *Russia Intercessory Prayer Network* (August 1999). Available http://www.ripnet.org/strategies/religions/newmuftis.htm [June 21, 2002].

102. For example by Marina Latysheva, "The Eurasian Movement: Mystics, Priests and Secret Service Agents," *Versiya* 19, May 29, translated online in *Johnson's Russia List* 5275 (May 30, 2001). Available http://www.cdi.org/russia/johnson/5275.html [June 17, 2002].

103. "An SVR Veteran and a Chechen Separatist Urge that Russia and Chechnya Join Forces Against the Wahhabis—and the United States," *Chechnya Weekly*, July 10, 2001. Available http://chechnya.jamestown.org/pubs/view/che_002_007_001.htm [June 17, 2002].

104. The source is "FSB Blows Up Russia," extracts from a forthcoming book by Alexander Litvinenko and Yuri Fel'shtinsky published in *Novaya Gazeta* on August 27, 2001. The extracts concentrated on establishing FSB responsibility for an attempted pseudo-terrorist action in Ryazan in late 1999. See *The NIS Observed: An Analytical Review,* September 12, 2001 [online]. Available http://www.bu.edu/iscip/digest/vol16/ed0614.html [June 17, 2002].

105. Mavra Kosichkina, "Putin's New Style: Moderation and Precision, against the Backdrop of a 'Soviet Mentality' Renaissance," online at *Politruk* 56 (June 6, 2001). Available at http://www.wps.ru:8101/chitalka/politruk/en/20010606.shtml [June 17, 2002].

106. Dorofeyeva, "Eurasia Movement Created in Russia."

107. "Body Set up in Moscow to Promote Peace in North Caucasus," ITAR-TASS dispatch from Moscow, January 8, 1999.

108. "An SVR Veteran and a Chechen Separatist."

109. Dugin, "The Swallows of Apocalypse," communique of the Eurasia Movement, September 12, 2002, online at http://www.eurasia.com.ru/swallows.html [June 17, 2002].

110. Dugin, "Swallows."

111. Defined as China, India, Iran, and certain Arab countries.

112. Dugin, "The Eurasia Movement at a Difficult Stage."

113. Dugin, "The Eurasia Movement at a Difficult Stage."

114. Anastasia Matveeva, "This Kind of Eurasian Putin Will Be Supported by Us," *Gazeta* March 4, 2002, p. 2.

115. Dugin, "Landmarks of Eurasianism."

116. MAOF, "Who We Are" [online]. Available http://rjews.net/maof/maofabout21.html [June 19, 2002].

117. The section is actually called "Geopolitics"—http://rjews.net/maof/geopolitics/geopolit.htm.

118. Lev Gorodetsky, "Risky Ruskies: Russian Fascists's Troubling Cry: 'Euroasia [sic] Above All' Is His Platform," online at *Jewsweek* (June 17, 2002). Available http://www.jesweek.com/politics/009.htm [June 17, 2002].

119. "Russian Foreign Ministry Criticizes Retrial of Former Soviet Partisan," AP dispatch from Moscow, May 20, 2002.

120. "Demonstrators at Latvian Embassy in Israel Tear Apart Latvian Flag," Baltic News Service dispatch from Moscow, April 5, 2001.

121. "Russian Ambassador to Latvia Presents Russian Passport to WWII Resistance Fighter," Interfax dispatch from Riga, April 26, 2000.

122. "Latvian Court Sends Russian Radicals to Confinement for Illegal Border Crossing," Baltic News Service dispatch from Rezekne, Latvia, June 6, 2001.

123. Arseni Volkov, "They Called Him Nikita. . . ." Interview with Abraham Shmulevich [online]. Available http://www.jewish.ru/4025.asp [June 17, 2002].

124. See Aviezer Ravitzky, *Messianism, Zionism, and Jewish religious Radicalism* (Chicago: University of Chicago Press, 1996).

125. The figures are of course disputed. Those used here (235 and 40,000) come from "Not Intifada, This Time It's War," *The Economist*, November 16, 2000. If the inhabitants of neighboring Kiryat Arba are included, the number of settlers is of course higher; my point here is to emphasize the precariousness of the central Hebron settlements.

126. "Eskin Gets Four Months for Curse on Rabin," *Jerusalem Post*, July 21, 1997.

127. He was found guilty of soliciting arson and conspiring to deface a grave but was acquitted on the Temple Mount charge. His accomplice, Damian Peckovich, was found guilty on all counts; in the case of the Temple Mount plan, he was convicted of sedition. Elli Wohlgelernter, "Eskin Held in Foiled Temple Mount Pig Plot," *Jerusalem Post*, December 28, 1997, p. 1; Sari Bashi, "Israeli Convicted of Defacing Muslim Grave with Pig's Head," AP dispatch from Jerusalem, October 5, 1999; Moshe Reinfeld, "Court Acquits Man in Pig's Head Plot on Temple Mount," *Ha'aretz*, October 6, 1999; Reinfeld, "Pig's Head Plotter Gets 30 Months Jail," *Ha'aretz*, November 12, 1999.

128. Alexander Sherman, "Here Everything Is as Usual: They're Shooting" (interview with Avraam Shmulevich, April 5, 2001). Online at http://www.jewish.ru/edit/obzorp/view.htm?id=106 [June 17, 2002].

129. AP dispatch from Tel Aviv, July 16, 1979.

130. Larry McShane, "Allen: Administration Will 'Redefine' Actions to Help Soviet Jews," AP dispatch from New York, May 31, 1981.

13. THE ISLAMIC WORLD

Parts of this section were originally delivered as a paper "The Imperial Iranian Academy of Philosophy and Religious Pluralism in the Islamic Republic of Iran," at the Annual Meeting of the Middle East Studies Association, San Francisco, Cal., November 17–20, 2001. A version of this paper was published in *Historian in Cairo: Essays in Honor of George Scanlon*, ed. Jill Edwards (Cairo: AUC Press, 2002).

1. Between 11 and 20 million out of a total Russian population of 150 million. Traditionalism in Malaysia is not dealt with in this chapter, for practical reasons, but would certainly repay further study. The leading Traditionalist there is Osman Bakar, probably a Maryami. There is a master's program in Civilizational Studies at the Universiti Malaya that is, to judge from its reading list, thoroughly Traditionalist. Course homepage, online at http://www.cc.um-edu.my/fcivil.htm [September 22, 1999].

2. Discussed in chapter 9.

3. Rachid ben Eissa, interview. Ben Eissa is the source of all information on Traditionalism in Algeria.

4. Garaudy described his enthusiasm for Guénon in conversation with Alain de Benoist (de Benoist, interview).

5. Fawzy Sqali, interview.

6. Many of the aspects of French culture that members of the Francophone elite have adopted distance them from Islam as well as from Sufism: the wearing of Western clothes (especially for women), closer social contact between the sexes than the Sharia permits, and in some cases even the regular drinking of wine. The consumption of alcohol has become especially prevalent in North Africa.

7. Thami Afailal, "René Guénon: un modèle soufi du XXème siècle [Interview with Zakia Zouanat]," *Demain*, July 1, 2000, p. 17.

8. Afailal, "René Guénon," and Zakia Zouanat, "Sidi Hamza, le saint vivant," *Le Journal* [Casablanca], May 27, 2000, p. 55.

9. Ahmad Qustas, interview.

10. Visits to bookshops in Casablanca. The "Livre Service" bookshop did stock one book by Idries Shah, however.

11. These comments are based on visits to a selection of bookshops in Casablanca in January 2001. The largest of these stocked Schuon (*Comprendre l'Islam*), du Pasquier (*Découverte de l'Islam*), and Sqali (three books), but not Guénon.

12. Where no other source is given, information concerning Fawzy Sqali derives from interviews with him.

13. Rumi's *Le livre de dedans* [*Fi-ha ma fi*], Henry Corbin's *L'imagination créatrice d'Ibn Arabi*, and Jean-Louis Michon's *Ibn ʿAjiba et son miʾraj*. Sqali, interview, supplemented by Faouzi Skali, "Eva de Vitray, ou la rencontre des deux rives," *Soufisme* 4 (2000), 11–14, esp. p. 14.

14. Qustas joined the Budshishiyya in 1971.

15. He is the regional president of the Fondation Internationale de Synthèse Architecturale, the founder and president of Habitat Culture Développement.

16. *Soufisme* 4 (2000). Attali's interest is reflected in his *Chemins de sagesse* and derives in part from the fact that he was born in Algiers. After a distinguished administrative and academic career, Attali became a special advisor to the French president in 1981, and in 1991 he became the first (and controversial) president of the European Bank for Reconstruction and Development.

17. References here are to the 1995 edition (Paris: Albin Michel). In French, Sqali spells his name Faouzi Skali. *La voie soufie* was for some time widely on sale in Sqali's home country. Even in 2001 Sqali was one of the best represented contemporary authors in the "Spirituality" section of the French-language part of a major Casablanca bookshop. Three of his books were on sale in that section of Livre Service.

18. Sqali, *Voie*, p. 56. Titus Burckhardt's distinction between the cosmological and metaphysical meanings of Ibn al-ʿArabi's use of the word *qabil* [receptacle] is also used (on p. 25), for example.

19. Sqali, *Voie*, p. 13.

20. Sqali, *Voie*, pp. 149–53.

21. Sqali, *Voie*, pp. 67–69. This view might well be justified but seems to me less clearly correct than the previous one.

22. See chapter 3.

23. In France he changed from sociology to anthropology and moved his studies from the University of Lisieux (Paris VII) in order to have the Traditionalist Muslim Najm al-Din Bammate as the supervisor of his *thèse de troisième cycle* [approximately, M.A. thesis]. He expanded his readings of Guénon, making extensive use of them in this thesis, and he also expanded his contacts with other Traditionalists in Paris.

24. Sqali, interview.

25. Advertisement in *Soufisme* 4 (2000).

26. Sqali has spoken in Barcelona on a number of occasions (though through an interpreter), and some of the events of the 2000 Rencontres took place in that city. A Budshishi *zawiya* in Birmingham, England, is run by Hamid Lee, a British Budshishi. The United States is handled by Qustas.

27. Unsigned editorial, *Soufisme* 5 (2000), 2.

28. Jean-Louis Girotto, "Sacrées émotions: Retour sur les 5èmes Rencontres Méditerranéennes sur le soufisme," *Soufisme* 5 (2000), 4–5, esp. p. 4.

29. Girotto, "Sacrées émotions."

30. Sqali, interview.

31. Denis Gril, interview.

32. The academy initially passed under the control of the office of the prime minister, and was for a while administered by Chihil Tani, a revolutionary who was sympathetic to its aims but was in no way a philosopher, continuing its activities as best it could

33. Observation of books in the academy's library, January 2001.

34. Yahya Alawi, interview, and Ashtiyani, *Sharh-e moqaddeme-ye Qaysani*, quoted in Christian Bonaud, *L'Imam Khomeyni, un gnostique méconnu de XXe siècle* (Beirut: Al-Bouraq, 1997), p. 16.

35. Hadi Sharifi, interview. The foundation was funded principally by Shaykh Yamani, the Saudi Arabian oil minister, and the necessary introductions were made by Nasr. The foundation's work became well known and highly respected among Western scholars; what was less known was that many of its staff were Traditionalists.

36. A'avani and A2 (see list before bibliography), interviews.

37. Various reports suggest it had about 50 persons.

38. Shahram Pazuki, interview.

39. Pazuki, interview.

40. Pazuki, interview.

41. Muhammad Legenhausen, interview.

42. Marcia Z. Nelson, "Islamic Publishing Is Poised for Growth," *Publishers Weekly*, November 13, 2000.

43. Nasrullah Purjavadi, interview.

44. Daryush Shayegan, *Asia dar barabir gharb* (Tehran, 1977).

45. Hamshahri Maah, "One Foot on Water, One Foot on Earth: Interview with Dariush Shaygan," online at *TehranAvenue.com* (August 2001). Available http://www.tehranavenue.com/ec_interview.htm [November 4, 2001].

46. Laleh Bakhtiar and Nader Ardalan, *The Sense of Unity: The Sufi Tradition in Persian Architecture* (Chicago: Chicago University Press, 1973); Pazuki, interview.

47. See AN 1.

48. Ashk Dahlén, e-mail, November 9, 2001.

49. Legenhausen and Pazuki, interviews.

50. See Wilfried Buchta, *Who Rules Iran? The Structure of Power in the Islamic Republic* (Washington, D.C.: Washington Institute for Near East, 2000) for a succinct and fascinating account of this struggle. Note, however, that Buchta is dependant mostly on reformist sources and so presents a somewhat one-sided (and occasionally alarmist) picture.

51. Mahmoud Sadri, "Intellectual Autobiography [of Soroush]," May 3, 1999 [online]. Available http://www.seraj.org/interviewI.htm [May 17, 2000].

52. Vol. 4, nos. 3–4, summer and fall 1998.

53. These questions may also be treated in later publications. The debate continues at the present time.

54. For both debates see Mehrzad Boroujerdi, "The Encounter of Post-Revolutionary Thought in Iran with Hegel, Heidegger and Popper," *Cultural Transitions in the Middle East*, ed. Serif Mardin (Leiden: Brill, 1994), pp. 236–59.

55. For example, by Boroujerdi, "Encounter," p. 239.

56. I have no definite proof of Davari's debt to Traditionalism, but from circumstantial evidence (including his biography) it seems clear.

57. Alawi, interview.

58. See AN 2.

59. A Western philosopher who had made a number of visits to the academy from abroad spoke very highly of the quality of the work done there. Ernest Wolf-Gazo, interview.

60. On another occasion he described any philosophy that lacked a transcendent element as "futile." Interview.

61. Sadiq Larijani, interview.

62. Pazuki and Legenhausen, interview.

63. These arguments are developed more fully in Muhammad Legenhausen, *Islam and Religious Pluralism* (London: Al-Hoda, 1999).

64. Legenhausen, interview.

65. Guénon is referred to, for example, in Hilmi Ziya Ülker's *İslam Düşüncesi*, first published in about 1946. Ülker was a professor of philosophy, latterly at Ankara University. Like other intellectuals of the late Ottoman and early Republican period, he read French (English began to replace French among educated Turks in the 1950s). A 1970s mention is in one volume of Sâmiha Ayverdi's encyclopedic *Türk Târihinde Osmanli Asirlari* [Turkish History of the Ottoman Age], 1954–75. There were also mentions of *Crise du monde moderne* and *Orient et Occident* in newspaper articles.

66. "Tavhid," *Kubbealti Akademi Mecmûasi* 8 (1979).

67. Where no other source is given, information on Traditionalism in Turkey is taken from interviews with Mustafa Tahrali and Mahmud Kiliç.

68. This impression is due in part to the nature of the two books translated so far (see AN 3). A translation of his *Métaphysique de la guerre* was launched in 1999, however, and may change this situation.

69. The exception is an indirect impact, through the Turkish branch of Nuevo Acropolis. Nuevo Acropolis's somewhat Traditionalist conception of the Holy Roman Empire was "naturalized" into the idea of a Holy Ottoman Empire, but this is not a significant movement.

70. See AN 4.

71. One exception is Yeryüzü Yayinlari, a publishing house owned by Ahmet Kot, a Traditionalist journalist. Another publisher, İz Yayincilik, also specialized in Traditionalist works. Print runs were initially 2,000–3,000, and in the late 1990s went down to 1,000–1,500, sometimes with new editions after a year or two but sometimes selling over five years—A4, interview (see list before bibliography). Many Turkish bookshops, self-consciously secular, do not have significant sections on Islam.

72. Fritjof Capra, *The Tao of Physics* (Berkeley, Cal.: Shambhala, 1975); Paul C. W. Davies, *God and the New Physics* (New York: Simon and Schuster, 1983); Kiliç, interview.

73. The literal translation, *gelenek*, is also used by some translators but has unfortunate connotations of a fashion that has passed. A similar problem was encountered in Arabic: the literal translation of "tradition," *taqlid*, would imply outdated social custom. Ben Eissa, like some Turkish translators, decided on *din* (the Turkish word is of Arabic origin). Arguably, the standard Persian translation is the best one: *sunnat*, a term borrowed from Islamic law, where it indicates exemplary past practice.

74. *İnsanin Yüceliği Guenoniyen Batinilik* (Istanbul: Fikir, 1992).

75. Kiliç, interview.

76. Mahmud Kiliç, "Ölümünün 37. Yildönümünde R. Guénon'u Anmak" [Remembering R. Guénon on the 37th anniversary of his death], *İlim ve Sanat* 18 (1987), 40–42. My thanks to Thierry Zarcone for this reference.

77. Ken'an Rifa'i attended the Galatasaray school in Istanbul, and then took the Rifa'iyya from Hamza al-Rifa'i in Medina.

78. The other academics are Nabi Avci, who teaches at the department of film and television at İstanbul Bilgi university and who has written four Traditionalist books and also translated Guénon, and Ersin Gürdoğan, an economist, who has had seven books published by İz. The Islamic philosopher is İlhan Kutluer.

79. These have included a Turkish-born Greek who wrote from Athens.

80. A successor to Ahmad al-Alawi with *zawiyas* in Algeria as well as Switzerland, Bin Murad does not recognize the Maryamiyya.

81. Yaacov Ro'i, *Muslim Eurasia: Conflicting Legacies* (London: Frank Cass, 1995), pp. 43–44.

82. Gejdar Jamal, *Tawhid: Prospettive dell'Islam nell'ex URSS*, trans. and ed. Danilo Valdorio (Parma: Insegna del Veltro, 1993).

83. Jamal, *Tawhid*, pp. 16–17 and 18–19.

84. "Islam and the Right," *Giperboreja* [Vilnius], 1 (1991), translated into Italian in Jamal, *Tawhid*, pp. 31–36.

85. Ro'i, *Muslim Eurasia*, p. 44.

86. Leonid Berres, "The Wahhabis are Ready to Make an Alliance with Makashov and Ilyukhin," *Kommersant*, July 24, 1999, pp. 1 ff.

87. Berres, "The Wahhabis." The title of this article makes an identification between Jamal and the "Wahhabi" Islamists who were at that time in conflict with Russian forces in Daghestan, an identification which the text of the article does not really support.

88. "Krasnoye i Zelyenoye: vozmozhen li yedinyi front kommunistov i musul'man?" [Red and Green: Is a United Front of Communists and Muslims Possible?], *Zavtra*, August–September 1999, p. 6. See AN 5.

89. Hostilities were beginning in Daghestan when the alliance was announced, and soon afterward spread to Chechnya.

90. Colonel Bondarenko, chair of the Movement in Support of the Army in Kabardino-Balkaria (a small republic in the western Caucasus), asking a question at the Ilyukhin-Makashov press conference.

91. Federal Information Systems Corporation, press conference given by Viktor Ilyukhin and General Makashov, September 2, 1999.

92. *Zavtra* interview.

93. Such theories are not always entirely wrong, of course, especially in Russia.

94. Islamism is progressive, has no interest in Perennialism, and commonly rejects Sufism.

95. Alexander Dugin, interview.

96. Gaydar Jamal, interview.

97. "The true representative of the right is neither an ascetic nor a mystic [as Evola saw him]. The right is not a religious movement" (Jamal, *Tawhid*, p. 33).

98. Franco Ferraresi, *Minacce alla democrazia: La Destra radicale e la strategia della tensione in Italia nel dopoguerra* (Milan: Feltrinelli, 1995), pp. 103 and 344.

99. Claudio Mutti, "Pourquoi j'ai choisi l'Islam," *Eléments: Revue de la Nouvelle Droite* 53 (Spring 1985), 37–39, and Mutti, interview.

100. Mutti, "Pourquoi j'ai choisi l'Islam," p. 38.

14. AGAINST THE STREAM

1. Douglas Allen, "Mircea Eliade's View of the Study of Religion as the Basis for Cultural and Spiritual Renewal," in *Changing Religious Worlds: The Meaning and End of Mircea Eliade*, ed. Bryan S. Rennie (Albany, N.Y.: SUNY Press, 2000), p. 223.

2. Antoine Faivre, "Histoire de la notion moderne de Tradition dans ses rapports avec les courants ésotériques (XVe–XXe siècles)," *Aries*, vol. hors série, "Symboles et Mythes" (c 2000), p. 39.

3. During the twelfth century the Norman kings of Sicily first tolerated and then oppressed their Muslim subjects in the island they had recently conquered from the Arabs, but they always acknowledged the superiority of Arab culture, dressing their women in Islamic fashion, keeping eunuchs, and using Arabic for official purposes. After the Normans were driven out of Sicily by Germans, the thirteenth-century emperor Frederick II Hohenstaufen continued to use eunuchs to guard the ladies of his family and continued to patronize Arab scholars. He sponsored the translation of Averroes and Avicenna, questioned scholars such as Alam al-Din al-Hanafi about cosmology (as well as optics and medicine), and commissioned a treatise from the celebrated Murcian Sufi philosopher Ibn Sabain, *Al-ajwiba an al-asila al-saqaliyya* [Answers to Sicilian Questions]. Among the questions Frederick II put to Ibn Sabain were ones dealing with the immortality of the soul and the eternity of the world. Although at the same time he was completing the extinction of Islam in Sicily, Frederick II was eager to learn from the East about matters that we would today class as religious. See Aziz Ahmad, *A History of Islamic Sicily* (Edinburgh: Edinburgh University Press, 1975), esp. pp. 63–66 and 85–91.

4. Edward Said, *Orientalism* (New York: Pantheon, 1978).

5. The revolution did involve evils, even by the admission of its supporters—though they argue that they were necessary and few. I do not mean to suggest that the revolution itself was evil.

6. Evola is usually described as a baron, but his entitlement to this title has been questioned by some.

7. Faivre, "Histoire de la notion moderne de Tradition," pp. 38–39.

Glossary

Bismillah: the formula "In the name of God the most merciful, the compassionate" (starting with the word "bismillah," in the name of God) with which devout Muslims begin all actions, statements, and writings.

Confession of Faith: the formula "I confess that there is no god save God [and] I confess that Muhammad is the prophet of God," used on multiple occasions, including during the ritual prayer.

Dhikr: repetitive prayer, normally using short formulas often drawn from the Koran. *Dhikr* may be done either individually (usually silently) or congregationally, in which case it is usually said aloud.

Esoteric: aspects of religious practice and of knowledge relating directly to the relationship between believer and God. Used especially in connection with the search for mystic unification with God in Sufism.

Exoteric: externally visible religious practice and knowledge.

Fard: obligatory. When applied to religious acts, denotes acts the omission of which is a sin.

Hadith: the reported sayings and actions of the Prophet Muhammad, one of two main sources (the other being the Koran) of the Sharia.

Hajj: the annual pilgrimage to the Kaba in Mecca. It takes place only once each year and involves various complex rites in Mecca. All Muslims are obliged to perform it at least once in their lives, circumstances permitting.

Hijra: emigration, originally that of the Prophet Muhammad and his earliest followers from Mecca (where they were under threat) to Medina. Muhammad and his followers returned triumphant to Mecca after victory in a series of armed engagements with the Meccans. *Hijra* is thus the model for Muslim tactical withdrawal.

Hijri: adjectival form of *hijra.* Hence the Islamic lunar calendar, which starts at the *hijra* of the Prophet Muhammad.

Ijaza: authorization, in Sufism an authorization to admit persons to a particular Sufi order.

Islamism: a political philosophy with religious implications, derived from Islam. Alternatively, the persons and groups dedicated to the implementation of that philosophy.

Islamism, radical: the version of Islamism that endorses or requires the use of force to achieve its ends. Alternatively, the persons and groups dedicated to implementation of Islamism through force.

Jalabiyya: an article of male clothing, often white, familiar in the West as the common attire of Saudi Arabians, but also worn in other Arab countries, in slightly different forms and in a variety of colors.

Kaba: the small, ancient temple in Mecca believed by Muslims to have been built by Abraham.

Kali yuga: the fourth and final age of the temporal cycle, lasting 6,000 years, when all is reduced to its most base elements.

Koran: the holy scripture of Islam, believed to be the literal word of God given to the Prophet Muhammad through the angel Gabriel. Muslims believe the Koran to be of entirely divine origin.

Kufr: disbelief in God's revelations, the opposite of Islam. If committed by a Muslim, *kufr* in theory incurs the death penalty.

Muqaddam: a lieutenant, in Sufism usually the official in a Sufi order who runs a branch *zawiya* on behalf of a shaykh. Various terms are used for this function in different orders.

Order, Sufi: a group of Sufis and their shaykh, who leads them along a spiritual path distinct (often only in minor ways) from that found in other orders.

Perennialism: the belief that all religions share a common origin in remote antiquity, usually including a belief that as a consequence all religions are different paths to the same destination.

Prayer, Friday: the congregational version of the daily ritual prayer, held every week on Friday and including a sermon. Attendance is obligatory for every male Muslim and optional for females.

Prayer, ritual: the precisely defined rituals of prayer which every Muslim must perform five times every day, at specific points during the day.

Primordialism: a version of perennialism that concentrates on the original, primordial religion.

Salamat: greetings of peace between one Muslim and other, required by the Sharia and not (at least in theory) to be used with non-Muslims.

Sharia: the code of Islam, believed by Muslims to be the sum of the will of God for the conducting of life on earth. The Sharia includes law, rules for ritual, and ethical and moral prescriptions.

Shaykh: a learned man, in Sufism the spiritual master running a Sufi order.

Sunna: the exemplary practice of the Prophet Muhammad—hence, acts that will be rewarded but that are not *fard.*

Syncretism: the combination of elements from different religions, whether of doctrine or practice, whether intentionally or accidentally.

Ulama: scholars, especially scholars in disciplines related to Islam.

Umra: a pilgrimage made to the Kaba in Mecca made voluntarily at any time of year, the rites of which are less complex than those of the *Hajj*.

Universalism: the belief that all religions are much the same, or syncretism on this basis.

Wird: a set of nonritual prayers, often with elements of *dhikr*, assigned to Sufis by a shaykh.

Zawiya: an area or small building set aside for ritual prayer, in Sufism the premises of an order or of one of a number of geographically separate sections of a larger order. Hence the local branch of a larger order.

Interviewees

A1. Anonymous informant, a Traditionalist since before 1945, who knew leading Traditionalists well.

A2. Anonymous informant, once a senior member of the Imperial Iranian Academy of Philosophy.

A3. Anonymous informant, an early member of the Maryamiyya in Switzerland.

A4. Anonymous informant, working with Traditionalist works in the Turkish publishing industry.

A5. Anonymous informant, a former member of the Maryamiyya in America.

A6. Anonymous informant, a member of the Maryamiyya in America until 2002.

A7. Anonymous informant, a former member of the Maryamiyya in America.

A8. Anonymous informant, a former senior member of the Maryamiyya in America.

Aʿavani Gholam Reza. Director of the Iranian Academy of Philosophy. Interviewed in Tehran, January 2001.

Alawi, Yahya. Former student of Jalal al-Din Ashtiyani. Interviewed in Mashhad, Iran, January 2001.

Al-Hitami. See under *H*.

Badawi, Ahmad. Nephew of Moin al-Arab. Interviewed in Cairo, October 1998.

Ben Eissa. See Eissa, Rachid ben.

Benoist, Alain de. "New Right" theoretician and publisher. Interviewed in Paris, January 2000.

Bentounès, Khaled. Shaykh of the Alawiyya and grandson of Adda Bentounès. Interviewed in Alexandria, April 2003.

Braire, André. Proprietor of Editions traditionnelles from 1985. Interviewed in Paris, January 2000.

Chodkiewicz, Michel. Follower of Michel Vâlsan. Interviewed in the Loire Valley, France, January 2000.

De Benoist. See Benoist, Alain de.

Dugin, Alexander. Russian Traditionalist. Interviewed in Moscow, August 1999.

Eissa, Rachid ben. Algerian Traditionalist. Interviewed in Paris, March 2001.

Fadae, Mary-Anne. Widow of Victor Danner, ex-Maryami. Interviewed in Washington, D.C., November 1999.

Faivre, Antoine. Senior French scholar at the Sorbonne. Interviewed in Paris, March 2001.

Falikov, Boris. Soviet-era independent intellectual. Interviewed in Moscow, August 1999.

Forsaith, Richard B. Former Maryami. Interviewed by mail, fax, and e-mail, April–May 2000.

Gagne, Claude. Venerable master of the Grand Triad. Interviewed in Paris, January 2000.

Gril, Denis. Son of followers of Michel Vâlsan, and French Islamologist. Interviewed in Cairo, December 2000.

Guénon, Muhammad. Youngest son of René Guénon. Interviewed in Cairo, July 1997.

Hartung, Sylvie. Widow of Henri Hartung. Interviewed in Fleurier, Switzerland, August 2001.

al-Hitami, Faruq. Successor of Muin al-Arab. Interviewed in Cairo, April 2001.

Jamal, Gaydar. Russian Islamist and Traditionalist. Interviewed in Moscow, August 1999.

Kiliç, Mahmud. Turkish academic and Traditionalist. Interviewed in Istanbul, April 1999.

Koslow, Mark. Former member of Maryami "inner circle" at Inverness, Indiana. Interviewed by telephone, November 1999.

Larijani, Sadiq. Hujjat al-Islam, professor at the Madrasa-yi Vali-yi Asr, Qom. Interviewed in Qom, Iran, January 2001.

Legenhausen, Muhammad. Instructor at the Imam Khomeini Research Center, Qom. Interviewed in Qom, Iran, January 2001.

Lings, Martin. British Maryami and once Guénon's secretary in Cairo. Interviewed in London, September 1996.

Lory, Pierre. Former student at the Imperial Iranian Academy of Philosophy. Interviewed in Paris, January 2000.

Meyenburg, Harald von (de). Early follower of Schuon and brother-in-law of Burckhardt. Interviewed in Lausanne, September 1998.

Mollier, Pierre. Archivist of the Grand Orient of France. Interviewed in Paris, January 2000.

Mutti, Claudio. Evolian Muslim and former follower of Franco Freda. Interviewed in Parma, Italy, September 1998.

Nasr, Hossein. Leading Maryami. Interviewed in Washington, D.C., May 1996.

Pallavicini, Abd al-Wahid. Traditionalist shaykh of the Ahmadiyya. Interviewed in Milan, January 1996.

Pazuki, Shahram. Professor at Tehran University and member of the Iranian Academy of Philosophy. Interviewed in Tehran, January 2001.

Purjavadi, Nasrullah. Past member of the Imperial Iranian Academy of Philosophy. Interviewed in Tehran, January 2001.

Qustas, Ahmad. Budshishi *muqaddam* and Traditionalist. Interviewed in Fez, Morocco, January 2001.

Richardson, Jim. Former police sergeant in charge of the Schuon investigation in 1991. Interviewed by telephone, November 2001.

Salim, Ali. Former *muqaddam* of Shaykh Abd al-Rashid ibn Muhammad Said. Interviewed in Singapore, March 1996.

Schneuwly, Jean-Paul. Former Maryami. Interviewed in Geneva, September 1998.

Schutz, Ali. Director of Il Fondaco and one of the leaders of the Muslim community in Milan. Interviewed in Milan, January 1996.

Sharifi, Hadi. Former deputy director of the Imperial Iaranian Academy of Philosophy. Interviewed in Tehran, January 2001.

Sqali, Fawzy. Budshishi *muqaddam* and Traditionalist. Interviewed in Fez, Morocco, January 2001.

Soroush, Abd al-Karim. Leading Iranian intellectual. Interviewed at Harvard, November 2000.

Tahrali, Mustafa. Turkish academic and Traditionalist. Interviewed in Istanbul, April 1999.

Vâlsan, Muhammad. Son of Michel Vâlsan. Interviewed in Paris, January 2000.

Von Meyenburg. See Meyenburg, Harald von.

Wolf-Gazo, Ernst. Professor of philosophy at the American University in Cairo. Interviewed in Cairo, October 2000.

Zabid, Muhammad. Ahmadi shaykh and son of Shaykh Abd al-Rashid. Interviewed in Kuala Lumpur, April 1996.

Bibliography

Current editions and translations into English are given on www.traditionalists.org.

Accart, Xavier. "Du *Jardin enchante* à l'ermitage Saint-Jean: La réception de l'oeuvre de René Guénon par Henri Bosco." In *Henri Bosco, Actes de colloque international de Narbonne, 13–14 juin 1997,* no editor. Narbonne: Les cahiers du CERMEIL, 1997.

——, ed. *L'Ermite de Duqqi: René Guénon en marge des milieux francophones égyptiens.* Milan: Archè, 2001.

Afailal, Thami. "René Guénon: un modèle soufi du XXème siècle" [interview with Zakia Zouanat]. *Demain,* July 1, 2000, p. 17.

Alibert, Pierre. *Gleizes: biographie.* Paris: Editions Gallérie Michèle Heyraud, 1970.

Alleau, René, and Marianne Scriabine. *Actes du colloque international René Guénon et l'actualité de la pensée traditionnelle (Cérisy-la-Salle, 13–20 juillet 1973).* Braine-le-Comte, Belgium: Editions du Baucens, 1979.

André, Marie-Sophie, and Christophe Beaufils. *Papus, biographie: la Belle Epoque de l'occultisme.* Paris: Berg International, 1995.

Aslan, Adnan. *Religious Pluralism in Christian and Islamic Philosophy: The Thought of John Hick and Seyyed Hossein Nasr.* Richmond, U.K.: Curzon, 1998.

Aymard, Jean-Baptiste. "Frithjof Schuon (1907–1998). Connaissance et voie d'intériorité. Approche biographique." In *Frithjof Schuon,* ed. Chevilliat, pp. 1–79.

Baker, Rob. "Merton, Marco Pallis, and the Traditionalists." In *Merton & Sufism,* ed. Rob Baker and Gray Henry, 193–265.

Baker, Rob, and Gray Henry, eds. *Merton & Sufism: The Untold Story.* Louisville, Ky.: Fons Vitae, 1999.

Benoist, Alain de. "Bibliographie de Julius Evola." Unpublished typescript, property of M. de Benoist.

Berger, Adriana. "Mircea Eliade: Romanian Fascism and the History of Religions in the United States." In *Tainted Greatness: Antisemitism and Cultural Heroes,* ed. Nancy A. Harrowitz, pp. 51–74. Philadelphia: Temple University Press, 1994.

Berres, Leonid. "The Wahhabis Are Ready to Make an Alliance with Makashov and Ilyukhin." *Kommersant,* July 24, 1999, pp. 1ff.

Blanch, Lesley. *The Wilder Shores of Love.* London: John Murray, 1955.

Bonaud, Christian. *L'Imam Khomeyni, un gnostique méconnu de XXe siècle.* Beirut: Al-Bouraq, 1997.

Bono, Salvatore. *Orientalismo e Colonialismo: La ricerca di consenso in Egitto per l'impresa di Libia.* Rome: Istituto per l'Oriente C. A. Nallino, 1997.

Boroujerdi, Mehrzad. "The Encounter of Post-Revolutionary Thought in Iran with Hegel, Heidegger and Popper." In *Cultural Transitions in the Middle East,* ed. Serif Mardin, pp. 236–59. Leiden: Brill, 1994.

Boulet, Nöele Maurice-Denis. "L'ésotériste René Guénon: Souvenirs et jugements." *La pensée catholique: Cahiers de synthèse* 77 (1962), 17–42; 78–79 (1962), 139–62; and 80 (1962).

Brown, Joseph Epes. *The Sacred Pipe: Black Elk's Account of the Seven Rites of the Oglala Sioux.* Norman: University of Oklahoma Press, 1953.

Brudny, Yitzhak M. *Reinventing Russia: Russian Nationalism and the Soviet State, 1953–91.* Cambridge, Mass.: Harvard University Press, 1998.

Bryan, G. McLeod. *Voices in the Wilderness: Twentieth-Century Prophets Speak to the New Millennium.* Macon, Ga.: Mercer University Press, 1999.

Buchta, Wilfried. *Who Rules Iran? The Structure of Power in the Islamic Republic.* Washington, D.C.: Washington Institute for Near East, 2000.

Burckhardt, Titus. *Fes, Stadt des Islam.* Olten: Urs Graf-Verlag, 1960. Translation, *Fez: City of Islam.* Cambridge: Islamic Texts Society, 1992.

Camicas, Yves, and Claude Camicas. *Les gens du blâme: une secte au quotidien.* Milan: Archè, 1995.

Campbell, Bruce F. *Ancient Wisdom Revived: A History of the Theosophical Movement.* Berkeley: University of California Press, 1980.

Chacornac, Paul. *La vie simple de René Guénon.* 1958. Reprint, Paris: Editions traditionnelles, 1986.

Chatwin, Margret. "Fronte Nazionale," July 29, 2001. *Informationsdienst gegen Rechtsextremismus* [online]. Available http://www.idgr.de/lexikon/stich/f/fronte -nazionale/fronte-n.html [October 23, 2001].

Chevilliat, Bernard, ed. *Frithjof Schuon, 1907–1998: Etudes et témoignages.* Avon: Connaissance des Religions, 1999.

Christensen, Damascene. *Not of This World: The Life and Teachings of Fr. Seraphim Rose, Pathfinder to the Heart of Ancient Christianity.* Forestville, Cal.: Fr. Seraphim Rose Foundation, 1993.

Clavelle, Maurice [Jean Reyor]. "Document confidentiel inédit," unpublished typescript. Private collection.

Clover, Charles. "Dreams of the Eurasian Heartland." *Foreign Affairs* 78, no. 2 (March–April 1999), 9–13.

Coen, Antonio, and Michel Dumesnil de Grammont. *La Franc-Maçonnerie Ecossaise.* Nice: SNEP, 1946.

Cook, Deborah. "Origins and Metamorphoses of the New Right: An Interview with Pierre-Andre Taguieff." *Telos* 98–99 (Winter 1993 / Spring 1994), 159–72.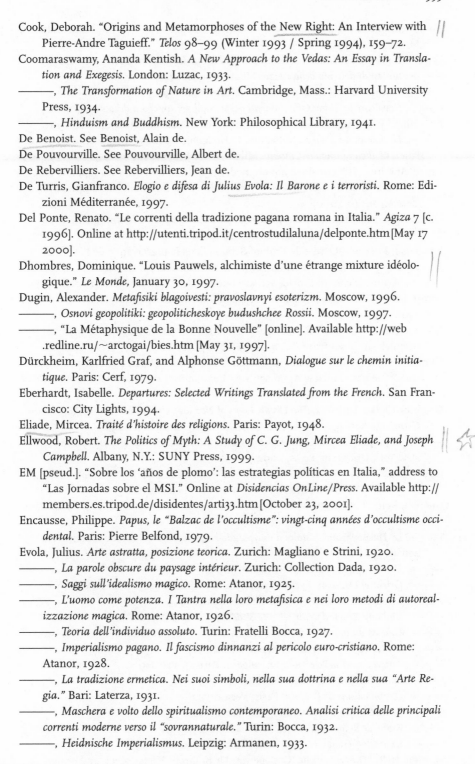

Coomaraswamy, Ananda Kentish. *A New Approach to the Vedas: An Essay in Translation and Exegesis.* London: Luzac, 1933.

———, *The Transformation of Nature in Art.* Cambridge, Mass.: Harvard University Press, 1934.

———, *Hinduism and Buddhism.* New York: Philosophical Library, 1941.

De Benoist. See Benoist, Alain de.

De Pouvourville. See Pouvourville, Albert de.

De Rebervilliers. See Rebervilliers, Jean de.

De Turris, Gianfranco. *Elogio e difesa di Julius Evola: Il Barone e i terroristi.* Rome: Edizioni Méditerranée, 1997.

Del Ponte, Renato. "Le correnti della tradizione pagana romana in Italia." *Agiza* 7 [c. 1996]. Online at http://utenti.tripod.it/centrostudilaluna/delponte.htm [May 17 2000].

Dhombres, Dominique. "Louis Pauwels, alchimiste d'une étrange mixture idéologique." *Le Monde,* January 30, 1997.

Dugin, Alexander. *Metafisiki blagoivesti: pravoslavnyi esoterizm.* Moscow, 1996.

———, *Osnovi geopolitiki: geopoliticheskoye budushchee Rossii.* Moscow, 1997.

———, "La Métaphysique de la Bonne Nouvelle" [online]. Available http://web.redline.ru/~arctogai/bies.htm [May 31, 1997].

Dürckheim, Karlfried Graf, and Alphonse Göttmann, *Dialogue sur le chemin initiatique.* Paris: Cerf, 1979.

Eberhardt, Isabelle. *Departures: Selected Writings Translated from the French.* San Francisco: City Lights, 1994.

Eliade, Mircea. *Traité d'histoire des religions.* Paris: Payot, 1948.

Ellwood, Robert. *The Politics of Myth: A Study of C. G. Jung, Mircea Eliade, and Joseph Campbell.* Albany, N.Y.: SUNY Press, 1999.

EM [pseud.]. "Sobre los 'años de plomo': las estrategias políticas en Italia," address to "Las Jornadas sobre el MSI." Online at *Disidencias OnLine/Press.* Available http://members.es.tripod.de/disidentes/arti33.htm [October 23, 2001].

Encausse, Philippe. *Papus, le "Balzac de l'occultisme": vingt-cinq années d'occultisme occidental.* Paris: Pierre Belfond, 1979.

Evola, Julius. *Arte astratta, posizione teorica.* Zurich: Magliano e Strini, 1920.

———, *La parole obscure du paysage intérieur.* Zurich: Collection Dada, 1920.

———, *Saggi sull'idealismo magico.* Rome: Atanor, 1925.

———, *L'uomo come potenza. I Tantra nella loro metafisica e nei loro metodi di autorealizzazione magica.* Rome: Atanor, 1926.

———, *Teoria dell'individuo assoluto.* Turin: Fratelli Bocca, 1927.

———, *Imperialismo pagano. Il fascismo dinnanzi al pericolo euro-cristiano.* Rome: Atanor, 1928.

———, *La tradizione ermetica. Nei suoi simboli, nella sua dottrina e nella sua "Arte Regia."* Bari: Laterza, 1931.

———, *Maschera e volto dello spiritualismo contemporaneo. Analisi critica delle principali correnti moderne verso il "sovrannaturale."* Turin: Bocca, 1932.

———, *Heidnische Imperialismus.* Leipzig: Armanen, 1933.

———, *Rivolta contro il mondo moderno*. Milan: Hoepli, 1934. Reprint, Rome: Edizioni Mediterranee, 1993.

———, *Il mistero del Graal e la tradizione ghibellina dell'Impero*. Bari: Laterza, 1937.

———, *Sintesi di dottrina della razza*. Milan: Hoelpi, 1941.

———, *Orientamenti. Undici punti*. Rome: Imperium, 1950.

———, *Cavalcare la Tigre: Orientamenti esistenziali per un'epoca della dissoluzione*. Milan: Vanni Scheiwiller, 1961. Reprint, Rome: Edizioni Méditerranée, 1995.

———, *Le chemin du cinabre*. Milan and Carmagnola: Archè and Arktos, 1983. Translation of *Il cammino del Cinabro*. Milan: Vanni Scheiwiller, 1972.

Faivre, Antoine. "Histoire de la notion moderne de Tradition dans ses rapports avec les courants ésotériques (XVe–XXe siècles)." *Aries,* unnumbered volume, *Symboles et Mythes* (c. 2000).

Ferraresi, Franco. *Minacce alla democrazia: La Destra radicale e la strategia della tensione in Italia nel dopoguerra*. Milan: Feltrinelli, 1995.

Fitzgerald, Michael. "Le rôle de Frithjof Schuon dans la préservation de l'esprit de l'indien peau-rouge." In *Frithjof Schuon, ed. Chevilliat, pp. 186–94.*

——— "Frithjof Schuon: Providence without Paradox." *Sacred Web* 8 (2002), 19–34.

Forest, James H. *Living with Wisdom: A Life of Thomas Merton*. Maryknoll, N.Y.: Orbis, 1991.

Girotto, Jean-Louis. "Sacrées émotions: Retour sur les 5èmes Rencontres Méditerranéennes sur le soufisme." *Soufisme* 5 (2000), 4–5.

Glinski-Vassiliev, Dmitri. "Islam in Russian Society and Politics: Survival and Expansion." Program on New Approaches to Russian Security, Harvard University, policy memo no. 198, May 2001.

Goodrick-Clarke, Nicholas. *The Occult Roots of Nazism: The Ariosophists of Austria and Germany, 1890–1935*. Wellingborough, U.K.: Aquarian Press, 1985.

———, *Black Sun: Aryan Cults, Esoteric Nazism, and the Politics of Identity*. New York: New York University Press, 2002.

Götz von Olenhusen, Albrecht. "Zeittafel zur Biographie Rudolf von Sebottendorfs (1875–1945)." Printed after 1969 in an unidentified journal.

Guénon, René. *L'introduction générale à l'étude des doctrines hindoues*. Paris: M. Rivière, 1921.

———, *Le Théosophisme, histoire d'une pseudo-religion*. Paris: Nouvelle Librairie Nationale, 1921.

———, *L'erreur spirite*. Paris: M. Rivière, 1923.

———, *Orient et Occident*. Paris: Payot, 1924. Reprint, Paris: Guy Trédaniel, 1993.

———, *L'ésotérisme de Dante*. Paris: Charles Bosse, 1924.

———, *L'homme et son devenir selon le Védânta*. Paris: Bossard, 1925.

———, *La crise du monde moderne*. Paris: Bossard, 1927. Reprint, Paris: Folio, 1999.

———, *Le Roi du Monde*. Paris: Charles Bosse, 1927.

———, *Autorité spirituelle et pouvoir temporel*. Paris: J. Vrin, 1929.

———, *Saint Bernard*. Marseilles: Publiroc, 1929.

———, *Le symbolisme de la croix*. Paris: Vega, 1931.

———, *La métaphysique orientale*. Paris: Chacornac, 1939.

———, *Règne de la quantité*. Paris: Gallimard, 1945.

———, *La grande Triade*. Nancy: Revue de la Table Ronde, 1946.

Hansen, H. T. "Die 'magische' Gruppe von Ur in ihrem Historischen und esoter-

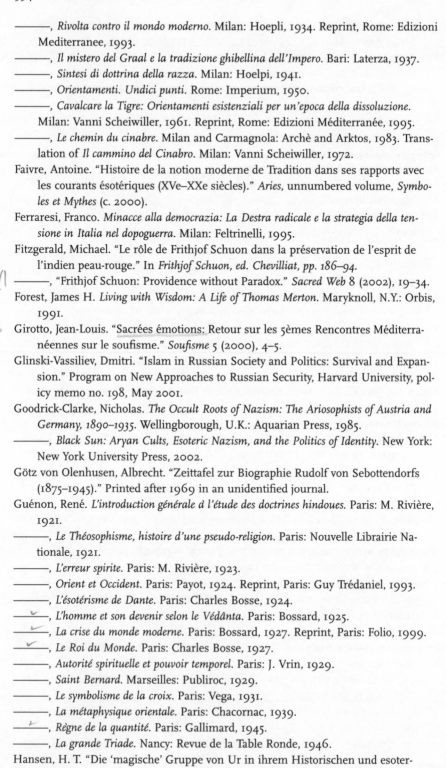

ischen Umfeld." In Julius Evola, *Schritte zur Initiation*, pp. 7–27. Bern: Scherz-Ansata, 1997.

———, "Der Ritt auf dem Tiger: Anmerkungen zum Buch." In Julius Evola, *Cavalcare la Tigre / Den Tiger reiten*. Engerda: Arun, 1997.

———, "Julius Evola und der Sexus." In Julius Evola, *Die Grosse Lust—Metaphysik des Sexus*. n.p.: Fischer Media Verlag, 1998.

———, "Julius Evola und die deutsche konservative Revolution." *Criticon* [Munich] 158 (April/June 1998), 16–33.

———, "Mircea Eliade, Julius Evola und die Integrale Tradition." In Julius Evola, *Über das Initiatische*. Sinzheim: AAGW, 1998.

Hartung, Henri. *Pour une éducation permanente*. Paris: Fayard, 1966.

———, *Ces princes du management: le patronat français face a ses responsabilités*. Paris: Fayard, 1970.

———, "Articles et conférences." Unpublished manuscript, July 1, 1983. Private collection.

———, "Rencontres Romaines au milieu des ruines." Unpublished manuscript, March 1984. Private collection.

Hocking, Hilary, and Ingrid Holmgren. *Ivan Aguéli*. Sala, Sweden: Sala Art Society, n.d.

Hue-Tam Ho Tai. *Millenarianism and Peasant Politics in Vietnam*. Cambridge, Mass.: Harvard University Press, 1983.

Ioanid, Radu. *The Sword of the Archangel: Fascist Ideology in Romania*. Boulder, Col.: East European Monographs, 1990.

Jamal, Gejdar. *Tawhid: Prospettive dell'Islam nell'ex URSS*. Trans. & ed. Danilo Valdorio. Parma: Insegna del Veltro, 1993.

James, Marie-France. *Ésotérisme et Christianisme: autour de René Guénon*. Paris: Nouvelles éditions latines, 1981.

———, *Esotérisme, Occultisme, Franc-Maçonnerie et Christianisme aux XIX et XX siècles. Explorations bio-bibliographiques*. Paris: Nouvelles éditions latines, 1981.

Johnson, K. Paul. *The Masters Revealed: Madame Blavatsky and the Myth of the Great White Lodge*. Albany, N.Y.: SUNY Press, 1994.

———, *Initiates of Theosophical Masters*. Albany, N.Y.: SUNY Press, 1995.

Koslow, Mark. "Schuon and Thomas Yellowtail." Unpublished typescript.

Kristeller, Paul Oskar. Introduction. In *The Letters of Marsilio Ficino*. London: Shepheard-Walwyn, 1975.

Lardinois, Roland. "Louis Dumont et la science indigène," *Actes de la recherche en sciences sociales* 106–107 (March 1995), pp. 11–26.

Laurant, Jean-Pierre. *Le sens caché selon René Guénon*. Lausanne: L'Age d'homme, 1975.

———, *Matgioi, un aventurier taoïste*. Paris: Dervy livres, 1982.

———, *L'ésotérisme chrétien en France au XIX siècle*. Lausanne: L'Age d'Homme, 1992.

———, "La 'non-conversion' de René Guénon (1886–1951)." In *De la conversion*, ed. Jean-Christophe Attias, pp. 133–39. Paris: Cerf, 1998.

Laurant, Jean-Pierre, and Paul Barbanegra, eds. *René Guénon* [Cahiers de l'Herne]. Paris: Editions de l'Herne, 1985.

Le Forestier, René. *L'Occultisme en France aux XIXe et XXe siècles: L'église gnostique*, ed. Antoine Faivre. Milan: Archè, 1990.

Le Mire, Béatrice. *Sauvez-moi, sauvez-moi!* Paris: Albin Michel, 1977.

Le Mire, Henri. *Le voleur d'âme: réponse a Beatrice Le Mire.* Paris: Société de production littéraire, 1978.

Lindqvist, Viveca. *Ivan Aguéli 1869–1917: centre culturel suédois, Paris 11 mars–24 avril, 1983.* Paris: Centre culturel suédois, 1983.

Lings, Martin. *A Moslem Saint of the Twentieth Century.* London: Allen & Unwin, 1961.

Lipsey, Roger. *Coomaraswamy,* 3 vol.s. Vol. 3: *His Life and Work.* Princeton, N.J.: Princeton University Press, 1977.

Mayer, Jean-François. *Confessions d'un chasseur de sectes.* Paris: Cerf, 1990.

Mélikoff, Irène. *Hadji Bektach: un mythe et ses avatars.* Leiden: Brill, 1998.

Merton, Thomas. *The Seven Storey Mountain.* New York: Harcourt, Brace, 1946.

Michon, Jean-Louis. "Dans l'intimité de Cheikh Abd al-Wahid—René Guénon—au Caire, 1947–49." *Sophia* 3, no. 2 (1997). Reprint, *L'Ermite de Duqqi,* ed. Accart, pp. 252–59.

Mila, E. "Charbonneau-Lassay y el esoterismo católico en el siglo XX." Online at *Disidencias: OnLine Press.* Available http://members.es.tripod.de/disidentes/arti44.htm [June 1, 2000].

Monastra, Giovanni. "Ananda K. Coomaraswamy: de l'idéalisme à la tradition." *Nouvelle Ecole* 47 (1995), 25–42.

Muir, Kate. "The Selling of the Prince of Wales." *The Times* [London], March 30, 1992.

Mutti, Claudio. Introduction. In Vasile Lovinescu, *La Dacia iperborea,* pp. 5–13. Parma: All'insegna del Veltro, 1984.

———, "Pourquoi j'ai choisi l'Islam." *Eléments: Revue de la Nouvelle Droite* 53 (Spring 1985), 37–39.

———, "Evola e l'Islam." *Heliodromos: Contributi per il fronte della Tradizione* [Siracusa] 6 (Spring 1995), 41–55.

———, "La vita e i libri di Vasile Lovinescu." In Vasile Lovinescu, *La colonna traiana* [sic.], pp. 19–24. Parma: All'insegna del Veltro, 1995.

———, *Julius Evola sul fronte dell'est.* Parma: All'insegna del Veltro, 1998.

Nasr, Seyyed Hossein. *Ideals and Realities of Islam.* New York: Praeger, 1966.

———, *The Encounter of Man and Nature: The Spiritual Crisis of Modern Man.* London: Allen & Unwin, 1968.

———, *Sufi Essays.* New York: Schroder Books, 1972.

———, "Frithjof Schuon et la tradition islamique." In *Frithjof Schuon,* ed. Chevilliat, pp. 123–39.

———, "Intellectual Autobiography." In *The Philosophy of Seyyed Hossein Nasr,* ed. Lewis E Hahn, pp. 3–85. Chicago: Open Court, 2001.

———, ed. *Islamic Spirituality.* 2 vols. New York: Crossroad, 1987–91.

Neihardt, John. *Black Elk Speaks.* New York: William Morrow, 1932.

Ornea, Z. *The Romanian Extreme Right: The Nineteen Thirties.* Boulder, Col.: East European Monographs, 1999.

Pallavicini, Abd-al-Wahid. *Islam interiore: La spiritualità universale nella religione islamica.* Milan: Arnoldo Mondadori, 1991.

———, *L'islam intérieur: La spiritualité universelle dans la religion islamique.* Paris: Christian de Bartillat, 1995.

Pas, Julian F., and Man Kam Leung. *Historical Dictionary of Taoism.* Lanham, Md.: Scarecrow Press, 1998.

Quinn, William W. *The Only Tradition.* Albany, N.Y.: SUNY Press, 1996.

Raine, Kathleen. *Stone and Flower.* London: Nicholson and Watson, 1943.

Rawlinson, Andrew. *The Book of Enlightened Masters: Western Teachers in Eastern Traditions.* Chicago: Open Court Press, 1997.

Rebervilliers, Jean de. Afterward. In Camicas and Camicas, *Gens du blâme,* pp. 279–311.

Rennie, Bryan S. Introduction. In *Changing Religious Worlds,* ed. Rennie, pp. ix–xxiv.

———, ed. *Changing Religious Worlds: The Meaning and End of Mircea Eliade.* Albany, N.Y.: SUNY Press, 2000.

Rigal-Cellard, Bernadette. "La religion des sioux oglalas." In *Le facteur religieux an Amérique du Nord: Religion et groupes ethniques au Canada et aux Etats-Unis,* ed J. Beranger and P. Guillaume, pp. 245–67. Bordeaux: CNRS, 1984.

Rittlinger, Herbert. *Geheimdienst mit beschränkter Haftung: Bericht vom Bosporus.* Stuttgart: Deutsche Verlags-Anstalt, 1973.

Rocca, G., ed. *'Abdul-Hadi: Ecrits pour* La Gnose. Milan: Archè, 1988.

Ro'i, Yaacov. *Muslim Eurasia: Conflicting Legacies.* London: Frank Cass, 1995.

Roman, Denys. *René Guénon et les destins de la Franc-Maçonnerie.* Paris: Les éditions de l'oeuvre, 1982.

Ross, Kelley. "Mircea Eliade (1907–1986)." *The Proceedings of the Friesian School,* Fourth Series, 1996– [online]. Available http://www.friesian.com/eliade.htm.

Ruby, Walter. "Of Russia, 'Memory,' and the Jews" [interview with Dmitry Vasilyev]. *Jerusalem Post,* March 7, 1989.

Salzani, Stefano, and PierLuigi Zoccatelli. *Hermétisme et emblématique du Christ dans la vie et dans l'oeuvre de Louis Charbonneau-Lassay (1871–1946).* Milan: Archè, 1996.

Schumacher, E. F. *Small Is Beautiful: Economics as if People Mattered.* 1973. Reprint, New York: Harper & Row, 1989.

———, *A Guide for the Perplexed.* 1977. Reprint, London: Vintage, 1995.

Schuon, Catherine. "Frithjof Schuon: Memories and Anecdotes." *Sacred Web* 8 (1992), 35–60.

Schuon, Frithjof. *De l'unité transcendante des religions.* Paris: Gallimard, 1948.

———, *Understanding Islam.* 1961. Translated, London: Allen & Unwin, 1963.

———, *In the Tracks of Buddhism.* London: Allen & Unwin, 1968.

———, *Erinnerungen und Betrachtungen.* [Switzerland]: privately printed, 1974.

———, "Paradoxical Aspects of Sufism." *Studies in Comparative Religion* 12 (1978), 131–75.

———, "Quelques critiques." In *René Guénon* [Dossier H], ed. Pierre-Marie Sigaud, pp. 56–80. Lausanne: L'Age d'Homme, 1984.

Sebottendorf, Rudolf von. *Die Praxis der alter türkischen Freimaurerei: Der Schlüssel zum Verständnis der Alchimie.* 1924. Reprint, Freiburg im Breisgau: Hermann Bauer, 1954.

———, *Der Talisman des Rosenkreuzers.* Pfullinger in Württemberg: Johannes Baum Verlag, 1925.

———, *Bevor Hitler kam: Urkundlichen aus der Frühzeit der nationalsozialistischen Bewegung.* Munich: Deukula-Verlag Grassinger, 1933.

Sénard, Jean. "Pour se cultiver: d'abord savoir couper le téléphone." *Figaro Littéraire,* February 24, 1962.

Shenfield, Stephen D. *Russian Fascism: Traditions, Tendencies, and Movements*. New York: M. E. Sharpe, 2000.

Sherrard, Philip. *Constantinople: Iconography of a Sacred City*. London: Oxford University Press, 1965.

Skali, Faouzi. *La voie soufie*. Paris: Albin Michel, 1995.

Smith, Huston. *The Religions of Man*. New York: Harper, 1958. Reprint, New York: Harper Collins, 1991.

——, *Forgotten Truth: The Primordial Tradition*. New York: Harper & Row, 1976.

——, *Beyond the Post-Modern Mind*. New York: Crossroad, 1982.

——, "Bubble Blown and Lived in: A Theological Autobiography." *Dialog* 33, no. 4 (Fall 1994), 274–79.

Snell, Marilyn. "The World of Religions according to Huston Smith." *Mother Jones* 22, no.5 (November–December 1997), 40–43.

Spineto, Natale. "Mircea Eliade and Traditionalism." *Aries* NS 1, no. 1 (2001), 62–87.

Sqali. See Skali.

Steadman, J. M. "The Asiatick Society of Bengal." *Eighteenth Century Studies* 10 (1977), 464–83.

Stevenson, David. *The Origins of Freemasonry: Scotland's Century, 1590–1710*. Cambridge: Cambridge University Press, 1988.

Tabandeh, Ali. *Hurshid tabande*. Tehran: Haqiqat, 1998.

Tourniac, Jean [pseud.]. *Johannes Eques A Rosa Mystica. La Franc-maçonnerie chrétienne-templière des Prieures Ecossais Rectifies: Réflexion sur l'organisation prieurale et l'esprit du rite*. Paris: SEPP, 1997.

Trent, Alice Lucy [pseud.]. *The Feminine Universe: A Complete Outline of the Primordial Feminine Essentialist Philosophy*. London: Golden Order Press, n.d.

Tsipko, Alexander. "Russia's Difficult Path Toward Democracy: Moral and Ideological Preconditions for Overcoming the Legacies of the Communist System in Russia." *International Review of Sociology* 7 (1997), 267–318.

Vâlsan, Michel. *L'islam et la fonction de René Guénon: recueil posthume*. Paris: Editions de l'Oeuvre, 1984.

Vatsyayan, Kapila. "Kathleen Raine Speaks" [interview with Kathleen Raine]. *IGNCA [Indira Gandhi National Center for the Arts] Newsletter* 3, no. 3 (October–December 1995). Available online at IGNCA website, http://ignca.nic.in/nl_00902.htm [June 14, 2001].

Von Sebottendorf. See Sebottendorf, Rudolf von.

Waite, Arthur Edward. "The French Mystic and the Story of Modern Martinism." Online at *Martinist Information Page*. Available http://www.icbl.hw.ac.uk/~bill/TFMSOMM.html.

Washington, Peter. *Madame Blavatsky's Baboon: A History of the Mystics, Mediums and Misfits Who Brought Spiritualism to America*. New York: Schocken Books, 1995.

Wasserstrom, Steven M. *Religion after Religion: Gershom Scholem, Mircea Eliade, and Henry Corbin at Eranos*. Princeton, N.J.: Princeton University Press, 1999.

Waterfield, Robin. *René Guénon and the Future of the West: The Life and Writings of a 20th-century Metaphysician*. [UK]: Crucible Press, 1987.

Watts, Larry L. *Romanian Cassandra: Ion Antonescu and the Struggle for Reform, 1916–1941*. Boulder, Col.: East European Monographs, 1993.

Whicher, Stephen E., ed. *Selections from Ralph Waldo Emerson: An Organic Anthology.* Cambridge, Mass.: Riverside Press, 1960.

Wilson, Peter Lamborn. "The World of Islam." *Sophia Perennis* [Tehran] 2, no. 2 (Autumn 1976), 108.

Wirth, Oswald. *La Franc-Maçonnerie rendue intelligible à ses adeptes.* 3 vols. Vol. 2: *Le compagnon.* 1931? Reprint, Paris: Dervy livres, 2000.

Wood, Barbara. *E. F. Schumacher: His Life and Thought.* New York: Harper & Row, 1984.

Yakovich, Yelena. "Kontinent in Moscow: Voice of Russian Culture" [Interview with Igor Vinogradov]. *Literaturnaya Gazeta,* July 22, 1992, p. 5.

Zarcone, Thierry. *Mystiques, philosophes et francs-maçons en Islam: Riza Tevfiq, penseur ottoman (1868–1948), du soufisme a la confrérie.* Paris: Institut français d'études anatoliennes d'Istanbul, 1993.

———, "Relectures et transformations de Soufisme en Occident." *Diogène* 187 (January 2000).

Zoccatelli, PierLuigi. *Le lièvre qui rumine: Autour de René Guénon, Louis Charbonneau-Lassay et la Fraternité du Paraclet.* Milan: Archè, 1999.

Zoccatelli, PierLuigi, and Stefano Salzani, *Hermétisme et emblématique du Christ dans la vie et dans l'oeuvre de Louis Charbonneau-Lassay (1871–1946).* Milan: Archè, 1996.

Index

Quotation marks around proper names indicate that a name was adopted in later life. Thus Aguéli, Ivan (John Agelii, "Abd al-Hadi," 1869–1917) means that the person most often referred to as Ivan Aguéli was born John Agelii, and also used the name Abd al-Hadi (in this case, taking that name on his conversion to Islam).